CW01521391

Come with me through
THE GOSPEL OF JOHN

Come with me through
THE GOSPEL OF JOHN

David Pawson

Anchor Recordings

First published in Great Britain in 2012
by Anchor Recordings Ltd.
72 The Street, Kennington, Ashford TN24 9HS

The text of this book is edited versions of a series of sermons originally
given in 1972. For more of David Pawson's teaching, including MP3s,
DVDs and CDs, go to www.davidpawson.com
For further information, email info@davidpawsonministry.com

Editor: Martin Manser www.martinmanser.com

www.davidpawson.org

ISBN 978-0-9569376-4-3

Printed in Great Britain by Imprint Digital, Exeter
Printed in USA by CreateSpace

Contents

This book is based on a series of talks. Originating as it does from the spoken word, its style will be found by many readers to be somewhat different from my usual written style. It is hoped that this will not detract from the substance of the biblical teaching found here.

As always, I ask the reader to compare everything I say or write with what is written in the Bible and, if at any point a conflict is found, always to rely upon the clear teaching of scripture.

David Pawson

INTRODUCTION

Have you ever wondered why the New Testament has four Gospels? Why did God not give us only one account of the life of Jesus Christ? The four Gospels are not photographs, but portraits. Each of them brings out the personal experience and impression of a different apostle and together the four portraits give you a wonderful variety of approach to the Lord Jesus Christ. The Gospel of Mark was probably the first to be written and is very clearly dependent on the experience of Simon Peter who passed onto the young boy Mark what he had known of the Lord Jesus. It is a simple brief account of what Jesus did. Some years later Matthew and Luke wrote their Gospels and they concentrated not so much on what Jesus did but on what he said. Matthew was most interested in what Jesus said for the Jews whereas Luke was most interested in what Jesus said for the Gentiles. A theme emerges from each of the four Gospels, a picture of Jesus that's different yet the same. In Mark's Gospel you see Jesus as the Son Of Man. In Matthew's Gospel you see Jesus as the King of the Jews. In Luke's Gospel you see Jesus as the Saviour of the world.

DIFFERENCES FROM SYNOPTIC GOSPELS (MATTHEW, MARK AND LUKE)

When we turn to John there is a difference. John was writing many years later and he seems far more interested in what Jesus was. Not what he did, like Mark, or what he said like Matthew and Luke, but what he was, the real person, who he was, Jesus' innermost character. And so John is the deepest Gospel of all: it brings you closer to Jesus than any other. It enables you to understand who he is as a person so that at the end of the Gospel you know Jesus, and to know Jesus is to know life eternal.

Going through Matthew, Mark and Luke, we see they are so similar that they can be harmonized. They synchronize; they syncopate. That is why they are called the Synoptic Gospels. It is like going through different counties in one country but when you step into John's Gospel you are in very different country. There is a different atmosphere, a different feel. John's Gospel is quite different from the others.

John is concerned to look at Jesus from the *inside*. He writes primarily about who Jesus was.

Omissions

The way John differs from the synoptic Gospels is especially evident when we consider the content of his Gospel. It is not just that John writes with a special viewpoint on Jesus, but he omits a number of areas considered significant by the other Gospel writers:

- the conception and birth of Jesus
- his baptism
- his temptations
- the casting out of demons
- the transfiguration
- the Last Supper
- Jesus' struggle in prayer in Gethsemane
- the ascension

These are surprising omissions, especially if we note the prominence which the other writers give to some of these events. The transfiguration, for example, is seen as a pivotal event in the synoptic Gospels. And John was asked by Jesus at the cross to look after his mother, so perhaps he omitted the birth story to save Mary from more publicity. The main reason for these omissions, however, is simply that such details did not suit John's purpose. He set out to tell us something quite different from the other Gospels and there was no point in including what he regarded as unnecessary material.

Not only are there omissions, but there is also an underplaying of some themes regarded as important or worthy of more space in the other three Gospels. Miracles proliferate in the Gospels of

Matthew, Mark and Luke, for example, but in John there are just seven. John also makes little mention of one of the major themes of the preaching of Jesus: *the kingdom of God*. The word only occurs twice, when Jesus tells Nicodemus that unless he is born again he cannot see the kingdom of God, and when he tells Pilate that his kingdom is not of this world. Again, this does not mean that miracles or the kingdom are unimportant, but just that John has a different purpose from the other writers, and a different way of achieving it.

Additions

Miracles
Just as there are omissions, there are also some important additions. Of the seven miracles that John mentions, five are completely new:
- the water into wine at the wedding at Cana
- the man by the pool at Bethesda
- the healing of the nobleman's son
- healing the man blind from birth
- the raising of Lazarus

Only two, walking on water and feeding the 5,000, are repetitions.

Furthermore, John uses a different word for miracles, referring to them as "signs." A sign always points to something beyond itself. So he does not record fewer miracles because he believes them to be less important, but in order to highlight the way in which the miracle or sign points to Jesus.

Individuals
John includes more stories about individuals and a number of these are unique to his Gospel. Peter's initial refusal to have his feet washed, the conversation with the Samaritan woman at the well and the conversation with Nicodemus are all included. Indeed, these one-to-one dialogues are given more prominence than the meetings with crowds which seem to dominate the other three Gospels. The words of John the Baptist in this Gospel are all in private conversations, not public proclamations.

Statements about Jesus

There are also seven big statements about Jesus himself which appear in John, known as the "I am" sayings:

- I am the living bread
- I am the light of the world
- I am the door
- I am the good shepherd
- I am the resurrection and the life
- I am the way, the truth and the life
- I am the true vine

These statements only occur in John's Gospel and they serve to emphasize his purpose as he gives us an insight into how Jesus viewed himself.

Emphases

The synoptic Gospels are based on the outline of Mark and tend to use his framework of 30 months in the north in Galilee, followed by six months in the south in Judaea, focusing especially on Jerusalem. But John is quite different. Almost all of his Gospel is in the south and includes material from Jesus' early ministry. He chooses to emphasize the occasions when Jesus went to Jerusalem for the feasts (maybe as often as three times a year). Much of John therefore surrounds the Feast of Tabernacles, the Passover and the dedication of the temple, and ignores much of Jesus' ministry in the north.

Style

The style differences in John can be seen especially in two areas. First, the language of John is different from the other Gospels. They have considerable overlaps, with identical wording being used in places. John's language suggests that his work is completely independent. For example, when the synoptic Gospels describe the feeding of the 5,000, they have 53 words in common with each other but just 8 in common with John. Even the word for "fish" is different.

Secondly, the synoptic Gospels major on the parables of Jesus. Longer teaching sections are rare. In John, however, Jesus seems to be involved in endless arguments, with long discourses focusing more on issues of belief than behaviour. Since these are largely from his southern tours, it does seem that when Jesus went south he changed his style of teaching, probably because he was involved in more arguments with the Judaeans about his identity.

Take the long discussion in John 8, for example. Jesus has been speaking of his relationship to his Father, God. The Pharisees ask Jesus, "Where is your father?" – the inference being that Jesus could not speak confidently about his parentage and was rumoured to be illegitimate.

"You do not know me or my Father," Jesus replies. "If you knew me, you would know my Father also." So Jesus tells them that he does know who his father is, and turns the argument back on the Pharisees. They should know him too, but are far from him.

This raises an interesting issue concerning Jesus' opponents, which is often not understood. When we read in John's Gospel that the "Jews" hated Jesus, that Jesus was always arguing with the Jews and that the Jews crucified him, we make a very big mistake if we apply the name "Jews" to the whole nation. Indeed, this misunderstanding has stimulated anti-Semitism for 2,000 years. When John refers to "the Jews" he means the southerners, the Judaeans, as distinct from the Galileans in the north, whose attitude (with a few exceptions) was altogether different and more positive towards Jesus.

Outlook

John's outlook is very different from that of the synoptics. John was conscious of the need to communicate to a Greek world as well as a Hebrew one. He was writing his Gospel in Ephesus in Asia (western Turkey today), where there was a meeting of Greek and Hebrew thought. An understanding of the difference between them is necessary if we are to grasp some of the approaches John uses in arranging his material.

Put simply, the Hebrews used a *horizontal time line* in their thinking, holding the common ideas of past, present and future. They knew God as the One who was, who is and who is to come. All their thinking was on such a time line, where time has both purpose and progress. The Greek mind, by contrast, thought of a *vertical line in space* and was concerned with life above and below, in heaven and on earth.

If you think in Hebrew terms, therefore, you have a concept of time travelling in one direction, with God deciding where things are heading. The first three Gospels assume this sort of time line, and John does not abandon it entirely. After all, he is Jewish himself. He includes, for example, the concept of the "hour" five times.

However, he also uses the Greek approach, with a vertical line between heaven and earth, above and below. Therefore he sees Jesus as the One from heaven, quoting Jesus' words in 3:13: "No man has ever gone into heaven except the one who came down from heaven – the Son of Man." And in 6:33: "For the bread of God is he who comes down from heaven and gives life to the world."

We saw earlier that there is little mention of the kingdom of God in John's Gospel. Whereas the synoptic Gospels emphasize the kingdom breaking into this present evil age and awaiting the consummation, John focuses more on the vertical aspect of God loving the world and sending Jesus down to earth. We could say that John is primarily an "up and down" Gospel, whereas the others are "now and then" Gospels.

UNDERSTANDING JOHN'S GOSPEL

Having considered the ways in which John's Gospel stands apart from the other three, we should take a closer look at John himself.

Who was John?

A fisherman

Before being called to follow Jesus, John was a fisherman involved in both sides of the business, both catching and retailing. We know he had connections in Jerusalem and it is likely that these included a retail business for selling the fish which had been caught in Galilee. So he was a man of two worlds, the rural north and the urban city of Jerusalem in the south. As such, he stood out from most of the apostles, who were exclusively northerners – the only native southerner being Judas Iscariot.

A relative of Jesus
He was a cousin of Jesus and the brother of James, one of the other disciples. Indeed, at least five, and probably seven, of the Twelve were Jesus' relatives, though his own brothers remained sceptical until after the resurrection, when James and Jude not only became believers but penned two of the books of the New Testament. This closeness was evident at the cross, when Jesus asked John to look after his mother.

Jesus' closest friend
John, however, was not just close to Jesus because he was a cousin. He was also part of an inner circle, along with James and Peter, of those who were particularly close to Jesus. He refers to himself as "the disciple whom Jesus loved," intending to deflect attention from himself by not actually giving his name, but nonetheless providing us with the insight that, of all the Twelve, John was nearest to Jesus. At the Last Supper it was John who was seated next to Jesus as they reclined to eat their meal. Jesus wanted his good friend at hand as they shared this momentous event together.

The last apostle
Not only was John the closest to Jesus, but he was also the last surviving apostle. He writes his Gospel as an old man, reflecting on Jesus with unique insight. At the end he records the story of how Peter learned from Jesus that he would be crucified, and how Peter asked Jesus about John's death. Jesus replied that it was none of his business and that if Jesus wanted to keep John alive until he returned, that was up to him. From that day a rumour went round that Jesus would come back before John died, but that is not what Jesus said, and John makes this clear at the end of his Gospel.

"Why did John write his Gospel? 'These are written that you may believe that Jesus is the Christ, the Son of God, and that by going on believing you may have life in his name' (20:31)."

The closeness of John to Jesus is reflected in the way in which he feels free to expand Jesus' actual words. John paraphrases some of his discourse to bring out the full meaning, because he believes he knows Jesus' mind well enough to explain what he meant. So, for example, if you read John 3:16, "For God so loved the world that he gave his only begotten Son," it is not clear who is speaking. Is it Jesus in conversation with Nicodemus, or John expanding the section with reflection of his own? It is certainly a strange thing for Jesus to say, and sounds more like a third person talking about Jesus, in a rather indirect way. This is typical of John throughout the Gospel. He expands what Jesus said because he really understands what he meant. He draws out the implications under the guidance of the Holy Spirit. For this reason Eusebius, one of the early Church Fathers, called it "the spiritual Gospel," and it is easy to see why.

John's purpose

What exactly was John's purpose in writing? Looking at this question will really open up our understanding of the book. Already we have seen John's concern to look at Jesus' inward being, but this was all part of a wider concern which he makes explicit at the end of his Gospel. He tells us that he selected the material so that readers might believe that Jesus is the Christ, the Son of the living God, and that by believing this, they might have life in his name. This is a clear enough statement, but it is important that we grasp the *full* meaning of what John says.

Exact meaning
We need first of all to understand the precise wording in the original Greek language. Greek has a "present continuous" tense for verbs

which is not easily translated into English, but is so often crucial to a proper understanding of the text. It means to be continually doing something. To translate the sense into English it is necessary to add the two little words "go on." For example, Jesus did not say, "Ask and you will receive, seek and you will find, knock and it will be open to you," implying that each action need only be done once. He actually said, "*Go on asking* and you will receive, *go on seeking* and you will find, *go on knocking* and it will be open to you." So if someone does not receive the Holy Spirit when they first ask, they should not panic: they should go on asking.

This present continuous verb is used by John in 20:31, so that the verse is more properly translated: "'These are written that you may *go on believing* that Jesus was the Son of God and by *going on believing* you will *go on having* life." This same construction illuminates the best known verse in the Gospel. John 3:16 is better understood as, "For God so loved the world that he gave his only begotten Son, that whoever *goes on believing* will never perish, but *go on having* eternal life."

For non-believers or believers?
John was not written so that his readers might *start* believing that Jesus is the Son of God. It was written that they might *go on* believing it. Much of the content of John is inappropriate for people who come to the Gospel with no prior knowledge of Jesus. The book is written for mature Christians, to help them hold on to their faith so that they do not depart from their understanding of who Jesus is, but go on believing and therefore go on having eternal life.

This was John's principle for the selection of his material. The Gospel was not intended to be comprehensive, but aimed to provide readers with what they needed to know in order that they might continue to have life through constant believing. Put simply, the end for which John was writing was life – and the means to that end is ongoing trust and obedience.

Life is the end
John describes the life which Jesus offered as a present continuous life. Eternal life includes quantity – it is everlasting; but also quality – it is abundant. It is not just an insurance against death, but a life

we are to enjoy here and now. John's statement of purpose in 20:31 implies that this life is something we possess but may lose if we do not continue to have faith. So the themes of life and belief are pivotal to John's overall purpose. Life is the end for which he is writing – that his readers may go on having life – whereas belief is the means to having this life. If we go on believing, we go on having life.

Faith is the means

That John was concerned with believing is confirmed by the frequency with which he uses the word – 98 times. This is far more than the other three Gospels put together. But we need to be careful, for he does not mean the same thing every time. For John there are three stages or phases of belief.

Credence

To give credence means to believe that something is true. The operative word is "that." So we believe *that* Jesus died, *that* he rose again. It is believing in certain historical facts, accepting the credibility of the gospel, accepting its truth. Credence is based on the words and works which establish Christ's claims. This is not by itself saving faith, for at this stage anyone can say they believe that something is true. It is only the *beginning* of saving faith to accept the truth. (The devil believes the truth too; he accepts it and he trembles, but he is not a believer.)

Confidence

Confidence is the second stage of belief: having accepted the truth, we then put our confidence *in* Jesus by trusting and obeying him. It means taking the truth and acting on the basis of what we say is true. Jesus said to Peter towards the end of the Gospel, "Follow me" – an activity of confidence, based on trust and obedience. We may claim to believe in someone, but if we do not have confidence in them, own "faith" is superficial.

Continuance

This third dimension of belief concerns the ongoing aspect that we considered above when looking at John's main purpose. We are to go on believing. In both the Greek and the Hebrew languages "faith" and "faithfulness" are the same word, and sometimes we do not know which is meant. If you really trust someone you will go on trusting them. If you are really full of faith then you will be faithful. You will go on believing in someone whatever happens and whatever it costs. Faith, therefore, is not a single *step* (instantaneous) but a *state* (continuous). Jesus makes this explicit when teaching his disciples in John 15. He uses the imagery of the vine to describe himself and tells them that they are the branches of the vine. He warns them that they must stay, abide, remain in him. If they do not, they will become unfruitful, be cut out and burned. So while John teaches that no one can come to Jesus unless the Father draws him, he also teaches the necessity of the believer *abiding in Christ* if he or she is to enjoy eternal life. This life is in the vine, not the branches (cf. 1 John 5:11). To summarize what we have noted about John's purpose, therefore: his aim is that readers continue to believe in Jesus so that they will continue to have eternal life. This belief involves the three stages of accepting the truth, acting on the truth and holding on to the truth. Jesus himself is the Truth.

The truth about Jesus

There is a further aspect to John's purpose which will help us understand some of the details of the text. By the time John was writing, around AD 90, there was considerable speculation concerning Jesus, even about his early life. A number of "non-canonical" gospels were written purporting to describe Jesus' childhood. One describes Jesus as a little boy playing in the street in Nazareth. Someone pushed him over into the mud and Jesus cursed him with leprosy. There is also a story of the boy Jesus fashioning little birds out of clay, blessing them and watching them fly away. Actually Jesus did not do a single miracle until he was 30, because he could not do them without the power of the Holy Spirit. Jesus did miracles not as the Son of God but as the Son of Man, filled with the Spirit. Given the erroneous teaching which was being spread about, John was concerned to silence once and for all speculation concerning Jesus' identity. Just who was he? There were in particular two notions circulating in Ephesus which John felt the need to correct.

Too high a view of John the Baptist

We know from Acts 19 that there was a group in Ephesus who were followers of John the Baptist but had not believed in Jesus until Paul corrected them. In John's day, it seems, there were still those who venerated John the Baptist to the point where there was a danger that they would become a sect of Christianity, focusing on repentance and morality as John had but without the emphasis on the Holy Spirit which Jesus brought.

The apostle John set out to write a Gospel that would correct this exalted view of John the Baptist. Every time he mentions John the Baptist he puts him down. He says that John was not the light of the world – he only pointed to the light. He says that John did no miracles. He records John's own words that he must decrease and Jesus increase, that Jesus was the bridegroom while he was just the best man.

John the Baptist said two vital things about Jesus:
- He will be the Lamb of God who takes away the sins of the world.
- He will be the one who baptizes in the Holy Spirit.

Both these things need to be taught if followers are to get a proper balance in their understanding of Jesus. John the Baptist made it clear that only Jesus could take away sin and baptize in the Holy Spirit. But in spite of what John had said, his followers had not remembered much of this and Jesus was not given his special place.

Too low a view of Jesus

Much more serious was the fact that in Ephesus they were already holding too low a view of Jesus. This can be understood in part by reflecting on the strong influence of Greek philosophy. As noted earlier, Greek philosophers divided life into two spheres. Various terms are used interchangeably for this: above and below, the physical and the spiritual, the temporal and eternal, the sacred and secular. Not only did they divide these two, they exalted one above the other. Plato said that the spiritual is more real, Aristotle said that the physical is more real. This being so, the Greeks had a real problem with the teaching that Jesus was both physical and spiritual, earthly and heavenly, human and divine. In their thinking physical and spiritual could not be put together like this, and so they developed a number of variations in order to decide which side of reality Jesus was.

More divine than human?
Some said Jesus was more divine than human, that he was never truly human but just *appeared* as a human being. This heresy was known as "docetism,", from a word meaning "phantom," i.e. Jesus only seemed to be human. According to this view Jesus never really experienced humanity, for his deity always overshadowed his human side.

More human than divine?
Others said he was more human than divine, a man who responded perfectly to God and developed fully the capacity of the divine that is in all of us. This is termed "adoptionism", i.e. Jesus was only adopted as God's Son, usually thought to have happened at his baptism when he was filled with the Spirit. Sadly, this is a heresy still being taught today.

Partly human, partly divine?
Some argue that he was partly divine and partly human without saying he was more one than the other. This view is still current today. The Jehovah's Witnesses argue that we must view Jesus as a demi-God, semi-human, the first *created* being. Since the first verse of John explicitly states that he was God, and was with God in the beginning, the Jehovah's Witnesses translate the passage to say that he was *a* God, inserting an indefinite article that is not in the original Greek.

Fully human, fully divine?
John's Gospel clearly asserts that Jesus is both fully divine *and* fully human. It was crucial for this to be demonstrated if John's purpose was to be achieved. Only one who was fully divine and fully human could save mankind from sin – his *humanity* enabling

him to die on our behalf and his *divinity* ensuring that he would conquer death and offer life to those who would believe in him. If John's readers were to have life in Jesus' name, they must know the *same* Jesus the apostles knew.

John therefore wanted people to know the truth about Jesus and so he deliberately focused on these two areas, on Jesus' humanity and divinity.

"John wrote his Gospel that we might think of Jesus as fully divine and fully human."

His real humanity

Jesus is actually "more human" in the fourth Gospel than in the other three. Take, for example, the shortest verse in the Bible: "Jesus wept." It shows Jesus as fully human, standing at the grave of one of his best friends, knowing that soon he would be calling him from the grave, yet weeping at the situation. John records Jesus being hungry and thirsty, tired and surprised, all thoroughly human characteristics. Pilate unwittingly sums up what John was portraying with the words, "Behold, the man!" In Jesus, John shows us what humanity is really like, or what it should be.

This humanity is also seen in John's emphasis on Jesus' prayer life, where more detail is given than in the other Gospels. John depicts a truly human Jesus who needed to pray, depending on his Father to direct what he said and what he did. Some of his most beautiful prayers are in this Gospel.

Furthermore, the Gospel's focus on the death of Jesus emphasizes as no other that he really died. John records how one of the soldiers pierced Jesus' side with a spear, bringing a sudden gush of blood and water. Then John adds the sentence, "He knows that he tells the truth, and he testifies so that you also may believe." It was important to John that his readers should know that Jesus was really dead.

By the same token, John also provides eyewitness evidence of the resurrection, recording his observation of the strips of linen and the head cloth in the empty tomb. Not only was Jesus really dead, but he was really raised from the dead.

His divinity

The main emphasis in John, however, is on the full divinity of Jesus. This takes us back to John's purpose for his Gospel, and gives us the opportunity to look closely at the intriguing way in which John develops this. We have seen already how John recognizes that faith begins with credence, the belief that something is so. John makes the case for belief that Jesus is fully divine by organizing his evidence around the figure seven, the perfect number in Hebrew thinking. John includes in his Gospel three complete bodies of evidence for Jesus' divinity: seven witnesses, seven miracles and seven words.

Seven witnesses

The word "witness" is used 50 times in the fourth Gospel. John stresses that we have personal testimonies to the truth about Jesus. There are seven people who attribute divinity to Jesus in this Gospel:

- John the Baptist
- Nathanael
- Peter
- Martha (the first woman to do so)
- Thomas
- John, the beloved apostle
- Jesus himself

In Jewish law two or three witnesses would be enough to establish the truth, but here John includes the perfect number of people to testify that Jesus really is the Son of the living God.

Seven miracles

We noted earlier how John records just seven miracles in all, and he calls them "signs" because they point to who Jesus was. He actually includes the seven miracles (signs) which were the most supernatural and sensational works that Jesus performed. He does not include casting out demons, because there were plenty of people doing that in the ancient world, including the Pharisees. Instead he highlights miracles no one else could do:

- Turning water into wine – an unmistakable miracle.
- Healing the nobleman's son while miles away from the sick

person, without seeing or laying hands on him.
- Healing the man by the Pool of Bethesda who had been there for 38 years, clearly suffering from a chronic condition.
- Feeding the 5,000, a miracle which all four Gospels include – a creative miracle, producing a lot from a little.
- Walking on water.
- Giving sight to the man blind from birth.
- Raising Lazarus from the dead – not the resuscitation of a corpse soon after death, as with Jairus' daughter or the widow of Nain's son, but the raising of a man whose body would already have started to rot.

John is saying that these are "signs" pointing to the divinity of Jesus. As Nicodemus said, no man could do the things Jesus was doing unless God was with him.

Seven words

John uniquely records for us seven "words" which Jesus gave about himself, mentioned earlier. To Jewish ears his claim was unmistakable, for each time he began with the Hebrew word for God, YHWH, meaning "I am." John carefully includes these sayings in settings which demonstrate that Jesus' claim was legitimate.

"I am the bread of heaven" was delivered following the feeding of the 5,000 with five loaves and two fish.

"I am the light of the world" followed his giving sight to the man born blind.

"I am the resurrection and the life" was said as he brought Lazarus out from the grave.

He also said, "I am the door", "I am the good shepherd", "I am the way, the truth and the life" and "I am the true vine." This is a man who knew himself to be God in human flesh and these seven words, placed deliberately throughout the Gospel, are crucial to John's case that Jesus is worthy of the readers' trust.

Open relationship to the Father

In John's Gospel, Jesus' relationship to the Father is far more open than in the synoptics. John records that Jesus was sent by the

Father, one with the Father, and obedient to the Father in the words he speaks and in the works he does. So much of Jesus' controversy with the Jews concerned his identity and this was what created the greatest animosity, especially when he claimed to be God: '"I tell you the truth," Jesus answered, "before Abraham was born, I am!" At this they picked up stones to stone him, but Jesus hid himself, slipping away from the temple grounds.' In fact, John is the only Gospel directly to describe Jesus as God, though the implication is there in the other three. John begins with the statement "the Word was God" and towards the end Thomas confesses Jesus as "my Lord and my God".

THEMES

We come finally to consider the themes which are integral to John's overall purpose that faith in Christ might be continued.

Glory

"Glory" is a key word in John, for it was a word which the Old Testament reserved for God himself. In the very first chapter, John uses the same word for the Word dwelling among humanity as is used of the *shekinah* glory of God when he revealed himself through the tabernacle at the end of Exodus. John saw this splendour of God in Jesus throughout his whole life, death, resurrection and ascension. Even the cross was a place where Jesus was glorified. From the very start, therefore, we are introduced to a man who is utterly distinct from his contemporaries and set apart from all other men of God.

Logos

John starts his Gospel in a unique way. When Mark wrote his account of Jesus, he began when Jesus was thirty years of age, since this was when he first sprang into public view. Matthew was the author of possibly the next Gospel to be written, but decided to go further back, arguing that it was necessary to include Jesus' conception and birth, and because he was a Jew, the genealogy had to go back to Abraham. Luke felt that, since Jesus was the Son of Man, he must be seen as a human being belonging to the whole human race, and so he started his genealogy with Adam. In contrast to the other three, John decides to begin even earlier, emphasizing that Jesus existed before creation. So he takes the words from Genesis 1:1 as the basis for his opening to the Gospel: "In the beginning was the Word, and the Word was with God, and the Word was God."

Life

If the Logos theme commences the Gospel, "life" is also an important theme which runs throughout, mentioned 34 times. As we saw earlier, the Gospel is written so that Christians might go on believing and go on having life in Christ. We noted too that this life is *abundant* and *present* as well as *everlasting*. John draws a series of contrasts as to what this life will mean for the believer.

Life/death

He explains that having this life means that believers will not see death. Life will just continue beyond death. Death cannot touch it. So he contrasts those who are certain to die with those who will never die. "For my Father's will is that everyone who looks to the Son and believes in him shall have eternal life, and I shall raise him up on the last day."

Light/darkness

John also uses the contrast of light and darkness. When Jesus speaks of "never walking in darkness," he is referring to moral darkness. He says that if we walk with him we will not have things to hide, for we are walking in the light with everything above board and no secrets. Darkness, however, is the metaphor for death and an absence of God. Jesus says, "I am the light of the world. Whoever follows me will never walk in darkness, but will have the light of life."

Truth/lies

We have noted how John highlights the three stages of accepting the truth, doing the truth and holding to the truth, if faith is to be genuine. But he also contrasts truth with lies and includes a whole section in chapter 8 where this theme dominates a discussion between Jesus and his opponents. The word for "truth" and the word for "real" are the same in the Hebrew and Greek languages. If we live in the truth, we are also living in reality. Jesus says, "If you hold to my teaching, you are really my disciples. Then you will know the truth, and the truth will set you free."

Freedom/slavery

This was a discussion point between Jesus and the Pharisees, who claimed never to have been slaves to anyone but had clearly forgotten the slavery in Egypt! Jesus said that whoever sins is a slave to sin, because every time you sin you help to strengthen the chain of habit that will be your master. He had come to set them free. True life, therefore, meant freedom from spiritual bondage. "So if the Son sets you free, you will be free indeed."

Love/wrath

John is clear in his understanding of two contrasting aspects of God's activity. A person is either in God's love or under his wrath. There is no middle way. The eternal consequence of one as opposed to the other is made very clear. Jesus says, "Whoever believes in the Son has eternal life, but whoever rejects the Son will not see life, for God's wrath remains on him."

Real life

Real life, therefore, is a personal relationship with Jesus and his Father. It is life in the light and the truth, in freedom and love. Praying to his Father, Jesus says, "Now this is eternal life: that they may know you, the only true God, and Jesus Christ, whom you have sent."

Holy Spirit

No Gospel tells us as much about the Holy Spirit as John. As such, it is well placed before the book of Acts, in spite of Acts having such strong links with Luke's Gospel. It is through the Holy Spirit that we can enjoy the life which John describes. The teaching on the Holy Spirit is therefore prominent in John's writing:

- In chapter 1 John the Baptist testifies that Jesus received the Holy Spirit and that he will baptize others in Holy Spirit.
- In chapter 3 Jesus talks about the necessity of being born of water and Spirit, before we can enter the kingdom.
- In chapter 4 Jesus speaks of the Spirit as living water and says we must worship God in Spirit and in truth.
- In chapter 7 Jesus goes to the Feast of Tabernacles in Jerusalem, the feast being held in September or October at the end of the dry season. On the last day of Tabernacles the Jews enacted a ceremony in which the priests filled up a great pitcher with water at the Pool of Siloam, carried it to the temple and poured the water on the altar, while praying for the early autumn rains. On this occasion Jesus stood up and called out, "If anyone is thirsty, let him come to me. I will give him a spring of living water, gushing up in his innermost being." The text tells us that he was speaking about the Holy Spirit, whom those who already believed in him were later to receive.
- Chapters 14 to 16 are full of the new "Comforter" who is going to come, the Spirit of truth. The Greek name for the Holy Spirit is *paraclete* (*para* meaning "alongside", *cletus* meaning "called") – the one who stands by you, or the one who is called alongside. The Holy Spirit is also described as one who is just the same as Jesus. He will continue the work of Jesus after he has left, convicting the world of sin, righteousness and judgment, empowering believers and reminding them of everything Jesus said.
- In chapter 20 Jesus prepares his followers for the Day of Pentecost by giving them a sign and a command. The sign was Jesus blowing on each of them, and the command was, "Receive the Holy Spirit." They did not receive anything at

that moment, but it was a rehearsal for Pentecost a few weeks later. That day, when they were seated in the temple, they heard the sound of the wind, reminding them of what Jesus had done. Then they obeyed his command and received the Holy Spirit he had promised.

CONCLUSION

John is a remarkable Gospel, utterly different from the other three. It reflects the unique insights of the man who was closest to Jesus while he was on earth, and is full of a concern that we should not just know about what Jesus did, but should also realize who he was. It reflects, too, John's burden that believers in Jesus should not be sidetracked by erroneous teaching, whether concerning Jesus' identity or the veracity of his claims. He wanted believers to be absolutely sure that eyewitnesses, Jesus' own words and his astonishing works all point to one who was truly God come in the flesh, the living Word, the very glory of God among humanity. John's collected evidence and proof all make the most compelling testimony to Jesus' right to demand our ongoing trust and obedience.

1

JESUS: THE ETERNAL WORD
John 1:1-4, 14, 18

THE BEGINNING OF JOHN'S GOSPEL (1:1-4)

JESUS' ETERNAL PERSONALITY AS GOD (1:1-2)

Jesus' eternity
Jesus' personality
Jesus' deity

THE WORD (1:1-4,14, 18)

The simple answer: what it means to readers today
The profound answer: what it meant to readers then

The significance of the Word
He was the agent in creation (1:3)
He is the source of life (1:4)
He became a human being (1:14)
We have seen his glory (1:14)
He has made God known (1:18)

THE BEGINNING OF JOHN'S GOSPEL (1:1-4)

One of the problems in writing the biography of someone is to know when to begin. Do you begin with the contribution they've made to public life? Or do you go back to their birth and talk about their parents and grandparents, and if so, how far do you go back in their family? It's interesting to see how different biographers answer this question in different ways.

The Bible has four biographies of Jesus, each beginning differently in describing Jesus' life. Mark decided to limit his biography to those three years when Jesus was in the public eye and influencing men and women for good and for God and so he began with John the Baptist. Matthew said, "I'm going further back. I'm going to begin with his birth and include his ancestors," and he went back to the ancestor of our Lord called Abraham: the beginning of Jewish history. Luke said, "I'm going further back than that. I'm going back through his ancestry as far back as Adam." All these answers were in line with the purpose for which each Gospel writer wanted to give of Jesus' life. Mark wanted to show Jesus as the Son of Man, so he showed Jesus as the man among humanity. Matthew showed Jesus as the King of the Jews, and so he went back to the beginning of Jewish history with Abraham. Luke shows Jesus as the Saviour of the world and so took his family tree right back to the first man, Adam.

Then John came, this eighty-year-old man, who had known Jesus for sixty years and he wanted to show Jesus as the Son of God. He thought where to begin and he said, "I'm going back further than the other three, beyond Abraham and Adam, right back to the beginning of the Bible where it says, 'In the beginning God created the heavens and the earth.'" That was as far back as his mind could go. You can't think of a time when there was nothing; our minds cannot cope with that.

JESUS' ETERNAL PERSONALITY AS GOD (1:1-2)

Jesus' eternity

We assume this universe has been here for ever, but both Scripture and science tell us this universe had a beginning, that it wasn't always here. There was a day when there was nothing and now there is a universe. That's as far as we can go because my mind cannot imagine nothing. We know that space is limited, that you can't go on into space for ever, that you reach its end. As soon as you say that, somebody says, "But what is there beyond that?" and you reply, "Nothing." The difficulty is that we can't imagine nothing; the human mind can't imagine the infinite, and so we can't go back beyond the beginning of our universe: that is the limit of our thinking.

John said, "I'm going to begin my Gospel there but I fully realize that I haven't started at the beginning of Jesus' life even then," and so he said, "In the beginning he already was." If you go back as far as the human mind can go, until your imagination stops – he was there: he was already in existence. Before everything was created, he already existed. You're still not at the beginning of Jesus' life and the truth is that you never can get to the beginning of his life, not if he's the Son of God.

If he's just a great man he must have had a beginning. Everyone has a beginning. There was a time when I did not exist. But Jesus never felt that way: if Jesus is the Son of God, you can go back as far back as you want and he's still there. He always was. God always was, and if Jesus is God's Son, he always was. So there can't ever be a beginning to his life.

Notice he doesn't say, "He began before everything else"; he says, "Before everything else began, he was," and that's completely different. This is something our puny little minds cannot grasp and so we get asked the silly question, "Who made God?" There is a simple answer and it is, "That's a silly question." It's the same kind of question as asking, "Where does a circle begin?" You can't answer that question because a circle goes on and on: it has neither beginning nor end. So it's nonsensical to ask such a question. Equally, it's nonsensical to ask who made God, because the Bible says, "God is from everlasting to everlasting," and I can't understand that. And if Jesus was God's Son, then he was from everlasting to everlasting. He was always there and so you could never begin to write Jesus' life at the beginning.

The first phrase in verse 1 of John's Gospel talks about the eternity of Jesus. If you go back as far as your imagination can take you, he was there. The eternity of Jesus – these first few verses of John leave us utterly out of our depth. We can't cope with it and so I'm glad that John said, "I won't take you back beyond what you can imagine. Just go back to the beginning of the universe. Go back to the time when everything was created and he was already there."

"In the beginning was the Word, and the Word was with God, and the Word was God" (1:1).

Jesus' personality

The second thing stated in verse 1 is the *personality* of Jesus. "He was with God." The word translated *with* means literally "face to face with; talking with; looking at." As two friends talk together, Jesus was face to face with God. He was a real person. Do you realize the revolutionary implications of this? For example, we say that God is love. You couldn't say that if God had been all alone in eternity, if there was no other person for him to meet face to face. But because Jesus was there all the time, because Jesus was God's Son and because they were face to face, God is love. He always was and always will be. Love is real and all the crying out for love is feeling after what God is. He always was love.

Jesus was with God from the beginning. It also means we can say that God is Father, always was Father, and always will be Father. You can't be a father unless you have a child. For many years of my life I was not a father but now I am a father, but God was not like that. God always was a father because he always had a Son and that Son had personality and they were face to face. He was with God.

Jesus' deity

The third thing this verse tells us is the deity of our Lord Jesus. He was God. There is no higher statement about Jesus in the whole of the New Testament than this. There is no qualification, saying he was a bit like God or he was full of God. No, he was God. He was the same as God. Exactly the same. What you say about God you can say about Jesus: "and the Word was God."

These are the three things said in verse 1 and if you drop any one of those three you destroy Christianity. If there is no eternity in Jesus, then he can't give you everlasting life. If there is not personality in Jesus, then he can't be your friend and Saviour. If there is not deity in Jesus, then he can't forgive your sins because only God can forgive sins. It's because of these three things that the man we call Jesus can do for you what no other man could do.

THE WORD (1:1-4. 14, 18)

At this point we need to look at the word *Word*. Why did John not begin his Gospel by saying, "In the beginning Jesus was and Jesus was with God and Jesus was God." Why did he introduce this extraordinary phrasing, "In the beginning was the Word, and the Word was with God, and the Word was God"? *The Word* is the first title in John's Gospel given to Jesus, and every title is given for a purpose.

There are two purposes why he calls Jesus the *Word* here. The first reason is that the name *Jesus* was only given to this person when he was born in Bethlehem. It was not the name that he had before. It was a human name to describe what he came to earth to do. It did not describe what he did before he was born. So the word *Jesus* is never used of him before he was born at Bethlehem, and it would therefore seem silly to say, "Jesus was there at the beginning of the creation" – that's not quite correct. He changed his name when he came to earth.

The second reason why John doesn't use the word *Jesus* until later in chapter 1 is that he wants to give Jesus a title that will describe exactly what he was before he came to earth. He felt around in the Greek language he spoke, and the Holy Spirit gave him this thought: "I'm going to call him *the Word*." Now why? John is the only man in the New Testament to call Jesus *the Word*.

"Jesus is the communicating link between God and people."

The simple answer: what it means to readers today

What does *the Word* mean? I'm going to give you two explanations: a simple and a profound one. Let's take the simple one first. What does word mean to you? It is the connecting link between two people, a pattern of sound that expresses the thought of one person's mind and enters another person's mind, so providing a link between them. A word expresses one person and enters another. I'm sure that was one of the meanings John had when he called Jesus *the Word*. He expressed God perfectly and entered people. And in this way God and God's thoughts, which were so much higher than ours, were able to enter our minds. Jesus is the communicating link between God and people. God expresses himself in Jesus and in Jesus God enters people. He's the communication between God and people. You'll never find God until you find Jesus. "No-one comes to the Father except through me" (14:6, NIV). God has spoken in Jesus and through Jesus God can enter our lives. That's the simple meaning.

The profound answer: what it meant to readers then

But I'm not sure that's the real reason why John chose this title. I'm going to have to go back into Greek history and historical linguistics. I want to take you back to about six hundred years before this book was written in Ephesus, where a Greek man called Heraclitus lived. Heraclitus looked out on the world and he saw that nature was changing; people were changing; history was changing. Everything was changing, and he asked, "Is there any meaning to it? Is there any purpose to it? Is there any pattern to it? Is there any logic to it? Is there any *logos* to it?" And the Greek word *logos* means "word".

Now people today are asking the same question Heraclitus asked. They read their papers and they say, "Is there any purpose, pattern, meaning, logic to it all? Or is it all chaos?" I tell you this, that if the world is nothing more than chaos then I think I would be tempted to take my own life. There is no point, no meaning if there is no pattern to all that is happening, if there is no purpose, if it's all chance and not choice. Is there any logic? Is there any *logos*? Heraclitus said there must be. There must be a pattern, a reason, a meaning. There must be some logic behind life and the pattern life takes. He searched and he studied nature, history and individual people. But he couldn't find what he called the *logos*, the word, reason, meaning, the pattern behind it all. Now that's where it started.

Do you know that people are still looking for this *logos*? Every time they investigate a new subject they use the word *logos*. The word *biology* contains the word *logos*: *bios* "life" + *logos* "reason, logic, pattern." Students of biology are looking for the pattern, the meaning, the logic, the purpose in life. Psychology is the study of the logic, the *logos*, the pattern of individual behaviour. Sociology is the study of the meaning and pattern of group behaviour. So we have all our -ologies: archaeology, zoology, entomology, etc. They've all got *logos* in. People still haven't found it: they're still looking for the meaning of life. They're still asking why it all happened. Is there any pattern at all or is it just chaos? And Heraclitus never found the *logos*, the word.

Many centuries later there lived in Egypt a Jew called Philo. He studied Heraclitus. He said, "There must be a *logos*. There must be a word. There must be a reason." But he also knew his Bible, his Old Testament, and as he thought about this, he remembered God said, "Let there be light," and there was light. God didn't merely think, "Let's have light and light appeared"; God *said the word*. Philo saw that God created the world by the word, the *logos*. Philo realized he was beginning to see something, and he began to say something new about the word, thinking that it wasn't in nature, but that it was the connecting link between God and nature. God gave a word and nature came to be. God speaks and the pattern of nature flows.

He was beginning to see it, he was getting so near and then John came, saying, "The meaning you've been looking for, the reason, what holds the world together, what explains the reason and the pattern of life, *I know him. I can tell you his name*." Isn't it exciting? So he says, "In the beginning was the *logos*, the Word, the reason, the pattern, and he was always there." This *logos*, this pattern of life you're looking for, is personal. He was a person face to face with God. You'll not find this *logos* in nature because this *logos* was God.

You know, with all our advanced knowledge we still can't find the meaning of the universe. We still can't see what holds it all together. But listen to the New Testament: "The Son ... sustaining all things by his powerful word" (Hebrews 1:3, NIV). Once you find him, you've found why it all hangs together. You have found the Person who is the reason for it all. "All things were created by him and for him. He is before all things, and in him all things hold together" (Colossians 1:16-17, NIV). God made the whole universe for Jesus. God flung the planets into space. We are just beginning to find out they are all there but they were put there for Jesus. He's the *logos*. He's the One who holds it all together. And he was the One who was busy making it all.

The significance of the Word

He was the agent in creation (1:3)

Here John moves on to an amazing thought. He says, "You know when God made the world he didn't make one single thing without Jesus." I looked out of the room in which I was writing this and I looked at the trees. Jesus made the trees before he made chairs and tables out of them. Do you understand that? Before Jesus walked the mountains and climbed those paths of Galilee, he made the mountains. Jesus made the seas before he sailed in a boat on the Sea of Galilee and then stepped into it. What a vision of Jesus! That's not the Jesus of *Godspell* or *Jesus Christ Superstar*. They don't start early enough or go on long enough: they're too limited. I want to take those two operas and stretch them both ways and say begin at the beginning. Show Jesus making a tree or a mountain.

And then you'll see my Jesus. Long before he came down here to help me, that's what he was doing. He was the contractor that God employed to bring into being the universe in which we live.

He is the source of life (1:4)

John began his Gospel here because this is the first thing Jesus did that affects me. There is something more wonderful than making trees and mountains: making life. Even when they manage to make life, they're doing something Jesus did thousands of years ago. We now know that the first little cell of life was more complicated than one of our best computers. They used to think when they taught evolution as fact that the first cell of life was a simple cell and that it became more and more complicated until finally we have life as it is today. We now know that that is not scientifically true. We now know that the very first life cell was so complex that we can't understand it. How do you think that first little cell of life appeared so complicated straightaway? Science has lost the answer to this or never found it.

I will tell you. In him was life and this is the big view of Jesus that John wants you to begin with. Before you look at a baby in a manger at Bethlehem, before you look at a young man of thirty being baptized in the Jordan, or someone who went around doing good, who died aged thirty-three – before you consider all those facts, consider he was always there. He was with God. He was God and he was with God making everything that is and giving life. What a thought!

He became a human being (1:14)

Maybe some of you feel I'm making Jesus too great or remote. You think that somebody who made all of space is too big for me to understand – and if that's all he had remained we would never have known him personally any more than you can know God personally if he'd remained out of touch. But now let me say I have good news for you. The Word became a human being; "the Word became flesh" (1:14). Consider the marvel of this! I can't understand how that could happen. The logos behind the whole universe, the meaning that people have sought, the One who brought it all into being stepped into what he'd made.

We have seen his glory (1:14)

He came right here as a human being and John says, "We have seen his glory" (1:14, NIV). If you've seen Jesus properly, you've seen somebody unique: the only Son of God. It could only be him, the radiance of his personality, the glory shining from his face and life – these could only belong to the Son of God. It couldn't belong to anyone else and we've seen his glory, the glory of the One and Only, the Only Begotten Son of the Father. John says, "We know the secret of the universe personally. We don't what's behind it all but we personally know who's behind it all."

"Jesus is the key that unlocks life and its purpose."

He has made God known (1:18)

This is what John means as he sums up in verse 18 of his introduction. No one has ever seen God. The God who was for ever beyond the reach of our senses has been made known by Jesus. Later in John's Gospel, John tells how a man said to Jesus, "You've told us many things but there's one thing you haven't done: you haven't shown us God. Just show us God. Let's see God and that'll be enough. We'll be satisfied then." And Jesus said, "Philip, I've been with you three years. Don't you know me yet?" Now the most staggering thing in that answer is that Jesus didn't say, "Don't you know God yet?", but rather, "Have I been with you, Philip, so long and don't you know me?" (See 14:1-9.)

Have you been looking for God? Have you been searching for the meaning to life? Do you look out on the chaos? Do you read your newspapers and wonder where it's all heading, what it's all about? You look at nature and you ask, "Is there any pattern to it or is it just pure chance?" Your life is chaos and you're trying to find a meaning. You may study science until you're blue in the face but you won't find it because the logos is not to be found there. The *logos* is with God. The reason for it all is in him. I tell you that as soon as you find Jesus, you've found the meaning: you've found the key that unlocks life and its purpose. Isn't that exciting? And that's where John began his Gospel. He said, "I'm beginning by telling you about something you're all searching for – only it's not some*thing*; it's *Someone*.

2

JESUS: LIFE AND LIGHT
1:4-18

THE LIFE IN HIS LIGHT (1:4-13)

Light conquers darkness
Mental darkness
Moral darkness

Light causes division
Rejected
Received

THE LIGHT IN HIS LIFE (1:14-18)

Shining glory

Shared grace
Enabling grace
Enlightening grace

One of the questions that has puzzled scientists for centuries is the question of where life came from. Scientists used to believe life on earth began as a kind of spontaneous chemical reaction. Charles Darwin believed life began "in some warm little pond with all sorts of ammonia and phosphoric acid salts, light, heat and electricity." He believed this mixture produced a chemical reaction which was a simple form of life and all life developed from that simple little cell until it became increasingly complex and now we have life in all its varieties – animal, vegetable and human. We now know from science this view is inadequate: the first tiny life cell was more complex than today's most complicated computer. That first living cell was made up of two components, neither of which could exist without the other. So how could they ever come together? One part was the basic material of life, a complex protein, and the other was a kind of taped code that controlled matter; these two proteins were so complex that the earth is not old enough for these two things to have happened by chance.

The fact is that science is no nearer finding out where life came from than it ever was. And the reason? Because "in him was life" (1:4, NIV). That statement means Jesus gave life. It didn't happen by chance as a spontaneous chemical combustion in a little pond. Life was in Christ: the revolutionary implications of that simple statement are mind-boggling. Every living thing owes its life to Jesus. That means, whether you acknowledge it or not, every living person is only alive because Jesus gave them life. In that sense, every living thing owes its existence to Jesus.

"Life was in Christ: the revolutionary implications of that simple statement are mind-boggling. Every living thing owes its life to Jesus."

In verse 3 John said that nothing in all creation would have existed without Jesus, but now John moves beyond inorganic things to life; every living thing came into being because of Jesus: "in him was life".

Jesus gives life. On two other occasions in this Gospel he gave himself the title "I am the life"; both were situations in which he confronted physical death. The first was when he stood at the graveside of one of his best friends and knew that a rotting, stinking corpse was inside the grave. Jesus said to those who stood at the tomb, "I am the life" (11:25). "I can bring that corpse from the tomb because I gave life to that body in the first place. Since I gave you life the first time, I can give it to you again. I am the resurrection and the life." Then he said, "Roll the stone away from that grave … Lazarus, come out." And there standing in the dark mouth of a gaping grave was a corpse, but its eyes could move. And when they unwound the shroud he was alive. "I am the life." "In him was life." The fact that I live and breathe is due to Jesus Christ, whether I know it or not. The fact that flowers bloom is due to Jesus Christ even though they don't know it. When I take my dog for a walk, that dog owes its life to Jesus. What a conception of Jesus!

The other time when Jesus said, "I am the life," was when he was about to die. He was talking about a beautiful place beyond the grave and he said to his friends, "I want you to be there with me. After death there is somewhere I live and I want you to come and be with me." And they said, "But how, where?" They couldn't understand it and he told them, "I am the way, and the truth, and the life. If I could give you life once I could give it to you twice. If I could cause a lump of matter to live then I could cause the dust of the earth to live again."

This is our hope. Beyond the grave, my body is going to live again. I'm going to have physical life and that's because he said, "I am the life." "In him was life." So whenever you see a living thing, you can say Jesus gave life to that thing.

THE LIFE IN HIS LIGHT (1:4-13)

But in a distinctive sense, life in Jesus becomes something more to humanity than the life of Jesus is to flowers or to animals. The life that was in him becomes light to me. "In him was life, and that life was the light of men" (1:4, NIV). The light shines because "God is light; in him there is no darkness at all" (1 John 1:5, NIV). If God were not light, this universe would be pitch black: there would be no light at all.

All light finds its origin in him, but there is a light in the life of Jesus that we are now going to consider. In what sense is the life of Jesus light to humanity? Flowers get their light from the sun not directly from Jesus, but if people are to know light, they will get it directly from Jesus, not from the sun.

Light conquers darkness

When Jesus said, "I am the light of the world" (8:24), he was not speaking of physical light. The sun is the physical light of the universe. Our electric light bulbs draw their power from the sun's buried energy from centuries ago. They are physical light. But Jesus doesn't light us physically. He's lighting us in a different way. In what sense is he light to mankind? The first thing light does is to conquer darkness. I remember going down a coal mine and the miner who took me 1,500 feet below ground put out his lamp. I couldn't even see my hand in front of my face. It was thick darkness. But as soon as that miner lit his lamp, all the darkness couldn't do anything about it. The darkness couldn't extinguish it, couldn't swallow it up, couldn't absorb it. That's what the word *understood* means in 1:4. The light shines in the darkness and the darkness can do nothing about it. The tiniest little light can conquer darkness and darkness can't put it out.

Mental darkness
People are walking about today thinking they can see, but they are actually in mental darkness: they cannot distinguish what is real. Why is it that the cleverest people can't find that God exists?

Why is it that you listen to discussions of brilliant professors of philosophy on television, but they haven't discovered that God is real? They are in mental darkness: they cannot distinguish the real from the illusory. We live in an age when it is obvious that humanity is completely bewildered. We've got amazing scientific discoveries on the one hand but appalling superstitions on the other, even in the same people. There's hardly a popular daily newspaper or magazine today that doesn't print a horoscope. This is the darkness in which we live. People say that a trip on a jumbo jet and a trip on heroin are both real. We can't distinguish the real from the illusory.

"Come out of the dark, come out of the shadows and walk in the light. Know a life that is not debased, but a life that can be lifted up into the light of his presence."

Moral darkness

You would have to be bold to say that humanity has become better, to say we have evolved where we are far better than our great-grandparents. We know what is right; we know how to live at peace; we can span space; we can send messages and pictures around the globe but we still haven't learned to live together. We know that selfishness is the bedrock on which all human ideals are wrecked and yet we still can't build the world we want our children to have. And our problems get bigger every year.

It was into this mental and moral darkness that a light – the life of Jesus – has shone. That light shines on humanity, not on flowers or animals, who haven't rebelled against God. But the light has shone on mankind and here is a life that is shining, telling us what is real and right so that we can begin to see. Anybody who looks at Jesus will begin to see the light. They will say, "Now I can see. I've seen the light." All that moral and mental confusion in the world can't put the light of Jesus out. He will continue to shine to the end of history.

It is that light that shines on everyone in the world. It's a universal light and that's why Jesus' teaching and his life, death and resurrection must be proclaimed to the whole world. He is the only light of the world: "I am the light of the world. Whoever follows me will never walk in darkness" (8:12, NIV). Come out of the dark, come out of the shadows and walk in the light. Know a life that is not mentally and morally debased, but a life that can be lifted up into the light of his presence.

Light causes division

Rejected

But light also causes division. Light cuts the dark from the light. Once when I was preaching, the lights failed. Somebody in the gallery had a torch and shone it on me during the service – that was all the light we had. I was in the light and the congregation was in darkness. Light has this divisive effect. The tragic truth is that when light shines, not everybody wants it to shine. Have you ever picked up a stone in your garden and seen lots of little creepy-crawlies underneath it? What do they do? They scuttle away into the dark. They don't want the light. They don't want to feel the warmth of the sun on them. They dig under another stone or under the grass. When Jesus shone, that's what happened.

We're now going to look at this sad truth. John says, "He was in the world … and the world didn't recognize him" (1:10). That was true even before his birth. Before he was born at Bethlehem, Jesus was in this world. If every tree owes its life to Jesus, he was in this world. If he not only created all things but sustains them by his powerful word, he was in this world. He was not in the form in which he came at Bethlehem, but he was in this world and the world hadn't a clue. They never recognized him. Who would know that Jesus was controlling all things before he was born at Bethlehem? But the tragedy is when he did come in a form they could recognize, they still didn't receive the light. They just saw a baby in a manger at Bethlehem; even his own parents didn't see him as they should, the Son of God, and he had to rebuke them when he was twelve years old. Later in Nazareth, they still said, "Isn't this the carpenter?" They just thought he made stools: they didn't realize he made stars.

Out of all the countries that he had made, there was one country prepared to receive him. Out of all the nations he had given life to, there was one nation that was just prepared for him and he came to his own country and his own people would not have him. The Jews have faced the memory for two thousand years that they rejected the light. But Jews are not alone in doing this, Gentiles did so too. When someone first hears about Jesus, they are at a fork in the road. Either they can walk in the light and follow this through or they prefer to go back into the darkness and scuttle away like a creature under a stone.

Received

But not everybody rejected him. Some received him, opening up their lives to him (1:11-12). They believed in him. They said in all the mental confusion of human opinion, this man is the truth. In all the moral confusion, this man is the way. And in all the deadness, this man is the life, and so they believed in him.

What happened to them? He changed their status and he changed their state. He changed their status by giving them the right to become children of God. Do you know this means that people are not the children of God? Some people talk about "the universal brotherhood of man" and "the universal fatherhood of God" – that is nonsense. The Bible doesn't teach that. The true children of God are those who receive this light, who believe in Jesus. Then they have the right to call God *Father*. Do you know you haven't got the right to use the Lord's Prayer until you believe in Jesus? "Our Father." He is not your Father until you've come into the light. When you believe Jesus, you have the right to become a child of God. You'll never be alone again, never an orphan without a father to care for you.

Is it only a change in status? No, it's more than that; it's a change in state. Because you become children of God by being born. Here is one of the mysteries of John's Gospel, which we will come back to in chapter three. A man can be born twice. The first time, when he's born physically, Jesus gives him physical life. But he can be born all over again. This time not in the way that babies are born. There are two ways babies are born: unwanted and wanted. Some babies are expected, some are not. John says when you believe in him you are born not as an unwanted or wanted child. You are born of God and he wanted you: new life is born within you. You are starting life all over again. You are born of God, so you are able to be a child of God. You've been born into the family. You can call God *Father*, and know he will look after you.

So when Jesus shines and someone steps into that light, something happens. That person knows a life that they never knew by being born into this world. They become a child of God. How should such a thing be? The answer is simple. Jesus Christ was the Son of God and the divine being in him became a human being so that human beings might enter divine being. "The Word became flesh" (1:14, NIV), that flesh might be born of God. He was born of flesh so that we might be born of Spirit. Do you understand? God took the first step that we might take this one. God came to us and then he said, "Now you come to me."

THE LIGHT IN HIS LIFE (1:14-18)

So far we have been thinking about the life in his light. When he shines, he gives new life to people, but now let's look at the light in his life. This is John's version of the Christmas story. Matthew and Luke take chapters over it. John tells the Christmas story in one phrase. "The Word became flesh" (1:14, NIV): the Word became a human being. That should make you gasp. How can you get all of God in a body that length? But that's what happened. Here is one of my favourite hymns:

> *Glory be to God on high,*
> *And peace on earth descend!*
> *God comes down, he bows the sky,*
> *And shows himself our friend:*
> *God the invisible appears!*
> *God, the blest, the great I AM,*
> *Sojourns in this vale of tears,*
> *And Jesus is his name.*

Him the angels all adored,
Their Maker and their King.
Tidings of their humbled Lord
They now to mortals bring.
Emptied of his majesty,
Of his dazzling glories shorn,
Being's source begins to be,
And God himself is born!

See the eternal Son of God
A mortal Son of man;
Dwelling in an earthly clod,
Whom heaven cannot contain!
Stand amazed, ye heavens, at this!
See the Lord of earth and skies;
Humbled to the dust he is,
And in a manger lies.

We, the sons of men, rejoice,
The Prince of peace proclaim;
With heaven's host lift up our voice,
And shout Immanuel's name:
Knees and hearts to him we bow;
Of our flesh and of our bone,
Jesus is our brother now,
And God is all our own.

(Charles Wesley)

"The Word became flesh and made his dwelling among us. We have seen his glory, the glory of the One and Only who came from the Father" (1:14, NIV). They actually saw Jesus with their eyes. He came and lived among them. He didn't come like a human being, he *became* a human being. He had a body like mine. He knew what it was to be hungry, thirsty, tired, angry, surprised and sad. He was just like me, but not like me because when they looked at his life they saw a shining glory in it that you've never seen in anybody else. It was a glory that was of human life at its best.

Shining glory

He lived in difficult circumstances in an occupied country, full of turmoil, violence and terrorism, but in that situation there is a life that's full of glory. It's the glory of a perfect human life, which the world had not seen until then, but it's the glory that's not only human, it's also divine. He radiated God. As people looked at him, they said, "That is the Father's one and only Son." The glory that shines out of his life is a glory that you'll see in no other person. That's why the study of his life is more important to you than the study of the greatest person who ever lived.

"The great contrast between the Old and the New Testament is 'the law was given through Moses; grace and truth came through Jesus Christ' (1:17). The law came with demands; Jesus came with an offer."

Shared grace

The glory shining in Jesus' life is a glory made up of two things that rarely go together in human beings: grace and truth. Some people are gracious but there isn't the strength of truth or justice in them. Some people have all the strength and justice of truth but not enough grace: "full of grace and truth" (1:14, NIV). The glorious thing is that Jesus shares his grace with us. There's a wonderful little phrase here: "From the fullness of his grace we have all received grace instead of grace." Jesus has everything you need. "From his fullness": he's got everything. He made everything, so he has got everything: therefore everything you will ever need you will find in Jesus. And he is willing to give it. To think that someone who has got everything is so generous. He is a multi-millionaire and he just longs to give it away.

The phrase "grace instead of grace" is extraordinary. I can best explain it to you by thinking of milk bottles. Every day in our house there is a ritual. We put empty bottles out on the front doorstep and the next morning they are full. It's marvellous! We drink it and the next day the bottle is full again and it continues. That is exactly what this phrase in Greek means. It means when Jesus has given you a grace gift of his love and you've used it up, it's full again, replaced as regularly as your daily milk: grace instead of grace, grace upon grace. "Of his fullness we've received grace after grace, wave upon wave of blessing." The blessings just pour into the lives of those who walk in the light, one blessing after the other. He wants you to share and give the glory that shone in Jesus.

Enabling grace

We have seen his glory, but we've also received his grace and that's even more wonderful. Otherwise you would just look at Jesus and say, "I could never be like that. That life is too high an ideal. The glory is too great. I could never be like that." But Jesus says, "No, you can't, but I can give you grace to be like that." This is the glory of the gospel. The great contrast between the Old and the New Testament is "the law was given through Moses; grace and truth came through Jesus Christ" (1:17, NIV). The law came with demands; Jesus came with an offer. The law said, "This is how you should live. Here are the Ten Commandments. Now live like that or you'll die," and every one of us knows that's a sentence of death on us. The law told us what to do but it didn't help us do it, but Jesus came with grace and said, "I'll help you. I will lift you. Don't try and be patient. Let my patience live in you. Don't try and be pure – let my purity fill you. Don't try and be this or that. Let me give you blessing upon blessing, grace upon grace." This is the difference: his grace enables us to do what his Father demands of us.

Enlightening grace

His grace not only enables us to live rightly; it also enlightens us. No one has ever seen God. How can we get to know someone we can't see? We meet each other. How can we get to know God? Here is the grand climax of John's introduction. He says, "Don't you see, if Jesus is the same as God; if Jesus is at the Father's side, if he is this nature and in this relationship with God, if you could get to know Jesus, you will know his Father?" He who is the same as God and is at God's side has made the Father known. "Don't you know me, Philip, even after I have been among you such a long time and yet do you not know the Father? Do you not know me?" (14:9). So we have now come to the amazing privilege of knowing God.

3

JOHN THE BAPTIST
POINTS TO JESUS
1:19-34

MESSENGER OF THE LORD - JOHN (1:19-28)

Self-humbled
Saviour exalted

MISSION OF THE LAMB - JESUS (1:29-34)

Sin emptied
Spirit filled

MESSENGER OF THE LORD – JOHN (1:19-28)

Have you heard of Annie Sullivan? From the age of twenty-one she gave her whole life to a little girl of seven, spending the rest of her life with that blind, deaf and dumb girl. Annie Sullivan was Helen Keller's tutor. More of you have heard of Helen Keller, but you would never have heard of Helen but for Annie. Annie spent years patiently teaching that girl to speak until she could talk with the world's great men. By the age of ten she could read Braille in Latin, Greek and English. Helen Keller became a great and wonderful lady. By 1936 Helen Keller had no problems of communication but Annie Sullivan was totally blind and her health had gone and she died in 1936. Somebody visited her just before she died and said to her, "Teacher, get well. Without you, Helen Keller will be nothing." Annie Sullivan replied, "Then I have failed." But she had not failed. Helen Keller spent World War II comforting blinded soldiers, opening homes for blind people. All over Israel there are Helen Keller Homes for Blind Children. She ministered in the Foundation for the Blind in New York for many years. Annie Sullivan had not failed but it is Helen Keller who is remembered.

Annie Sullivan and John the Baptist would have got on well together. They would have understood each other for the wonderful qualities in Annie Sullivan are seen similarly in John the Baptist. John was a man who gave his life for the sake of one other person and counted it his duty to leave that other person centre stage.

I think John the Baptist is one of the loveliest men in the whole of the Bible. I think Jesus was right when he said, "Among all those born of women he's the greatest" (Matthew 11:11). At the time, people would not have thought he was the greatest. Many would have dismissed him as a dropout or a hippy. He wore his hair longer than everybody else. He wore an old coat made of tent cloth, camel's hair. He lived in the wilds on a weird diet of insects and sometimes wild honey.

But in his late twenties this young man who had lived a lonely life apart from others, but who'd had wonderful spiritual communion with God, stepped into the public eye, not by coming back to town, but staying out in the wilderness and he began to do two strange things, preach sermons and dip people in the river.

At first, a trickle of people came and then the trickle became a stream and then the stream became a river and the river became a flood, until thousands of people were journeying miles to go and see this young man, to listen to what he had to say, and they usually finished up in the river.

Why did they go? What was it that drew hundreds of people? For a thousand years Israel had been in trouble; they always looked back to peace and prosperity of when David had been king. They had never had such large borders then; everything was right. But after David died, everything went wrong; there was civil war and they were invaded. They were taken off as slaves to a foreign land. Even when some of them struggled back years later they still found they were invaded, overrun by one nation after another. The Greeks, Egyptians, Syrians, and Romans came, and pent up within them were hopes and dreams for the future they hoped God would fulfil. They searched their Bibles looking for clues. They began to believe because the Scripture said God was going to do something about it all one day and that he'd do it by sending men to help them. They searched their Bibles to see what kind of a man and they found different promises. They found that in Malachi (4:5) God promised that one day he would send Elijah back to them, and they thought Elijah was their greatest prophet. They looked for Elijah to return. They read in Deuteronomy 18:15 that Moses said, "One day God will send to you a prophet like me." So they used to talk about and look for the prophet, but above all they looked for a king like David, a king anointed by God as David was anointed. The Hebrew for "anointed" is *Messiah* and the Greek for "anointed" is *Christ*. So they looked for a messiah.

These hopes had lasted nearly 1,000 years. When you've waited that time you get excited if you think something is happening. During this time, for 400 years, God had been silent. That was unknown in their history. For 400 years not a word had come from heaven. That's why there's a gap of 400 years between the Old and the New Testaments. The records were kept but God wasn't talking, so there was nothing to listen to. For 400 years they had waited for God to speak again. Was the God who had spoken through the prophets from Moses to Malachi ever going to talk again?

So we reach a generation that had never heard a prophet speak, who didn't know what prophecy was. That could be true of many Christians today also. Many don't know what prophecy is: they have never heard God speak directly using the human mouth.

They looked for someone like Moses, Elijah or David. Can you now see why, when this young man with his long hair and his old clothes got up and preached, they listened, they heard God? It was the first time they had heard God in years. No wonder they came. Do you know, when God is talking, people come. So they came in ever-increasing numbers. Could this young man be one of the three they'd been looking for? Could it be Elijah? He's wearing the same kind of clothes. Could it be the prophet like Moses? Could he even be the Messiah who's going to reign over us? So the rumours spread, and this young man in the centre of all the controversy and discussion went on preaching. His message was simple: "You're all dirty, so I'll wash you." As he preached that message, people realized they were dirty inside. To go down into that Jordan River, with everybody watching, and be washed was an open acknowledgement of inward dirt. But that was his sermon: he said, "Get washed, get clean quick, because the King is coming."

The more God is talking, the more external things become secondary. When God begins to move, he sometimes has to go outside the religious establishment. It's new wine, and the old bottles would crack. Sometimes he's got to start up a completely new work, something the religious establishment may not be ready for and may be disturbed by. And they were. A young man with long hair down by the Jordan … and people were going to listen to him speaking about God. The Jews were worried. Congregations were dwindling and when they asked, "Where's Mrs So and So today?" they were told, "Oh, she's gone to hear the new preacher at the Jordan River." So they sent a deputation of priests and Levites to go and examine this young man (1:19). They came down the Jericho road and met this young man in his late twenties.

"Who are you?" they asked. It was a confrontation between a human religion and a new move of God's Spirit. They came down and we read about the confrontation. What did John think about himself?

"They came to John the Baptist and asked , 'Who are you? Are you the Messiah?' 'No, I'm not.' 'Then are you Elijah?' 'No, I'm not.' 'Are you the Prophet?' 'No.' Do you notice his answers get shorter and shorter, as if he doesn't want to talk about himself?   He's saying, 'Let's not talk about me at all.'"

John was mentioned twice in the first 18 verses: look at 1:6-8. John says, "This John was not the Light. He only came to tell people about the Light." He pointed to the Light. The next mention is in verse 15. John cried out, "This is the One I was talking about when I said, 'He comes after me but he is greater than I am because he existed before I was born.'" John says he must have the pre-eminence because he had the pre-existence. "He was before me so he is above me." John was actually born on earth six months before Jesus, his cousin, but he says, "He existed long before I did." How did he know that? What an extraordinary insight! But he'd lived with God in the wilderness and God tells you lovely secrets when you're there to talk to him.

Self-humbled

Everybody who dares use the name *Baptist* should go back to John and discover what it is to be a Baptist. It is a nickname for those who take people and plunge them under water. The word *baptize* is Greek for "plunge, submerge, dip". When they wanted a nickname for this John to identify him, they called him "John the Dipper," "John the Plunger," "John the Baptist". If you use the nickname "Baptist" we say with John, "We baptize with water." But there's more to a Baptist than that. A Baptist should be someone who humbles himself, who doesn't draw attention to himself but who draws attention to Jesus. Look how he did this (1:20-25). They came to him and they said, "People think all kinds of things about you ... who are you? Are you the Messiah?" "No, I'm not." "Then are you Elijah?" No, I'm not. "Are you the Prophet?" "No." Do you notice his answers get shorter and shorter, as if he doesn't want to talk about himself? He's saying, "Let's not talk about me at all." Here he is in marked contrast to Jesus. John said, "I am not," but Jesus said, "I am." That's the difference between a man and the Son of God.

None of us should go around beginning every other sentence with, "I am". The Son of God should and did. So John the Baptist said, "I'm not." And they said, "Look we've got to report back with something to a council meeting in Jerusalem tomorrow morning. Tell us who you are." And John said, "You've got it all wrong – it's not *who* I am; it's *what* I am. I will tell you what I am: I'm just a voice, that's all… a voice."

That's what a good Baptist is: a voice, saying, "The Lord is coming – get ready;" a voice crying out, "Get ready. Make the road straight." This goes back to something that happened regularly in the Middle East and still does sometimes. It did more then before the roads were paved. Now tarmac roads cross the Arabian desert but where the roads are not paved, they get rutted and rough with holes, bumps, ridges and rocks. So whenever a king or other VIP is going to visit a town, somebody goes running ahead shouting out, "Make the road straight." They run out, take the rocks off the road and fill up every valley in the road and bring down every mountain in the road. They fill up the potholes, clear off the bumps and take the rocks away to get a smooth road. A VIP is coming. And John said, "That's all I am … and nothing more matters." He was a forerunner shouting out, "Get ready, he's coming, make the road straight, get it smooth." Jesus wants you to be a voice, saying, "Get ready for the coming of the Lord," for he is coming back to earth a second time.

This didn't satisfy them and they began to speak threateningly and switch the subject from the One who was coming later to what John was doing (1:24-25). "Why are you baptizing? What's all this about? This is a religious symbol you shouldn't be doing. This is for the priest to do." The priest baptized but they never baptized a Jew. Baptism was observed by the Jews for the Gentiles. It was always for a dirty Gentile, never for a Jew. When a Gentile wanted to join their religion, to come into the temple and worship their God, they said, "Fine, but you're dirty – you need to be washed," and they baptized them from head to toe. The priests knew all about baptism and they asked, "John, why do you baptize? You're not a priest and you shouldn't be doing this. Above all, why are you doing it to our people, the Jews? We never do it to our people. They already belong to God." John was saying, "No, Jews are just as dirty as Gentiles, and if the Lord is coming we've got to be clean. We've all got to get ready." What a ministry! He knew it would offend people and it did.

Saviour exalted

"Why do you baptize?" John replied (1:26-28), "Yes, I baptize them with water, but I don't want to discuss that. There is One standing here in this crowd whom you don't know and I'm not worthy to untie his shoes." The Jewish rabbis had a saying: "Everything a servant does for his master a pupil should do for his teacher except untie his sandal." That was the most undignified, humiliating task. The lowest slave in any large household had the job of untying people's shoes and I wonder if John had to kneel down and undo his sandals and felt that even that was too good a job for him.

John is saying, "Look, stop discussing me, stop looking at me. There is Somebody far greater, far more wonderful, than me. I want you to think of him."

"Let's humble self and exalt Christ!"

Can I plead with those who call themselves Baptists that we should be known as those who humble self and exalt Christ? Not as those who exalt Baptists and debase Christ! Let's follow John if we use his title and let's tell people if they ask what Baptists are, "We're just people saying, 'Look to Jesus.' We don't want to discuss ourselves. We want you to look to him. Yes, we baptize with water, but there is One who is greater."

MISSION OF THE LAMB – JESUS (1:29-34)

The next day Jesus came. John saw him coming and said, "Look, that's the One," and he gave him the extraordinary title of *lamb*. Unfortunately, that title has lost most of its meaning for us today. We use the word *lamb* of a little child or a little, harmless cuddly animal. You think of something young rather than older, but a lamb to a shepherd and in the Bible was a yearling: strong and grown, a ram. The other wrong impression of *lamb* is that it conveys a live animal because nearly every lamb you've seen is alive. But to the people then it would convey a dead animal. Most lambs they saw were dead; they had had their throats slit and were lying in a pool of their own blood. Every morning and evening hundreds of lambs were brought into the temple and slaughtered. Every Jewish household once a year took a lamb and cut its throat on Passover night. The major content of the word *lamb* to those people would have been of an animal that had died a violent death.

When John called Jesus "the Lamb," it would have been inevitable for them to have thought that Jesus would die soon. Both John and Jesus died a bloody death. A few months later John was beheaded at the whim of a despot and the wish of a dancing girl. Three years later Jesus was strung up on a cross with the blood flowing from the wounds in his body. John's death accomplished nothing. His ministry was his life but Jesus' death was most amazing. There has never been a greater claim for Jesus than the one John made then. "Look, the Lamb of God who takes away the sin of the world!" (1:29, NIV).

Sin emptied

If you wonder why Christians make so much of the cross and why we think the greatest thing Jesus ever did was to die, it is that when Jesus died that violent death, he was taking away the sins of the world. To take away the sins from one life would be a major achievement, but it's something no one could ever do. You can't take the sin away from your life. Not just one life, never mind taking it away from anybody else's. But Jesus took away – removed – the sin of the world, all human selfishness and wilfulness. "The Lamb of God who takes away the sin of the world." It doesn't say he'll *reduce*, *neutralize* or even that he'll *forgive* the sin, but he takes it away. That's a tremendous claim!

One day there will be a heaven and an earth in which righteousness and peace will dwell and no sin. And it will be because Jesus died. The Lamb of God taking away the sin of the world. Look at him.

"Jesus Christ didn't just come to empty your life of all that's wrong; he came to fill it with all that's right. This is the glorious news!"

Spirit filled

But some people could say that if you took away all the sin, then life would be empty and dull. If you took away all evil and selfishness, what would be left? The tragedy is that some people have illustrated precisely this. The emptiness and the narrowness of a life that's had sin taken away with nothing put in its place is an empty hollow life, but John knew better. He knew that if this Lamb of God was going to take away sins he would not leave the world empty. He would not leave life hollow, narrow and limited. And so John spoke of something else. He said, "I baptize you in water, but this man – this Lamb, this Son of God – will give you another baptism that will fill you up with something else. He will baptize you in the Holy Spirit."

Here is the positive side of our Lord's ministry. He didn't come just to take away sin. He came to fill with the Spirit. He didn't just come to empty your life of all that's wrong; he also came to fill it with all that's right. This is the glorious news that Jesus didn't just come to empty us of sin but he came to fill us with the Spirit. You can become so obsessed with baptism in water that you neglect being baptized in the Spirit. You wash away the past and the sins go, but the life that results is not a life that's attractive to others. They say, "Well, if that's Christianity, I don't want it. It's boring."

One philosopher said, "You've got to fill a man with something." That's why Paul said, "Don't get drunk with wine but be filled with the Spirit" (Ephesians 5:18).

It's no use just taking something away that's wrong; you also have to replace it with what's right. So John said, "I'll tell you something else about Jesus. He'll not only take away what's wrong, he will also baptize with the Spirit. I know this from experience." It's said of John – and of no one else in the Bible – that he was filled with the Holy Spirit from the day of his birth. Can you imagine what that would be like? To be filled with the Holy Spirit all your babyhood, boyhood, adolescence, young adulthood? John knew from experience what it was to be filled. He hadn't got a house to live in, any decent clothes or friends. He'd got nothing, but he had got everything: he was filled with the Holy Spirit.

He also knew it from observation. He said, "God told me something. He told me that when I was baptizing people I would see the Holy Spirit come down on one man and stay with that man, who would be the One who will baptize others with the Holy Spirit." He said, "I saw that happen to my own cousin. I didn't know that that was the One God was going to choose. He was there and I didn't know it and he came and I baptized him and I saw the Spirit like a dove, something so pure and white, come to rest on him."

It is no wonder John finishes (1:34) by saying, "I tell you he must be the Son of God." Nobody else can take away your sins and fill you with the Spirit. The most I personally can do is what John the Baptist did. I can baptize you in water but that's all I can do. That's only one of the baptisms. But he can cause that dove to alight on you and fill you to overflowing with his Spirit. He must be the Son of God. He couldn't be anyone else and that is the testimony.

I have spoken to those who are believers and I have told you to take your cue from John the Baptist. Point to him. Let's stop talking about Baptist things and talk about Jesus.

Now a word to those who are not yet believers. You are listening to a Baptist but that's not enough. I can't take your sins away. I can't take my own away. And I can't fill you with God's Spirit. I can't fill myself with the Spirit. So I would say, "Don't just join the Baptists. Don't just come to a Baptist. Come to Jesus and let him do what he longs to do." Would you really like Jesus to take away your sins? All the pride, selfishness and self-will that spoils your life and spoils other people's lives. Would you really like to be filled with the Spirit, so that the empty void has been filled with Someone beautiful?" Come to Jesus, the Lamb of God, who takes away the sins of the world.

4

FOLLOWING AND FINDING JESUS
1:35-51

A DAY IN THE SOUTH (1:35-42)

Andrew follows
The question
The quest

Peter found

A DAY IN THE NORTH (1:43-51)

Philip follows
The command
The companionship

Nathanael found
The law
The ladder

Three things strike me about the beginning of the church in this passage: first, how *low* it started: 1,600 feet below sea level! It started at the bottom but it won't finish there; it will finish in highest heaven. Secondly, how *small* it started: with just two members. It may have started small but it's already so large that nobody knows except God how many millions are in the church. It's going to finish as a multitude that no one can number. Thirdly, how *simply* it started. No conference or committee was set up to decide how to have a church. It started by one person going and finding another person. That is so simple but it's still the most fruitful way of growing the church. If we could match Andrew finding Peter and then Philip finding Nathanael, there would be exponential growth.

Who started the church? We could say Jesus but I'm going further back. John the Baptist started the church of Jesus Christ by telling two men, "That's the Lamb of God" (1:29) and they left John and followed Jesus. The greatness of John's character is never seen so clearly as when he said to his own followers, "Follow Jesus." The followers of Jesus increased because the followers of John decreased. John was big enough to say, "He must become greater; I must become less" (3:30, NIV). Happy is the person who is not concerned about whether they have a lot of friends but is concerned whether Jesus has friends and who is big enough to say, "Follow him, not me."

A DAY IN THE SOUTH (1:35-42)

Andrew follows

We're going to look at the first two days in the life of the church. On these two days you have exactly the same pattern but different personalities. The first day, John is standing by the Jordan with two disciples, and Jesus walks by. This is the last occasion when John was going to see Jesus with his earthly eyes. It was also the first occasion when these two men saw Jesus. One glimpse was enough to transfer their allegiance from one leader to another. Imagine the scene: the river, the riverbank, Jesus walking away, two disciples following him along the bank, leaving John alone, standing still. It's a poignant moment. John said, "Don't look at me. Look at him," and they took one look and followed Jesus. One good look at Jesus is enough to make you dissatisfied with anyone else. If you really look at Jesus, no one else can ever be your Saviour.

The question

As they followed Jesus, he opened the conversation, asking a leading question. Jesus nearly always drew someone out by asking them a question, so they had to describe their inner thoughts. He asked, "What do you want?" (1:38). Not "Who do you want?" but, "What do you want? Why are you following me?"

I ask you: What do you come to church for? What is the desire of your heart as you come? Is it simply to go through another service? What do you want? Some people come to Jesus first because they're looking for excitement. Or they come looking for comfort or for the answer to a question. Not many come to Jesus first for the deepest reason. It may be mere curiosity as in the case of these two disciples.

"I ask you: what do you come to church for? What is the desire of your heart as you come here? Is it simply to go through another service? What do you want?"

John had said, "Look, the Lamb of God, who takes away the sin of the world!" (1:29, NIV) and Jesus said, "What do you want?" They could have said, "We want our sins taken away," but they didn't say that – it wouldn't have been true. Not then, but later, that's what they wanted. I first began to look for Jesus, not to have my sins taken away, but because I met a group of young people who'd got something I hadn't got but wanted – I wanted to know who gave it to them, where they got it, what it was. Then

I discovered that it wasn't an *it* but a *he*. I didn't come to Jesus first to take away my sins, but I soon began to realize that's what he wanted to do.

They asked, "We'd like to know where you live. Could you give us your address please?" They're saying, "We're curious. We would like to know where we can contact you again." They were honest. Jesus didn't answer them, "Look, I came to take away sins, not to give people my address." He said, "All right – come and see." He could have said, "Go and see: it's number 35 High Street, Bethany. If you're interested in the house and circumstances I live in, go and see." But he didn't. He said, "Come and see." He started right where they were and said, "Come on, let's travel together." This was a better answer. He didn't answer their question in so many words. But he said, "I see you want to know the person rather than the place, so come home with me." Jesus was the kind of person who says, "My home is open to you. I don't shut myself off in privacy. Come and see and share; get to know me. Spend the rest of the day with me." There was an openness in Jesus here which should characterize every Christian. There was an openness that encouraged those two.

The quest

They still did not call him "the Lamb"; they simply called him "Teacher" (1:38). That was as high as their faith could rise. Many start by looking at Jesus purely as a human being: they are fascinated by his life but it doesn't stop there. If you follow this through, if the question becomes a quest, if you look at Jesus and share his life, you will soon say something more than "Teacher".

Their question became a quest and it made such a deep impression that 60 years later John could tell you the exact time they arrived at that house: four o'clock in the afternoon. The moment you first really meet Jesus and start looking at him is a moment you never forget. I remember the time and place where I first met Jesus. It was quarter to nine at night – the same time John Wesley first met Jesus!

Peter found

One of the immediate results was that one of the two who is named, Andrew, (the other is unnamed but is probably the writer of this Gospel) just had to go and find someone else. It is one of the true marks you have met Jesus that you have to go and tell someone else and say, "I've found." That implies you were looking for something and you found what you're looking for.

"The first thing Andrew did was to find his brother Simon and tell him, 'We have found the Messiah' (that is, the Christ). And he brought him to Jesus." (1:41-42)

Andrew had an advantage over us. Simon Peter, his brother, was already seeking and it's lovely to tell someone whose seeking that we've found. We're living in a day when many people are seeking; many are waiting for someone to go and say, "We've found; we know what you're looking for." You'll not find it in Zen Buddhism or your horoscope. We've found Jesus. Like Andrew, we would discover if we talked about Jesus that there are people waiting to hear, who will come and see, and who will taste and see that the Lord is good. So Peter was found.

It says "Andrew bought Simon to Jesus." The great Archbishop Temple wrote a commentary on John's Gospel. Against most texts he has quite a long paragraph, but against verse 42 "He brought him to Jesus," he has only one sentence: "The greatest service one man can render to another." The greatest thing you could ever do for someone else is to bring them to Jesus. You could do other things for which they would be grateful, but to bring someone to Jesus is the greatest thing because it is the one thing that will last for ever. Everything else would not last, but this would help them for ever.

The greatest thing you could ever do for someone else is to bring them to Jesus.

When Jesus saw Peter, we see the four kinds of sight that Jesus had: sight, insight, foresight and oversight. It says first of all, "He looked Peter over." That's the literal translation of verse 42. When you first come into contact with Jesus, it is a bit uncomfortable. He looks hard at you. He has insight as well as sight: he looked right into this man and said, "You really are a Simon." That name means "unreliable." One of the twelve tribes of Israel, one of the twelve sons, was Simeon. It means "a reed; easily blown around; weak, shaken, bendy, unreliable." When Jacob died, he cursed his son Simeon for his unreliability. Jesus looked into Simon and said: "You're unreliable. You're a reed. But I've not only got insight into your past, I've also got foresight into your future. You're going to be a rock." Christ's oversight is seen in the fact that Jesus said he was going to give him a new name. "You're now going to belong to me, so I have the right to call you by a new name and I'm going to call you 'Cephas' [*'rock'*]."

Although Peter's temperament was not changed, it became strong. His temperamental weaknesses vanished under the influence of Jesus over the next three years. Don't ever make an excuse of your temperament when you come to Jesus. "I can't help worrying – I'm the worrying sort." Jesus said, "You of little faith, do not worry. Your heavenly Father cares for you." Or, "I'm bad-tempered; I can't help it. My father and grandfather were like this; it runs in the family." Jesus says, "I can change all that."

The reed can become a rock but it's still Peter. It's not a machine; it's Peter. Not a robot who's been brainwashed, but still Peter, yet Peter without his instability. To this impetuous, impulsive, unreliable, unstable personality, Jesus said, "Let's call you 'rock'."

Suppose Andrew had not told Peter. What a loss to the church! Peter was not the first pope but he was the first pastor. He was the first preacher on the Day of Pentecost and he has left us two of the loveliest letters in the whole of the New Testament, and it was all because Andrew said, "I've got to tell my brother," and he did.

A DAY IN THE NORTH (1:43-51)

From verse 43 the scene shifts from the south to the north, from the Jordan to Galilee. What happened the second day is almost a repeat of the day before. Here is the pattern: a man follows Jesus and then goes looking and finds someone else. Is that the pattern of your life? If it's not, then how can you call yourself a disciple? This is the pattern: follow and find. Philip followed and found Nathanael. Is your Christian life unbalanced? You can become so caught up with Jesus that you ignore the people around you. You have a kind of private fellowship but it won't be healthy. It will become ingrown because it's not being shared.

Philip follows

The command
In Galilee it was much more crowded and cosmopolitan, much less quiet, than the Jordan River. Philip follows Jesus, but this time it is a direct call from Jesus as a command: "Come." It is not: "Would you like to come?" No one has the authority to tell anyone else to leave what they're doing and come except the Son of God. At the time I became a Christian I thought I chose to follow Jesus, though I realize now I had no choice. Had you? When Jesus says, "Come with me," what else can you do?

The companionship
"Come" is a command, but at the same time it is an offer, for the next two words are "with me." The heart of the Christian life is not to try and live *like* Jesus; it is to live *with* Jesus. It isn't to try and do something hard; it is to come and do it *with* him. He used the figure of the yoke, a beam of wood with two hollows carved out of it so that it goes from neck to neck of two animals. He says, "Take my yoke" (Matthew 11:28-30). He's saying, "Be linked with me. Let's pull together. Come along with me."

This is the best offer anybody can make to you: not to tell you how to do something but to say, "I'll do it with you." If you are a bit frightened about going from door to door visiting, then find someone else and say, "Would you come with me? Do it with me." You'll soon find you want to go on your own. You've done it with someone and have been encouraged and Jesus says to Philip, "Come." That seems to be a demand. With me that's an offer. The more I think about it, the less I think it's a demand and the more I think it's an offer.

Nathanael found

Now look at Nathanael. He is one of the most interesting among the disciples. He is a man who did something rare today: he thought; he meditated. He sat quietly under his fig tree and thought. I remember once I went to preach at a tiny chapel in Yorkshire. A little old lady took me home to her cottage for lunch and tea. Immediately after the service she put me in the front room, sat me down on an old chair and said, "I'm going to get the dinner ready; you'll be all right with your own thoughts, won't you?" She walked out of the room and left me there for over an hour: no thought of entertaining, of giving me a book or a magazine to read. She just said, "You'll be all right with your own thoughts, won't you?" I knew I had met a lady who meditated, a lady who was still, who sat and thought about God. It's a lost art, for it takes time and quiet and we live in a noisy, busy world.

"Nathanael did something rare today: he thought; he meditated."

But Nathanael was such a man. The favourite place in the Middle East to get alone and quiet is to sit under a fig tree to give you some shade from the sun for a few hours. Why don't you try it? You may not have a fig tree but you've got another sort of tree. Go and find a quiet place. Meditation is no use if it's empty. Nature abhors a vacuum. I'm not now talking about the meditation of the Maharishi, the meditation that says make your mind a blank and sit there. There is something nice about feeling hollow inside, but I'm not talking about that. I'm talking about meditation that begins with something to think about.

Nathanael was the kind of man who thought about God. He thought about God's word and thought about the Old Testament. I know he not only had a favourite place to meditate; he also had a favourite person to meditate on: Jacob. Nathanael thought a lot about Jacob, the man whose name was changed to Israel and became the father of the people of God. Nathanael used to think about Jacob and he thought Jacob was a man who was full of deceitfulness. He was too clever by half, subtle and deceitful. His name meant "supplanter": someone who could push someone else out of the way and climb the ladder of life instead, and Nathanael didn't like that. The more Nathanael thought about Jacob, the more he asked why God should choose such a man who was so full of deceit. Then God gave Jacob the blessing of a dream of a ladder stretching from heaven to earth with angels coming up and down so that Jacob at the bottom of the ladder said, "I'm just outside heaven."

Why does God give such an experience to such a man? Nathanael thought about this long and hard as he sat under his fig tree, and then Philip brought him to Jesus. Jesus looked at him with sight and insight and said, "There's a real Jew. In him there is nothing false; no deceitfulness, one who is honest and open, a man of integrity" (1:47).

The law

I'm going to say a word about Jews here. William Shakespeare has done more damage to the image of Jews in England than anybody else with his picture of Shylock in the *Merchant of Venice*. He has spread abroad that a Jew by nature is a man who's full of deceit, too clever by half, a supplanter, who, if you're not careful, will take over your job and your business. It is a picture of Jacob in his early days before God touched his soul. But that is not a true Jew. A true Jew is not like that. We must get rid of anti-Semitic prejudice. A true Jew is an honest, open man of integrity. Jesus said, "Look at Nathanael." If you've ever met a true Jew you know what I'm talking about. Jesus said, "Here's a real Jew. There is nothing false in him; he's honest."

Nathanael immediately proved that Jesus was right because he accepted a compliment. What would you do if somebody came up to you and said to someone else, "Now let me introduce you to a really sincere man." What would you do? You'd say, "Oh no, no." Would you accept it? What would you say? Do you know what Nathanael said? "How do you know that?" Here's an open man. He's a man who can say, "It's true, but how did you know?" There is no mock modesty here because mock modesty can be as deceitful as mock pride. Jesus said, "Here's a true Jew, one who is straight, open and honest." Nathanael said, "How do you know me?" It's the unsophisticated, open honest response of a man who really was what Jesus said he was. An honest man can accept a compliment if it is true. So Nathanael asked, "How do you know me? Did Philip tell you about me before he told me about you?" But Jesus replied, "Look, I've been watching you. When you were all alone by yourself just thinking I was watching you. Do you think you were by yourself sitting under that fig tree? You weren't. I was there" (1:48).

That is why, in a sense, Christian meditation is so different from any other. You can get alone up onto the hills; you can go for a walk in the woods. You can get absolutely alone but under the tree Jesus is watching. "Nathanael, I saw you under the fig tree." Nathanael suddenly realized you can't hide anything from Jesus, that he already had a relationship with him, that Jesus was already interested in him and it just burst out of his lips. "Teacher, you really are…" (1:49).

He had to get over a mental prejudice to say this. Nathanael was a man who said, "Unless a thing lines up with the Bible I can't believe it." Happy is the person who says, "The Bible is my rule of belief. You may tell me something about Jesus but if I can't find it in my Bible, it's not true." Unfortunately, Philip had said two things about Jesus that were not true. Philip wasn't to know but he said, "We've found the Messiah. Moses wrote about him. The prophets wrote about him. It's in your Bible. And he's the son of Joseph." That wasn't true. "And he's from Nazareth," and that wasn't true. In all innocence, Philip passed on false information. Nathanael didn't know but Nathanael said, "Look, my Bible doesn't say that. Can anything good come out of Nazareth? It doesn't fit."

The ladder

Philip wisely didn't argue. He couldn't have. He just said what Jesus said: "Come and see." If you meet somebody who says, "I can't fit it all in. I can't see how Jesus is this, that and the other," the best thing to say is: "Why don't you try?" Why don't you come and see? Why don't you open your life to him?" There are many things in the Bible I still don't understand; many questions I still can't answer. But I'm sure of Jesus. I came and I saw and I believe that one day he'll answer some of those questions. Which is better: for someone to say, "Until all my questions are answered I won't come and see" or "I will come and see even though I can't see it all"? It is far better to come to Jesus with your questions, and he will deal with them one by one. Nathanael came and said, "You know me. You must be the Son of God. No mere man has seen me under the fig tree. You must be the Son of God. The King of Israel" (1:49).

Jesus replied, "Nathanael, you love Jacob, don't you? You love that story. You think Jacob felt near to heaven because he saw a ladder with angels going up and down on it. I'll tell you what you'll see. You'll see me and angels and ascending and descending on me, the Son of Man" (1:51). In other words, Jacob said, "I'm just outside heaven." "You will have the same feeling in my presence. Not a ladder but a person. I am the link between heaven and earth." But when did Nathanael see that? The answer is he hasn't fully seen it yet, for the phrase Jesus uses, *the Son of Man*, points us to the future, when the Son of Man will come with clouds of glory and we will all see the angels ascending and descending.

"If you think Jacob's dream was wonderful, it's nothing compared with what you will see. You'll see the Son of Man coming with all his angels and you'll realize that heaven and earth have kissed each other." Heaven is so near and so real through Jesus Christ. So Nathanael found his favourite story of Jacob's ladder was going to come true for him through Jesus.

"If you think Jacob's dream was wonderful, it's nothing compared with what you will see. You'll see the Son of Man coming with all his angels and you'll realize that heaven and earth have kissed each other."

I close with two things. The two greatest thrills I've had in my Christian life are these. One, my first contact with Jesus at the age of 17, which I can still remember vividly. The second was my first convert for Jesus. I remember him too and how we knelt together in a room and I said, "I've found and I want you to find." I hope those two thrills belong to you. You could never have two greater moments: your first contact with Jesus and your first convert for Jesus.

"Andrew found Peter and said, 'We've found the Christ. Come and see." Philip found Nathanael and said, "We've found the Christ. Come and see."

5

JESUS CHANGES WATER INTO WINE
2:1-11

SUPERFICIAL STUDY: EMBARRASSING
His presence at the wedding
His provision of wine
His words to his mother
His use of his power

SERIOUS STUDY: ENCOURAGING
Jesus honours marriage
Jesus helps people in trouble
Jesus rewards obedience
Jesus blesses abundantly
Jesus stimulates faith

SYMBOLIC STUDY: ENLIGHTENING
Christ: the Word
Christianity: the wine

Weddings in the Middle East last for up to seven days, so it's easy to run out of refreshments. There also isn't the same formal etiquette about receiving printed invitations; it's all freer – here Jesus dropped in. It must have been a relative of his being married and brought with him five unexpected guests which may have contributed to the crisis.

As we read this story, I want to show you we can look at it superficially and see certain things. We can then go a little deeper and study it seriously and see other things. Then we go deeper still and look for a deeper significance and we find even deeper truth.

SUPERFICIAL STUDY: EMBARRASSING

His presence at the wedding

Many Christians find things here that disturb them. Some are disturbed that Jesus spent time at a social occasion. Some think when Jesus had just been baptized and had started his ministry that to spend time at a wedding reception was a waste. Jesus was there, and it doesn't say he spent all his time preaching. He was there enjoying people. I'm sure they enjoyed him too – that's why when somebody came to Jesus the first thing they often did was throw a party for their friends and invite Jesus. That's a great thing to do for your friends and neighbours.

We shouldn't be embarrassed that Jesus spent so much time at a purely social occasion. He didn't come to be a killjoy and spoil our social life. He came to enable us to be friendly towards one another. It's part of God's will that we not only love him but also love one another.

His provision of wine

Some temperance advocates are embarrassed by this. A huge amount of wine was drunk: 120-150 gallons of alcoholic wine. The Bible warns us about drunkenness, telling us not to get drunk; so it wasn't a harmless wine. Here Jesus drinks wine at a wedding reception: something many Christians today don't feel able to do, including me. It's always rather embarrassing to read this at a wedding service and then go to a reception that's teetotal! But we must have a balanced view in everything: we must face the fact that although John the Baptist was a total abstainer, Jesus was not.

We are also told, however, two things: First, that self-control is to be a mark of the Christian life and that Christians are not to get drunk and behave like animals. Second, we are told that if there is in your fellowship a Christian brother who has difficulty with this thing then the loving attitude is not to drink wine: that you become a total abstainer for the sake of your Christian brother who would otherwise be caused to stumble. So there is a Christian reason for total abstinence and it is a reason that is not embarrassed with Jesus providing wine here.

His words to his mother

The third embarrassment is how Jesus spoke to his mother. It seems a little harsh, something of a rebuke (2:4). Literally, it's "Woman, what is there between me and you?" "Woman" is not a derogatory term; it's not an insult. It was a lovely word, the normal word used in the Middle East. When Jesus was saying farewell to his mother from the cross, he called her "Woman" (19:26). So that's not the embarrassing thing; it's what he said: "Don't tell me what to do." It was a definite rebuke. We must ask why she spoke to Jesus like this; then we'll be able to ask why Jesus replied as he did.

What was Mary saying by "They've run out of wine" (2:3)? Jesus and his mother knew each other well. Presumably, Joseph had died many years before since he's not mentioned and so she had come to rely completely on her elder son. He had been a tremendous help to Mary and so it was instinctive for her to tell him they had run out of wine and to bring the need to Jesus. But there is more to it than that. As Jesus looked into her eyes, he realized she was saying more: "Show all your relatives who you really are." A mother's pride is speaking. She wants all the relatives to know her son is the Messiah. "Go on, show them: do something miraculous. You've started your mission now; you've been baptized. You've

come preaching. Well, show them and show your relatives first.
I'll be so proud of you, Jesus, if you will do something that's a
real miracle." You can tell that's what she's saying by Jesus' reply.
She believed in him, but Jesus said, "I must take my orders from
a heavenly Father not from an earthly mother" (2:4).

**"She believed in him, but Jesus said, 'I must take my orders
from a heavenly Father not from an earthly mother'" (2:4).**

He did something about the need but in such a way that the
relatives were unaware a miracle had taken place. It all happened
out in the pantry. So the relatives never knew it had happened;
they were just enjoying the wine. It was not yet the moment for
Jesus to display his heavenly power and so he said, "My time has
not yet come. Don't you tell me what to do, dear woman. My
heavenly Father will tell me the right moment to step into centre
stage and even a mother's pride mustn't deflect me from the will
of God" (2:4).

His use of his power

The fourth embarrassment is that he used his power for something
ordinary. With all the power of the universe at his fingertips, the
first thing he does is simply provide a little wine at a wedding
reception. Well, not a little, but what a little thing to do with his
power! Surely this contradicts his temptation where the devil
said, "Turn these stones into bread." Jesus said, "No, I'm not
going to do that – that's the wrong way to go about things." Why,
then, is he within a few weeks turning water into wine? It seems
the same kind of miracle. But is it? When the devil said to Jesus,
"Turn these stones into bread," he was saying "to meet your own
need. You are hungry. You've had nothing to eat for six weeks ...
here's a ready-made answer." But Jesus refused, not because it was
wrong to turn stones into bread but because it was wrong to use
his miraculous power for his own physical needs. If he had once
done that – even for the physical need of hunger – he could never
have stayed on the cross later, when his physical body was crying

out for release from pain and the devil was saying, "You've got the power – step off the cross." Jesus would never use his miraculous power for his own needs. But when it came to someone else in need, he was glad to do so.

SERIOUS STUDY: ENCOURAGING

So far we have looked at the story superficially and dealt with its embarrassments, but now let's go deeper. This is a story about Jesus, and Jesus is the same yesterday, today and for ever, so what Jesus is like here he is like now. So let's see that this story tells us some wonderful things about Jesus.

Jesus honours marriage

The fact that Jesus' first act in his public ministry was to attend a wedding shows what Jesus thinks of marriage. God made marriage: it is a high and a holy estate. It is a lovely thing and Jesus upholds it. It is true he was not married while on earth, but he is going to be. When he spoke about himself and John the Baptist, he said that John the Baptist was the best man and Jesus was the bridegroom. Jesus honours marriage. And that is why he will attend any wedding where he is invited. He may bring a few of his friends too. But what a joy it is to start a marriage, two people in Christ, with Jesus himself at the wedding and his disciples gathered around. That is the way to start a marriage. Jesus honours marriage.

In 1 Timothy 4:3, Paul says those who teach abstaining from marriage are wrong. Don't twist Paul's teaching to say he degraded marriage: he did not. In certain circumstances he said it is better not to marry because of the responsibilities and ties it brings when there is pressure and persecution. But let no one say that the Bible looks down on marriage. Jesus honours marriage, and by his presence at Cana and by his preaching, he lifted marriage to a new level of spirituality, love and loyalty.

Jesus helps in trouble

We see here Jesus helps people when they are in trouble. That sounds so simple. That couple little realized how soon they would get into trouble in their married life but it was Jesus who got them out of trouble. Happy are the couple who turn to Jesus in difficulties. Of course it doesn't seem to us a serious crisis, but for them it would have been. It would have been talked about for the rest of their married life. They would never have lived it down: "You know they were the couple whose refreshments ran out at their wedding. Wasn't it dreadful?"

It was in a crisis of social embarrassment that Jesus stepped in and eased the situation. That tells me that it doesn't need to be what the world calls a huge problem before you trouble Jesus about it. Whatever your problem, you can take it to him. He helps in time of trouble.

Jesus rewards obedience

This story tells us that Jesus rewards obedience. Mary said one thing right: "Do whatever he tells you without question" (2:5). They were going to have to do something silly, something that might have cost them their jobs and even their lives. The servants were going to have to give people water and that would have been considered a great insult. They did what he told them, and he rewarded their obedience. Mary's words are still true: "Do whatever he tells you." You will find that even before you've done it, he has already acted. As you take the water to the feast, it's wine.

"Mary's words are still true: 'Do whatever he tells you.' You will find that even before you've done it, he has already acted. As you take the water to the feast, it's wine."

Jesus blesses abundantly

His gifts are the best; his wedding present exceeded expectations. Jesus talking about God's blessings likened it to buying corn in the marketplace where you have taken your own container along. You see this is in markets in Africa still. People present their basin and a good merchant will shake it together, press it down and pour more on, until it's running over and that will be the measure. That's how God gives: pressed down, shaken together, running over. But here? They had run out of wine. I don't know how much longer the wedding reception lasted, but 2,400 half-pint glasses were filled. You and I would have to testify that God has dealt with us far more abundantly than we have ever asked or imagined.

God gives more and more. He not only gives you more in quantity but he gives you more in quality. There is a little social custom here which is the world's way: to put the best first, to give a good impression, and when people's sensibilities are dulled you bring out the rough stuff. The world always offers you the best first. The world will put the best on first but then gradually the quality peters out. In almost every respect, the older you get the poorer life gets. But those who live with Jesus will say that he brings on the best last and that is supremely true of heaven. The world says, "Enjoy yourself now and pay later," but Jesus said, "It's a cross now, but there's a crown later." Life may be hard now but look where it leads: the best comes last.

"This, the first of his miraculous signs, Jesus performed at Cana in Galilee. He thus revealed his glory, and his disciples put their faith in him" (2:11).

Jesus stimulates faith

Jesus stimulates faith, not in the guests or even in the servants, as far as we know, but his disciples – those five men who came with him – believed in him (2:11). He is always doing things to stretch our faith a little. Do you know what a joy it is at a weekly prayer meeting to hear what God has been doing? He stretches our faith a little. We hear of a miracle here and there, and our faith grows a bit and we say, "We could ask for something bigger." He has a lovely way of increasing our faith. The one limitation to God's miracles is our faith, but when you have seen one you could believe he could do it again. When you have seen two, you believe more still.

SYMBOLIC STUDY: ENLIGHTENING

We now come to the deepest level of the story. John's Gospel has a way of calling miracles *signs*. A sign points beyond itself to something or someone else. You can become so involved in looking at a sign that you miss its significance. You would be foolish if you came to a signpost on a country hike and said, "Look at that signpost – it's just been painted: all nice and white in lovely lettering!" and then you just wandered on. Here, this miracle points to a person and a thing:

Christ: the Word

This miracle points to Christ. I've heard five explanations as to what happened in those water jars. The first tells me wine leaves a sediment in the bottom of jars and when they poured water in, the sediment got all mixed up and that's how it changed into wine. Apart from the fact that these jars were not wine jars, I don't think anybody would say the mixture of water and sediment was the best wine yet. The second explanation is that the people were by then so drunk they couldn't tell the difference between water and wine, but I've never yet met a drunk in that condition! The third is that it was just water and they all agreed that Adam's ale is best: I simply cannot believe that! The fourth is that all Jesus was doing was speeding up a natural process, as rain from the sky is soaked up by the vine in the soil and is transformed into wine juice in the grape. Jesus simply speeded up a natural process. That is just not true, for there was no vine. A fifth is that Jesus or Mary slipped out to the nearest shop and came back with wine. What lengths people will go to, to explain away miracles! They will try any ingenious explanation.

What does this miracle point to? It points to the fact that Jesus is the Son of God. Who else could do such a thing? Only God has the power to create what is not there. Only God has the power to do this. That's why the disciples saw his glory and believed (2:11). It's a sign that Jesus is the Son of God. There can be no other explanation. If you do not want to believe that Jesus is the Son of God you will have to resort to the most incredible explanations for these events. You will have to twist your thinking until you can explain it away. But to those who look at these things with an open mind, they will say Jesus is who he said he was. Jesus is the Son of God.

Christianity: the wine

The other sign this miracle points to is Christianity. This little miracle summarizes for us a most lovely truth about our religion. Why were those jars there? They were not there for drinking; they were washing jars. The Jews are particular and they were more particular then with all their many laws about washing hands before meals and between courses and so they had these jars full of water. That was a symbol of their religion washing the outside. Jesus took the heart of their religion, which consisted in external ceremonies, and he changed the water of washing outside to the wine that makes glad the heart of man inside.

"Here's a tremendous sign and symbol of our faith. The difference between religion and Christianity is the difference between water outside you and wine inside you. It's the difference between duty and delight."

Here is a tremendous sign and symbol of our faith. The difference between religion and Christianity is the difference between water outside you and wine inside you. It's the difference between duty and delight, between doing something because you've got to and doing something because you want to. It's the difference between enslavement and enjoyment, between obeying rules and rejoicing. Here we have summed up for us what Jesus can do: change the water of external religious rite into the wine of gladness.

That's what he came to do; that's why on the Day of Pentecost people said: "They are drunk." That's why Paul said, "Don't be filled with wine but be filled with the Holy Spirit and sing and make melody to the Lord in your heart" (Ephesians 5:18-19). The Lord's people should show signs of being drunk, yet without any loss of self-control, but certainly all loss of reserve, all loss of self-consciousness that accompanies the drinking of wine.

Here then is the sign of our faith, that our religion should be more a matter of the wine inside than the water outside.

6

JESUS CLEANSES
THE TEMPLE
2:13-22

THE ATTITUDE HE EXHIBITED
His use of physical force
His display of emotional anger
His act of spiritual intolerance

THE ABUSE HE EXPELLED
Laziness?
Exploitation?
Nationalism?
Misappropriation?

THE AUTHORITY HE EXERCISED
The Son of the Father
The Messiah of Israel
The temple of God

CONCLUSION

You can't really love someone unless you know them. You must love them as they are, not as you want them to be or as you think they are, but as they really are. If you are going to love someone, you must find out what they are really like and love them as they are. This applies supremely to the Lord Jesus Christ: if we are to love Jesus, we must know him as he really is. We must see him in all his character. Not the Jesus we would like him to be, but Jesus as he really is.

THE ATTITUDE HE EXHIBITED

John disturbs many people in this story. It shows traits in Jesus' personality that puzzle many: they say they are not like him, they are out of keeping with the Jesus I know. Three things in particular may disturb us.

His use of physical force

At the end of our Lord's life he was whipped and the whip was in someone else's hand. But when you see Jesus with a whip in his own hand, it is difficult to understand. Here Jesus has a whip of cords tied together. In this account it says he used it on animals. That in itself contradicts some people's idea of Jesus. We have been used to pictures with Jesus surrounded by farmyard animals looking lovingly into his face, as if they would follow him anywhere. But here is Jesus using a whip on animals. The Greek is even rather ambiguous and suggests he used it on people also, for the previous sentence says "he found men selling cattle" (2:14), and money changers. The next bit in the Greek says he made a whip from cords and drove them out of the temple with the sheep and the oxen. Jesus whipping men? Now we've got to love Jesus as he is. Do you know him well? Do you know him well enough to understand what made him take a whip and use physical force to deal with the situation?

His display of emotional anger

Anger is generally bad. When you and I have lost our temper, we have had regrets about what we've said and done. Anger is felt to be an emotion which should not characterize a mature person. And Jesus was angry. We know from the other Gospels that he blazed with anger on this occasion, that his eyes were on fire, he was dreadfully angry. Had he lost his temper? Maybe we do not know Jesus well enough if we find it difficult to imagine him angry, but we are told in Revelation that one day the whole world will see the wrath of the Lamb and his eyes will be so terrible that people will cry for the rocks and the mountains to fall on them rather than see his emotion than see those blazing eyes. How well do you know Jesus? Have you ever seen him angry or felt him angry? What makes him angry?

"Here Jesus shows a spiritual intolerance: he will not have certain things under the disguise of religion."

His act of spiritual intolerance

Tolerance is widely thought as a Christian virtue, that we should "live and let live", that if we really love people we would let them do what they want and we get on with our own lives. If that is their religion, that's all right – and you keep to yours. But here Jesus shows a spiritual intolerance: he will not have certain things under the disguise of religion. Jesus says about certain things, "Take them out of here." At times Jesus is intolerant. That puzzles people. They can't see here the gentle Jesus in whom they were brought up to believe.

THE ABUSE HE EXPELLED

What explains these features we find difficult to fit in with our image of Jesus? Let's look at the background. In Israel in April 2,250,000 people migrated to one city. Every able male Jew travelled up to 100 miles and camped outside the city. For seven or eight days there were celebrations – it was the year's biggest celebration. Our nearest equivalent is Christmas. It was *the* festival. It had been done every twelve months for 1,400 years.

Naturally it centred on the house of God, the temple the people made for that four acres of beautiful buildings and courtyards where God lived. They were coming to say thank you for something that had happened 1,400 years before. We tend to thank God for what happens in our life; maybe when we come to church we thank God for something that happened last week. But one of the reasons we take bread and wine is to thank God for something that happened 2,000 years ago. We need to go back in history to the roots of what God has done for us. If things had not happened as they did centuries ago, you wouldn't be worshipping as you do now. So thank God and celebrate that God began your salvation centuries ago, even before the foundation of the world – that's what they were doing.

They needed two things when they went into the temple: money and an animal. The money was to pay the temple tax, to keep the whole temple going, and you weren't allowed in unless you paid your half-shekel. In a day when the daily wages were 3p, the temple tax amounted to £75,000 a year. You can imagine how much came in. Furthermore, it had to be brought in Jewish money, which was not the normal money used. They used Roman money in the shops, and so before you could get into the temple you had to go to a money changer and get your Roman money changed into a Jewish shekel. Then you needed an animal; if you were wealthy you took an ox or a sheep; if you were poor, a pigeon, but you had to have a life to sacrifice.

Before they could offer them, the priest had to inspect the animals and to see that they were good, that they were without spot or blemish. I'm afraid it was comparatively easy for the inspectors to say, "Your lamb is no good, I've got a better one here – you buy this one." That's what was going on. The price of animals within the temple was up to twenty times as much as you paid outside. The whole thing was becoming a racket. The religious leaders, the priests, the Sadducees, loved money; they were behind the racket and you couldn't get near to God without money. The money changers took some of it; the priests took the rest of it. You came with nothing but your little animal and your half-shekel to worship God. It was a dreadful situation.

Jesus came and saw that. When something like that is going on inside God's temple, Jesus blazes with fury. All his holiness is filled with indignation. If you want to see Jesus angry then show him something like this. Now why was he so upset? The commentators argue what was the basic reason: four reasons have been given.

Laziness?

It could have been laziness that made him cross. Why were they doing it inside the temple? It was the most convenient place. There was plenty of room there; that's where the pilgrims were; where the business was; the streets were crowded. It was convenient. They were too lazy to do it anywhere else, so they said, "All right, we'll just do it here." Now is that the reason? Were these men putting their own convenience before anything or anyone else? If that is the reason, it is certainly a wrong attitude to God, and I will return to it later. But I don't think that's the real reason, although it could be part of it.

Exploitation?

The second reason could have been exploitation: the monopoly of the money changers and priests were bleeding the people of money. Christ is angry with exploitation. Exploitation by monopolies of human need and shortage are things that make Jesus angry. When you begin to apply that to modern life there are many examples of things that must make Christ cross in our day. What would he think of gazumping of house prices? It could have been exploitation.

Nationalism?

The third reason could have been nationalism. I'd almost have to draw a chart here. Right in the middle of the temple area of four acres was the building that contained the Holy of Holies and the Holy Place. Then a courtyard outside it and another courtyard and another, until you came to the big Court of the Gentiles; it was the only part of the house of God an outsider could come into. God intended his temple to be a house of prayer for all nations. The very place that should have been a house of prayer was noisy, dirty and so full of coming and going that nobody could pray there. Have you ever walked through an eastern bazaar? Have you ever tried to pray in the middle of the smells, shouting and pushing? It's not an easy place to pray. Maybe Jesus was saying, and he did say in another Gospel, "My Father's house was to be a house of prayer for all nations, and this is stopping any but God's people coming to worship." The Jews could go on into the quiet area – is that what's wrong? Well it could be and he says that in Mark's Gospel.

Misappropriation?

It could be misappropriation – using something for the wrong purpose. He said, "Here was a den of thieves, not a house of prayer for all nations. You've taken my Father's house and made it a marketplace; you've used this building for the wrong purpose. It was never intended for this. That's what making me so angry."

"They came and asked Jesus, 'Who do you think you are? What right have you to do this? What do you think you're doing to interfere with what we have set up?'" (2:18).

THE AUTHORITY HE EXERCISED

Now they soon came and said, "By what authority do you do this?" If you went into a market now and started turning over the stalls and telling everybody to remove their merchandise, somebody will ask, "Who do you think you are? What do you think you're doing?" And they came and asked Jesus precisely this. "Who do you think you are? What right have you to do this? What do you think you're doing to interfere with what we have set up?" (2:18). Jesus gave them three answers. We're going to see three things about our Lord Jesus. He is:

The Son of the Father

He is the Son of the Father and the Son has a right to tell the servants of the Father what to do. I suppose that Prince Charles as a boy could have wandered into Buckingham Palace garden and told a gardener, "Take that rubbish away." And the gardener could have said, "Who do you think you are talking to me like that?" But Prince Charles would have replied, "My mother's house is here." Presumably royal children have the right to speak to royal servants. Jesus was doing just this. The Prince of Peace had come and he's saying, "This is my Father's house. Who am I to do this? This is my Father's property. How dare you do this with it?" This is the Son of the Father speaking.

The Messiah of Israel

The second right he had to do it was as the Messiah of Israel. They had been expecting the Messiah for hundreds of years. Certain predictions about the Messiah in the Old Testament made it clear that one of the things he would do when he came would be to clean up the temple. For example, Malachi 3:1-4: "The Lord will suddenly come to his temple but who can stand his appearing? You all want the Messiah to come to the temple of God but will you like it when he comes? He will come as a blazing fire and he will put the priests right and he'll put the people right so that God can enjoy his house again." The most important thing about the Father's house is that it's for the Father to enjoy. God wasn't enjoying the temple when Jesus came to it, and so he said, "I am the Messiah." That text from Malachi was not remembered on this occasion but another one was. Psalm 69 includes amazing predictions about the coming Messiah. Look at verse 21: "They gave me vinegar to quench my thirst." One of the other things said in Psalm 69 about the coming Messiah was: "The zeal of God's house is burning me up" (verse 9). When Jesus took a whip and went through that court and flogged them out of the temple, his disciples said, "You know that's what the Messiah's going to do. The zeal of God's house will burn him up. There needs to be this kind of fire if we're going to be endured by God." Zeal for God, not half-heartedness. He wants piping-hot zeal, "Lukewarm people make me sick," said Jesus to the church at Laodicea," (Revelation 3:16), "I'd rather you were a cold than lukewarm."

The temple of God

He says, "I am the temple of God. I have the right to deal with this temple because I am *the* temple." What did he mean? They asked him, "Give us a miracle, a sign. If you're who you claim to be, give us a miracle that will prove your credentials," (2:18), and he replied, "All right, I'll give you one miracle. Destroy this body and in three days I'll build it up again" (2:19). Only he didn't say *body*; he said, "Destroy this *temple*, and I'll build it up again in three days." They misunderstood what he said. They asked, "This temple?" The temple at Jerusalem took 46 years and 18,000 workers to build. Can you imagine the craftsmanship that went into it? It was still being built when Jesus said this. It was Herod who started it, but he didn't live to see it finished. It was the third temple on that site. Forty-six years and still armies of little workers were building, decorating and carving, but Jesus said, "Destroy this temple and I'll build it in three days." They responded, "Build it in three days? You're talking through your hat! It took us forty-six years to build this." You see, they weren't listening to what he said.

That was the only sign he ever promised to give the Jews. They were always asking for miracles and signs. He said, "I'll give you no sign but the sign of Jonah, three days and three nights in the belly of the earth and then resurrection" – that is *the* proof of the Son of God's authority to cleanse his temple. But why did he call his body the temple? The temple that had stood there for many years, first of all the temple built by Solomon, then rebuilt in Ezra's and Haggai's day, then the temple built again in Herod's day on the same spot. Why did they set up this building? It was somewhere for God to live: it was where God lived on earth and if you wanted to meet with God you came to this building. This was where God's glory shone. It is where you could approach God and your prayers were always directed to his house.

Jesus is now saying, "If you destroy me, you destroy this." Do you understand? The day that Jesus died, the temple became obsolete. God ripped the veil of the temple from top to bottom. God took his invisible hands and ripped a seventy-foot high curtain from top to bottom, and when they looked in it was empty.

"Destroy this temple: destroy me and you destroy yourself. Destroy this temple, and you destroy this one. Destroy this temple but I will raise up a new dwelling place of God on earth." Do you see what he's saying? "I have the right to deal with this temple because I am *the* temple. From now on God is dwelling in me. If you want to see God's glory, come to me. If you want to pray to God, pray to me." So we no longer pray towards Jerusalem; we pray towards Jesus. He is the temple of God. A temple destroyed and in three days rebuilt. That is his authority for cleansing every human temple.

CONCLUSION

On Ascension Day, Christians throughout the world remember that Jesus left this earth and the temple that was his body was taken up into the high heavenly temple. Where that heavenly temple is stands a great high priest. Well, where is God's temple on earth now? The answer is it's here. Not a lovely church building here. Again and again the New Testament makes it clear where the temple of God is now: "You are the temple of God. Do you not know that your body is the temple of the Holy Spirit? You are being built together in a fellowship to become a dwelling in which God lives by his Spirit" (1 Corinthians 6:19; 2 Corinthians 5:1; 2 Peter 1:13; Ephesians 2:21-22). *You* are the temple.

So let's apply this: is your body just a library to be stuffed with knowledge? Is your body a bank, a place for gathering money? Is your body a playhouse, simply for pleasure? Is your body a pigsty where slimy passions rule? Or is your body a temple where God lives? "Do you not know that your body is the temple of the Holy Spirit?" So Jesus must come and cleanse the temple if God is to enjoy it.

Let's look briefly at those four things I mentioned earlier and apply them. Laziness: making a convenience of religion or a religion of a convenience. That is not a temple fit for God. Our faith must not be a convenience. It is tragic if we only worship God, or only witness, when it's convenient and fits in with our plans, rather than fitting ourselves into God's plan. It could be laziness that could need cleansing from the temple.

Exploitation: am I living only for what I can get out of other people, to get the better of my neighbour; am I just living to grab all I can? If I am just part of this affluent society that just wants more and more – then I'm not a fit temple for God.

Nationalism: am I just interested in *my* worship, in *my* faith? Or do I want all nations to come and know my God? Am I concerned that others should come into the temple or do I just go on worshipping God unconcerned my life has things that make it impossible for others to get near my God?

Misappropriation: this is the main thing. If I am the temple of God, then everything in my life has got to be sacred. Every courtyard – not just the central shrine of devotion, but every courtyard. It is so easy, but so tragic, to let the secular swallow the sacred in my life, to become so busy even in the things that arrange worship that there is no longer the peace of worship in my heart. These people were turning the temple into a marketplace even though they were doing things to help people worship, to enable them to get the tax and the sacrifices. It is possible to misappropriate part of the temple and make it no different from anybody else's life. If the feverish busyness of life is crowding increasingly into my life so that it is no longer the place of worship everywhere, then I am misappropriating the temple. Am I as irritable as everybody else in the office? As feverish as everybody else? Do I lose my temper as much as everybody else? God says, "Let the whole temple be sacred, so that at work you're a little pool of worship, so that in the feverish busyness of life you don't lose me, so that your life is my Father's house and not a marketplace, and is somehow different."

One final word – some people are puzzled that the cleansing of the temple comes at the beginning of John's Gospel, whereas it is at the end in Matthew, Mark and Luke. People have asked when this event took place – at the beginning of his ministry or the end? The answer is that it needed to be done twice. At the beginning of his ministry, Jesus came on the first Passover to Jerusalem, and he saw this going on and said, "That's not what my Father wants," and so he cleansed the temple. He was away for three years and he returned at the third Passover, when he saw the same thing going on in the Father's house. It had all crept back in.

The temple of our lives needs to be cleansed repeatedly. Living in today's hectic pressures, with all the rushing round, commuting, travelling, and the television, newspapers, etc., shouting at us so much, it's very easy for the Father's house gradually to revert to a busy marketplace. Jesus has to return and say, "It's my Father's house, not a marketplace. Nothing in your life is to be common; nothing in your life is to be secular. Nothing in your life is to be the same as it is in the world outside. Everything is to be holy to the Lord."

7

YOU MUST BE BORN AGAIN
2:23-3:21

RELIGION—BY MAN (2:23-3:1)

REGENERATION—BY THE SPIRIT (3:2-8)

REVELATION—FROM THE HEAVENS (3:9-13)

REDEMPTION—THROUGH THE CROSS (3:14-17)

RETRIBUTION—FOR THE UNBELIEVER (3:18-21)

For further explanation of Chapter 3 of the Gospel of John, see my book entitled *Is John 3:16 the Gospel?* (Terra Nova, 2007).

RELIGION — BY MAN (2:23-3:1)

John's Gospel contains some extraordinary statements about Jesus, for example: "Many people believed in Jesus but he would not believe in them" (2:23-24). They trusted him, but he wouldn't trust them. You would have thought that when people took a step towards him he would meet them more than halfway. But Jesus can see through people. He knows when faith is deep and real and when it's shallow. He looks into the human heart and asks, "Why do you trust me; what is the foundation for your faith?" The reason he wouldn't trust himself to these people was that they only believed him because of his miracles. That kind of a faith produces a faith that is dependent on sight rather than hearing. Miracles don't give you a deep enough faith by themselves. They believed Jesus could perform miracles. They said, "We would trust you with any situation. You could do anything." But Jesus knew in their hearts they had come to that faith by seeing, not hearing, and their faith wasn't deep enough.

Miracles take place in the material realm. Every miracle Jesus performed was a physical miracle – changing water into wine; stilling the storm; making a lame man walk and a blind man see. They are all material things, but the change in a man is not necessarily moral. A leper may be cleansed of his leprosy but there may be no change in his heart. It is therefore not deep enough. It is not enough to ask Jesus to perform material miracles for us if we are going to come real faith. Their faith was inadequate also because, since it was based on Jesus' miracles, it was entirely concerned with their worldly needs. It was not a faith that believed him for the next world: and that's the faith that Jesus looks for. So he saw through their professed faith.

People may say, "I believe in Jesus," but you've got to ask why. What kind of faith is it? Is it a shallow faith that springs up in a moment of excitement but soon withers and fades away? Or is it a deep faith that has really got deep down inside? Jesus didn't trust himself to people until there'd been an inward, not just an outward, change. The miracles were all outward changes, but what Jesus came to do was to change people inside.

Now isn't this true of human nature? Many of our prayers may be concerned with outward changes: "Lord, change my husband/wife, and then I can get on with them." "Lord, change my children, make them better behaved." "Lord, change my health; change my income." We ask him to change our circumstances and then we'll be all right. But the prayer he's waiting for is, "Lord, change me ... because I could be the one who's making life difficult." I have never yet come across a marriage that was breaking that was not due to faults on both sides. If only the person who had complained most about the other started by saying, "Lord, let's start with an inward change. You can leave me in this house with this husband or these children, but change me." That's the beginning of real faith, and that's what Jesus is looking for.

Now of all those who saw his miracles during the Passover in Jerusalem in April AD 27 was one man who wanted to go deeper. He watched Jesus, heard him speak, saw him do miracles. That man said, "I need what he's got," but he didn't know how to approach Jesus because he was in such a prominent position that if he had come publicly it would have been to admit he was needy. This man was Nicodemus, who thought, "How am I going to find out what that man's secret is?" Nicodemus was a public teacher in Israel. Everybody looked up to him as a religious leader. People came to him with questions about God and philosophy. He was looked up to by the whole nation; he was the teacher in Israel. But for all his knowledge, he saw in Jesus the power of God. And Nicodemus knew nothing about the power of the Holy Spirit. He could answer questions; he had all the doctrines right, but he knew nothing about God's power. So one night after sunset, he crept through the streets with his hood over his head to go and talk to Jesus. He went in the dark because he was ashamed; he didn't want anybody to see. He was afraid of being identified with Jesus because Jesus was already unpopular. But he came. They spent a few hours talking together on the flat roof of a house in the evening breezes.

Their conversation is wonderful; it covers almost every major aspect of Christian belief. Nicodemus was to learn not only about God but about the Son of God and about the Spirit of God, about some of the most important truths of Christianity.

Nicodemus' religion was the religion of good deeds, the religion of 95% of the people in England. So what Jesus has to say to

Nicodemus is relevant to us. This religion says, "Try your best, to be kind, be good, help people, not harm anybody, and one day you'll arrive in the kingdom of heaven." You can soon find out if your religion is of good works by asking yourself, "If you were to die tonight and stand before God, who asked, 'Why should I let you into heaven?' what would you say? 'Well, Lord, I may have had my faults but I've done my best. I helped Mrs So and So when she was ill.'" If that's how you would talk, your religion is that of good deeds. It was the religion of every devout Jew, but the sad truth is the religion of good deeds doesn't get you anywhere.

Nicodemus knew he was no nearer the kingdom than when he had started. He had tried very hard and he had also taught others the same. He was no nearer any assurance God was going to receive him into his kingdom than when he had started.

Trying to get to heaven by doing good is a long, lonely and disappointing trail. You'll never make it, and there's no joy or love of the Lord because you are not sure whether you are near, whether you've done enough good deeds or missed one out. It is the basic religion of the world: you study Islam or Buddhism, and you will find deep down it's all the same religion: "Do your best."

Nicodemus had tried it and he said, "Teacher," – that's all he called Jesus at first – "God is with you, and he is not with me. Why not? Why is it you know God and the power of God is working through your life, not mine? We're both Jews and teachers. We both believe in the same God. What's the difference?" Jesus took Nicodemus where he was and he said there are four things you need to know. "Unless you've learned these four simple lessons, you're nowhere near even seeing the kingdom of God, never mind entering it.

REGENERATION — BY THE SPIRIT (3:2-8)

Interestingly, Jesus knew Nicodemus' question before he asked it. Nicodemus didn't ask a question, but Jesus said, "Here's your answer." He showed again he could see through someone. He says, "I know why you have come; you are disappointed with your religion; it's not doing for you what you had hoped. It hasn't brought you to the kingdom of God or given you power and life. All right, I'll tell you the secret. Nicodemus you need such a radical change that is being born all over again."

I want you to imagine a birth. The baby's body exists before the birth; it moves before the birth. But what a change takes place at birth! Before birth, the embryo knows nothing about this world; it cannot see or hear this world, cannot communicate with this world, and yet this world was all around it. But the moment of birth brings that embryo into a new world ... a world that existed all along and was near. The baby begins to be aware, opens its eyes, begins to communicate and breathe, and begins to connect. The baby has been born into our world and increasingly becomes aware of a new world.

Do you know people who say, "God isn't real to me; I can't communicate with him; I don't feel he's there." "They're like an unborn baby," says Jesus. God is all around them; 'In him we live and move and have our being'" (Acts 17:28, NIV). Heaven is even nearer than that. But they are not aware of it because they have not been born again. "Just as my birth in the flesh introduced me to this world," says Jesus to Nicodemus, "you will need another birth to introduce you to the next one. If you are ever going to see the kingdom of God, communicate with that kingdom, you'll need another experience like physical birth. You'll need a spiritual birth; as you have been born of the flesh, you will need to be born of the Spirit."

Did Nicodemus really misunderstand? He said in effect, "I'm too big to be born again; I can't get back inside my mother's body." Was this great intellect deliberately being obtuse or was he saying something more subtle? Was he really saying, "I'm too old to change, to start life again. I can't go back to the beginning and start all over again"? How can a man be born again when he's old? But thank God a man or woman can be born again when they're old. It's never too late. "Nicodemus, you may say you're too old to start life all over again, but what is impossible with man is possible with God!" In his heart of hearts, Nicodemus wished he could start again on another road and find the kingdom. He realized all his journeying had been wasted. There are people who'd give anything to go back and start all over again, now that they've made mistakes and got their regrets. Jesus is saying, "Nicodemus, you must be born again which means you can be born again. You can start a new life."

" 'You must be born again' (3:7). It's the only hope."

One thing Jesus says has puzzled many. Jesus says, "Unless you are born of water and of the Spirit...." There is a double agency. What does he mean? Some point to the fact that when a baby is born physically, a moment comes when the waters break and the baby (having been cradled in waters) is born soon after. Some have thought Jesus was saying, "Unless you are born physically with the breaking of waters, and spiritually, then you can't enter the kingdom of God." That would seem a possible explanation but I think it is unlikely. Why would Jesus say something superfluous? Of course you have got to be born physically before you can be born spiritually. You have to have been born in the first place before you could go anywhere else.

We must ask what would have come into Nicodemus' mind when Jesus mentioned water. The big talking point at that time was John the Baptist: he was saying to all the Jews, not just the dirty Gentiles, "You need a clean start. You need to repent of your sins and wash them away and then start all over again. And there is someone coming after me who will flood you with the Spirit."

Now Nicodemus would think of that and every mention except one of water in the first few chapters of John's Gospel refers to baptism.[1] That doesn't mean there is anything magical in baptism. Jesus doesn't say, "Unless you are born of water." But the message I think Nicodemus would receive was, "I need to make a clean start; I need to be washed of all the past, of my good deeds as well as my bad deeds." Do you realize if you are ever going to start on the road to the kingdom of heaven you have got to repent of your good deeds as well as your bad deeds, if you've been putting your trust in them?

So, "Nicodemus, you need to be born of both water and the Spirit. You need to make a clean start, to wash away the past, and you need the Spirit to create new life in you." Poor Nicodemus with his brilliant mind says, "I can't understand this. I know the things of the flesh, which I can see and handle, but I can't understand the things of the Spirit; they're invisible, intangible." Jesus said, "Come on, Nicodemus, pull yourself together, can you feel that wind? Can you explain that wind to me? Can you answer all my questions about it; can you tell me where that bit of wind came from that just blew on our cheeks? Can you tell me where it's going to next? Nicodemus, you felt an invisible power pushing on us just now, didn't you?" That's how everybody born of the Spirit feels; just as one day on the top of a hill you feel the wind pushing you, blowing you, an invisible power pressing you, so when you are born again of the Spirit you feel the breath of God breathing inside you, moving you. You can't explain where it came from, where it's going to lead to. But you know something is happening; so it is with everyone who's born of the Spirit – you know when the wind of God is blowing.

Nicodemus said, "I'm sorry, you're talking in riddles, I cannot understand." Jesus said, "You – the great teacher of Israel who tell people how to find God – and you don't know this." How ignorant even religious leaders can be of the elementary truths of the Christian faith! "You need to start all over again, not just to learn the truth but to unlearn what you have thought and which is wrong."

REVELATION — FROM THE HEAVENS (3:9-13)

"You must be born again" (3:7, NIV): it is the only hope. But how do you start? You need *revelation*: somebody to talk to you who knows what he's talking about. Unfortunately, most of us pick up our knowledge second hand. Time and again people talk to me about the Bible, and I ask them, "Have you read the Bible?" "No," they reply, "But I've been told the Bible is full of contradictions." My response is to give them a Bible and ask them to show me one. We pick up our opinions second hand. There's only one person to go to if you want to know the truth about the kingdom of heaven and that is the only person who has been there. Don't listen to anybody else's ideas about life after death unless they have been there and come back to tell you. Why is it we will listen to what philosophers, film stars or pop stars have to say about life after death, but we won't listen to the one person who can tell us?

Let me illustrate this. Very few people take hell seriously. They use it as a swear word and make jokes about its temperature, but people say, "I don't believe in hell." But I have to believe in a hell because Jesus did. He is the only person in the Bible who talks about hell. If I want to know about heaven and the kingdom of heaven, what it's like and so how to get there, I need to go to Jesus. I need to listen and so Jesus says, "Nobody's been to heaven except the One who came from heaven: the Son of Man; here I am. You must listen to me now. I'll tell you all about it." But Nicodemus couldn't even believe what Jesus told him about earthly things, so how could he believe what he told him about heaven? If you don't believe what Jesus said about life here, you'll not believe what he says about life hereafter. You must start with what he says about life here and now. You ask if what he says about the earthly is true; if what he says about us now is true, can we not accept what he says about heavenly things too?

REDEMPTION — THROUGH THE CROSS (3:14-17)

The third R you need is *redemption*. Nicodemus knew his Bible and he knew the story of the bronze snake (Numbers 21:4-9): the people sinned against God, they grumbled against God, saying, "Why did you bring us here; why did you put us in these circumstances?" It's just like us: "God, why do you let this happen?" They grumbled and God punished them by a particularly horrible death by a plague of snakes. They realized they had sinned and said, "God, why do we have to die?" God had a perfect right to say, "Why should you live? I've done so much for you: I've brought you out of slavery, I've fed you every day. I've led you every step of your journey. Why should you live?" But God didn't say that. He said, "I'll give you a way to be saved." He said, "Moses, make a snake out of bronze and put it on a pole and stick it up on that hill outside the camp. When anybody's bitten with a snake, just tell them to look at that." They did and they were saved. That is one of the simple ways in which God has taught us how he copes with a situation.

We say to God, "Save us," and God would be perfectly just to say, "Why should I? Why should you live? My goodness and mercy have followed you all the days of your life and what have you done for me? What have you said to me? You're complaining now. You're saying I've messed up your circumstances. Why should you live?" God doesn't say that. He says, "I'll give you a way to be saved so that you needn't die. I'll hang my Son on a stake on a hill outside the city. When you realize you are dying, look at it. Look at the cross."

Here is the most amazing truth, which I can't fully explain. I don't know how the bronze snake on the pole worked for the children of Israel and I don't know how it is that when a man realizes he is dying and deserves to die because of the way he has treated God – but when a man looks at the Son of Man lifted up on a cross, he is saved from the penalty of past sins. I don't know how, but it works. We can't explain it any more than we can explain the wind, but it's God's chosen way of saving men and women. You see it is God's way, because it enables a person to come to a realization of their need before they look. God doesn't just say, "I'll take the snakes away"; he says: "I'll leave the snakes there so that you realize the seriousness of what you've done, but there's a way out." In the same way, God doesn't just forgive everybody and say, "All right, I'll have you all in heaven; I'll overlook everything you've done." He says, "Realize what you've done will lead you to die, and then look at my Son on the cross for you."

Jesus said to Nicodemus, "You need redemption, Nicodemus. You'll see me lifted up like that snake was on the pole you are to look at." Do you know Nicodemus did look then? He looked and he came right out for Jesus. He was the one who buried Jesus' body. He looked. He saw Jesus lifted up on a cross.

Do you know that eternal life would not appeal to anybody until they have been born again? Not only could you not enter the kingdom of heaven if you're not born again you wouldn't enjoy it if you could. Until you are born of the Spirit, you don't want to live for ever. But once you have tasted God's love, you want eternal life – you never want to let that go. It's too wonderful.

FINALLY, RETRIBUTION — FOR THE UNBELIEVER (3:18-21)

There us another, serious side to all this: the fourth R is *retribution*. Retribution for the unbeliever means punishment. The greatest sin you can ever commit is to throw God's gift back in his face. What a gift he gave: God gave his only Son. To say, "No thanks" is the most terrible thing you can do: not to believe God gave his precious Son for you. But it is true that many hear about Christ, turn and walk away. When they hear the story of the cross, many are not interested.

Your reaction to the story of Christ and the cross reveals what kind of a person you are. A man who hears about Jesus and the cross and who does not welcome that gift is evil. It says, "The cross shines like light; Jesus was the light of the world, but people loved darkness rather than light because their works are evil" (3:18-20). If a man does not respond to this story, it means there is something in his life that he loves more than God. It means there is something evil that is a barrier between him and God. Other people may not know it. He may not even be fully aware of it himself but God knows about it. Someone who can listen to the story of Christ and the cross and not embrace it as the greatest good news he has ever heard is a man who is covering up some evil. It may be pride, ambition, self-will or an unwillingness to humble himself and be changed. But there is evil there. When someone has heard it and does not respond, we must assume that their works are evil. One day, what is hidden that is preventing him from coming will be revealed. That is one side of it: he is already condemned. You don't need to wait till judgment day to know that a man is condemned. A man who hears this story, who says, "It's not for me" is already condemned.

Somebody will ask about those who have never heard the story. Jesus deals with those also: "If a man is already following what is true he will welcome the light. If he is sincere in seeking God, if he really has responded to God's existing witness to him when you tell him about Christ, he will come to the light and prove that he's been obedient to God all along" (3:20-21). This is going to happen to someone who's never heard about Jesus. Think of Cornelius.

He'd never heard of Jesus, but when Peter told him about Jesus, Cornelius said, "This is what we've been looking for." Peter said, "I can see that those in every nation who fear God really follow him and want him. God accepts them" (Acts 10). Missionaries tell stories like this. Stanley Jones told many times in his Indian books of going to a new village where the gospel is not being preached and preaching, and then having a man come to him and say, "I've been worshipping this God all my life, and now you have told me his name!" They have embraced the truth.

God witnesses to every person through creation, through the things he has made, through the human conscience. If a man honestly and truly is obedient to what little light he has had, then as soon as he hears about Christ and his cross he will respond: "This is what I've been looking for." But a man who is evil does not respond. A man who's got something he doesn't want exposed, who doesn't want to be changed, who is self-sufficient running his own life, not wanting God to run it – that man doesn't welcome the light. He may go on listening month after month, year after year, and that is proof that he is under condemnation already. He is not sincere in wanting God.

Here then are the four Rs we need to know. *Regeneration*: have you been born again? If you have not, as Bishop Ryle once said, "If you have not been born again, a day will come when you wish you had never been born at all." The second truth: *Revelation*. Where have you taken your ideas of heaven and hell from? From other people, from yourself, or from the only one who is in a position to talk: the Son of Man? *Redemption*: have you looked at the cross, seen your Saviour and said, "He died so that I can live"? Finally, have you realized that the future is that those who choose to live in darkness here will live in eternal darkness without even the sun, moon and stars? They have chosen darkness, so God says, "All right, live that way."

---

[1] I expand on this view of one birth with physical and spiritual aspects in my *The Normal Christian Birth* (Hodder & Stoughton, 1997), pages 108-115 and *Jesus Baptises in one Holy Spirit* (Terra Nova, 2010 edition) pp. 84 ff.

8

HE MUST BECOME GREATER
3:22-36

JESUS THE BAPTIST (3:22-26)

Continuity of mission (3:22-24)
Competition of ministries (3:25-26)

JESUS THE BRIDEGROOM (3:27-36)

Transfer of loyalty (3:27-30)
Truth of life (3:31-36)

Christianity has two sides: the inside and the outside. Which do you think is more important? Let's think about two extreme views. There are those content only with the outside of Christianity. Such people think that as long as you go through the outward motions of being a Christian then that's all that God requires. If I've been christened, confirmed, go to Communion, have been through all the ceremonies and do my duty, that is all that is needed. But the Bible comes out strongly against that: "You must be born again. You may have been through all the outside ceremonies, but that may not have changed your inside."

Throughout the Bible, God says he is not interested in a person who has only got outward godliness. The Old Testament prophets said to the Jews, "Don't bring any more sacrifices – God is fed up with them. You honour him with your lips but your heart is far from him. You are doing it on the outside; you are there every Sabbath; you are going through the motions of worship but it is only on the outside and God isn't interested. He wants a heart that's full of love for him." When Jesus came, he spoke more severely about hypocrisy than about any other sin, because it was the outside without the inside.

The trouble is that when people realize this truth they can swing to the opposite extreme. They can say the important thing is that you have everything inside: as long as you've got the inside right, as long as you've been born again and believe in the Lord Jesus and have him in your heart, that's all that's needed – the outside doesn't matter. Such people become impatient with outward ceremonies and outward showing of what is inside. At an extreme are Christian groups like the Quakers, the Society of Friends, who have abolished all the outward side of Christianity. They do not baptize or have the Lord's Supper, because these are outward. It's possible for us to fall into the error of thinking that once you have the inside the outside doesn't matter. It is God's will that Christians should have it inside *and* outside: not only in their hearts but also letting it show.

John chapter 3 emphasizes the inward side of Christianity: the work of God in the heart through his Spirit bringing new life, believing in the Lord Jesus, being born again. This chapter, however, also has much to say about baptism. Baptism is not unimportant. Somebody could say, "I love Jesus in my heart; I don't need to be baptized. The Bible doesn't talk like that; the Bible talks about the outside and the inside as being two parts of the same thing. In this chapter, belief is the inside and baptism is the outside of the same response to Jesus. After all, I have two sides: an inside and an outside, and God wants both. He isn't content only with my inside; he wants my outside too. If I am baptized, I am showing him I want him to have the outside as he has already got the inside.

To illustrate this from marriage, I think you would agree it would be wrong for two people to marry unless they love each other. I know that some marriages are arranged in the hope that some day in the future the married couple will live happily and love each other. But to us that is "putting the cart before the horse". Surely they should love each other and then get married? The inside should be there or the outside is meaningless. On the other hand, we now live in a day in which young people are saying, "The inside is all that matters, why bother with getting married? Why go through an outward ceremony? We love each other – that's all that counts." Those who say love without marriage is all right are as one-sided as those who say marriage without love is all right. The inside and the outside go together. After I have conducted a marriage ceremony I often say to the bridegroom, "You can kiss the bride now." I don't have to tell some bridegrooms – they immediately do it, but to some I say, "Go on – you can kiss the bride"; they look embarrassed, stand there and kiss the bride. I would be worried if a bridegroom said, "No, I don't want to express it outwardly. I'm just loving her in my heart – that's all that's needed." Similarly, it's not enough to say to Jesus, "I love you on the inside"; Jesus says, "Show it on the outside."

You have an inside and an outside and the two go together. But the important thing that the Bible says is that the inside must come first. If the outside is presented first, it is offensive to God. This is our supreme ground for baptizing believers: this is why baptism follows faith. Believing comes first, the inside and then the outside follows – we express our love by doing what Christ commands.

People know John 3:16 very well: "For God so loved the world that he gave his one and only Son, that whoever believes in him shall not perish but have eternal life" (NIV). "… believes in him" [which would be better translated *goes on believing in him*]: that is the inside. But only six verses later it talks about baptism, about water. That is why I believe Jesus said to Nicodemus, "Unless a man be born of water and the Spirit..." (3:5). If you believe only in inward Christianity you are embarrassed by the word *water*. But Jesus is saying there's an outside and an inside to this, and to Nicodemus *water* would speak of baptism.

John 3 goes on to talk about baptism. These few verses tell us certain things about baptism: it needs a lot of water. Did you notice that phrase in verse 23? John was baptizing at a place called Aenon, meaning "Fountains" which had seven springs that fed the Jordan River, near a place called Salim meaning "Peace." There was plenty of water there, which you need if you're going to baptize. The word *baptize* means "plunge, immerse, dip." John baptized in that place because there was enough water to do it. We read also that people came to be baptized: they made the decision. Nobody decided for them; they were responsible, mature people. They were old enough to have sinned and to need cleansing from sin. They came and were baptized. Here is a picture of baptism as immersion, a responsible adult act. That's the picture of baptism right through the New Testament.

JESUS THE BAPTIST (3:22-26)

Continuity of mission (3:22-24)

Now let's look at two titles of Jesus in this study. First, Jesus was a Baptist. I'm not trying to be partisan. The word *Baptist* shouldn't be a denominational label; it is a title that goes back to John the Baptist, who did what God told him and immersed people to get them clean, who did this outward act because inside they were repenting of their sin. But this chapter tells us clearly that Jesus also was a Baptist. He continued this ministry: there was no break between John and Jesus. Baptism was not a temporary ceremony that would die out when Jesus brought inward religion. Jesus continued where John left off.

This continuity of mission has come down 2,000 years to us.

Christianity is not solely an inward religion. Throughout the New Testament, the deeper they got inside, the more they wanted to express it outside. Religion never became more inward than on the Day of Pentecost. The Holy Spirit got right inside 120 ordinary people: they were filled up. But that same day ended when they said to Peter, "What must we do to have this religion you've got? How could we have this Spirit you've got?" He said, "Repent," – that's inside work – and: "be baptized" – that's outside. That day 3,000 people were baptized (Acts 2:37-41). Throughout the New Testament these two things are perfectly matched: the inside first, and the outside second. See also Acts 16:31-33. That's the emphasis. Get the inside right and then express it on the outside.

So Jesus continued John's ministry in baptism. We sometimes forget that during his earthly ministry our Lord not only preached, taught and healed, he also baptized. Even more amazing is the statement that Jesus didn't just take over where John left off but that they overlapped for about six months. They were both baptizing in the same river, about five miles apart: how extraordinary! Jesus was baptizing at the bottom of the river Jordan and five miles up river near Aenon John was baptizing too (3:22-23). Something significant was happening: everybody was leaving John and moving down river. The new people who wanted to be baptized preferred Jesus, which led to an argument (3:25-26). It's unfortunate that baptism should ever divide the Lord's followers but it did here. It was because they focused attention on the wrong thing, on the person who baptized instead of baptism. A Jew who had gone to Jesus for baptism met some of John's followers and said, "We've had a better baptism than you'd get. Jesus baptized us." Actually we're told that Jesus himself never actually baptized but his disciples did. He stood by, and they did it for him, but he approved it. The argument arose as to whose baptism was better. John's followers said, "Ours is," and Jesus' followers said, "No, ours is." That's dreadful. It's baptism that's important, not the person who baptizes. It reached such proportions at Corinth that they used to stick labels of past ministers on each other: "I am of the Reverend Paul"; "I am of the Reverend Peter," etc. Paul wrote to them, "I thank God I didn't baptize any of you if that's how you're going to talk" (1 Corinthians 1:12-15). Baptism is one; it doesn't matter who administers it. It is a burial and a rising to the

Lord. They should never have argued like this.

"A congregation is God's gift to a minister. It's not due to his gifts but to God's gifts. No one could have a following unless God gave it. Woe betide the man who thinks he's got it. It is God who gives it, and if God moves a congregation down river it doesn't matter, as long as God is getting people."

Competition of ministries (3:25-26)

They came to John and said, "People are talking. There are bigger congregations five miles down river. Everybody's going there now, John. We've been defending you; we're jealous for your reputation." Baptism should never be made the ground of competition. Thank God that out of a horrible rivalry come some wonderful words: "I must get smaller; he must get larger. I must become less important; he must become more important" (3:30). Here is John the Baptist's greatness: his humility. He's a man with a big heart who says, "Aren't you forgetting something? Firstly, a congregation is God's gift to a minister. It's not due to his gifts but to God's gifts. No one could have a following unless God gave it. Woe betide the man who thinks he's got it. It is *God* who gives it, and if God moves a congregation down river it doesn't matter, as long as God is getting people." It takes a man with a big heart to say that, but John said it. He said, "Aren't you forgetting God gave me my ministry and God gave me the people to come? We mustn't talk about our church, our denomination, our followers. Let's talk about *his* gifts."

JESUS THE BRIDEGROOM (3:27-36)

Transfer of loyalty (3:27-30)

John also said, "Have you forgotten what I've preached?" They had; they even said, "The One you spoke about has started up down river." But he said, "The One I spoke about ... do you remember what I said about him?" It's terribly easy to remember a minister and forget his sermons. But the important thing is to remember what he said, not the man. So John said, "Don't you remember what I said about this other man? I said, 'I'm not the Messiah, I've been sent ahead of him.'" He then gave Jesus the lovely title of *bridegroom*. It tells me that Jesus loves. He's seeking someone to live with him for ever. He's come to woo and win his bride. We are all the bride of Christ and the bridegroom comes to us.

John used this title to say, "I'm nothing more than the best man." In fact John was too humble to use the word *best*, so he said, "I'm the bridegroom's friend (3:29). Let us think about the best man, because in weddings today his function is completely different from New Testament times. Nowadays, the best man invariably spends the previous night with the bridegroom; it is his job to get the bridegroom to the wedding punctually; at the reception he reads out cards, etc., tries to make jokes and generally keeps things going well. But in New Testament times, the best man's job was not to get the *bridegroom*, but the *bride*, to the wedding. The best man had to go and propose. If you fell in love with a girl and wanted to marry her, you got hold of a person and asked him, "Will you be my best man and negotiate with the family? Will you take my proposal and make an arrangement and decide on a dowry?" The best man had to go and get a bride, but that was only the beginning of his task. Between the betrothal and marriage, the best man was responsible for the bride's holiness, to keep the bride away from other men. Sometimes that was difficult; the best man was always relieved when he got the bride finally to the bridegroom punctually.

John said, "I am Jesus' best man. A wedding is coming, and I've been sent to get the bride ready. My task is to bring the bride to the bridegroom. Can't you see in telling me Jesus has a bigger congregation than I have that you've completed my happiness? I've delivered the bride to the bridegroom." It's a great privilege for every Christian: bringing someone to Jesus is like bringing a bride to a bridegroom. That was John's task. He said, "It's wonderful that people are leaving me and going down river to Jesus. Did you think I'd be jealous or unhappy? Far from it! My happiness is complete – my job as the best man is to get the bride and when I hear the bridegroom's voice, I'm thrilled!"

Wouldn't it be terrible if a best man ran off with the bride? If the bride never turned up at the wedding and the bridegroom was told, "I'm sorry but the best man's fallen in love with your bride; he's too fond of her and he's run off with her"? That's what would have happened if John had clung to his congregation. But John said, "No; I'm here to serve the bridegroom. When I see them together, my job's done. My happiness is complete." That's every Christian's job.

So we come to these great words: "I must become less, I must fade out of the picture, and Jesus must step into the picture" (3:30). If you're the best man, that is your job. John said, "I must do this, my congregation must go down and his must go up, so people will turn to the bridegroom." You may have been at a wedding reception where the best man has constantly drawn attention away from the couple to himself. That's a bad best man. His task is quietly to direct all the attention to the loving couple, to conduct the reception so that their happiness is complete, and his is complete by fading out of the picture. This involves a transfer of loyalty.

"'He must become greater; I must become less.' This is the secret of the Christian life, the secret of happiness. The only hope of being happy in Jesus is for me to become less and for him to become greater. It's also the secret of holiness. If I tried to be holy, it doesn't work; I become increasingly proud of what I achieve. But if I become less and he becomes greater, that's how I'm going to achieve holiness. It's the secret of effective Christian service and evangelism: if we're ever going to win anybody else, it's not by pushing ourselves, but by allowing Jesus to become greater and have centre stage."

Truth of life (3:31-36)

But why should people transfer from John to Jesus? What has Jesus got that John hasn't? After all, they are both baptizing; they are both preachers. What has Jesus got that John hasn't? In John's last sermon about Jesus, he gives us four thoughts about the Lord that show there is no one like Jesus.

Firstly, Jesus' *origin*. John says, "I was born on this earth; I belong to this earth. My experience is limited to this earth. But that man who's baptizing down river came from heaven, his experience is heavenly. He knows what he's talking about, he is above all because he started above all. Jesus is above everyone. Don't think highly of any of his ministers; think highly of Jesus."

Secondly, Jesus' *knowledge*. John says: "My message is second-hand but his is first-hand. I can tell you only things God has told me but that man can say what he has seen and heard." If I preach about heaven, I'm talking about something I have never seen. I don't know what heaven is like. I can only tell you what I have heard and read. But Jesus had seen that, and it was too incredible and nobody believed it, and still they don't – the things Jesus teaches are so amazing that nobody believes them. He talks of heaven, and people don't believe it. He talks of hell and people don't believe it. He talks of God and people ask: is there a God? He's speaking about what he's seen and heard and no one receives his message. But those who do prove that God is true. John says, "Go and listen to Jesus: he's telling you first-hand what he's seen, and if you believe what he says, you'll prove God is true. This means if you don't believe what Jesus said, you're saying God is a liar. But those who believe the message of Jesus say God is true."

Thirdly, Jesus' *inspiration*. Jesus is filled with the Holy Spirit without any limit. The Holy Spirit was there throughout Jesus' life. At his birth, the Holy Spirit brought the body of Jesus to birth. He's there at his baptism, anointing Jesus with power to do good. He's there in the temptations: the Spirit leads him into the wilderness. He's there in every miracle. Jesus says, "If I by the Spirit of God drive out demons, then the kingdom of God has come upon you." He's there at the resurrection: it was the Spirit of holiness who raised Jesus from the dead. The Spirit! The reason why you should go to Jesus is that Jesus was filled with the Holy Spirit without limit. Unfortunately, our human cowardice and faithlessness puts limits on what the Holy Spirit can do. There isn't one person who hasn't limited the Holy Spirit's activity in their life, but Jesus walked this earth and he never set any limit on the Holy Spirit, and God gave him the Spirit without limit. Every word he said and every act he did was filled with the Holy Spirit.

John says, "Go down river to Jesus, for God gave him the Holy Spirit without limit."

Fourthly, Jesus' *power*. John says God so loves his own Son that he's given him power over everything. Power is what the world dreams of, but the power of the universe is in Jesus' hands because the Father loves the Son. Sometimes an earthly father has taken his son into a room and said, "Now son, I'm going to put the family business in your hands. I intended that. I love you and I want you to have the family business." God the Father said that to Jesus, "I want you to have the business. I've made the universe; I want you to have it. I'm going to make a church; I want you to have it. I want all power in the universe to be yours." So he gave all power to Jesus. He never gave it to John, to me, any other minister or anyone, but he gave it to his Son. That's a fourth reason why you should turn away from people and turn to Jesus: the power to handle your future is in Jesus.

The last thing John the writer of the Gospel said was that John the Baptist *preached faithfully*. He did not mind that people would be offended by his preaching; John the Baptist told the truth. Jesus' power will decide whether you spend eternity in heaven or hell; his power will decide whether you live with the love of God or the wrath of God. For whoever believes [*is believing* or *goes on believing*] in Jesus *is having eternal life*. Whoever doesn't is going to live under God's anger for ever.

Verse 36 deals a mortal blow to many modern notions, including the idea that everybody will be saved and get to heaven some day. John never taught that. He talked about God's eternal wrath. There is an idea that heaven is real but not hell, but John never talked like that.

9

THE STORY OF THE BAD SAMARITAN
John 4:1-42

THE CONTRAST (4:1-6)

THE CONVERSATION (4:7-26)

His request—her indifference
His statement—her scepticism
His offer—her flippancy
His challenge—her evasion
His accusation—her diversion
His demand—her procrastination
His claim—her silence

The Bible has two famous Samaritans: the good Samaritan (about a man) and the bad Samaritan (about a woman). The story of the Good Samaritan is fiction because good Samaritans are rare, and Jesus made up that story. The story of bad Samaritan is fact, because badness is common.

THE CONTRAST (4:1-6)

What a complete contrast between Nicodemus (John 3) and this woman: they couldn't have been further apart in morals, in race, in everything else. This clearly shows us Jesus isn't tied to any type of person. Some people think religion is a matter of temperament, as if you have to be a certain type to believe in Jesus. But Jesus was at home with everyone. Whoever you are or whatever you have done, Jesus would like to talk with you, and if you listen, you will feel at home with him.

Then there is the contrast in place. Jesus made a journey; he left the Jordan, about 1,000 feet below sea level in that hot valley, and went hundreds of feet up to the open hills of Samaria, with two great mountains, Mount Ebal and Mount Gerizim, standing like sentinels against the skyline. In the valley between the mountains is the town of Samaria, now Shechem. Another little town lies at the end of that valley: Sychar. You can still stop at a well and they let a bucket 150 feet down into the ground to get a drink of water! That well was dug thousands of years ago by a man called Jacob. It's still there.

Jesus not only moved from the deep valley to the hills, he also moved from Jewish to Samaritan territory. We need to think about the Samaritans as the background to this story. About 500 years before this, the Jewish nation were taken away into exile. But a few men managed to hide and were not taken prisoner. They survived in the little land of Israel, but they had no one to marry: what were they going to do? Were they going to wait until the exiles found their way home again? They were not happy to wait so they took local girls from other tribes and entered into mixed marriages, something God had told them not to do. They married people who didn't belong to God. They were called Samaritans because they lived around Samaria in the north. Now when the pure Jews came back after the exile, the Samaritans said, "Could we link up with you again now?" but the Jews refused, saying, "You've mixed the blood; you're not pure." From then, Jews and Samaritans hated each other. A Jew would deliberately go seventy miles out of his way to avoid going through Samaria, the quickest way from Galilee to Judea.

Jews and Samaritans hated each other. So when Jesus told his disciples, who were all Jews, "We're going to walk through Samaria," can you imagine how they felt? I am sure they hoped they wouldn't meet anybody or get involved with the people and that they would travel as quickly as possible to the north, to Galilee. About noon they reached this well. You can still go there today and meet Samaritans who live on that mountain, Mount Gerizim, where they still worship and offer their sacrifices to the same God as the Jewish God. They don't have the whole Old Testament, however; they only have the first five books of the Old Testament: Genesis, Exodus, Leviticus, Numbers and Deuteronomy.

Jesus met these people by meeting one of them first. It was noon – the time of day when you rest. He was hot, tired, hungry and thirsty. Thank God the Bible says that: it shows he was really human: a real man as well as the Son of God. His disciples could see he was worn out. They told Jesus, "You stay here. We'll go into town and buy some food. You rest here."

A woman then came out at noon, but no woman would usually do that. It was the hottest time of day to make the mile-long journey with a water pot on your head. She came then because she didn't want to meet other women. You can tell that from later: she was a loner. She liked men but not women. So she came alone at noon and met a strange man. That's the setting.

THE CONVERSATION (4:7-26)

As we look at the conversation, we shall see the woman tried every possible evading tactic to stop. Time and again she tried to close the discussion, but she couldn't. Notice too that Jesus progressively goes deeper and deeper. Everything he says is a further step into her heart.

His request—her indifference

Jesus begins with a simple request, and that was a good way to begin. It would put him under obligation to her. This is not a patronizing approach. Have you ever thought about starting that way? Not by going patronizingly to help someone but asking, "Would you help me?" Jesus said, "I'm thirsty – could I have a drink?" He began the relationship. To do this, he ignored convention, etiquette and racialism. He strode right through these artificial human barriers. It was not the done thing for a man to address a woman in public if he did not know her. Some even thought a man should not talk to his own wife in public. But Christ went straight through that etiquette. It was certainly not the done thing for a Jew to talk to a Samaritan, but he strode right over that racial barrier. This is an example to us: if you can help someone, go straight through etiquette or convention. Go and talk them; don't wait till you're introduced. You might wait forever; just go and talk! He took the first step. Now she gave him the cold shoulder; she knew how to do that with strange men.

Notice she never gave him that drink. In fact, later it says when she ran back to her village she even left her water pot behind. She got so absorbed in the conversation but she never gave him a drink. She said, "Who do you think you are speaking to? You're a man; I'm a woman; you're a Jew; I'm a Samaritan. We don't have dealings with each other. Don't try and get friendly with me." Indifference: she didn't want to know. An interesting note is in the footnote of verse 9: Jews and Samaritans never use the same dish. They wouldn't drink out of something that the other had used to drink.

His statement—her scepticism

Jesus then stated, "If you really knew who you were talking to, you wouldn't talk like that. You would be asking something from him, not letting him ask something from you." It was a mild rebuke. He said, "I could give you living water. If you knew what God can do, I could give you living water – if you only asked." To her, living water would mean spring water, as opposed to pool water, dead water, stagnant water, as you get in a well. Living water is a spring that's bubbling like a brook. "If you only knew who you were talking to, you would have asked him for living water." Having made this statement, she now tries a second way to close the conversation: she is sceptical. She doubts whether he could do it. Logically, she's reasonable: her arguments were right; she says, "The well is deep." It was – it's about 150 feet down. She said, "You haven't got a bucket – there's no other water near here. How can you give me water?" Logical, yes, but like Nicodemus she's bound to her own experience of material things so she cannot look deeper. She didn't ask him where he would get it or what it was. She just argued. Haven't you found sometimes when you make a statement that's true about God somebody says, "Logically it's impossible. I don't see how that could happen."

His offer — her flippancy

So her scepticism leads to a question which must have embarrassed her. "Do you think you're bigger than Jacob? Jacob dug this well; he was a great man, and this well is still going. Do you think you're greater than him?" "Well, yes," Jesus thought, but he didn't say so. He dealt gently with her. So he next made an offer to her. He enlarged what he said about living water. She didn't ask him to but he continued, "I'll tell you what I'm talking about. If you drink this water, you'll be thirsty again and you'll have to come all the way from the village with water pot to get more." Do you know we don't know what thirst is in this country? I didn't know what thirst was till one day I was stranded in the Arabian desert with a broken down Land Rover. You begin to dream of a glass of water, to think you'd sell your soul for just a little bit of water – that was real thirst, when there's no water available.

Jesus says, "I'll tell you what, instead of you having to come to the well, I could give you water that would bubble up like a spring inside you." He wasn't talking of literal water, of course, he was talking about the Holy Spirit, rivers of living water (John 7:37-39). He tells this woman, "Instead of having to fetch it, I will give you the convenience of running water in your heart, so that you've got it on tap. You'd never be thirsty again." He doesn't mean you drink once and that's it for ever, but when there's a spring of living water in your heart you don't need to keep going to other people's wells to drink.

"Jesus challenged her: 'Go and get your husband.' What memories came through her mind as he said that? Which one? She'd been through five men and the one she was living with then wasn't her husband. Jesus was getting too near the bone, touching her conscience. The conversation was taking a turn she didn't like, so she deliberately evaded it."

Now she tried flippancy. This conversation was getting too serious, so the deeper he went, the shallower she became. She make a joke of it. She said, "This sounds great; running water – lead me to it! I'm all for the easy life. Sir, give me this water, then I don't need to come here with buckets every day!" She's laughing at him.

His challenge—her evasion

However, it is a mistake to laugh when Jesus is trying to help you with the deep things of God. So Jesus becomes serious and challenges her. He says, "Bring your husband and I'll talk to both of you." It's a command. Jesus has the right to tell us what to do. "Go and get your husband." What memories came through her mind as he said that? Which one? She's been through five men and the one she was living with then wasn't her husband. This man was getting a bit too near the bone, touching her conscience and making her feel uncomfortable. The conversation was taking a turn she didn't like, so she deliberately evaded it. She told a half-truth: "I have no husband." That was true but it was only half-true. You can put people off with a half-truth when they are getting near the bone.

His accusation—her diversion

She assumes his challenge was a guess, but now he makes an accusation. You can't put Jesus off with half-truths. He knows everything, so he said, "Yes, what you said is true – but it's only half-true, isn't it? You've had five, in fact, six men." Like Peter, like Nathanael, this woman realized Jesus knew everything she had done. That's a horrible moment because each one of us falls into the same trap of thinking nobody knows what we've done, because nobody was there. But Jesus knows.

Jesus turned her life inside out, and she tried the oldest trick in the book: she raised a theological controversy, after a touch of flattery. She's clever. She says, "You know a lot. You're a prophet. All right, here's a question I've always been troubled by. Who are right: the Jews or the Samaritans? You Jews have got your temple in Jerusalem and we've got our temple on Mount Gerizim. We like to worship God here; you like to worship God there. Who's right?" People play off one religion against another; it's astonishing how many English people suddenly become interested in comparative religion when you get near the bone!

His demand—her procrastination

Jesus answered her question: "If you're going to press me, the Jews are right. You've only got a little bit of the Bible; you don't know enough about God, you're still ignorant of a lot. And if you're going to be saved it'll be through the Jews that you get saved." I am glad to wear a little badge with the Jewish word *shalom*, "peace", because I owe everything to Jews: the Bible I read is a Jewish book, my Saviour was a Jew. The apostles who started the church were Jews. Yes, "Salvation is of the Jews," even if they don't realize it themselves always. Their greatest gift to the world was a Saviour.

"So," Jesus said, "if you're going to press me, then we are right and you are wrong. But I tell you this is an obsolete issue. It's a question that will soon be out of date, and you won't even be able to ask it in a few years," and that was true. A few years later, both temples would have gone. But he says, "I'll tell you what real religion is. You've got the wrong dimensions: it's not time and space that are important: God is spirit." You can't tie him down to this or that building. You cannot say you have got to worship God in a cathedral, church, chapel or synagogue. You can't say that, because God is spirit and you can't tie spirit down to dimensions. Spirit is everywhere and so it's an obsolete question. "Madam, you've got to rethink your attitude to religion and realize you've got to enter the dimension of the spirit to worship God. You're only concerned with the material, with water you can drink from this well. You need the dimension of the spirit if you're going to meet God who is spirit. Furthermore, the Jews and you both worship God, but the Father – do you know the Father? [do you notice the switch?] – wants people of a different kind."

Most people in this country believe in God, according to opinion polls, but not many of them know the Father. The Father seeks people who have entered the dimension of spirit. The Holy Spirit is given so that you can cry out, "Abba, daddy, father." The Holy Spirit puts you in a new dimension in which you're not dependent on a building. It's not here, there, cathedral or chapel; it's anywhere! We are to know the Father and worship him in spirit and reality. That's what the word *truth* means: knowing God as he really is. Not as you think he is, but as he is. The Father is looking for a different kind of worship: Jesus is saying, "Woman, what God wants from you is not to worship here or here, but to get into the dimension of spirit and worship God as he really is. God is for real, he's true."

"The woman tried one last thing: procrastination. It's like those who say, 'That's interesting. I'll think about it some day. Some day the Messiah's going to come and he'll answer all my questions ... some day.' She was trying to put it off. She's gone so far and didn't want to go further."

The woman therefore tried the last thing. "Some day": procrastination – don't do today what you can put off till tomorrow. It's like those who say, "That's all very interesting and challenging. I'll think about it some day. One day I'll look into it more deeply." She said, "Some day the Messiah's going to come and he'll answer all my questions … some day." She was trying to put it off. She's gone so far and didn't want to go further. So she said, as Samaritans believed with Jews, that one day the Messiah would come and change all religion and make it real. "It's all very interesting but some day I'll really listen to the Messiah."

His claim — her silence

Then Jesus finally said: "I am." He didn't say, "I am he," – that's how it's translated into English. He said simply, "I am." Back in the Scriptures the Samaritans had, the first five books of the Bible, Moses said to God, "What is your name?" and God said, "I am." She knew that. Jesus said, "I am." In other words, "Now's the time – you're dealing with God right now. You're dealing with the great I am." In fact, she might never have had another chance to deal with the Lord, he was there: "I am. I'm talking to you. Let's get it all settled now."

THE CONSEQUENCES (4:27-42)

Jewish disciples

The disciples blundered in at that point, but enough had been said. The disciples came back and they were in for three surprises: firstly, he was talking to a woman, a strange woman, in public, a Samaritan. But they didn't dare ask him for fear that he thought they thought bad things about him, so they kept quiet.

The second surprise was that he wasn't hungry any more. They had been a mile to get some food, but he wasn't interested. When you're busy in the things of God, physical needs somehow become secondary: you are refreshed. We become absorbed in the task to finish it. Jesus says (4:34): "My food is to finish the job. I've got to get this finished, I'm not hungry any more, I'm finishing the job God gave me to do." He'd done wonderfully with that woman: he'd led her step by step to the point where she just had to make up her mind about Jesus. He'd finished the job, so he was satisfied, not hungry.

Their third surprise was that he began to talk strangely. It was January and he says, "Look around the fields": they could see people beginning to sow the corn. He continued, "You say it's another four months before you'll see harvest. I tell you look at those fields again. The harvest is just ready to pluck. One person sows, another reaps – it doesn't matter, they all rejoice together as long as there's a harvest. Can't you see?" And they looked around but couldn't see. If you'd been there, however, you'd have seen half a mile across the fields a field full of people all running and ripe for harvest.

Samaritan believers

Jesus always saw the spiritual; he looked beyond the material to the spiritual. He said, "Look at them. I've been sowing, you're going to reap." He told that woman to go and bring her husband. She brought every man in the village! She brought the whole village, and they came. See the results of one woman who can simply say, "Come and see." You don't need to be as clever, brilliant, wise as Jesus in that conversation. You can start by just saying to someone, "Come and see." I know we've seen Jesus brilliantly steer the conversation rightly, and you read it and wish you could talk to people like that. But you don't need to, to start; you can start by saying what the woman said, "Come and see."

Everybody in that village knew her life but they didn't think the Jews knew about it. But she told them, "I've just met a Jew and he knew all about me ... and you know what I've been like. He told me everything ... come and see him!" They came and said, "We believed you at first because of what you said but now we believe because we've met him for ourselves." Nearly everybody's faith goes through two stages. They believe what somebody else says about Jesus so they come. They try him for themselves, and then say, "It's true. We believe it now not because you said so but because we know for ourselves."

They finished up saying something about Jesus that had never been said before. They said, "We know he's the Saviour of the whole world" (4:42). The word *world* is one of the most fascinating words in John's Gospel, which begins by saying Jesus created the world. It goes on to say though the world came into being through Jesus, it did not recognize him, but nevertheless Jesus came into the world. Then it says he came to take away the sins of the world, then that God loved the world and that he gave his one and only Son. All this builds up to this simple fact: Jesus is the Saviour of the world.

It took the Samaritans to say that. Everybody else called him the Messiah of the Jews, but the Samaritans said, "He's the Saviour of the world." That is why we've got to go to the whole world and tell people about Jesus Christ. He's not a Middle East Messiah; he's the Saviour of the world. He's not the English Christ; he's the Saviour of the world. He's for every person, for everybody, for every nation, beginning at Jerusalem to Samaria and to the ends of the earth.

10

HOW TO GROW TO
A MATURE FAITH
John 4:43-54

FAMILIARITY BREEDS CONTEMPT (4:43-46a)

FAITH BRINGS CONFIDENCE (4:46b-54)

He had faith in the presence of Jesus
He had faith in the power of Jesus
He had faith in the person of Jesus

We have five senses: sight, touch, hearing, taste and smell, and everything we know and believe comes to us through one of those five senses. We rely on some of them more than others. Generally, it is our sight that convinces us of the truth of things. We may hear about things but until we've seen them we find them difficult to believe.

With the power of television, we can see pictures of what is happening all around the world – and we remember seeing man walking on the moon – but we are still one of the most unbelieving generations ever. We are so used to seeing things that we can't believe without seeing. Here, we've much in common with the ancient Jews. The great contrast between the Samaritans in the early part of chapter 4, and the Jews in the second part is that the Samaritans were content to believe what they heard. The Jews, however, always wanted to see before they were convinced. There is an English proverb: seeing is believing, but that isn't true. All of John's Gospel was written to help us believe even when we do not see.

One of the stories at the end of this Gospel concerns Thomas, the sceptical disciple who said, "You don't expect me to believe, do you? Until I've seen, until I've touched, I won't believe my ears. I'll believe my eyes and then I'll believe my hands but I won't believe my ears." Jesus said to Thomas, "Thomas, you've had to see before you believe, and blessed – happy, to be congratulated – are those who've never seen but who believe." In fact if you have seen something, you don't need to believe it: that's the message of this passage.

Every single miracle in John's Gospel is carefully selected with a message, and the message of this story is: believe without seeing. That's the faith that overcomes the world, that's going to move mountains. To be able to believe where you didn't see.

FAMILIARITY BREEDS CONTEMPT (4:43-46a)

This was my favourite Bible story as a boy. Whenever my mother offered to tell me a Bible story I would ask her for this one. I don't know why; what affected me deep down was the amazing coincidence of time, at least that's what I thought it was: that the little boy should get well at exactly the moment Jesus said he would. I never cease to love this story.

"The most difficult place to be a Christian and to witness is where you are known best, because unfortunately people know you and your weaknesses. You're the person they know only too well. Jesus deliberately went from Samaria to Judea saying, 'I know it's going to be harder. I'm a prophet, and I realize a prophet isn't appreciated by those who know him well. But I'm still going there.'"

Let's consider the background of this story. Verses 43 to 45 tell us that Jesus deliberately moved from one place to another. That sounds ordinary until you realize he was moving from an easy to a difficult situation, which takes real strength of character. He was in Samaria where they believed on hearing only, where everybody wanted to know him, where he was welcomed and a revival was going on. But Jesus left Samaria to go to Galilee. He said openly and honestly, "It's going to be tough going back to where I live."

This shows us that God often calls us to go and witness in the hardest place. You may be having a good time in one area but he may want you to go elsewhere. In Acts 8, Philip was called away from this same Samaria where revival and miracles were happening, with hundreds of people being converted, and God sent him into the desert: Philip had to go to a lonely place for the sake of one man.

The most difficult place to be a Christian and to witness is where you are known best, because unfortunately people know you and your weaknesses. You are the person next door; the person they know only too well. Jesus deliberately went from Samaria to Judea saying, "I know it's going to be harder. I'm a prophet, and I realize a prophet isn't appreciated by those who know him well. But we're still going there."

Look at that proverb: I want you to notice it's a prophet who is not appreciated, because in the next verse (4:45), it says they welcomed him, not as a prophet, but as a miracle worker. The world will always be glad to see miracle workers who can relieve them from sickness, troubles and pain. But a prophet isn't as welcome: someone who talks about God, morals, sin and future judgment – that's not popular. A prophet may achieve some honour in a place where he's not known, but the honour doesn't come where he lives and from the people who know him, which Jesus knew perfectly well but he still didn't shy away from it.

Do you ever feel that your friends, family and the people you work with don't appreciate you? It seems easier to go off to Timbuktu and be a missionary, to go somewhere else and conduct a crusade. But to be a Christian where people know you isn't easy. If they know you, they won't come running with open arms if you talk to them about God, sin, judgment and salvation. They might listen to a stranger but not a friend. Jesus knew that, so he said, "That's where we've got to go." I think it's lovely that Jesus deliberately chose the most difficult place to go and preach to. He wanted to be right where he was most needed, even though he wouldn't be received as a prophet.

The other possible reason why he went to Galilee was that he was already getting too famous. He wanted time with his disciples, so he deliberately took them north to Galilee where he wouldn't create such a stir, where he could obtain comparative peace to train them.

You can take either reason; the important thing was that they wouldn't appreciate his message but they would love his miracles. So he went back to Cana in Galilee, and by now word had spread that he was the man who turned water into wine. Some of the Galileans had been south for the Passover and had seen him do miracles in Jerusalem: a story in the *Nazareth Chronicle* under the headline "Local boy makes good" would have been about the miracle worker from their own country coming back. They welcomed him for what he had done for them, but not for what he had said about them: this is the great tension – familiarity does breed contempt.

We need to remember God has put us where we are not only to do good but also to speak about him. Doing good will be welcomed by your neighbour, but speaking about God may not be. "A prophet is not without honour except in his own town." The subtle pressure on us therefore is not to talk about the Lord to our neighbours and friends, but only to do good to them, because they will welcome that. But Jesus came preaching and teaching as well as healing. He did good, but he also spoke about God, even though it was difficult.

FAITH BRINGS CONFIDENCE (4:46b-54)

Jesus came back to Cana and their minds were only full of what he was going to do for them, to deal with their problems and heal their sickness. But in all the stir in Galilee there was one man in whose heart a spark of hope is struck. We know very little about him; we don't even know his name. We know he was rich and that he had a prominent position at King Herod's court in Galilee. We also know that, as he travelled around Galilee, his heart was heavy. He had a little boy who had been ill for a long time. The Greek verb means that he was not ill occasionally or just once but that he had continued being ill, and that he had got worse and worse. This man still travelled around on business but he had to return home as quickly as possible at the end of the day. He tried not to stay away from home too often but he had watched his boy's condition became increasingly worse over the years and he knew his son would die soon.

But then this man who travelled round Galilee on royal business heard that the One who had done miracles elsewhere is in town. The father was desperate and went to Jesus. Let's trace the story of this man's faith, which passed through three stages. I want to share this with you in the hope that God will grow your faith to make it mature and strong.

He had faith in the presence of Jesus

That's where he began. His faith wasn't very big but it was a first step. This man believed Jesus could heal his boy, but he believed Jesus could only do it through physical touch. It was faith in Jesus simply as a faith healer, so he said, "I've got to get him to my son. I've got to bring them together physically. Jesus' body must somehow touch my son's body if there's going to be healing." So he begged Jesus to come.

His faith lacked two things. First, he believed that distance prevented God's power from operating, and secondly, he believed death prevented God's power from operating. He was wrong in both. He said, "You've got to come quickly [to overcome the distance barrier]. If you don't, he'll die and be beyond your reach." He was saying, "My boy is within your reach now but will be beyond your reach unless you come quickly." He was limiting God's power.

But he was talking to Jesus. Jesus could heal at a distance of miles. He didn't believe that, however; he believed in physical power, and so he wanted Jesus to come and touch his boy. He didn't yet realize that Jesus could speak to a dead body and say, "Get up." He had faith, but it was limited. It was real and he had gone to the right person but it wasn't big enough. If we ever set limits on what Jesus can do either by distance or death, then our faith is no greater than this official's.

Jesus' reply was unusual. The poor man was anxious and desperate, saying, "Come quickly." Jesus answered, "Why will you not believe unless you see?" The man is frustrated and disappointed with him. It's a real blow for him that Jesus longs for people to believe without limits. He's waiting for someone to say, "Lord, you can do anything. I don't need to tell you how to do it." When we come and tell the Lord how he's got to act, we show our faith is limited. Instead of saying, "Here's the need, Lord – you do what's right, whatever you see is best," this official said, "You've got to come quickly ... you've got to do it this way, or it won't work." Jesus responded, "Why don't you believe? You've got to see me come and touch, have you? Why don't you believe without seeing? Hearing is all you need to believe. You don't need to see me touch your boy."

The official was impatient – he didn't want a theological discussion, a long enquiry about belief – he wanted practical help for his boy, so he said, "Come, I haven't time to discuss faith with you." That's step number one – it's not very great faith is it – or is it? Some would say it was tremendous faith, at least to believe that Jesus could cure the boy. But it wasn't big enough.

He had faith in the power of Jesus

One comment on this story was that the Lord wanted to heal the father's soul as well as the son's body. The Lord wanted to stretch his faith, to take that father further, to make the father grow so that he really believed. How did he do it? Jesus magnificently dealt with both father and son together. He helped them both by making a simple statement. I don't think it comes across properly in the English in v. 50. Jesus looked at the father and said, "Your son is already living. I've done it." His statement put the poor father on the spot: he was in a dilemma. If he went home and it hadn't worked out, the whole thing would have been wasted and precious time would have been lost. But if he had stayed there and said, "Well, I don't believe you," that would have been an insult to Jesus. The poor father's heart must have been in turmoil. The father said, "Come," but Jesus said, "Go."

"You could summarize this whole story with: 'He says it; I believe it; that settles it.' What faith! Do you have faith like that when God says something to you? Do you say, 'That settles it,' or do you say, 'I'll wait and see'?"

The father had to make up his mind whether the power of Jesus was greater than he had thought or not. He had to venture a step of faith without any proof, evidence or anything to see. What would he do? We're told he believed Jesus, turned around and walked away. That is a wonderful sentence: "He believed Jesus and went" (4:50). No proof or evidence, nothing for his eyes to see and nothing to touch. Just a word: that's all he had, but he believed and he went.

The word of Jesus is as good as anyone's action. Others may do something for you but Jesus just has to say something and that's all you need. The power of Jesus' word is amazing; this is now the second miracle he performed in Galilee. Did you notice both of them were performed only by word and by nothing else? How did he change water into wine? He said, "Fill the water pots up."

Did he then say, "Abracadabra" over them? No! Did he go and take his hand and swish round the water inside? No! He simply said, "Fill them up and take the water to the master of the feast" and it was done (2:7-8). This is why we still believe in preaching; this is why we don't replace preaching with a television screen and have pictures for you all the time. *God's word* is enough. If God says something, it's done.

Someone has said you could summarize this whole story with: "He says it; I believe it; that settles it." Isn't that wonderful? What faith! This man took a further step in his faith and said, "He says it; I believe it; that settles it." He turned round and went home. Would you have had faith like that? Do you have faith like that when God says something to you? Do you say, "That settles it," or do you say, "I'll wait and see"?

Do you realize if you only believe what you see that so many things God says are lost on you? You have no assurance of heaven, if you're going to wait till you get there before you believe in it. What a loss to your Christian life! Look how much God has said about heaven. Every Christian has the right to say, "I believe it; that settles it. I have no doubts about heaven. I'm going towards heaven before I've seen it just as that man went towards Capernaum long before he had seen his boy well again."

That is the second stage of his faith – his faith had to act. His walking home was an act of faith that proved he believed. That's how you prove whether you believe or not, according to James too (James 2:14-26). If you really believe something, then you act; you go ahead and trust the Lord.

He had faith in the person of Jesus

There's a problem here: it was about fifteen miles but he didn't get home till the next morning. Where did he spend the night? Why did he delay? I admit I don't know the answer. It could be that his faith was so strong that he said, "Everything is all right; I can spend the night where I am and go home in the morning." If he had business to do in Cana perhaps that was the reason.

As he approached home the next morning, he saw the servants running out, I wonder if his heart missed a beat. Did he think,

"Have they got bad news?" If I had been that man, I'd have thought I would have known what they were going to say. But they came and said the same thing Jesus said: "Your son's alive!" He was on the road to recovery, improving all the time; he was going to survive the long illness that seemed to have been leading to death. He was now starting to get better, as we can see from what the official asked the servants, "When did he begin to get better?" Literally the Greek says, "When did he begin to mend?"

The official wants to tie his faith down to fact; he wants to know, was it a coincidence? Was it that Jesus had clairvoyance and knew the fever had reached its peak and the boy was going to get better? They replied, "He began to get better at one o'clock." One o'clock? Then it must have been Jesus. If a boy has been ill a long time and suddenly gets better at one o'clock and sixteen miles away the Lord Jesus has said it's all right, that is not a coincidence; that is stretching coincidence too far.

Those who live by faith in the Son of God statistically live beyond coincidence. The world might say about one or two intercessory prayers that they were coincidence but when it comes again, again and again – when you have evidence that events taking place miles apart are related exactly in time – then it's not coincidence or clairvoyance: it's Jesus Christ. When your faith grows up, this is the kind of thing that happens all the time; you discover things that the world would say are mere chance but they are not. They correspond too closely to the word of God.

"The great men of faith in the Bible are those who said, 'I can't see but I've heard God speak and that's enough for me.' That's the faith God longs to see in his people: the faith that goes beyond sight, goes further than reason, that says, 'If he says so, I believe it – I'm absolutely sure.'"

So now they said what Jesus had said: "Your son is living." The text then says he and all his household believed (4:53): he believed now. This is strange; we thought he believed in Cana; it now says he believed in Capernaum. It means his faith has gone to an even deeper level: it is now faith in a person. From this day forward that whole household were believers in Jesus. He believed with all his household. Have you noticed they didn't see Jesus? As far as we know, the household had never met Jesus, but they believed. The whole story is telling you this: even if you can't see, believe.

What is faith? "Faith is being sure of what we hope for and certain of what we do not see" (Hebrews 11:1, NIV). The great men of faith in both the Old and New Testaments were those who said, "I can't see but I have heard God speak and that is enough for me." That's the faith God longs to see in his people: the faith that can go beyond sight, that can go further than reason, that says, "If he says so, I believe it – I'm absolutely sure."

Let me finally deal with a modern difficulty of faith. In Jesus' days, the Jews said, "If we see, we'll believe." People still say that. If you talk about miracles, if you tell them about some of the wonderful things God is doing today, they say, "I don't believe it. I'll only believe it if I see it." I spoke to six hundred senior boys in Eton College chapel. I told them about some of the things God is doing. Two teachers came to me afterwards and said they could not believe it. What was the evidence? After we talked, it was obvious that unless they *saw* things – they were so rational and intellectual – they wouldn't believe. That's one tragic outlook we meet today.

There is another viewpoint I am constantly coming across: those who say, "I won't believe until I feel." This is the modern version of this cry for signs. But as with sight so it is with feelings. God says "Believe first, and then we'll let you see and feel later. I've said it; you believe it; you don't need to wait until you've seen or felt something." To rely on either sense or sensation is not to believe. Let me repeat that simple phrase: "God says it; I believe it, that settles it."

Jesus' first two miracles in Galilee are so different from each other. One is a miracle that changed things; the other is a miracle that changed people. One is a miracle that he performed in the room where he was. The other was a miracle he performed sixteen miles away. One was a comparatively trivial need – running out of refreshments at a wedding reception – the other was a matter of life and death. But they both have in common the fact that Jesus spoke and people acted on what he said and they saw the miracle.

May I say to you if Jesus is going to do anything for you today, he's got to do it at a distance? Jesus is no longer physically able to come here and touch your body. You are no longer able to see him with your eyes or hear him with your ears, because Jesus is in the highest heaven at the right hand of God the Father. Nevertheless, he is still able to do miracles at a distance. That's the glory of it. We can ask Jesus to touch us, to bless us, to save us, and he does all the way from highest heaven. He does it when a person says, "He says it; I believe it; that settles it."

11

DO YOU REALLY WANT TO GET WELL?
John 5:1-16

THE HANDICAP OF A PHYSICAL SICKNESS (5:1-4)

THE HAZARD OF MENTAL SLOTH (5:5-9a)

THE HORROR OF SPIRITUAL SIN (5:9b-16)

THE HANDICAP OF A PHYSICAL SICKNESS (5:1-4)

In 1888 they decided to renovate an ancient church in northeast Jerusalem. As they scrubbed the whitewash off a wall, they discovered a faded fresco. It showed a pool of water and an angel standing in the water, stirring the waters with his hand. They began to excavate the churchyard. You can now gaze down a hole 40 feet deep and see the pool of Bethesda. They found it: it has five porches. I remember looking down into that pool trying to visualize how dreadful it must have been. Hundreds of poor people with no hope. The blind, lame and paralysed, with no doctor or nurse.

Here the people gathered at the waters, but they weren't looking for a natural cure. We come to something puzzling I don't understand but have to accept. Any speculation leads to too many questions. The statement is that sometimes an angel came and the water bubbled and the first person – and only the first person – into the pool after the water was stirred was healed. I find that difficult; how frustrating it must have been to the people gathered around the pool: that only one person at a time – and that only occasionally – could be healed and the place was packed. If it wasn't so tragic, it would be laughable. The blind people couldn't see when the water was stirred but they could get there. The lame people could see when it was stirred but they couldn't move. Isn't it pathetic? They all lay there, and you can imagine the appalling selfishness that must have been revealed when the water was stirred. Everyone shouting, pushing and shoving. All these poor invalids scrambling for this pool of water.

One day Jesus came to these poor people. They were helpless but not hopeless. There was a glimmer of hope that one of them might be cured next time and each of them hoped it would be them. One man had been there longer than Jesus had lived on earth. He had been there five years when Jesus was born. Now, about thirty years later, Jesus came to this pool, and he looked at that man and healed him out of all the people: Jesus healed only one person that day.

Some people say Jesus always healed every sick person he met, but that's not true. In this situation he healed one and then got away quickly from the crowd that would have besieged him. But why did he heal this one? What was it about this person that drew his attention? This is the handicap of a physical sickness: when a person is helpless and nearly hopeless but just has a little glimmer that something might happen that would relieve their need.

"Jesus asked, 'Do you really want to get well?' It seems a silly question: a man who's been sick for 38 years and is lying at the only place where there's any hope of him getting better and somebody asks him does he want to get well."

THE HAZARD OF MENTAL SLOTH (5:5-9a)

Now let's look at something more serious: the hazard of mental sloth. This poor man had been lying there for thirty-eight years. Jesus knew all about him: he only had to look at a person and he knew everything. Jesus opened the conversation as he often did. He asked him this awful question. Jesus asked, "Do you really want to get well?" It seems a silly question: a man who's been sick for 38 years and is lying at the only place where there's any hope of him getting better and somebody asks him does he want to get well. Isn't that a ridiculous question?

But we know the man didn't want to get well because of his reply. He doesn't answer, "Yes," or, "Of course I do." He doesn't answer the question. He blames his circumstances. He blames other people. But he doesn't say, "Yes, I want to get well. I want health." He says, "No, well, you see it's like this. I can't help my condition, you see, and I can't help lying here. I just can't help it." Now that's not an answer to Jesus' question. This man evaded the question and answered ambiguously by saying, "I can't." The real problem with this man at this stage is that his will is paralysed. It's not his paralysed body that is his greatest handicap – it's his paralysed will. Jesus is really asking, "Have you the will to get better?" any nurse or doctor will tell you this is one of the critical factors in any serious illness.

I have known people who have been seriously ill but have had a chance to get better. The doctor has told me they could get better but they don't seem to have the will to live. The nurses and doctors then just had to wait and watch them get worse and die. I know others – I'm thinking of a lady aged 94 who fell and broke her hip, but was walking again in six weeks – because she had the will.

The will plays a great part in our life, more than we are prepared to admit. Nowadays we have become used to thinking of the will as something old-fashioned, so we say, "I'm not responsible for what I am; it's my background, my environment. I'm just a victim. I can't help being what I am." We have been told so much about amateur psychology that we all think we're victims and that we have no will any more, that we can't help what we are, that we're pushed around by circumstances and nobody will help us. So if somebody asks, "Do you really want to get well, do you really want to be a saint, do you really want to be whole?" we reply, "Well, you see, I can't help being like this – it runs in the family. I've had a very difficult and unfortunate upbringing." "Do you want to get well?" asks Jesus.

This applies in many directions. It applies physically, as I have said, in hospitals. It applies emotionally: all of us have emotional problems. Each one of us has inhibitions, fears, and complexes, but it is what we do with them that matters. It is whether we have the will to say, "I'm going to get over this complex. I'm not going to be a victim of this. I'm going to rise above my circumstances. I'm determined to overcome this emotional handicap."

Think of Mary Slessor, the great missionary who went out to Africa. When she lived as a girl in Glasgow she was so frightened of people and things that she dare not cross the road alone. That was in the days before it was dangerous to do so – she couldn't even cross the road without her parents taking her hand, even when she was in her teens. But years later Mary Slessor was sailing alone in a canoe in cannibal territory in west Africa. She had the will.

If we have emotional problems, it's not enough to say, "Nobody will help me. I can't help myself." Any psychiatrist will tell you there is hope if a patient is determined to get better. But there is very little you can do for someone who *enjoys* bad health and who would rather have sympathy and support than stand on their own two feet.

"Why do we still have any sins at all? The answer must be we that don't really want to be rid of them ... I'm afraid that is the truth. If I'm having real problems with a temptation, Jesus asks me, 'Do you really want to get well? Do you want to be free of this? Do you want to overcome it?'"

It applies morally. Jesus came to die to save us from our sins. Why then do we still have any sins at all? The answer must be we that don't really want to be rid of them – I am afraid that is the truth. If I am having real problems with a temptation, Jesus asks me, "Do you really want to get well? Do you want to be free of this? Do you want to be on top of it?" Or is it a case of a divided personality: the better part of you wants to be rid of it, the other part of you secretly enjoys it and hangs onto it.

It applies spiritually. Jesus can save any man, any woman, any time, anywhere. Why is it then that some people seem so long becoming Christians? Jesus says to them, "Do you really want to be saved? Do you want this more than anything else? Or is it that you like this but another part of you wouldn't like it?" In other words, if Jesus makes you well, you need to face up to the demands and responsibilities of life.

Now how does this apply to this man here? He had been there thirty-eight years, which means he had survived for those years without working for his living. I don't know how he did it. Presumably people with tender hearts gave him food or money. But he was a beggar. We don't see many beggars in this country now but I have seen them abroad. Unfortunately, some people would rather beg than work. It doesn't follow that just because a man goes to the Jobcentre every day he really wants a job. I've also learned the hard way that not everyone who asks for a job really wants one.

The reality is that if Jesus makes you well, you are going to have to work, you are going to have to face up to demands and responsibilities. It is easier to be an invalid spiritually, morally, mentally and in many other ways and enjoy the sympathy and support of others than to face up to the responsibilities of life.

This man had been there so long that he now enjoyed bad health and Jesus knew this – that's why he asked him, "Do you really want to get well?" He was a man who was resigned to accepting his condition and Jesus can do nothing with such a man. But I believe Jesus can do something for someone who says, "Yes, I want to get well. I want to be well morally, spiritually, emotionally. I want to be well."

Now look at what Jesus did. A man who was filled with resignation Jesus challenged to resolution. Jesus can sometimes be harsh, tough and firm. He didn't say, "Friend, take my hand and let me lift you up"; he said, "Get up." Jesus didn't offer him a helping hand at all. Then Jesus said, "Pick up", and then, "Walk away". Jesus gave him three commands, and in not one of them did Jesus offer help. He said, "Get up yourself. Pick up your bed. And walk away."

That's the way to deal with those who don't want to get well: it challenges them to make a decision. It reaches them at the point of their will and asks, "Are you ready to be made whole? If so, then you can be. Stand on your own two feet." It may seem a harsh demand, but in fact it was a glorious offer because Jesus was really saying, "I will get you up if you'll get up. I will enable you to pick up your bed if you'll pick it up. I will enable you to walk if you'll walk." It was an offer as well as a demand. Jesus never tells us to do something we can't do in his strength. But he does tell us to do things.

The man came face to face with the biggest decision of his life. He could have said again, "But I can't ... I can't," but if he had said that he would have lain there until he died. But he didn't say that again. If Jesus tells you to do something, you can do it by his strength. Who is equal to such things? I thank God through Christ who strengthens me. If you've ever refused something Jesus told you to do, it means you didn't want to do it.

It's rather like Peter walking on the water. Do you remember Peter and the boat? He saw Jesus walking on the water and asked, "Jesus, could I do that?" and Jesus replied, "Come on. Step out. You do it." If Peter had stayed in the boat and said, "No, I'm not sure ... that water doesn't look solid and I'm heavy," then I'm sure he would never have done it, but he stepped out onto the water and he did it. Many people in a congregation would say this too:

when they did something they thought impossible because Jesus told them to do it they found they could do it. Jesus commands us, but when he demands something of us he's offering to us his strength too. He says, "You do it. Stand on your own two feet." He asks for an exertion of our will in obedience to his will and this is the perfect balance between his will and our will. He doesn't say, "Lie there and I'll pick you up"; he says, "You get up. And when I tell you to get up, you'll find you can and this is the secret of true health." It worked.

" 'As I look into your face Jesus, I can.' It's that kind of faith that Jesus needs, that is obedience to what he tells us to do, that doesn't lie there helplessly and cry out, 'Lord, can I have your sympathy and support,' but says, 'Lord, when I look into your face, I know I can.' "

Once I was ten days in bed after an operation in hospital and when I got out of bed I felt like blancmange ... after just ten days! But this man had been lying there thirty-eight years and he could not only walk, he could even carry a bed. It works all right: supernatural strength was given him, but it was given him because he obeyed and didn't say, "I can't." He didn't say anything but in fact his heart was saying, "As I look into your face Jesus, I can." It's that kind of faith that Jesus needs. It's that kind of faith that is obedience to what he tells us to do, that doesn't lie there helplessly and cry out, "Lord, can I have your sympathy and support," but says, "Lord, when I look into your face, I know I can."

You may be struggling with what you are and saying, "I can't help it. I've been brought up like this. Life has treated me badly. No one has helped me as they should and I've been to lots of people and no one's been any good to me." If you're like that, then I say to you, "Take a good look at Jesus and say I can." You will find he will enable you to do so.

THE HORROR OF SPIRITUAL SIN (5:9b-16)

That might have been the end of the story, but it isn't. The poor man went out and got into lots of trouble. There is no guarantee that when you come to Jesus you have finished with troubles. In fact, you usually quickly run into trouble with others and this man did. By the end of that day he must have got tired of people telling him not to sin. The Jewish authorities told him not to sin. Jesus met him again and said, "Don't sin." He must have been in quite a whirl at the end of the day but let's see what happened.

He got up, carried his bed and ran straight into the Jewish leaders who told him he was breaking the Sabbath. Here we have the beginning of a clash of outlooks that is going to lead to the cross. It is a puzzle why someone like Jesus who went about doing good, healing the sick and helping people was so hated that he was assassinated aged thirty-three. But this is its beginning: this is the first hint of opposition in John's Gospel.

Two religions were meeting on this ground: the religion of the letter (regulations and the form of godliness) and the religion of the spirit (life and power). These two religions meet head on and when human tradition meets divine truth there is an explosion. This man was meeting those who had a very fixed and strict outlook in religious matters. It all happened on the Sabbath.

Isn't it incredible that something that God gave as a blessing should be used in this way? Let me tell you what the Sabbath was for. God gave the Sabbath to prevent humanity from being so wrapped up in their own work that they forget God's work. What a blessing the Sabbath is! I don't believe Christians are under any Sabbath law. It's the only one of the Ten Commandments never passed on to Christians in the New Testament. I am not under the Sabbath law. It's part of the Jewish shadows of things to come and the fulfilment of that shadow is Christ, in whom is perfect rest every day. That's the Sabbath rest that we are to enter into as Christians. So I don't believe in the Sabbath law. But I do believe it is good for a man to get away from his own work once a week and think about God's work. It is good for you: it is a blessing and God wanted us to have this blessing, so he gave the Sabbath as a blessing, when humanity should cease from their own work and turn their attention to God's work. Now Jesus had no scruples whatever about working on the Sabbath as long as it was God's work. And that's where he ran head into opposition. Their limited outlook could only see the letter of the law and they said a man carrying his bed was work. It wasn't. It was God's work. The Lord had told him to do this.

So these two religions met head on; they said: "You're sinning," and he then said something lovely: "The man who healed me told me to do it." The Jesus who saved you will tell you to do things. People may disagree; they may object and be offended. All you can say is, "The One who healed me told me to do this. Do you think I could refuse the One who healed me? Do you think I could listen to people rather than the One who made me whole?" No, you can't. It was a perfect answer.

But then he met Jesus again and as the Jews had said, "Don't sin," and he'd said, "But Jesus told me to," now Jesus met him and said, "Now I will tell you what not to do." He said, "Don't sin any more or something worse could happen to you."

Here we have to face a difficult question and I want to try and tackle it honestly. Is there a connection between sin and sickness? My answer is yes, always, according to the Bible. Now before you jump to any wrong conclusion and think that I am taking the part of Job's comforters who went to Job and said, "You must have been a bad to suffer like this," listen to me more. I do not believe that every sickness is due to the sin of the person who is sick. But according to the Bible, every sickness is due to someone's sin. It could be the person themselves. It could be someone else's sin or it could be Satan's sin but it's all due to sin.

Our hospitals are monuments to sin. They would never have been necessary if sin had not entered God's universe. Every doctor and nurse is fighting the results of sin, not necessarily the sin of the people who are sick but the sin that spoiled God's universe. We can't live as isolated units. We affect each other. What I do affects you, and what you do affects me. What Satan does affects us all. According to the Bible, if there'd never been any sin, there would never have been any sickness. When you think of all the sorrow and suffering that's been caused by sickness, you take sin seriously and you look forward to a day when there will be no more sorrow, suffering and pain. But that day will not come until sin has gone.

But what about this man? Why did Jesus say that to this man? There are two possible answers. One is that this man was ill because of his own sin, that he had done something thirty-eight years before which had led to this physical condition. That is possible. If that is so, Jesus is saying, "Don't put yourself back into that condition." When you are free from the effects of your sin, it is easy to go back to your sin, isn't it? As long as you are facing the consequences that keeps you sobered up, but as soon as the consequences of your wrongdoing are removed, it is easy to go back to what you did before.

But I don't think that's what Jesus is saying to this man because if I were to translate literally what he said, Jesus says, "Don't continue to sin or a worse thing could happen." I don't think he's referring to something thirty-eight years earlier but something happening recently. Now surely a paralysed man can't sin ... or can he? He may not be able to murder someone, commit adultery or go out stealing. But how many sins a sick person can commit. If you work with many sick people and you saw one person healed regularly and it wasn't you, you could easily commit the sin of envy, the sin of resentment and bitterness, or above all, the attitude of mental sloth I mentioned, accepting your circumstances by not fighting, but giving in. I think Jesus is saying, "My friend, you've been weak-willed. You've given in to this sickness. You've let this sickness conquer you."

I think Jesus was saying to this man: "Look, together we've mastered this thing, so don't slip back. Don't be weak any more. Go ahead in my strength from now or something worse could happen." What could be worse than lying in that pool, in that condition for all those years? I will tell you. Spending eternity with a paralysed soul, surrounded by sin-sick people. That's the end of those who will not put their faith in Christ and let him make them strong in will to get up, to pick up their responsibilities and to walk in the way that he wants us to walk.

12

THE IMPACT OF JESUS' MIRACLES
John 5:17-47

THE TRUTH ABOUT THE SON'S WORKS (5:17-30)

Healing the sick
Raising the dead
Judging the world

TESTIMONY OF THE FATHER'S WORDS (5:31-39)

Hearing the forerunner
Seeing the miracles
Reading the Scriptures

THE TROUBLE WITH THE PEOPLE'S WILLS (5:40-47)

Lacking the love
Wanting the praise
Disbelieving the prophet

Why is it that the One who went about doing good, helping people, healing them, should be put to death after three years? What offended the Jewish leaders that they had to assassinate Jesus at the age of thirty-three?

There are two answers: first in what he *did*. He trampled on their sacred traditions and nobody likes a man who does that. He ignored their traditions – and put himself above the religious leaders, which was considered sacrilege.

The second answer is in what he *said*. He didn't say God works on the Sabbath and so I follow his example. He said, "My Father works right now and so I do too." In their eyes he moved from the crime of sacrilege to the crime of blasphemy. He claimed to be God and to be equal with God. He didn't say, "God works on the Sabbath and so I follow his example." He said, "My Father works right now and so I do too."

The Jews hated him for this. It was not only what he did which they called sacrilege, trampling on their sacred traditions. It was what he said was considered blasphemy, calling himself God's only Son and making himself equal with God. This is the message. Jesus again and again claimed to be equal with God. He did not consider equality with God something to be used to his own advantage. But that was why they put him on a cross. They said that's blasphemy.

THE TRUTH ABOUT THE SON'S WORKS (5:17-30)

Here we understand the truth about the Son's works, the real meaning of his miracles and why he did them. Three times in this section (verses 19, 24, 25) he says, "I tell you the truth." Only he didn't speak English and he didn't say it like that. He said "Amen, Amen" three times which means "it's true; it's true." When you say Amen at the end of a prayer, you're saying it's true. Jesus said, "Amen, amen. I'll tell you the truth. I'm doing these things not only because God does them but also because I'm God and that's the truth."

Healing the sick

Jesus is challenged, "Why are you doing work on the Sabbath? Why are you healing people on the Sabbath? You could have waited till tomorrow. The man's been ill thirty-eight years so you could surely wait another day? Why did you do this on the Sabbath and trample on our precious observance?"

In reply Jesus tells them, "God doesn't stop work for the Sabbath." He said, "I'm only doing what God is doing. God works on the Sabbath, so do I." Now how do you line this up with the statement in the law of Moses that God rested on the seventh day? We must understand there were two kinds of work that God did. He did one during the six days and he did the other on the seventh day and the seventh day is still going on. In the six days, God was working for himself, for his own benefit and satisfaction. He made the earth and he said it was good. He made the sea, dry land, trees and plants, and he derived such joy from it. Finally, as the peak of his work, he made mankind in his own image and he said that was very good. He enjoyed making things for himself, working for himself creating things he wanted to.

Then he stopped working for himself and entered the seventh day which is still the seventh day. We are living in God's Sabbath rest. We are in his seventh day which is a long day and indicates that the other six were also long days but he is still resting from his own work, from doing things for himself. What is he doing now? He's now looking after others, helping others. Do you realize God is working today? He caused the sun to rise. He's keeping it all going for your sake. He's working for you.

"Every day thousands have been raised from the dead by Jesus. Every minute now somebody in the world is being given life by Jesus and they will do it only through hearing his word. That's all he has to do."

So Jesus is saying, "My Father is still working." Do you think that God has stopped doing things? Do you think he's now idle? He's stopped creating things for himself but now he's looking after you. He's helping. "And so I'm just doing what he does on the Sabbath." This is why we must not even think of Sunday as a day of idleness. It's a day to do something for him, to do something for somebody else. Go and visit someone sick, elderly or lonely on a Sunday. It's doing what God's doing today.

Raising the dead

Jesus says, "I can do anything God can do. You'll be more amazed at the other things I'm going to do." Healing the sick is comparatively easy to God: the God who made our bodies can heal them. "I'm only doing it because my Father showed me how." The relationship Jesus had with God is lovely. He says, "The Father loves me so he's shown me these things to do," as a father may take his boy and show him how to do something. "My Father took me," says Jesus, "and he showed me. Healing the sick was one thing I had to do but you'll be amazed at the other things he's going to give me to do. Because I'm his Son, I can raise the dead as he does." Everybody agreed God could raise the dead: the God who gave life can take it away and give it back again. "Well," Jesus said, "I'm going to do it too. I can give life to the dead. The time is coming and now is when I'll speak to a corpse and that corpse will get up and live," and Jesus did it again and again: to Jairus' daughter, the widow of Nain's son and Lazarus. Jesus is the only man I've ever heard of who can speak to a corpse and be obeyed. But he said, "God can do that and you'll be amazed because I'm going to do it too. The time is here when this will happen and I'll speak to the dead."

Jesus was clearly speaking in two senses: to the physically dead and to the spiritually dead. I don't know which is greater: to give physical life to a corpse or to give spiritual, eternal life to a dead sinner, but Jesus said he would do both. "As God is the source of life, he's now put life in me and I'm the source of life. Whoever hears my words and believes in the One who sent me has eternal life. He's got it right now." Every day thousands have been raised from the dead by Jesus. Every minute now somebody in the world is being given life by Jesus and they will do it only through hearing his word. That's all he has to do.

Judging the world

There's one other function we thought was just God's that Jesus now claims. He says, "God isn't going to judge the world." That cut right across their beliefs. He said, "God isn't going to be the judge. Do you know he's told me I'm going to judge the whole world? Everything God can do I can do and he's simply giving me the job to finish. He starts it but I finish it." Jesus talks about the tasks God has given him to finish. God started it; he gave you life; he created you. But Jesus will finish the job, when he heals the sick, raises the dead and judges the world. What is he doing but completing the work of God? So he now says, "I'm going to be the judge. Therefore you should honour me as you honour God. I am the One who will decide your eternal destiny, so you should think highly of me."

Let's look at what he says here. He states the simple fact that when you bury a person in a grave that is not their last resting place; it's only a temporary place. At every funeral – whether the body turns to dust slowly or to ashes quickly – you have not put the person in their final resting place in the cemetery or the garden of remembrance. These are simply temporary places for those people. Jesus said, "One day even the dead will hear the voice of the Son of Man. And they'll come out to judgment and they'll face me." All will come from their graves and face Jesus and answer to him for the decisions they made during their life. It is a solemn thought.

This teaching of Jesus in verses 28-29 is almost a word-for-word repetition of Daniel 12:2, said hundreds of years before. This verse demolishes so many false ideas about life after death. In just one verse he demolishes several wrong views.

That death is the end. Once a body has gone to dust and ashes, those is nothing more. That isn't true. Jesus says they can hear his voice and when he says, "Come," they must come. Some people say we all go to the same place afterwards, that everybody will finish up in heaven but Jesus demolishes that. He says some will rise to life and some to condemnation. Some think that evildoers will be annihilated, that only the good people will survive. This teaching is called "conditional immortality." But Jesus never taught that. We shall live in bodies for ever. He's going to raise everyone, the good and the evil. So we will have another body, and we will live in that for ever, either glorying and serving God or suffering for ever. Jesus never said there is no hell, no damnation, no condemnation. These are solemn, dreadful words and Jesus said, "I'm going to be the judge. I will be fair because I don't seek anything for myself. I don't want anything for myself out of this. I am just going to judge as the Father wants me to."

Here is something remarkable. Jesus says, "My Father has chosen me to be the judge because I am the Son of" – now what would you expect to be said there, "God"? He didn't say that; he said "because I am the Son of *Man*." To be absolutely fair in his mercy and wisdom, God says, "I want a man to judge humanity, someone who has shared human life, who's been tired and tempted, who's been through it all." That's only fair because on the last day of judgment people could say to God, "God you're judging us, but you don't know what it's like to be human and live in this world, to have these pressures on me." But God will say, "My Son knows what it's like. He's going to judge." The Father has given judgment to the Son because he is the Son of Man. Only One who is the Son of God and Son of Man could judge your life.

TESTIMONY OF THE FATHER'S WORDS (5:31-39)

So far Jesus has been talking only about himself and he freely admits that the testimony of a man about himself is not enough for a law court. We can say anything we like about ourselves but the world wants evidence, proof and witnesses. A man can get up in a court when he's accused of a crime and he can say what he likes about himself but the jury must have witnesses.

So Jesus says, "I know that I speak about myself and I know that isn't sufficient testimony but added to the truth about the Son's works is the testimony of the Father's words. As I talk about my Father, he talks about me. You've got someone else to tell you that what I say is true. I tell you the truth, but I don't expect you to believe me on my own words. Listen to what God has said."

He then talks about three ways in which God has given

testimony to his own Son and told the world that his Son is true: through John the Baptist, miracles and the Scriptures.

Hearing the forerunner

Jesus said about himself, "I am the light of the world," but he said about John, "He is a lamp burning and shining." A lamp shines on something or lights it up. What did John the Baptist light up? Jesus. Jesus says to the Jews, "You accepted John. You were willing to accept his preaching. Why did you not listen to what he said? Through John, the Father was talking about me."

Here are some of the lovely things John the Baptist said about Jesus: "He's the One who will take away the sins of the world." "He is the bridegroom." "He is the One who baptizes with the Holy Spirit." Above all he said, "He is the Son of God." So Jesus said, "God the Father sent the forerunner to speak about me – why didn't you listen to that evidence and believe it?"

Seeing the miracles

John did no miracle, but when Jesus came, the blind could see, the deaf could hear, the lame could walk: all this was the evidence of God the Father. Nicodemus came to Jesus and said, "No one could do the miracles you do unless God was with him." It is clear from Scripture that Jesus' enemies never doubted he did miracles. Have you ever noticed that? People 2,000 years later question the miracles because they weren't there, but the people there never questioned them but admitted they were real. The only thing they could say was, "It must be by the power of the devil, Beelzebub, that you did them." How perverted can you be that you can't accept miracles as proof of truth?

Reading the Scriptures

Words usually come from a face, but Jesus told the Jews, "You've never seen God's face. You've not heard his voice but you've got the words of God in your own home. Search them. You think that somewhere in these pages you'll find the secret of life and you will." Jesus is saying, "This is how the Father witnesses to the truth about me. You've got the proof in your own hands, and you think you've got the secret of life. You have, but you're looking the wrong way."

Do you know you can be a keen Bible student and miss the secret of life? You can know this book backwards but still not know the secret of life. The Jews did just that: they fingered through the evidence every day but couldn't see the truth. Why not? Because they didn't look in the Bible for a person. You could read the Bible every day but it could do you no good, unless you're looking for what it says about Jesus. You've got to search. Merely reading the Bible doesn't do much good. You've got to search until you find what you're looking for ... but what are you looking for? They were looking for a secret of life, for something they had to do, for a system, an institution, and all the time they should have been looking for a person.

I was out on the streets talking to people about Jesus. You'd be amazed how many people don't want to know about Jesus. One person said, "Well that's not quite my line of business"; another, "I'm just a visitor here and then I'm going away," as if Jesus was only in this town. I went up to an Indian man and I asked him if he knew Jesus and he replied, "I've been reading John's Gospel, which somebody gave me. I've been a Sikh. I've been searching for God all my life. I've been afraid of doing the wrong thing with God and I've found Jesus." He read the book for a person.

Remember that when Jesus spoke to the Jews they only had the Old Testament, not the New. We think the New Testament is about Jesus but Jesus says the Old Testament is about him. Is that how you read the psalms, the prophets and the history books and the law of Moses? It's full of Jesus, but you'll have to search, but he's there. The complete story of Jesus Christ is to be found in the Old Testament but it's in bits and pieces, like a jigsaw. In the New Testament you've got the whole picture on the lid, but in the Old Testament you've got all the pieces, which you can miss. You've got to search the pieces and pick one up and you say, "That's a bit of his glory." Do you read the Old Testament like that? Jesus said if you did, you'd get the evidence for him. The Father's testimony was there long before he came and so he says to the Jews, "You've got the evidence of John the Baptist, my miracles and your own Scriptures about me. Why don't you believe I'm telling the truth? Why are you putting me in the dock and saying I am breaking the Sabbath?" He makes himself equal with God as if these were crimes instead of the truth.

"The trouble is people don't want to believe in Jesus. Their will is the root problem. They've got too little willpower and too much won't power. It isn't that they *can't* believe it is that they *won't*. They're unwilling to come to Jesus that he might give them life."

THE TROUBLE WITH THE PEOPLE'S WILLS (5:40-47)

Why did so many people I met yesterday not want to talk about Jesus? Why do so few accept the truth although God has given all possible evidence? It's not basically an intellectual difficulty. The evidence is there for anyone with an impartial mind to examine. Anybody who will open-mindedly examine the evidence for the resurrection will be convinced of its truth. What's wrong? It's the will.

Jesus turned to the Jews and he said, "You're not willing to believe." That's the trouble. People don't want to believe in Jesus. Their will is the root problem. They've got too little willpower and too much won't power. It isn't that they *can't* believe it is that they *won't*. They're unwilling to come to Jesus that he might give them life.

Jesus doesn't want to harm people; he wants to give them life and release them from sin which will drag them down to hell, but they are unwilling to come. They will go to anybody else. Jesus said to the Jews, "If a man comes in his own authority you accept him. You'll go to anyone else." Do you know that within fifty years of Jesus' death the Jews accepted no less than sixty-five false messiahs? It is extraordinary that they accepted sixty-five false messiahs but when the only true one came they refused him. Why?

Why would they go to anyone else? Today, they'll go to a pop star, scientist or politician. Why won't they come to Jesus? Jesus says, "I'll tell you what makes you unwilling to believe in me."

Lacking the love

"God is outside your affections. You're not interested in him." If there's one proof that people don't love God it is that they're not interested in Jesus, his Son. What is the duty of man? People will answer, "To love your neighbour, that's all," but it isn't. That is the second duty of man. What's the first? "To love God with all your heart, soul, mind and strength." Jesus said, "You don't believe in me because you have no love for God, the God who gave you life, health and everything you have."

Wanting the praise

"You are more concerned about your reputation with people than you are about what God thinks about you." Does not that affect each of us? Are you more troubled when your neighbour criticizes, has something to complain about, or when God says what's wrong? We are more concerned with human praise; we are not really bothered about what God thinks of us. Jesus says, "As long as you're more concerned about praise from people than from God, you won't believe. You're unwilling because coming to Christ may damage your reputation." Jesus was hated and you may be too. So if you are more concerned about what other people are going to think, you won't get too religious. They will accuse you of religious mania or say you're mad.

Disbelieving the prophet

The third thing is intellectual pride. You will not believe what the Bible says. People say, "I believe in Jesus, but I don't believe everything the Bible says about him." What a contradiction! In their intellectual pride, people were saying they would decide what they're going to believe. "I will pass it all through the sieve of my reason and what I can accept I will and what I can't, I won't."

Jesus said, "Moses wrote about me. I'm not going to accuse you to the Father. I'm not going to stand as the Counsel for the Prosecution." Moses will do that job for me. Moses wrote about me. You say you believe in Moses, but you don't really. Read Deuteronomy 18:15. Just before Moses died, he said, "God is going to send you another prophet, just like me. Someone who will come and who will speak to you the words of God. Listen to him. If you don't, you'll die. If you do, you'll live." Jesus said, "Now I am here but you won't listen because you didn't really believe what he said." We have social and intellectual pride, but it all adds up to one word: self. We don't want to believe and so we can't.

You can say what you like about Jesus. You can accuse him of sacrilege or blasphemy. You can say he was this, that and the other, but a day will come when Jesus says, *"This is what I know about you*. Not what I think, what I know." So he said to the Jews "I know you. You don't love God. You love a good reputation and you will not bow your intellect before the word of Moses so you're not willing to believe."

In the last analysis that is why people are lost. Not because they don't get a chance, not because God hasn't chosen them, not because there isn't enough evidence, but because they are not willing to come to Jesus that they might have life.

13

CAN I REALLY BELIEVE IN MIRACLES?
John 6:1-21

EFFECT—ON THE PEOPLE

CAUSE—IN THE PERSON

Real character

His knowledge of people
His concern for people
His authority over people
His generosity towards people
His freedom from people

Remarkable control

In a church where I used to minister, as you came in you might have seen a lovely mosaic which one of our young men had made. It was based on an ancient mosaic at a little place called Tabgha on the shores of Galilee where there is an inlaid picture of the loaves and the fishes. It's there to remind you of perhaps the greatest miracle Jesus performed in his life: feeding 10,000 people, as that's what it must have been – 5,000 men plus women and children, with just five little round scones and two little sardine fish. It's quite a miracle.

When you had looked at that mosaic, if you had turned and looked out of the window across the river, you would have seen a red-brick house and a grey slate roof and white windows where Lewis Carroll lived, the author of *Alice in Wonderland*. It's the book in which you are asked to believe six impossible things before breakfast each day and in which anything can happen. For some people, the Bible is as difficult to believe as fact as *Alice in Wonderland*. To talk about feeding 10,000 people with a tiny little picnic lunch of one small boy is to ask them to believe the impossible.

"There are three things you can do with miracles. You can dismiss them as legend or myth. You can explain them away – but some of the explanations seem to require more faith than the story themselves! Or you can accept them as true."

Now I want to tackle honestly the problem of miracles in this study. I admit it's a problem; it's even a problem to me. If I wasn't a Christian, I couldn't believe them. It is what I've learned and known of Christ that enables me to read this story and say it must be true. But the difficulty is there in my natural reason, which just cannot understand it.

There are three things you can do with miracle stories. You can dismiss them as the kind of legend and myth that grows around any famous figure. Or you can explain them away – but some of the explanations seem to require more faith than the story themselves! Or you can accept them as true. When you read two stories such as these in which Jesus clearly acts contrary to all we know of the laws of nature, then you are faced with those three possibilities.

We can divide Jesus' miracles into two groups: his healing miracles and his nature miracles. We are prepared to accept the healing miracles today. We are familiar with psychosomatic illnesses, those in which the mind has an effect on the body. The mind can easily cause illness to the body: nearly half our hospital beds in England are filled with people with diseased minds; even the word *disease* is significant: minds that are "not at ease" with an effect on the body. People are in hospital with a sick body because the mind has controlled matter and has caused illness. I could give you half a dozen common illnesses that are caused by resentment, jealousy, lack of peace and guilt.

If the mind can bring illness to a body, the mind could also bring health. Many people say that and you will find many books on faith healing. It may not be faith in Jesus, but if a person through their own mind can have some control over their body, how much more can the mind of Jesus operating on the mind of the patient help that person's body.

As Jesus said earlier in chapter 5 to a paralysed man, "Get up and walk" and he did. Jesus' mind was controlling the matter of the man's body, so after thirty-eight years he was able not only to stand up but also to walk and to carry a bed straightaway.

We have some understanding of this but when it comes to telling nature what to do – that is beyond our experience. It is these miracles that people have most difficulty with today. Jesus could tell the wind and the waves what to do and they did it. His mind controlled the matter and the wind has no mind and the waves have no mind, so there could be no communication from his mind to the wind's mind. Or when he cursed a fig tree and it was dead twenty-four hours later. He said you could talk to a mountain if you had the faith and it would do what it told you but we haven't got that faith. We don't know of any situation in which a man is able to tell matter what to do and yet Jesus shows perfect control of matter. It is this that raises the question of miracles. We are going to look at these two miracles, in both of which Jesus controls matter. In the one case, bread and fish, in the other case the waves, by walking on them. Normally in my experience waves let you down rather badly but not with Jesus. He has perfect control of them too. Are these stories true? Are they credible? Let's look at these stories and ask whether they are credible, and I find that three-quarters of the way they are.

EFFECT – ON THE PEOPLE

Let's look at the reactions of the people involved. I don't believe human nature has changed in 2,000 years. Our fashions and circumstances have changed, but human nature hasn't. We face the same problems, we have the same feelings and thoughts as they had 2,000 years ago.

If we look at what happened to the people in these two miracles, what we find is entirely credible. It is how we would behave. Take first the feeding of the 5,000. Even just looking at Philip is typical of us. His calculating pessimism is everywhere: Jesus asked "Where shall we get enough food to feed these people?" and Philip replied, "It would take eight months' wages to buy enough bread for this crowd." That's precisely how the human mind still argues: we calculate the situation and say, "Statistically it's impossible," and that settles it for us. That's exactly how people talk about miracles today. They say, "I've weighed it all up, I've thought it through and it's impossible – and that's all there is to say." Poor old Philip, but he's just like you and me.

But let's now look at the crowd. They had walked about five miles around the northern coast of the Sea of Galilee because they had seen Jesus crossing in a boat. He was trying to get some rest from the crowd and take his disciples away but they were prepared to walk five miles round the shore to meet him as soon as he stepped off the boat. They were tired and hungry and wanted food. But look at the state of their mind. They were a crowd of people who lived in an occupied country, whose occupation they hated. They were a crowd of people who were about to celebrate a Passover – which means they were filled with nationalistic spirit. They were a crowd of people who were going to look back 1,500 years to a day when their ancestors had been set free. Their minds were full of freedom, nationalism, the possibility of having their own country again and their bodies are hungry.

If you were in that situation and someone came along with the power to feed all of you, what would you do? I'll tell you: you'd want to make him king – you'd say, "At last we've found our hero. We've found the man who can lead us to freedom. Here is a man who can do anything for us." V. 15 says that the crowd tried to kidnap him, take him by force and make him king – that's what crowds have done ever since.

Anyone who shows the power to feed the hungry will be followed. That was the appeal of communism in many parts of the world. People with empty bellies followed a man who could fill them. People who want to be free follow someone who shows the power to set them free. It's modern, credible and real.

Now look at the second story and see how they reacted. Look at their condition of body and mind again. They are fishermen. It's dark; they are on a storm-tossed sea. The Sea of Galilee is only thirteen miles long and eight miles wide, but it can be a terrible and dangerous place. They've been rowing for nine hours and only managed to get three and three-quarter miles across. They are worn out; they're wondering if they will ever make shore but they are tough and fighting hard to get to the shore. Then suddenly they see something that looks supernatural.

I began my ministry among fishermen and I know how they react. Superstition is just under the skin with them. You talk to sailors. I was talking to a trawlerman. He told me that with all their radar and modern electronic gadgets, just under the surface they are still superstitious. There are certain things that make them terrified. They imagine things at sea.

These tough men struggling against the storm thought they saw a ghost, the angel of death, coming for them. They were terrified – that's a normal reaction. It's entirely credible; the story rings true. This is how you would react in those circumstances. Nothing alarms human nature so much as a touch of the supernatural.

So the story is entirely credible if you look at the reactions of the people involved. I don't find any difficulty believing in it and it has the ring of truth of someone who knows, who was there and who saw the reactions.

"You're hungry. Maybe not in body but you're hungry for love, for purpose, for meaning, for a future – then he knows. Are you afraid? Afraid of insecurity, of loneliness, of failure, of all kinds of things? He knows. That is his character. It comes out in these miracle stories."

CAUSE – IN THE PERSON

Real character

Let's now look at the person who caused the miracle. Look at Jesus, because the story is about him. We see here a consistent picture of Jesus' character. It's the Jesus I know, the Jesus who appears in every other part of the New Testament. It is entirely credible. Here are five things about him that I see in the real character of Jesus:

His knowledge of people

Jesus always knew what was wrong with somebody before they told him. That comes out in story after story in the Gospels. I want to say that Jesus knows every need you have. You don't need to tell him even though he'd love you to do so but he already knows. It's here in this story: he knew they were hungry; he knew the men in the boat were frightened. He just knew.

You're hungry. Maybe not in body but you're hungry for love, for purpose, for meaning, for a future – then he knows. Are you afraid? Afraid of insecurity, of loneliness, of failure, of all kinds of things? He knows. That is his character. It comes out in this story.

His concern for people

Jesus not only knows; he also cares. Some people know but they don't care, but he knows and he cares. You see no sooner does he know they're hungry than he says, "What are we going to do about it? How are we going to feed this crowd? We've got to do something." No sooner does he see men frightened in the boat than he says, "Don't be afraid" – he was constantly saying that as if fear was one of the biggest burdens people carry. Don't be afraid. He cares. His concern for people comes out in these two miracle stories.

His authority over people

Have you ever tried to separate a small boy from his picnic lunch? That requires considerable character and authority over people but Jesus did it. Then he just took command of the situation and he said, "Sit the people down." Everything was done in an orderly fashion. Then he said, "Now give them something to eat," and so he went on giving orders. "Pick up what's left. We're not going to waste anything." Even though he could have produced another million tons of bread, he wasn't going to waste a crumb! That's Jesus: generous but not extravagant – giving you what you need. His authority over people is there. "Don't be afraid," and they weren't afraid any more. His authority over you could relieve you of the need you've got.

His generosity towards people

Isn't Jesus generous? He gives ... and he keeps on giving and giving. He goes on breaking the bread so that people can eat. In the same way, he allowed his body to be broken so that we might be mended. That is Jesus. He's generous. He goes on and on giving "pressed down, shaken together and running over," a picture from the marketplace where they sell corn in the Middle East by the bushel and where they shake it down and press it in and let it overflow. They give you as much as they can for the price. But Jesus gives it freely and generously.

His freedom from people

Could you resist an important offer of greatness? Only very few could resist popularity. When a crowd came to them and said we're going to make you king – very few could say, "No, I'm not going to accept what you want to give me." Jesus didn't refuse the throne here because of something or someone he wanted. He simply wanted to get away by himself with his Father and ask him, "Do you want this?" and God said, "No."

Do you know that within ten days of this happening Jesus could have been sitting on a throne with a crown of golden jewels on his head? A crowd could have swept him off to Jerusalem with two and a half million Jews there for the Passover who could have placed him on a throne with a crown on a wave of public feeling. Yet he knew it was God's will that it had to be a crown of thorns on a cross. So he was free from people. His complete independence from what people wanted him to do shines out in these stories.

Remarkable control

I've tried to make these miracle stories even more credible. They are credible because of the people in these accounts. They're credible because of Jesus' character. But now we come to the crux, to the part of the story that's left, and that is difficult: Jesus multiplying loaves and walking on the water.

Jesus is doing something no one could ever do or has ever done. No one. The first is an act of creating something out of nothing. I thought about the physical work involved in breaking a loaf for 10,000 people ... to go on and on and on doing it. But what was happening within those hands? Maybe the crowd didn't even realize at first what was happening, within those hands something was coming out of nothing. No man can do that. We can manufacture things but we've always got to take some raw material and make it into something else. No one can make something out of nothing. So that is a problem.

Then consider walking on the water. A man was doing that at Southampton, but he was only manipulating the laws of nature by building himself some floats like skis and allowing the law of buoyancy to counteract the law of gravity. But he couldn't walk on the water without those skis. Jesus was not manipulating the laws of nature which is all we can do. He was just cancelling them. Every law of nature said he had to sink but Jesus just cancelled those laws.

"This is the issue before us. Is Jesus God or is he man? If he's just a man, then these stories have to be cut out of the Bible, and Jesus can't perform any miracles for you either. But if he's God, then you can know miracles in your life. The first miracle you'll know when you come to Jesus is that he creates in you a heart and a life that were not there before."

So we've come to the crux of the matter and the question is this: if Jesus is just a man, then these two stories are myth or legend: you cannot believe them. But if Jesus was who he said he was, then he could do both these things. If he really was God, then God is the only person in the universe who can make something out of nothing, because that's precisely what he did when he made this world. God is also the only person in the universe who can cancel the laws of nature, because it was he who gave those laws. The person who made the laws can change them. The laws of nature that bind us completely as human beings are to God no more than a school timetable is to a headteacher. The students can't change it but the headteacher can, because headteacher made it.

This is the issue before us. Is Jesus God or is he man? If he's just a man, then these stories have to be cut out of the Bible, and Jesus can't perform any miracles for you either. But if he's God, then you can know miracles in your life. The first miracle you will know when you come to Jesus is that he creates in you a heart and a life that were not there before. You don't come to Jesus to have your old heart cleaned up. You come and say, "Create in me a clean heart, God." The Bible says, "If anyone is in Christ, there is a new creation." Something is now in that person that was never there before. Jesus has created within them a new life. That person has been born again. It's not the old life patched up; it's a new life created.

Only Jesus can do that for you because he's God. The Jesus who took a loaf of bread and made more bread out of nothing is the Jesus who takes an old life and says, "I will create in that life what is not there. I will make that life a new creature," and he does so. When he has done that, you begin to taste other miracles too.

One of the men to whom I owe a lot in my early days as a

Christian young man was a man who started his working life as a bookmaker on Durham racecourse. Jack was a rough, hard-drinking, hard-swearing man. He was asked by one of his workmates, "Do you believe that Jesus changed water into wine?" and he replied, "Well, he's changed beer into furniture in my house." What was the real miracle there? Beer into furniture? No; old Jack into new Jack – that was the miracle!

It is when you have had the big miracle happen that the others begin to follow. It is when you find out that Jesus really is alive and is able to create a new life in you that you come to a story like this and you say, "I have no difficulty with that. To do that with a loaf of bread, why the most marvellous thing is that he did it with me. He took what was not there and he created a new life with new desires, a new appetite, a new love of God, a new interest in his word, things that were not there before." Then after that you begin to discover all the other miracles that he does and can do, and you know he's the Son of God.

Credible? Believable? Well, to the person who isn't a Christian I don't blame them for not believing it. I don't see how they could believe it. It's against all their experience of nature and of themselves. But to the person who has come to Jesus Christ, they can't help believing it.

14

THE MORNING AFTER
THE NIGHT BEFORE
John 6:22-71

THE CROWD'S DEMANDS (6:25-40)

They want material satisfaction
The demand for good works
The demand for visible proof
The demand for immediate results

THE JEWS' DOUBTS (6:41-59)

His spiritual origin
His physical descent

THE FOLLOWERS' DIFFICULTIES (6:60-66)

THE TWELVE'S DEVOTION (6:66-71)

Miracles are exciting, but it is sad to see what happens the day after a miracle. Our last study considered John 6:1-21 when Jesus performed one of his greatest miracles: feeding ten thousand with five loaves and two sardine-size fish. Now let's see what happened the day after.

Here is some background: the Sea of Galilee is harp-shaped: thirteen miles from north to south and about seven miles from east to west. It lies in a deep valley; its surface is six hundred feet below sea level. Running down either side of that valley is a row of hills. Around the Sea of Galilee are shores and green flat areas covered with grass where people can sit on the sea edge. Jesus was in Capernaum, which is northeast, and he wanted to take a break with his disciples. They got into two boats, which crossed the sea from the northwest to the northeast coast, passing Bethsaida at the top of the lake. They landed on the side of the sea nestling up against the eastern hills.

The crowd saw him going but weren't going to let him have time off so they walked around the top of the lake. That took them hours, while the boat went straight across. So when Jesus and his disciples sat down on the grass, he saw a great crowd coming to him and said, "How are we going to feed this crowd?"

It would have been late afternoon when he fed them. After the meal, Jesus went further east up into the hills while he sent the disciples in a boat back to Capernaum. The crowd weren't going to let him get away: they were going to camp there for the night on the eastern shore, waiting for him to come down from the hills. However, when they woke up in the morning and looked around, they couldn't see him. The boat left behind for him was still on the shore. They were sure he hadn't passed them on land: they were baffled as to where he had gone. Finally, because they saw some boats from Tiberias out in the sea, they hired boats and crossed in this fleet of boats back to Capernaum to find the disciples and see if they knew where Jesus was. There Jesus was with them. Their first question to him was, "When did you get here? We've camped all night waiting for you." Jesus simply replied, "You're only interested in a free breakfast." That was the truth, and that's how one of Jesus' greatest sermons began.

"Jesus has a way of looking past the question a person asks to the question in their minds, which he answers. He deals with our inner thoughts, not our outward words."

THE CROWD'S DEMANDS (6:25-40)

The crowd made four demands. As we look at these four demands, we see typical fallen human nature.

They want material satisfaction

They asked, "When did you get here?" If he had given them the true answer, they would have been shattered. The real answer was, "I walked across the water." But he didn't tell them that; he said: "You're not asking the real question." That's only a question on your lips but I know the question that's in your mind: "When's breakfast? If you ask the real question, I'll answer that one."

Jesus has a way of looking past the question a person asks to the question in their minds, which he answers. He deals with our inner thoughts, not our outward words. So he rebuked them, "You don't really want to know when I got here – you're just a bit cross because I came without your knowing and I escaped your trap. You wanted to catch me this morning, for breakfast, didn't you? So I just came here."

Then he said, "Why are you so worried about food for the body?" Why are you so concerned about breakfast? The Bible talks about those whose God is their stomach. If you look at the advertisements all around us, you'd think we lived for what we ate and drank. We have become gluttons. We have got so much food that in almost every magazine we read how to slim and reduce our calories. We've all got freezers because, as Jesus said, it's food that spoils, and we've got to find a way to stop it perishing. "Why," Jesus asks, "do you spend so much energy and time on this?" He's saying strongly, "Man shall not live on bread alone. You're just an animal if you think only about food. Your god is your stomach and your end is destruction. Why do you work for food that goes rotten so quickly? You can't keep it. Make sure you obtain the food that lasts for ever."

The demand for good works

Jesus said, "Work for the bread that doesn't perish. I will give you this bread. I give it to you because I'm God's agent who distributes it. God has put his mark of approval on me so I can give you this very food I'm telling you to be concerned about" (v. 27). But they picked up the wrong word, *work*, and they dropped the word *give*.

Here's something profound about human nature: we spurn a free gift. If we can work for something, we'll take it. We hate charity; we would much rather achieve something ourselves. Free grace is one of the deepest barriers to receiving God's gifts. The food that really lasts is a gift. The Son of Man will give it to you.

"What must we do to do God's works?" How presumptuous to think we could do God's works! Only God can do God's works. But we all think we can get there by our own merits, that we deserve it. So they said, "You tell us to work for this food – what must we do to work for it?" It's strange that physically they were prepared to accept a free meal, but spiritually they weren't. Physically they would gladly take the loaves and the fishes, but spiritually they would not receive as a free gift the bread that lasts to eternal life.

"What must we do?" Jesus answered, "I'll tell you the good work God wants you to do. The first good deed God requires is to believe in Jesus," to trust. That cut the ground from under their feet. "What must we do?" He replied, "You let me do it. Believe in me."

The demand for visible proof

Their third question: "All right, if you want us to believe, you've got to let us see visible proof. What miracle are you going to do?" Amazingly, they asked this the day after they have been fed with two fishes and five loaves! How is it that so soon after seeing such a miracle they could ask for proof that he was sent by God?

They said, "You only gave us food from earth. The loaves and fish came from earth. You're not as great as Moses: he gave us bread from heaven, not loaves and fishes, but something new from the sky. If you do something as marvellous, we'll believe God sent you."

They demanded a sign, but Jesus wouldn't give them one. He replied, "What Moses gave you was bread, but it wasn't the real bread. I'm talking about something much more than what Moses gave." The real bread has two qualities the manna didn't have. First, the real bread is personal; it's *he* not *it*. Moses gave you *it*. God gives you *him*. Secondly, the bread Moses gave only *sustained* life, but the bread God gives in Jesus *gives* life. You try feeding a lump of bread to a corpse and see what happens. Earthly bread is of no use to a corpse, but heavenly bread is. Heavenly bread gives life to the world.

The demand for immediate results

They then said, "This sounds great – give it to us!" They wanted immediate results. They didn't even ask what it was all about, but like the woman at the well said, "Give me this water – it'll save me bringing the bucket here every day." "Give me this bread always. Give it to us." But Jesus won't. Jesus says, "I am the bread – come to me." In other words, "I can't give it to you; you have to come and get it. Come to me." "Sir, from now on give us this bread." "I am the bread of life. Come to me." It's all in that word *come*. What is it to be a Christian? It is to come to Christ.

Jesus says, "I can't pass it on to you; you have to come to me for it. You have got to come and get it in me. I can't produce it out of me as I did the bread. Come to me." This word *come* is the key word in his reply to their question. He talks about the result of coming. He said, "If you come to me, you'll have infinite resources. You'll never be hungry and thirsty again. You'll never have to go without again" (v. 35).

He not only talks about the result, he also talks about the cause: "You will never come to me unless the Father draws you" (v. 37; see also v. 44). Why is it that you can speak to a whole congregation and some come to Christ and some stay away? The answer is the Father needs to draw. It starts with the Father's will, his decision, his initiative. He draws someone to Jesus.

"'Don't think the Father isn't drawing you is an excuse for not coming. Anyone who comes to me I will receive. I'll never drive them away' (Jesus in John 6:37). Do you see how Jesus balances up predestination immediately? He says, 'Get this straight. No one comes to me unless the Father draws them. But come, and see if I'll accept you. It's your responsibility to come.'"

As soon as you talk like that about predestination, someone else says, "All right, I don't need to come. He's not drawing me, and so Jesus straightaway puts that right: "Don't think the Father isn't drawing you is an excuse for not coming. Anyone who comes to me I will receive. I'll never drive them away" (v. 37). Do you see how he balanced up predestination immediately? The trouble is that as soon as you mention predestination some people make that an excuse for not coming, but Jesus says, "Get this straight. No one comes to me unless the Father draws them. But come, and see if I'll accept you. It's your responsibility to come." Let no one say they've been turned away. Nobody has ever come to Jesus to be turned away because the Father wasn't drawing them.

The significance of coming to Jesus is that one day in the future Jesus will raise us up; that includes my body – so we're not just talking about spiritual things, we're talking about a bread from heaven that will actually do something for this body. The bread I ate for breakfast only keeps this body going for a while, but the bread of heaven that I've eaten will give me a new body. That's bread worth having! "Come and eat and I'll keep you until the last day."

THE JEWS' DOUBTS (6:41-59)

Jesus has finished with the crowd. They had raised four questions and Jesus had drawn them to consider deeper things. He did that in a synagogue. Now we hear about another group: the Jews, meaning the Jewish authorities, and Jesus had said all this in their pulpit. So they began to raise questions – but not to him, to each other. They asked two questions:

193

His spiritual origin

Jesus said, "I am the bread come down from heaven," and they asked, "How can that be? He didn't come from heaven but was born in Nazareth. We know Joseph and Mary, his father and mother, so how does he claim to have come down from heaven?" But they were wrong. They didn't know his father, and his father was not Joseph. His father was God. You can jump to wrong conclusions if you don't know and they assumed they knew where he had come from.

Jesus knew their questions. They didn't say it to him, but Jesus asked, "Why are you murmuring among yourselves? Why do you think I didn't come from heaven?" Notice in the next few sentences he keeps saying *the Father*, as much as to say, "You know my father, but it's not Joseph. It's the Father."

Jesus answered, "You may not be able to see the Father – there's only one person who's seen my Father and that's me – but you can listen to him and anybody who hears my Father can understand. Everyone will be taught the truth, as your own prophets have said, so even if you can't see my Father you could listen and if you did, you'd hear amazing things. Jesus then repeats his claims emphatically: "I tell you the truth, I am the bread from heaven. Eat this bread and you can live for ever."

His physical descent

Jesus then added something that upset them deeply: "The bread I'm going to give you to eat is my flesh." This really struck them forcibly. "It's my flesh for the world." Moses gave manna for the Jews. Jesus said, "I'm going to give my flesh for the world." The Jews became angry at this, asking, "How can he give us his flesh to eat. That's cannibalism. How can he do it?"

Crude literalism is one of the enemies of the gospel. When Jesus told Nicodemus, "You must be born again," Nicodemus replied with crude literalism, "How can a man get back inside his mother's womb?" Crude literalism is a feature of those who refuse to think more deeply about what Jesus says.

Jesus replied to those Jews, adding, "Not only will you have to eat my flesh you will also need to drink my blood." He could hardly have said something worse. You've seen kosher butchers. What's the difference between a kosher butcher and an ordinary butcher? Kosher butchers have drained off all the blood; no blood should pass the lips of a Jew. But here Jesus says to a Jew, "Drink blood." It was offensive. Notice something subtle: "Eat my flesh and drink my blood." How can you do that before a life has been slaughtered? The blood is in the flesh before that. You can't eat the flesh without the blood. The only way to eat the flesh and drink the blood is for the blood to be shed from that life and the flesh to die, for flesh and blood to be separated.

This is what Jesus was saying to them: "I've got to die – to be slaughtered – before you can eat, because you can't have the blood without the flesh until death has taken place." But they didn't listen.

The key word in all that Jesus is saying is *life*. Jesus again and again says *life*: "I am the bread of life. If you continue to eat me, I will live in you and you will live in me. This is the living bread."

THE FOLLOWERS' DIFFICULTIES (6:60-66)

We move to a third group, which may have numbered hundreds: the disciples who had followed him for some months. There were at least seventy, but may have been more. These followers said, "He's lost us. The sermon is too deep, too difficult to understand, we can't take it."

That's the point at which they should have tried to stretch their minds and listen further. It is tragic when we will only listen to sermons that are easy to understand. You never grow spiritually if you only listen to what you can understand. Thank God when you hear a sermon that loses you, which makes you think, "I didn't understand that – I'm going to have to work at that and think it through." But they said, "That sermon's too difficult. It's a hard saying, so I can't believe it and can't practise it. It's too much. We like your parables. Why can't you just talk to us in those simple stories? Why do you have to talk in these complicated ways about eating your flesh, drinking your blood and things like that?"

They didn't say it to Jesus, but Jesus knew what they were thinking. He said, "Do you find this difficult? Then I don't know what's going to happen when you see other things. If you find it difficult to think of me coming down from heaven what will you be like when you see me go back up? There is a lot more you're going to learn. If you're going to stop here because it's difficult, you're going to miss so much."

He says, "I know it may be difficult to understand but you've got to try because my words are spirit and life. You must grasp this if you're going to understand real life. You must stay with me. The flesh doesn't help at all. I've been talking about my flesh but it's God's Holy Spirit who gives life. Through eating my flesh, God's Spirit will give you life. It's something you must try and understand because my words will bring you life."

He's pleading with them to hold on. He's saying, "You need the Father's help – that's why I said to you, 'No one comes to me unless the Father draws them.' You need God's help." When you find a sermon difficult to understand, have you ever thought of saying, "God, give me your Spirit to help understand that," or do you just go home and say, "It was way above my head"? Unfortunately those followers of Jesus had got to the point where the difficulties were too much.

We come to one of the saddest sentences in John's Gospel: "Because of this many of his followers turned back and no longer walked with him" (v. 66). Confused heads invariably lead to wayward feet. If you don't understand something, your feet begin to go in the wrong direction. Unfortunately, they turned back. Notice you can't turn away from Jesus. You can only turn back from Jesus. We're either going forward with Jesus or back. You can't go in any other direction; you can't stand still. When the going gets tough, when things get difficult to understand and you feel you are out of your depth, you can either go on with him into the depths or turn back.

THE TWELVE'S DEVOTION (6:66-71)

Jesus was disappointed and discouraged. It's as if he looked sadly at the little group he had got left and said, "Are you going to go too? Are you going to go with me into something deeper or have you gone far enough?" This vast congregation of ten thousand who wanted to make him king had come down to twelve. "And you, are you going to leave me also?"

Dear old Peter, who always opened his mouth and put his foot in it said, "We've got no alternative." At least it was sincere, although it was hardly a compliment. He said, "If we had an alternative we might, but we've nobody else to go to." It was honest.

"Once you've really known Jesus can you go to anyone else? Anyone else would be an anticlimax. What other religion or philosophy would you turn to? What other person would you go to for help? You have no alternative once you've known Jesus."

As you go on as a Christian, you'll find the Christian life tough; the going will become difficult. Sometimes you feel out of your depth, that it's too hard to understand to go further. The Christian life begins with a simple gospel but it doesn't stay simple. It becomes deeper and you will get to the point where you're out of your depth and you're struggling. At that point what is your alternative? Is there anybody else you could go to? Once you've really known Jesus can you go to anyone else? Anyone else would be an anticlimax. What other religion or philosophy would you turn to? What other person would you go to for help? You have no alternative once you've known Jesus.

"Lord, to whom shall we go? We've no alternative. We're staying." Then, as he talked, his faith blossomed. He said, "Lord, I don't understand, I can't explain it, but I know what you're saying is true. I just know it's got life in it. You have the words of eternal life. Nobody else has. Everybody else talks about this life

197

and this life comes to an end. But you talk about a life that goes on for ever. Nobody else talks to us like that."

I don't know of anyone else in the world who can talk knowledgeably about eternal life and offer it to people. Everybody else tells me how to make the most of this present life, but Jesus says, "Whoever eats and drinks me has eternal life." Peter said, "I believe it's true." Then his faith flowered supremely. He says, "I may not be able to explain but I can experience. We believe and have come to know that you are the Holy One of God." Notice the order of these words. "We've believed and come to know." In other words, we've trusted you first and afterwards we understood. Some people say, "I'll understand first and then I'll believe. Show me a miracle to prove it and then I'll believe," but Peter says, "We've believed and now we know."

However, Jesus is still sad even with this lovely confession of faith. Jesus feels keenly that he's lost the crowd. So he said, "Peter, you're not speaking for all of them. I do thank you for speaking like that. I'm glad you felt you could say that but you said 'we.' I chose the twelve of you and yet one of you is a devil!"

What is significant here is that Jesus had no delusions about people. One thing was worse than all those disciples deciding to turn back and desert him: it was for a traitor to decide to stay. Jesus said, "I chose the twelve of you but I'm going to have to make do with eleven." Do you find this depressing? I don't: Jesus knew what he was doing. He could do more with eleven who believed than with ten thousand who wanted to use him for their purposes. We are not here to be popular; we are not here to play to the gallery. We're here to offer people the bread of life. If eleven people believe, come to Christ and eat, then through those eleven you can turn the world upside down.

15

WHY DON'T PEOPLE BELIEVE?
John 7:1-31

JESUS TRAVELLING PRIVATELY (7:1-13)

Relatives—not really believed
Rulers—not honestly listened
Rest—not finally decided

JESUS' PUBLIC TEACHING (7:14-31)

Messenger—not willingly obeyed
Miracle worker—not properly judged
Messiah—not intimately acquainted

I think the most shattering discovery that every new Christian makes is that not everybody else wants to be a Christian. You come to the Lord, you are full of it and want to tell the whole world. You are sure that as soon as you do they will come running to share the blessing. You tell them but the reactions you receive are one of the most depressing experiences of life.

What is it that keeps people away from Jesus Christ? He loves them and wants to help them. He doesn't want to harm them in any way but they will not come. He is calling today but the world is deaf. What are the reasons? What are the difficulties holding people away?

When I first read this passage, I thought there wasn't much in it: it seems an ordinary passage – no startling miracles, no exciting confrontations between our Lord and some needy individual. Just a lot of people discussing different things. But as I looked more closely, I saw six reasons, six barriers, why people do not commit themselves to Jesus Christ.

The Feast of Tabernacles is the background to this chapter. In verses 1-13, people are talking about him privately, and their private opinions reveal quite a lot. Then suddenly in verse 14 he strides onto centre stage in the temple in the middle of the Feast of Tabernacles, which I suppose was like a pop festival. About a million people on the hills around Jerusalem living in a way they could in little tabernacles made of rough branches and waterproof sheets and just there for the festival.

The Feast of Tabernacles took place in the autumn – it was a kind of harvest festival, but it was also a memorial of the days when for forty years they lived in tents and wandered through the wilderness trying to find somewhere to live when they were refugees. Then came the time when they came into the Promised Land, settled down, built houses and lived in their own land. But so that they would never forget the blessings of the wilderness and the blessings of the Promised Land, once a year everyone who could went back to living in the open air in a tent to remember the days when their ancestors were in the desert.

Jesus has six months to live: only six months more and he's only thirty-three. He's already living on borrowed time. There is already a plot to assassinate him and he knows about it and he has stayed in the north deliberately to avoid being killed. He did this not because he was a coward but simply because God had a timetable for him and his hour had not yet come.

When you read the story of the cross, you could jump to the conclusion that Jesus was the victim, but he wasn't. He was the master of it all. He died in the place that he decided, by the method he decided, at the time he decided – or rather he died in the way God decided, at the place God decided, in the way God decided. And God's timetable was not yet. Jesus had another six months to go.

JESUS TRAVELLING PRIVATELY (7:1-13)

Relatives – not really believed

First, we have the opinion of Jesus from his brothers. We often forget that Jesus was only one brother in a large family. After Mary had given birth to Jesus, she went on to have other children. One of the acid tests of any person is what their family think of them: the people who see you all the time, who see you at your worst and when you are tired. What did Jesus' brothers think of Jesus?

He was their elder brother but the way in which they talked to him here is not the way younger brothers should talk to older brothers. Look at what they say in verses 3 and 4. They said, "Jesus, now's your chance. If you really want to be famous, a million people are at the festival. Why don't you go? Just one or two miracles and you're in." That's how they talked, in a typical brother way. They pushed him on. They said, "Advertising pays. If you really want to be well known, here's a glorious opportunity. We're going – why don't you come with us?"

Why did they speak like this? Was it family pride? They wanted a feather in the cap of the Joseph family from Nazareth. After all, it's great to have somebody famous in the family. Or was it jealousy? I detect this tone: "You're getting a bit too big for your boots. You're only a carpenter's son, you know. You think you can perform a few miracles and then you'll be famous. All right – you go. Show them!"

"You can become too familiar with him, but familiarity is not faith. You may know all about Jesus. You may think you know a lot about him but you may still not believe in him."

Immediately (v. 5) they remark they didn't believe in him. That was tragic. They were too familiar with Jesus. You can become too familiar with him, but familiarity is not faith. You may know all about Jesus. You may think you know a lot about him but you may still not believe in him. I was brought up in a Christian home. I was familiar with Jesus. I was brought up in Sunday School, church, Christian books to read, the lot, but I didn't believe. I had to get away from home, from church and Sunday School and all that and then come back and believe.

This is the first barrier we come across here: someone who is too familiar with Jesus and doesn't believe in him, who has lived with the name of Jesus all their life but has never really believed that he is who he says he is. You have never trusted him as Saviour and Lord. Maybe you have to get right away from it and find how empty life is without Christ, then come back and find that he is who he said he is.

Look at what Jesus says to his own brothers (verses 6-8): "You belong to the world, you get on with the world. It doesn't matter where you go in the world, nobody is going to hate you, nobody is going to persecute you. You belong to them. You go to the feast. I can't go." If Jesus had gone to the beginning of the feast, he would have been crucified six months too early. Six months later when he went to the next big feast, the Passover, he went early and the result was they managed to get him on a cross just before the feast began. He knew perfectly well he could not go at this time and be safe. So he said: "You go. You can go at any time. You can go anywhere. You belong to the world. You may be familiar with me but you don't have any trouble from the world because you don't believe in me."

You may have been brought up to be familiar with Christ. You

203

may know a lot about the Bible. But I'll tell you this, you won't have any trouble from the world if you don't believe in Jesus. You can come to a church and then you go anywhere you like in the week. You can mix with anyone. They won't dislike you. They won't treat you as different or strange. Not unless you believe in Jesus. So Jesus said: "You go. They hate me; they don't hate you."

Why should anybody hate a good man? Jesus was perfect. Why did they hate him? Because he told them they were not perfect. The world can put up with saints if those saints mind their own business. The world can stand a good man – in fact the world likes a few good people around – provided they don't tell anybody else they're bad, and Jesus was always doing this. He was not content to live a good life himself. He told others they were not living a good life, and such a person will be hated.

Whoever goes round telling others they're not living a good life will be unpopular. You have got to do it in the Spirit of Christ, by the way. In fact, he alone can do it and he alone can do it through you. But Jesus went around, not only living a good life but also telling others they lived a bad life, and they hated him. If you are against the world, you are not going to be popular. If you are still popular with the world, still liked by everybody you meet, there is something wrong.

Are you too familiar with Jesus to believe in him? Have you been brought up with it, so you have never really made a decisive commitment towards Jesus Christ?

Rulers – not honestly listened

Let's look at the second group. The scene shifts to Jerusalem and even though Jesus isn't there, his presence is felt, or rather his absence is. They're all talking about him. Thank God that again people are talking about Jesus. It is healthy when people are talking about Jesus even if they think he's not around. In Jerusalem they were talking about Jesus; the rulers were asking, "Where is he?" Do you think they wanted to see Jesus? Do you think they wanted to welcome him with open arms? Not at all.

Where is he? They had no intention of believing in Jesus. What was the barrier in their minds? It comes out in what had happened earlier: he was a threat to their institution, to their traditions, to everything in which they put their security. They never really listened to Jesus. They were never honest enough to ask what he really meant when he answered their accusations. Do you know it's almost ludicrous. They asked Jesus, "What are you doing that for? Only God can do that." Isn't that incredible? "What are you doing that for? Only God can do that. Why did you tell that man his sins were forgiven? Only God can forgive sins."

The Jews were waiting for him and they asked, "Where is he?", but their minds were already made up even before he came. Their minds were prejudiced and blinded: they were not prepared to give an honest audience to Jesus Christ.

Why were they not honest enough to listen to what he was saying and realize he was God? Their minds were so closed that they would not listen honestly to Jesus. This is the second barrier I find in talking to people about Jesus. They will not listen honestly to what he says. They will tell you what they think about Jesus but if you ask them if they have ever read one of the Gospels to see what he really was like, then the answer is no. They have picked it all up second-hand. They have made up their minds first.

Rest – not finally decided

The rest of the people had not finally decided. It is interesting to study their opinions. They were divided right down the middle on one question: "Is Jesus good or bad?" Those who thought about what he *did* thought he was good; those who thought about what he *said* thought he was bad.

What did he do? He went about doing good: healing the sick, feeding the hungry and helping people – that makes someone good in the world's eyes. But a man who goes around talking about himself as God, who makes preposterous claims to decide the eternal destiny of every other human being, such a man is an impostor. He's a bad man, a fraud, a deceiver. He's trying to fool the people, and the world doesn't like being fooled. So their debate went on. They were discussing.

"There comes a point where discussion must lead to decision, where debate must lead to commitment. You can't go on debating Jesus for the rest of your life, because in the last analysis if you die still debating, then you die on the wrong side of the fence."

There was one thing they would not do, however. Verse 13 says they would not come out openly on either side. This is a third barrier. It is fine to have a discussion group, to debate Jesus, to talk about him – but eventually he asks, "Are you prepared to come out into the open on one side or the other? Are you prepared to be open and say I think he's bad? I think he deserved what he got, that he deserved to die, that he's not good. Or are you prepared to come out and say I'm for Jesus?" You see, there comes a point where discussion must lead to decision, where debate must lead to commitment. You can't go on debating Jesus for the rest of your life, because in the last analysis if you die still debating, then you die on the wrong side of the fence. You have not committed yourself openly.

Why would these people not commit themselves openly one way or the other? It says they feared what would happen to them if they did. Isn't this one of the reasons why people today are reluctant to come down for or against Jesus? It's because they are afraid of what will happen to them, of what others will think and do.

JESUS' PUBLIC TEACHING (7:14-31)

Jesus did go to the feast. Some people say he was a liar because he said he wouldn't go to the feast and then he did. It is a little problem. But he didn't go officially to the beginning and he didn't tell them he would go for the whole feast so they wouldn't tell others he was on his way. Moreover, he didn't go for the feast: he went halfway through and suddenly there he was teaching openly.

Messenger – not willingly obeyed

Any rabbi could stand up in the temple and teach. The Jewish pilgrims would gather around the rabbis in little groups and listen to them teaching. But a man who did this had to be theologically qualified, to have been through the seminary, to have the equivalent of a theology degree. But Jesus walked in and sat down like any other theologian and started talking about God. They were more worried about his theological qualifications than about what he was saying. They asked (v. 15), "How did he get to know God like this? He never came through our theological college. He never went to our school." Jesus replied, "I don't want you to think I'm a self-taught teacher. I did have theology: I did my theological degree in heaven." That's what he's saying (verses 16-19). "I'm not saying what I thought up myself; I'm simply passing on to you what God told me to say. That's where I got it from. If you want to test my credentials, if you want to prove whether what I say is true and from God, there is a simple way. If you are willing to do what God wants, you will soon find out whether I'm telling you the truth."

"Here is a simple reason why many people don't know whether Christianity is right or not. They are unwilling to do what God wants. The pathway to knowledge according to Jesus is obedience not education. We don't go wrong through ignorance but through wilfulness."

Here is a barrier: unless I am willing to do what God wants me to do, I have no proof this is true. There is no way of testing it, of checking the credentials of Jesus. But he says, "If you're willing to go along with God, then the barriers are down." You will find if you obey the little you do know that God will show you some more. Here is a simple reason why many people don't understand the truth and don't know whether Christianity is right or not. They are unwilling to do what God wants. That's a barrier. The pathway to knowledge according to Jesus is obedience not education. We don't go wrong through ignorance but through wilfulness. He says, "If you were only willing to do what God wants you to do, you would soon know where I got my theology and know whether it is true or not." It's a simple condition but Jesus accuses the Jews of not being able to understand because they haven't yet obeyed what little they do know. He says, "Moses gave you the Ten Commandments, but you don't even keep those. How do you expect to know whether what I say is true or not? You can't. You are not morally capable of judging my teaching."

If God shows you just one thing, and if you are obedient in that, you will know whether it's true or not and he will tell you something more. But if he shows you something today and you are disobedient and say, "No, I'm not going to do what he wants me to do," then you'll get stuck mentally. The Bible will go dead on you. You will be puzzled by it. You won't be able to grasp Jesus' teaching. Barrier number four is that those who are not willing to do what God wants will never understand that Jesus is God's messenger to humanity.

Miracle worker – not properly judged

Then the crowd said he was mad: "You must have a demon. You're possessed. You're now accusing people of breaking the Ten Commandments and in particular of breaking the commandment 'You shall not kill' because you're accusing people of wanting to kill you. Who's trying to kill you?" Unfortunately, the crowd had no idea that behind barred doors people were already plotting Jesus' death.

Jesus said, "You've got ten commandments and you're now breaking number six, 'You shall not kill.' You're planning to kill me. How dare you judge my teaching? You're not morally fit to do so." The crowd said, "You're deluded, you're possessed, who's trying to kill you?" Jesus replied, "Remember my miracles. Do you remember the man who was paralysed for thirty-eight years and I healed him on the wrong day, the Sabbath? You hypocrites! You don't judge me as you judge yourselves. You will take a little boy's body and you'll cut it, you'll circumcise that boy on the Sabbath and you're mutilating his body. You're making him sick for a few days. Yet you excuse that and when you look at me you judge me for making a man whole and well on the Sabbath."

This is the next barrier: the barrier of being hypocritical, of judging others more strictly than you judge yourself. The barrier of judging other people by appearances and not looking into the heart of the matter and not judging them by true standards. That is always a barrier. A man who is prepared to judge others more harshly than himself and a man who judges appearance and not reality is a man who can't go any further with Jesus Christ.

Messiah – not intimately acquainted

The crowd is still debating: is Jesus the Messiah or is he not? Is he the Christ? To a Jew the word *Messiah* sets his heart beating. The word *Messiah* sums up all his hopes for the future. I remember when I was in Israel soon after the 1967 six-day war, in a taxi. The taxi driver said, "I don't know how you feel sir, but I feel the Messiah is coming soon." His face lit up as he spoke. I said, "I do too." (I didn't at that point add I thought he had been once already but I wanted to share the man's joy.)

The word *Messiah* is wonderful and the crowd were asking, "Do you think he is the Messiah? He's talking openly. Does that mean the rulers have accepted that he's the Messiah? No, it can't be – there's no mystery about this man." They said, "We know where this man comes from – there is no mystery about that. We know where he lived: he's Jesus of Nazareth." Some people thought Jesus was too down to earth, that he didn't have enough mystery about him. Jesus answered them – and here comes the sixth and final barrier –"Do you really know me? Do you really know where I came from? Are you really thoroughly acquainted with me? You talk as if you know all about me, but you don't know me. Because you don't know me, you don't know the One who sent me. If you don't know me you don't know God."

This is the final barrier: an unwillingness to get to know Jesus intimately. You can know a lot *about* Jesus but not *know* him at all. To know Jesus is to be a Christian. Jesus said to these people,

"You're debating whether I'm the Messiah. So I don't have enough mystery? In fact, it's all mystery to you. You don't know me. You don't know God either. I know him. He sent me here."

That is the last barrier. The last question I want to ask you is: "How well do you know Jesus?" If you don't know him, one day he will say to you, "Depart from me – I never knew you." Just before that (Matthew 7:21-23) comes Jesus' words: "You will say to me, 'Look we did all this in your name. We went to church in your name. We helped the church in your name. We did good deeds in your name. We worked miracles in your name. We drove out demons in your name.' And I will say I never knew you. You were so busy doing things in my name that we never got to know each other." That's a barrier. You can be so busy doing Christ's work that you don't get to know him. How do you get to know a person? By doing a lot of things for them? No. By spending time with them. By talking to them. By listening to them. You never get to know anybody except this way and Jesus said, "You think there's no mystery about me. You don't even know me! So you don't know the One who sent me."

16

WHERE ARE YOU GOING TO?
John 7:32-52

WHERE WILL HE GO TO? (7:32-39)

Enemies—beyond their hands
Friends—within their hearts

WHERE HAS HE COME FROM? (7:40-52)

Friends—within their hopes
Enemies—beyond their heads

We're only a third of the way through John's Gospel, but already we read words like *arrest* and *kill*. No sooner had Jesus begun his ministry than almost immediately people began to plan his assassination. We are already facing the fact that Jesus is going to die. He's only thirty-three years of age and has six months to live. What does a man think about when he knows his time is measured in months? Some people would think of all they were going to lose. Others would think of all they wanted to do in the last few months. But Jesus is thinking about what lies beyond his death. The way in which Jesus talked to people shows his mind was living beyond his death. Even though he had another six months, it was only a little while. He says, "I'm only with you a little while longer and then..." (v. 32). He's already thinking about the future and what he was going to do.

WHERE WILL HE GO TO? (7:32-39)

Enemies – beyond their hands

Where was Jesus going to go after his death? The question arose because the soldiers were sent to arrest him and he said, "I'm only going to be with you a little while longer and then I'm going somewhere you can't come," and this caused much discussion. It is interesting to see who his enemies are: a coalition of two groups, the Pharisees and the Sadducees, who were not normally on speaking terms. Already among the Jews were two different denominations. They had split on a theological issue. They were divided over their beliefs about life beyond the grave. The Pharisees believed in the resurrection, that God was able to raise bodies from the dust and give people new life. The Sadducees did not believe in the resurrection. They raised all sorts of problems like supposing someone was married seven times and they get raised from the dead, "Who are they going to be married to?" But although they argued about life after death, as soon as somebody talked about life after death they could not understand. They were only able to think about this world. Here we have this extraordinary situation, not unknown today, where people talk about the next world and state their beliefs but in practice they live entirely for this one. We are told that both the Pharisees and the Sadducees loved money and they liked comfort and affluence. Even though they spent time arguing about life after death, the only world they lived for and were interested in was this one.

So when Jesus talked about going to a place they could not go to, they immediately thought, "Where do you think he's going to? Is he going to Greece, to the Jews who are dispersed in the Greek world? Is he going to try and get a following there?" (verses 35-36). Of course he didn't mean that. They could easily go there. He said, "You can't come." It would be sad if Jesus said to any of us, "I'm going somewhere you can't come." But the sad fact is that both the Pharisees and the Sadducees for all their beliefs about life after death were morally disqualified from going where he was. It doesn't really matter what you think about life after death; the important thing is can you go where Jesus goes? Can you follow him? He said to his own followers, "Where I am you will be also. I'll come and get you" (14:2-3). But he says to the others, "Where I am going you cannot come."

Friends — within their hearts

If Jesus was going to go to a place where his enemies could not reach him, what about his friends? We read now Jesus' glorious comment: "Even if I go beyond the reach of my enemies, I will be within the hearts of my friends." This is the unique relationship that is possible now that Jesus has died and returned to heaven.

Jesus is already looking forward to the day when he will be beyond the reach of his enemies but within his friends' hearts. "It is for your good that I go because if I don't go the Spirit can't come. It will be better for you when he's around and he will be within your hearts" (16:7). Jesus was beyond his enemies' reach. But that does not mean he's a long way away from our reach – in fact, he is nearer to us than he was in the days of his flesh. So he goes on to talk about being beyond their reach and within the hearts of those who believe in him. This is the new relationship.

Let's go back to the beginning of chapter 7 to consider why

he said that. We recall that it was the Feast of Tabernacles where every autumn about a million people would come to Jerusalem and live on the hills in little tents and booths they had built for themselves. They would spend eight days there. It was a memorial festival. They were remembering hundreds of years before when the nation lived in tents in a desert and survived on God's provision. Two and half million had survived forty years without their own food and water.

They did something significant at this feast: every day the high priest left the temple on the top of the hill and walked down the main street of the old city of Zion carrying an empty silver and gold chalice that held about two pints. People lining the streets watched him and he would come to the bottom of the hill to the Pool of Siloam. It is a pool that is filled from a spring outside the old city wall with a channel cut through the rock. It is only about eight feet high and two feet wide. The water runs through this channel for over half a mile through the rock into the Pool of Siloam. This brought water inside the city. The priest would dip the chalice in the water and would walk back up the hill carrying the chalice into the temple, through the different courts to the altar and there he would pour out the water.

Why did he do all that? He remembered the days when two and a half million people didn't have any water to drink. They were in a rocky, dry, barren, dusty place. They grumbled and asked, "Why did you bring us out to die here?" Moses struck a dry rock with Aaron's rod and water gushed out for them. They remember the fact that except for that water there would be no nation of Israel. There would never have been a Promised Land. There would be no history, no Jews and so no Jesus. But because God gave them water, they remembered it and every year afterwards they poured out the water.

This act had further significance. They all looked forward to the day when the Messiah would come and give them refreshment, that he would do what Moses did for them. As Moses gave them bread from heaven and water from the rock, they believed that one day the Messiah would come and give them bread and water. In John 6 Jesus gave them bread and talked about the living bread, but in John 7 on the last day of the feast – the eighth day, which was the only day the priest didn't go down for the water – Jesus stood in the midst of the crowd and cried out, "If anybody is thirsty, come to me and I'll give him water to drink. I'll give him a spring, a well, streams of waters, pouring out in his heart."

The people listened. Every day they had been thinking about Moses striking the rock and giving them water, which saved their life. Now Jesus makes such a claim. What's it all about? He's still thinking of the future. He's still thinking about what he's going to do as soon as he's dead. What was the first thing Jesus did when he went back to the One who sent him? Ten days after he went back to heaven, he filled them with living water. He's living in the future. The people around him are thinking about his last few months on earth but he's not.

Let me tell you about a pump I once used. It had a handle that went backwards and forwards. It had a round metal body with a handle running through the middle and a pipe down into the earth and another pipe coming up on top. Deep down was a well full of water and you could work the handle very hard but nothing would happen. You had to take a bucket of water with you and pour the water in the top until it was primed. As soon as the body of the pump was filled with water and you started moving the handle, you could go on and you would get far more than a bucketful. The pump had been primed. The water was now flowing: it just poured out.

"There are three conditions to pouring out. First, you believe in Jesus: you're fit and able to pour out. Secondly, you are thirsty, desperate for water, really sensing your need, and are able to drink. Thirdly, you drink, you receive. If you fulfil those three conditions, streams of living water – resources of spiritual refreshment – will pour out."

That seems a perfect picture of what Jesus is saying here: "If you drink from me, you will pour out streams of living waters. Take a drink and streams are the result." Christians cannot prime themselves. That's what he's saying. You need to drink of him and then you can pour out; otherwise you are just pulling the handle. Otherwise it's all effort. Otherwise you try so hard and nothing comes; you know it is there but somehow you can't get it out. Somehow it doesn't flow. Is that your situation? Is that how you feel?

You see Jesus is talking about believers here. There are three conditions to pouring out. First, you believe in Jesus: you're fit and able to pour out. Secondly, you are thirsty, desperate for water, really sensing your need, and are able to drink. Thirdly, you drink, you receive. If you fulfil those three conditions, streams of living water – resources of spiritual refreshment – will pour out. You have been primed. You have drunk, so you are full. Being full, you can now draw out more and more because now there is a stream, a spring of living water welling up within, just as Jesus said to the woman at the well.

Why is it that some Christians pour out and others don't? Why is it that some try so hard to share the love of God with others and it doesn't flow? It is because they haven't been drinking, because they're not thirsty enough or it may even be that they haven't yet fully believed.

Jesus was talking about the Holy Spirit whom those who had believed were going to receive. He is of course referring to Pentecost. There was another reason why they could not drink then: "that Jesus was not yet glorified" (v. 39). The Holy Spirit could only be poured out on people after Jesus had been lifted up on the cross, lifted up from the grave and taken to glory; only then could the Spirit be poured out.

So Jesus is here talking about something that could not happen for another six months. But we need not wait six months now! Any Christian can drink now. If they drink deeply of Jesus and of his Holy Spirit, they will find the pump begins to operate and streams of living water pour out. Jesus says, "Drink in, pour out."

Now a person who makes this kind of claim is a person who is claiming to be the Messiah. He told those Jews, "The water that has been poured out every day this week is ritual, but I want to give you the reality. That's a symbol. I want to give you the substance. That was looking forward, but I want to give you the real thing, and I claim to be able to do it."

WHERE HAS HE COME FROM? (7:40-52)

Friends—within their hopes

We now come to the people's reactions. Instead of saying, "Give us a drink," they asked, "Who is he?" Their attention was distracted into a debate about Jesus and they came to some wrong conclusions.

His friends found that their hopes were being fulfilled. They had two hopes: one was for a prophet like Moses and the other was for a king like David, a king after God's own heart. These two hopes had kept them going through enemy occupations. So they asked, "Could he be the Prophet?" "Yes," said some. "Is he the king like David? The anointed one, the Christ, the Messiah?" "Yes," said others. Then they ran into problems. People divided because some said, "The king like David has got to be born in Bethlehem. This man is from Galilee" (verses 41-43).

Here we come to the main lesson I want to draw out of this study: you're making a terrible mistake if you judge someone by their background instead of their destiny. It does not matter where someone has come from; what matters is where they are going to. We shouldn't ask where a man was born, how he was brought up, if he's had the right background. That doesn't matter; it's where he's going to after he dies that's important. A man can be born in a palace and finish up in hell and he can be born in a slum and finish up in glory.

So, having had the glorious opportunity to listen to Jesus talking about his future and where he would be after his death and what he would be able to do for people, they end up with a discussion as to where he came from. They said, "Galilee." Nobody famous comes from there, somewhere up north where people from different countries live. They were snobs; they said "Galilee." They tried to say it was the Scripture, but Scripture said that the Son of David would come from the south, from Bethlehem, the City of David, as Jesus did.

However, God's ways are so lovely that after Jesus' birth, he was taken as a refugee to Egypt, then up north to Galilee and everybody thought he came from Galilee. If they had only asked him, he would have said he was born in Bethlehem, but he never did. Why not? Because God has no room for snobbery. God has no room for those who are only interested if someone has the right background or comes from the right place. God comes so humbly that you have got to accept him for who he is, not because he fits your ideas. Those Pharisees show me that they were not just thinking of Scripture but that they were snobs because they said no prophet comes from Galilee. But I can find at least three prophets in the Old Testament who did: Jonah, Hosea and Nahum all came from Galilee, but such was their prejudice in the south that the people said, "Hmm, he comes from the north; he can't possibly be the prophet, the Messiah." They closed their minds to the possibility.

Enemies — beyond their heads

We now turn to the guards who were sent to arrest Jesus but returned, saying, "We couldn't do it." Here is an incredible mutiny among the soldiers. Imagine being sent to arrest a prisoner and coming back saying, "You should hear him talk! We couldn't arrest him. No one ever spoke as this man does" (verses 45-46). They were nearly right. No one speaks as Jesus does. No one in history has ever spoken as Jesus spoke: "Come to me all you who are thirsty. Come and I'll give you drink, and streams of living water will just pour into your heart. Whoever eats my flesh and drinks my blood will live for ever."

Have you ever heard anyone say such things? If you heard someone say them, you'd think they were mad. No mere man can say things like that. The soldiers couldn't arrest him. They said, "Yes, we know we've broken orders but we couldn't do it. You should hear him." It wasn't that the crowd had turned ugly; it wasn't that Jesus had soldiers behind him to protect him. The guards came back and said he defeated them with words – not weapons, but words.

When you listen to what Jesus says, you say, "This isn't a man talking. No man has the right to talk like this." Those Pharisees showed their bigotry and pride by their sarcasm. They said of the soldiers, "You're fooled – he's fooled you." They said of themselves, "We don't believe in him. You've never known one Pharisee believe." And they said of the crowd, "They're cursed anyway because they don't know what they're talking about" (verses 47-48). What pride!

They had closed their minds to Jesus, so they couldn't listen to him, even though others told them to listen. They were presumably meeting in the Council in the Sanhedrin with all the Pharisees gathering round and the leaders saying, "There isn't one Pharisee who believes in this man," but sitting there was one man who was feeling very uncomfortable, one man who in his heart did believe: Nicodemus. He was in a terrible situation, the same situation you're in if you're with people who are laughing at Christ or the church. You're afraid to openly say you believe in Christ and that you belong to the church.

Nicodemus was there and the leader of the Pharisees said, "You can't find one Pharisee who believes in Jesus," but Nicodemus believed. It was a horrible moment for him. He was still not a firm enough believer to declare himself fully but he said something. He had to speak; he couldn't keep quiet. What he said looks like an appeal for fair play: "Look, we're a council; we administer justice. You know it's only fair play to listen to what a man says and examine what he does before you condemn him." But was he just asking for fair play? I think in his heart, weak and cowardly though it was, he was trying to do more: trying to get them to listen to Jesus. It was bold, even though he didn't admit that a few months previously he had sneaked off in the darkness to talk to Jesus. He dare not say that. But he asked, "Are you going to condemn him before you've heard him?" They all turned on poor Nicodemus and asked, "Are you from Galilee by any chance? Are you one of those? Surely you know that no prophet comes from Galilee," but that wasn't true. Poor Nicodemus just shut up at that point. He got no further.

However, he must have told someone later or it wouldn't be in the Gospel. I think years later Nicodemus must have said, "You know I confess freely there was a horrible moment once in the Sanhedrin when they were all against Jesus. They were all saying that no Pharisee would believe in Jesus, but I sat there and my heart said, 'You do, don't you?' And I tried to get him a fair hearing, but hadn't the courage to say I believe in him."

Nicodemus is a man with whom we all have a lot of sympathy. What would cure Nicodemus of this cowardliness? Of this closing up when he could have witnessed for Christ? "Come to me and drink, and out of your heart will flow rivers of living water." It's the Holy Spirit's power flowing from you that enables you in that situation to say openly you belong to Jesus, that you believe in him, that you love him. Whether Nicodemus came to this later we never know. I know he asked for Jesus' body and gave him a decent burial, and that's the last we hear of him.

"Isn't it tragic when people are more interested in where someone comes from than in where they're going to? Someone's real significance is not where they born, not where they were brought up, not their background at all. Someone's real significance is where they're going to, where they will be five minutes after they've died."

But one other Pharisee came to believe in Jesus: Saul of Tarsus. He was a Pharisee with a closed mind who said, "Jesus can't be the Messiah. I'm going to arrest every one of his followers." The same attitude came out again. Then one day, when he was walking down a road harrying the church of Christ with letters in his hand giving him authority to arrest the Christians, he met Jesus and realized Jesus was the Messiah. Three days later, a man called Ananias came into the house where Saul was and said, "Brother Saul, I've been sent that you may be filled with the Spirit." In other words, Ananias said, "Saul, you're a Pharisee but I've come that you may be primed to flow with Jesus' love." Saul was filled with the Spirit and he fulfilled the predictions of the Pharisees here: Jesus in Saul went to the Greek cities, and to the Jews in those Greek cities, telling them about Jesus Christ.

To conclude: isn't it tragic when people are more interested in where someone comes from than in where they're going to? It misses the main significance of a person, for someone's real significance is not where they born, not where they were brought up, not the accent with which they speak English, not their background at all. Someone's real significance is where they are going to, where they will be five minutes after they have died. But the world still adopts this attitude to Jesus. They are still more interested in where he comes from than where he went to. They still celebrate Christmas every year. They still have the nativity plays. They still listen to the Bethlehem story. They still go back to his background and they know it all. But when you talk of where he is today they are not interested. Thank God some are. Thank God not a week passes by without men and women coming to Jesus and they drink and they begin to flow and the Holy Spirit springs up within them like streams of living water.

17

"I AM THE LIGHT OF THE WORLD"
John 8:1-12

DARKNESS OF THE WORLD (8:1-11)

The men
The woman

LIGHT OF THE WORLD (8:12)

The leader
The followers

This short story about Jesus and the woman caught in adultery is full of meaning. In fact, this story nearly didn't make it into our Bible. In many Bibles it is put in brackets; in some Bibles it is not even there. In some earliest copies of John's Gospel – and we have some very early copies: one in the John Rylands library in Manchester goes back to AD 110, about twenty years after it was written – this story is missing. Why was it left out? We can understand some of the fears people have about it. First, it looks as if adultery is all right: those who read this superficially might think it was condoning immorality. Secondly, it almost looks as if Jesus is saying no human being has the right to judge or punish another, which frankly means the end of the police, law courts and family discipline.

Why, then, is it included in some copies of John's Gospel? I think because it's true. Nobody would have invented such a story. It has all the marks of a genuine event and even if people were afraid of including it in early copies of John's Gospel, it persisted and was included later.

It's difficult to imagine the motive that anyone would have for inventing this story; in fact, it fits exactly the character of the Pharisees as we know them and it fits perfectly the character of Jesus as we know him. It has the ring of truth. I am going to assume it is true.

This story tells us that Jesus' primary concern is neither to punish the wrongdoer nor let him off but to put him right. That's its message. It is a perfect blending of justice and mercy. It shows Jesus' wisdom in escaping a trap set for him by evildoers. They were always doing it but they could never catch him.

DARKNESS OF THE WORLD (8:1-11)

Some years ago I walked through a township in Arabia called Ma'alla. I saw a crowd of men, excited, shouting. It was dusk so I couldn't see what all the fuss was about and then to my horror I saw they were dragging a half-naked Arab woman by the hair along the ground. I was paralysed by the whole situation and asked an Arab shopkeeper, "What's going on?" He replied, "She's been caught in adultery," and the whole scene of John 8 flashed into my mind. It was horrible.

Let's look at the background to this story. It was the Feast of Tabernacles. It was a real festival: they got excited and danced all night. They went back to their tents in the early hours of the morning and it was only too common to go into the wrong tent. This is what had happened here. They had found one man's wife in another man's tent, and they dragged her along to Jesus.

"Why did they bring her to Jesus? Because they were not really interested in the woman at all; they weren't interested in cleaning up Jerusalem or the morality or immorality of the situation. They were using this woman for their own purposes ... they were going to use her as bait to trap Jesus Christ."

The men

Look at these men. Notice first they brought the woman, but not the man. According to their own law of Moses, the man was as guilty as the woman and both deserved punishment, but they brought the woman, even though the man had been there as well. That shows their unjust attitude. They brought the woman along and seem almost to have been gloating over what they had seen: the act of adultery. They were judging her.

Why did they bring her to Jesus? Because they were not really interested in the woman at all; they weren't interested in cleaning up Jerusalem or the morality or immorality of the situation. They were using this woman for their own purposes and that in itself, if it was not a physical prostitution, was a spiritual one. They were going to use her as bait to trap Jesus Christ.

That was as bad as anything they had found her doing, but they were so callous they didn't realize it. Why was it a trap for Jesus? Because whatever he said, he was certain to offend one group of people. For example, he was known as the "friend of sinners", as the One that bad people could go to and find understanding and compassion. What would happen to that reputation if he was known to have condoned the stoning of this woman?

Another group could have been offended. Adultery was going on throughout the festival. The law of Moses was being widely and openly disregarded at the festivals in those days. What would happen to his popularity with the crowd if he took a strict line of censorship on this issue?

Another group – the Jewish leaders – stood for the law of Moses. What would happen if Jesus said the law of Moses didn't apply? They would immediately depict him as one who taught against the law, and he would be unpopular with the orthodox religious people. What about the Romans? The Romans had forbidden capital punishment by the Jews. They were not at liberty to do this kind of execution, so if Jesus said, "You must do it," he would have been unpopular with the Romans. They had him every way. There wasn't a single answer that he could make to their question, "What do you say?" (v. 5).

Here, Jesus wrote. This is the only time we are told that Jesus wrote. He stooped and scribbled in the ground with his finger. Soon, the passing feet would rub out what he had written so that the only thing we know that Jesus ever wrote was lost. We don't know what he wrote – it's not essential to the story or God would have told us. Why, then, did he stoop down and write? I can think of four reasons:

One reason is that he was disgusted and embarrassed at the situation and could not do anything but scribble. Secondly, by ignoring them and scribbling himself, he gained time for prayer with his heavenly Father about the situation. A third possibility is that like his heavenly Father, his eyes were too pure to look on evil (Habakkuk 1:13). It was not that he couldn't bear to look at the woman; he couldn't bear to look at the men either. They were just as bad.

But there's also a fourth reason: to express judgment. Back in the Old Testament, Moses went up a mountain and according to Exodus 31:18, "The finger of God wrote the commandments on tablets of stone." And if you move on to a banqueting hall in a royal palace with King Belshazzar giving a banquet. He's drunk and doing silly and blasphemous things – he picked up the cup that once graced the altar in God's house. He drank from it and laughed at God's people and cursed God. Suddenly he saw a finger writing on the wall: "You are weighed in the balances and found wanting" (Daniel 5:5). Maybe because Jesus knew they would remember what God's finger wrote, he was telling them the writing was there for them too: "I'm going to find you wanting": the finger of Jesus writing their judgment.

Whether that is the right explanation or not, I'll tell you this: the judges became the judged. They suddenly found the tables turned. When Jesus said, "Whoever is without sin can throw the first stone," he didn't mean you have to be perfect before you throw a stone at anyone else, because that would exclude all justice, all judgment, all legal cases, all courts. What did he mean? They would understand him to mean, "Whichever of you has not committed adultery can condemn this woman for it." This was shattering, because in the entire group of men of all ages – which gives you some idea of the kind of situation in Jerusalem in those days – there wasn't one of them who could say or do another thing. Jesus said, "You have no right to judge this woman for the things that you do." It's a principle that comes right through Scripture. Listen to the Sermon on the Mount. "Do not judge, or you too will be judged, for in the same way as you judge others, you yourselves will be judged. Psychologists tell us the sins we often shout loudest against are those we have most difficulty with ourselves. We recognize in others our own faults. Read Romans 2 and you will find Paul saying: "You Jews, you're always telling people not to do this and that but you do the same."

There was only one difference between that woman and all those men: they had never been found out. That's all; that put them all in the same boat. A man was once filling out an official form. When he came to the question "Have you ever been in prison?" he wrote, "No." The next question was "Why?" and he wrote, "I've never been found out," which was honest! The only difference between that woman and those men was that they had never been found out, so they thought they could judge another.

But Jesus knew everything and said, "You've no real desire to clean up this city or you'd have started with yourselves. You've no real desire to see justice done or you'd have judged your own lives." That's a challenging word.

Notice it was the eldest who went out first. Young men brazen it out. The older ones can't. It's easier to convict an older man of sin than a younger man. A man who can look back and see it all, and they went out one by one. They didn't even look at each other. They slunk away one by one.

The woman

The woman stayed. Why didn't she slip away? She had her opportunity to. I don't know what spirit she came in: sullen, defiant, angry? She almost lost her life very painfully: to be stoned to death is a horrible death. I wonder what she felt like. We know that in Jesus she had met a man who was different, who seemed to have justice and compassion. She was released: "Go."

Jesus was qualified to stone her yet not qualified to stone her. It's a strange legal position. He was qualified because there was one man in her presence who was without sin, one man who could have done it, but he didn't. However, on the other hand, he was not qualified. Legally, he wasn't bound to stone her because the law of Moses said the stones had to be thrown by witnesses who had witnessed the sin – and Jesus had not witnessed it. So if I can put it reverently, he was off the hook, out of the trap. If they told him afterwards, "You broke the law of Moses," he could reply, "I didn't – I wasn't a witness. I didn't have to stone her."

It's a marvellous moment: he was qualified to judge her and he didn't. The trap is sprung but Jesus isn't in it. Neither is the woman: they're both free. Only Jesus can find a way out of an insoluble problem. Only Jesus is wise enough to do what is right so that he did not break the law; nor did he insist on its terrible punishment.

She was released: "I'm not going to condemn you either." "There is now therefore no condemnation to those in Christ Jesus" (Romans 8:1). Jesus says, "I don't condemn you. That silences all your accusers. That takes away all those who would accuse you unjustly. "No condemnation now I dread / Bold I approach the eternal throne / And claim the crown through Christ my own [Charles Wesley]." She was released.

But forgiveness is more than being let off, more than being given a clean start. Forgiveness wants to put the future right. If you really love someone, you are not only concerned to get the past out of the way, you also want to get the future straightened. So Jesus added words that changed the whole situation: "Go, I release you, but I restrain you at the same time. Don't do it again." If you heard Jesus say that to you, you have got one of the strongest impulses not to do it again.

It's the difference between law and love. Law can only punish the wrongdoer, but love can put the wrongdoer right. Love will always be able to go further than law. "The law came through Moses, but grace and truth came through Jesus Christ" (1:17). Grace is operating now: she left.

LIGHT OF THE WORLD (8:12)

The leader

What do you think was going on in Jesus' mind as she went away? I think he thought something like this. "Why does it all have to happen? This is my Father's world; these are my Father's creatures. Why do they have to live like this? Why do they have to walk in darkness?" For darkness to Jesus was always moral darkness. It's at that point that the brackets end. We are certain that verse 12 is part of the original Gospel story. What is amazing is that the incident of the woman taken in adultery must have happened just before verse 12 or verse 12 doesn't make sense. It's a perfect comment on all that has happened and Jesus now says about himself, "I am the light of the world. Whoever follows me will have the light of life and will never walk in darkness." He gives the answer to this whole situation.

It's interesting that the autumn festival happening then was often called the festival of light because at the beginning of the feast in the temple, in the Courtyard of the Women, they lit two 14-foot-high gigantic candelabra, which they kept burning for eight days. The light they gave lit up not only the whole temple area at night but also the streets of the city and the hills around Jerusalem. Jesus takes all this up and says, "I am the light – follow me. I'll lead you through this dark world. If you keep close to me, you'll never get into such a mess again."

How do we know the woman would never sin again? How do we know that she wouldn't run after the next man she met? Jesus thought about that too, so he said to the crowd, "If you want to keep out of this kind of situation, follow me and I'll lead you where you should go."

Light does two things: it hurts and it helps. If you watch coalminers coming out of the pit shaft as they finish work, their eyes are blinking; the sun hurts. Physical light hurts the eyes but moral light hurts the conscience. When you first come to Jesus it hurts. The light exposes and shows you yourself.

But the light also helps: the light guides. Why do we have electric lights in a room? Why are there lamp posts along the street? They help you see where you are so you can go where you want. Jesus said, "I'm the light of the world. I'll hurt but I'll help. I'll expose but I'll guide." When those men brought that girl to Jesus, they little dreamt that his light would expose them too. But then he offered to help them. If only they'd come back and listened, he'd have said, "Now if you follow me, you won't be like this."

The followers

So Jesus, having witnessed an example of the darkness of human life and looking at those great lights in the Court of the Women said, "I am the light of the world. Whoever follows me will have the light of life and will never walk in darkness." At the Feast of Tabernacles the people remembered the pillar of fire by night, which moved along in front of them and led them for forty years through the wilderness. The pillar of fire cast light over the whole camp. When the pillar of fire moved, they followed.

"Those who follow Jesus need to keep up: the light of the world is on the move. It's not static. If you want to remain in the light you must keep moving and follow. Staying in Jesus' light depends on moving all the time with Jesus: not just one decision to come to Jesus but step after step, keeping up with him. Unless you keep up with Jesus, you'll quickly find yourself back in moral darkness."

Many know Holman Hunt's picture "The Light of the World." That picture is misunderstood: the text that inspired its picture isn't Revelation 3:20, "Here I am! I stand at the door and knock (NIV)." In the picture Jesus is standing with a lamp in his hand. It's true, he is knocking on a door and he's standing outside a door. It is a dark overgrown door with weeds, hidden in a wood. It was painted in an orchard not far from Guildford. But the point of the picture is that he is not trying to get in – he has come with a lamp to lead that person out. In the background of the picture, you can see the sun shining in the distance out of the trees. He's come into this dark little place to get a man out and lead him with his lamp into the light. That's why it's called "the Light of the World." He's saying, "Look where you're living. Look at the weeds, the darkness, the filth. I've come to show you the way out of all this. I am the light of the world."

Two things will be true of those who follow Jesus. First, they will need to keep up. Jesus as the light of the world is on the move; so if you want to remain in the light you must keep moving. You need to follow. Staying in Jesus' light depends on moving all the time with Jesus: not just one decision to come to Jesus but step after step, keeping up with him. Unless you keep up with Jesus, you will quickly find yourself back in moral darkness.

Secondly, those who follow him will be liberated from darkness: "If you keep close to me, you'll be free." This is a paradox. Many people say, "I want to be free; I want to go my own way." Then they land up in darkness and can't see where to go. They think that to submit their will to someone else and to follow someone else is going to be the opposite of freedom but they are wrong. Perhaps to submit yourself to the establishment, to the middle-class bourgeoisie may be bondage. But Jesus did not tell us to follow that group. He said, "Follow me. Submit to me. Walk in my footsteps. Keep close by my side, and you'll never walk in darkness. You'll be free. Really free." It's a promise. It's an offer.

Let me conclude by saying there's a wonderful offer in this verse. John's Gospel constantly mentions light and darkness. It came up in 1:4-9: "He is the light that gives light to everyone coming into the world and the darkness cannot overcome it"; in 3:16-21 when he said to Nicodemus, who came to see him at night, "It's only people whose deeds are evil who like the darkness and won't come to the light." In 9:4-5 he says, "The light will not shine in this world for ever. In 12:35-50 he talks about two places: one of light and the other of darkness.

Jerusalem is on a hill and it's surrounded by a U-shaped valley: in fact, two valleys: the Kidron Valley and the Valley of Hinnom meet south of the city and go down to the Dead Sea. The Kidron Valley is shallow. The Valley of Hinnom or Gehenna is deep as it curves round the west and south walls of Jerusalem. From Jerusalem you can see down into the old city of Zion down the hill. You can see the Valley of Kidron. You can see the Mount of Olives, and the ring of hills all round. There is one place that you cannot see from Jerusalem, however: the deep valley of Gehenna. It's so deep in the bottom that the sun never strikes it. Deep down in the bottom is the field where Judas tied a rope to a tree and hanged himself. It's a horrible place.

When they had rubbish to throw away in Jerusalem, they would take a bucket of rubbish to the west or the south wall and they would tip it over into the Valley of Gehenna. The rubbish tumbled down and worms ate the food that was left. When they lit the candelabra on the festival of light, the light couldn't reach that deep valley of darkness outside the city. When Jesus tried to describe hell to people, he gave it the same name as the valley they knew. He said it was the Valley of Gehenna, the valley of outer darkness where the fire burns all the time and the worms go on eating, where there is weeping, wailing and gnashing of teeth. Sooner or later those who choose to walk in darkness are going to go to a place where there isn't even any physical light.

Outer darkness: what a terrible description. But Jesus said, "Follow me and you'll never see it. You'll go to a place that's so bright it doesn't even need the sun." To follow Christ or not to follow Christ is as stark a contrast as between blazing light and utter darkness. Having witnessed that dark evil scene of a woman who'd done the wrong thing and men who were doing the wrong thing, Jesus said, "I can see where that's all leading: to a place of outer darkness. But I came to be the light of the world. Follow me and you'll never walk in darkness."

18

JESUS: MAD, BAD OR GOD?
John 8:13-59

THE CONSISTENCY OF RECOGNIZED TRUTH
(8:13-20)

Expert word
Extra witness

THE CONSEQUENCE OF REJECTED TRUTH
(8:21-30)

Fatal condition
Final confrontation

CONFIRMATION OF RECEIVED TRUTH
(8:31-47)

Real freedom
Reflected fatherhood

THE CONTINUITY OF REVEALED TRUTH
(8:48-59)

Endless effect
Eternal existence

Those who think Jesus was simply a great teacher have never studied his teaching properly or have dismissed many parts of it as unacceptable, because the main subject of Jesus' teaching was himself. In this passage the words *I*, *me* or *my* come 85 times. No other great teacher ever taught so much about himself as Jesus. The claims he makes about himself are incredible: to be the light of the world – he can keep a person out of moral darkness permanently – he can give people life that would last for ever, that the destiny of every person was in his hands A man who talks like this is mad, bad or God.

But are the statements Jesus made about himself true? How do you find out if something is true? In this sermon, Jesus makes four points about truth. But why do you accept truth? Why do you believe that anything is true?

THE CONSISTENCY OF RECOGNIZED TRUTH (8:13-20)

Think about things you have heard someone say that you accept as true. Why did you believe them? For example, why did you believe your schoolteacher? What makes the difference between accepting someone's word and not accepting it? The Pharisees said to Jesus, "We've only got your word for it. Nobody else is saying this about you. You have no proof; you can give us no evidence. Why should we accept that this is true?" Jesus talks about the consistency of recognized truth in two respects:

Expert word

If you know nothing about a subject, you can't tell whether a person is talking rubbish or whether what they say makes sense. But if you know a little, you say, "From what I know I recognize he's talking from an expert position. He knows what he's talking about because I know enough to recognize that. Jesus said to the Pharisees (verses 14-15), "You don't recognize whether I'm speaking the truth about myself or not because you don't know enough to know whether I'm an expert. I know where I came from.

I know where I am going. You don't know where I came from. You don't know where I'm going. So you cannot judge whether I'm talking the truth or not. In making these claims for myself you are not in a position to say whether they are true or false because you haven't enough knowledge already on which to base a fair judgment. So you judge in a human way but people judge what they have no knowledge about."

"The first thing someone should do before they say anything about Jesus is to study his life, read the records. You'd be amazed at how many people say what they think about Jesus but they've never even read the Gospels. They're judging in a human way. You've got to have some knowledge to say whether a statement is true or not."

I meet this attitude every week, talking to unbelievers about Christ, the Bible, the church and heaven. They are ready to judge but they know so little. They haven't enough knowledge to know whether what I am saying is true or false; they simply dismiss it out of hand. The fact is they can't recognize the truth when it is told them. They don't know enough.

So the first thing someone should do before they say anything about Jesus is to study his life, read the records. You would be amazed at how many people say what they think about Jesus but they have never even read the Gospels. They are judging in a human way. They don't know enough. You have got to have some knowledge to say whether a statement is true or not.

Extra witness

The second thing that makes you accept someone's word as true is if you hear somebody else saying the same thing independently. So Jesus said (verses 17-19), "Not only am I giving you an expert's word, but you also have an extra witness if you want one. Independently of my words, you can listen to my Father. My Father says the same thing about me as I do and in your law two witnesses agreed are enough [Deuteronomy 17:6; Numbers 35:30]. I am one witness and my Father is another. There's only one problem with that: you don't know my Father either. So you're not even in a position to listen to the witnesses."

No wonder they said, "We can't believe this! We've only got your word for it." They did not know Jesus well enough to know whether he was speaking the truth or not and they didn't know the Father well enough to listen to him. The Father was always witnessing to Jesus. When Jesus was baptized, the Father said, "This is my beloved Son with whom I'm well pleased." Later in Jesus' ministry God again said: "This is my beloved Son. Listen to him listen to him. I'm his witness. I'm telling you he's telling you the truth. Listen (Mark 9:7)."

If the Father and the Son both tell the truth to the world, why does the world dismiss it? Because they don't know enough about Jesus to judge and they don't know the Father to be able to listen. But those who study Jesus with an open mind know enough to recognize whether he's telling the truth and they can begin to hear God witnessing as well and they'll say, "It's true, it's consistent, I recognize it: something inside me says, 'That's right; it holds together.' It's integrated. It's truth."

Isn't that how you came to be convinced of the truth of Jesus' teaching about himself? You had a certain amount of knowledge, perhaps through Sunday School, coming to church, reading a Gospel or other book. Because you were open to that knowledge, you began to be able to judge whether Jesus was telling the truth. Later, another witness came, the witness of God's Spirit in your heart, confirming it was true. You can't prove it to someone else. They may ask you for proof or evidence, arguments for the truth of Jesus' teaching, but you say, "I can't give you them – you don't know enough and you don't know the other witnesses, but if you study and get to know enough, then you can judge the rest. Open your mind to some teaching; accept that Jesus came from God and has returned to God, then you're in a position to judge whether what he said was true."

What incredible impudence of the Pharisees when Jesus said, "You don't know my Father," and they replied, "Where is your father?" That's a subtle insult. Do you know in the Middle East among the Arabs the worst insult you can ever give another man is to imply doubt about his parenthood, to question his father? Most Middle Eastern insults are built around that; that's why the word *bastard* is an insult there, and when they said, "Where is your father?" there was a hint of rumours about Jesus' birth.

Jesus said, "If you only knew my Father, you'd listen. If you knew me better, you'd know my Father. But you don't know me and you don't know him. How can you judge the truth?" If someone isn't prepared to get to know Jesus and through him not prepared to get to know God, they have no right to say whether the teaching of Jesus is true or false.

THE CONSEQUENCE OF REJECTED TRUTH (8:21-30)

Fatal condition

This is the second thing that makes me accept what someone says is true. When doctors first suggested a link between tobacco and lung cancer, people didn't believe them, but we now know enough of the consequences of rejected truth. The medical statistics are clear. Some of those who didn't believe it have paid the price of rejecting truth.

Jesus pointed out to the Pharisees the terrible consequence of calling Jesus a liar. He said, "It means you and I will go to entirely different places." The consequence of saying what Jesus said about himself isn't true is eternal separation from God. He said, "I am going to a place where you will not be able to come," and they asked, "What's he going to do – commit suicide?" (verses 21-22). Where is he going that they can't follow him? Jesus said, "I'll tell you where I'm going. I belong to heaven, but you belong to earth. You think you can get to heaven by rejecting my truth. You don't belong to heaven, so you can't get there unless you believe I am who I am. I belong there. I came from there. I'm going back there. The only hope of you ever getting there is to believe that what I say about myself is true."

It's extraordinary that so many people believe they have a right to heaven, that they will all go there. Although they don't believe Jesus' teaching or obey it, they still assume everybody is going there "except of course a few terrible people in history: them, but not us." Jesus said, "You don't belong to heaven; you didn't come from there, you have no right to go there. The only hope is that you believe I am who I am. If you don't, you will die in your sins. You're in a fatal condition." The consequences of rejecting Christ's truth are eternal separation and the gates of heaven slammed tight.

Final confrontation

Jesus then spoke about the final confrontation he would give them: "One day you'll lift me up [referring to the cross] and you'll see that I do nothing for selfish reasons. I do nothing for myself. I only do what the God who sent me tells me to do. You'll see that I am who I am. That will be my final plea to you" (verses 28-29).

If you doubt whether Jesus is the Son of God then look at the cross. Why was he there? Do you know a tough regimental sergeant major in the Roman Legion stood at the foot of the cross and said, "Truly this man was the Son of God" (Mark 15:39). Jesus said, "I've spoken to you; I've told you who I am." They asked, "Who are you?" He replied, "I've told you from the beginning. But a final confrontation will come when you hang me on a cross and then you will know who I am. You will know what a mistake you have made then." And they did. Why could Peter preach so powerfully on the Day of Pentecost? Because they knew they had made a mistake. He said, "This Jesus whom you crucified God has made him both Lord and Christ. You hanged him on a tree. You murdered him by the hands of lawless men. You did this and now you know you were wrong" (Acts 2:22-36). Three thousand Jews recognized that fact that day.

Confirmation of received truth (8:31-47)

If you receive truth and act on it, you will find it is true from experience. Years ago, I needed to cut some glass for a picture frame. I hadn't got a glass cutter so I wondered how I was going to do it. Somebody told me you can cut glass with a pair of old scissors, provided you hold the glass underwater. My initial response was disbelief, but I did it and found you can cut glass underwater with some old scissors. The water absorbs the shock; it doesn't splinter and you can trim the glass. You don't get a perfectly straight edge but you can get enough to put in a picture frame. I heard that truth, acted on it and found it was true.

Verse 30 says, "Many were believing in him already," but their belief was only a belief in the mind. They said, "He might be right," and Jesus answered, "I'll tell you how to prove it: obey my truth. Do something about it; try it out and see what happens." This is a fair enough test. Two things will happen if you obey what Jesus says.

Real freedom

You will have real freedom. If you do more than accept Jesus' truth with your mind; if you do it, abide in it, continue to live in it, obey it, then you will be really free. Jesus said, "You won't be a slave any more," to which they replied, "We've never been anybody's slaves!" What short memories they had. They'd been slaves in Egypt, in Babylon, all over the place. And they added, "We're Abraham's descendants. We think we're free."

Jesus told them, "You think you're free. Everybody who sins is a slave. You think you're free when you do everything you want. But you're not – you've got to go on doing it. As soon as you do something wrong, a little link of a chain has been forged. When you do it again, there's a second link, and a third time, a third link and so on until you're chained. A young person says, "I want to be free; I'm going to take drugs." Free? Don't you realize that's a step into slavery? There will come a time when you are gripped by what you are doing.

"What is real freedom? It is the freedom to do good. Nobody is free to do good. We're all slaves of sin. But freedom is being free to want to do good, to be able to do good, to be free to be the person that God intended you to be."

If by *freedom* you mean freedom to do what is wrong, freedom to do what you want to do, that way lies complete slavery and Jesus says, "You're not free. What is your besetting sin, the thing that keeps coming back and gripping you? You call that freedom. You're a slave to it. You can't break it," and Jesus says, "Prove that what I say is true. Obey my truth and it'll make you free. Really free."

What is real freedom? It is the freedom to do good. Nobody is free to do good. We are all slaves of sin. But freedom is being free to want to do good, to be able to do good, to be free to be the person that God intended you to be. Jesus said, "If you obey what I say, you will know the truth by experience because the truth will set you free." "My chains fell off, / My heart was free; / I rose, went forth, and followed thee" [Charles Wesley]. It works. Believe that Jesus is who he said he is and you'll find he can make you free. If he is not who he said he was, then he can't be a Saviour.

Reflected fatherhood

You will reflect God's fatherhood. Here, the question of fatherhood came up again, with a nasty insinuation about the Virgin Mary. They said (v. 41), "We are not children of fornication. We know who our father is at an earthly level, Abraham and at a heavenly level, God." "But," Jesus replied, "just a moment; if you were children of Abraham you'd behave like Abraham. He didn't try and kill the truth but that's precisely what you're doing. More important than that, you think God is your father, that you're a child of his. So if you were a child of God, you would love his Son."

When I have met someone who loves my earthly father, they have an attitude towards me because of their love for him. Or someone will say, "Any friend of so and so is a friend of mine." The love often transfers to those connected with the person you love. Jesus said, "If you were a child of God, you'd love me. If you know the Father, you would love the Son. You would reflect the fatherhood; more than that, you would listen to my words." Here is the proof that a person is the child of God: they love Jesus and listen to what Jesus says. If that person doesn't love Jesus and doesn't listen to Jesus, they're not a child of God.

This idea that all people are brothers and sisters because God is the Father of all isn't an idea in the Bible. Those who love Jesus and listen to him are brothers and sisters, but not others. So Jesus says, "I'll tell you who your father is: the devil." Isn't that terrible? By nature, people are children of the devil. I've sat in a law court and heard a man in the dock say when the judge asked him, "Why did you do it?", "I don't know; the devil came into me." Came in? He was already there: he is in every person until they become a child of God. "You are of your father the devil."

The devil is a liar, slanderer and gossip; he maligns people and accuses our brothers and sisters. Isn't this what's happening all over the world today? People slandering, gossiping, maligning, lying, twisting the truth. The devil is the father of liars. It is disturbing to find out how early in life children learn to lie. You never had to teach your child to lie. You only had to teach them to tell the truth. They soon find they can cover up something they have done with an untruth. Why? Because their father taught them to. Unfortunately through their earthly father maybe, but even if the earthly father tries to teach them to tell the truth they will still learn instinctively.

"You are of your father the devil. You twist the truth. You won't listen to what I say. You tell lies about me," and they did: they called him a Samaritan (v. 48). He wasn't. They called him demon possessed. He wasn't. They said he was a bastard and he wasn't. They insinuated these things: the devil loves to do this. He is a slanderer. Not only is he a liar but he is also a killer: he loves to destroy people. He will destroy them with lies if he can. So Jesus challenges his hearers and says something no other person has ever dared say, "Which of you can find a single fault in me?" (v. 46). "I find fault in you. You are of your father the devil. You are like him: you lie, twist the truth, want to kill. Which of you can find anything wrong with me?"

This claim of Jesus was the only one they had no reply to. Isn't that amazing? Therefore he is saying, "Listen to me: I tell the truth. You've called me a liar. Are you really saying that that is my besetting sin?"

THE CONTINUITY OF REVEALED TRUTH (8:48-59)

Real truth is always true. Not human ideas, which change. I was taught evolution was proven fact. We now know that it is not. Human ideas of what is true change, but God's ideas of what is true stay the same. That is its glory. Jesus says more than "I tell the truth"; he says, "I am the truth," as he does in 14:6.

Endless effect

Jesus said, "If someone believes the truth I teach, they will never die" (v. 51). Its other side is: "Because I tell the truth and am the truth, I always existed." Truth was never born and truth will never die. So if I receive real truth, I will never die. Therefore the One who gives me real truth was never born. Jesus said, "If what I say is unchanging real truth and you do it, obey it, abide in it, you will live for ever."

No other teacher of so-called truth can say that. But Jesus said truth will always be true. So if you take truth into your life you will always be. That's an incredible claim. But if he was telling the truth it's true. And they said to him, "This is ridiculous! You must be possessed. Abraham died. The prophets died. Everybody dies. And you're saying that receiving the truth you can last as long as the truth. What rubbish!"

Eternal existence

Jesus answered, "You keep dishonouring me, don't you? You keep insulting me. I am trying to honour God and you do nothing but dishonour me. I tell you the truth. You call yourself the children of Abraham. I know Abraham. I knew him well. He was glad to see my day. He was glad to see me." They thought he had gone completely mad. They said, "You're not even fifty years old – how do you know Abraham?" He replied, "Before Abraham was born I am." Notice the verb tenses. The tense applied to Abraham was a once-for-all event. Abraham was born. Before that there was no such person as Abraham: he began as you and I began. But Jesus said, "I am the truth. I was always there because truth is always true and truth is always real. So I was always there." Here Jesus condenses a phrase he used earlier: "I am who I am" (verses 24, 28) into one phrase: "I am."

Do you remember when that was used in the Old Testament? God said to Moses in the burning bush, "Go and get my people out of Egypt," and Moses said, Who shall I say sent me? I don't even know your name." So God told Moses , "My name is I am ... I've always been. I always will be. I am what I am." Jesus is saying as clearly as possible, "I am God."

So we are back to the beginning of this study: the most important part of Jesus' teaching is Jesus himself. The most incredible claims he made can be summed up in Jesus saying, "I am God." It is a case of either Jesus was lying or everybody who says he is not God is lying. You have to choose. Thank God when you believe he is the truth, you are really free.

19

"TOUCH ME AND HEAL ME"
John 9:1-41

DISCIPLES: SUFFERING (9:1-5)

BLIND: SIGHT (9:6-8)

NEIGHBOURS: SENSATION (9:9-12)

PHARISEES: SCRUPLES (9:13-17)

PARENTS: SAFETY (9:18-23)

LEADERS: STATUS (9:24-34)

JESUS: SALVATION (9:35-41)

I don't think anybody ever got into so much trouble for doing good as Jesus Christ. Every time he helped somebody he seemed to have got into serious difficulties with others and this miracle is no exception. Here we have the miracle of giving sight to a blind man. This blind man had never seen anything – he had no conception of trees, the sky or clouds and had never seen people. The miracle should surely overwhelm everything else, but unfortunately, the miracle is almost lost sight of in the controversy that followed.

This miracle is unique in all the Gospels because it is of someone with a congenital defect. No other case in Jesus' miracles is of someone born with a handicap who is then cured years later. It is unique. When this blind man was healed I discern seven different reactions. I am going to ask you which response is yours.

DISCIPLES: SUFFERING (9:1-5)

The first response is that of the disciples who are primarily concerned with the question of suffering. Whenever I invite people to write down questions they want to ask, every time I receive "Why does God allow suffering?" It comes regularly in different forms. I've often asked myself "Why?" after I have visited many suffering people. When you look at a world in which millions are suffering terribly, that makes it even worse. It is very difficult to answer.

When the disciples saw this poor man suffering, their interest was intellectual and philosophical. They wanted to discuss the whole question: they were more concerned with the questions, "What causes suffering? Why does it happen?" This is the question I am often asked, but I am rarely asked it by the sufferers themselves. It is usually relatives or friends who ask it. The concern of the sufferer is different: how to cope with it and what to do about it.

"Jesus says, 'Don't look at suffering as something to debate, but as something to do something about. Stop speculating and start acting. See suffering as an opportunity to do something, because a time will come when that opportunity goes.' When you come up against suffering, don't say, 'This is an interesting question,' but ask, 'What can I do about it?'"

The disciples asked, "Lord, was it due to this man's own sin or was it his parents' sin that caused this suffering?" They were only concerned to have his authoritative answer to the question why. Of course they were wrong to assume it had to be one or the other. They were right in believing that all suffering is due to sin, but they were wrong in thinking it had to be the person themselves who had sinned or those nearest to them. There is a whole area of suffering that is not caused by my own sin or other people's sin but by Satan's sin; we tend to overlook that.

In reply (verses 3-5), Jesus said, "There's a more important question than 'Where does it come from?' and that is 'What is it going to lead to?'" He says, "Stop treating this blind man as a case and treat him as a person. Don't look at suffering as something to debate, but as something to do something about. Stop speculating and start acting. See suffering as an opportunity to do something, because a time will come when that opportunity goes. So: work for the night comes when no one can work." In other words, when you come up against suffering, don't say, "This is an interesting debatable question," but ask, "What can I do about it now while I can?"

Jesus gave a unique answer to the question of why God allows suffering. It's an answer that may not commend itself to you immediately but please think it through carefully. He said, "God has allowed this to happen in order that his power may be revealed. It's possible for God's power to be seen more clearly in a world in which suffering occurs than in a world in which no one suffers." That's Jesus' answer. It is extraordinary: it hits us squarely between the eyes. He is saying, "This has been allowed so that God's power may be seen." In other words, if you see suffering not as an opportunity for a philosophical debate as to where it comes from but instead see it as an opportunity of bringing glory to God, you're going to approach it differently.

Jesus' answer was profound; he said, 'Now, let's get on and do what we can do about it because while I am in the world I am the light for the world and here is a man in darkness and I must do something for him."

BLIND: SIGHT (9:6-8)

The second concern in this story was the blind man. His concern was not intellectual but practical. He was blind and he wanted to see. In fact, he had the simplest attitude to the situation of anybody there.

Look first at what was done for him. Jesus did something extraordinary: he spat. You've done that, to heal something, haven't you? When you cut or burnt your finger, what did you do? Immediately you have spat on it. Spittle can be used to hurt or to heal. Later, they spat on Jesus' body, to hurt and insult him. But when Jesus spat, it was to heal. It must have been wonderful for a blind man to feel that.

Jesus mixed his spittle with the mud, with the clay dust to make mud, and then he smeared it on the blind man's face which would hold the spittle against his eyes for some time. It was a beautiful act. There could be no better ointment in the world for eyes than Jesus' spittle.

That was done for him but notice also that Jesus helps those who help themselves. He invariably gives them something to do to cooperate with him. He demands an active not a passive faith. He said to a man lying on a bed, "Get up, take up your bed and walk. You do something. I will cooperate with you in this." Jesus doesn't treat someone as a passive victim but says, "Let's do this together." It's again the touch of the master that you can see because he would heal a man's will, faith and personality to know that he had cooperated with the Lord. So he acted and said, "Now I've done all I am going to do. You still can't see. Now you do your part." He then told him to do something extraordinary: to walk three-quarters of a mile, blind with mud smeared on his eyes, to the Pool of Siloam down the bottom of the hill.

This achieved two things: first, it tested that man's faith, whether he really believed it was worthwhile to pick his way, tapping his stick down the streets of old Zion. If he didn't believe it would work, he wouldn't do it. It stretched his faith, made him determined and convinced himself of his desire to see. Jesus drew out the man's cooperative faith, making him strong in his desire to see. Can you see the poor man with his eyes covered with mud tapping his way down the street, believing that at the end of it was a pool where he'd find sight?

It also ensured something extraordinary: when he did see, he could not see Jesus. I am sure that was partly why Jesus sent him all that way because we know from the end of chapter 8, they were ready to stone him for saying he was God. Jesus' life was in danger, and to heal a blind man publicly in his presence so that the blind man would see and say "Here's the man who healed me," was dangerous.

When the blind man could see, do you realize he would never have recognized Jesus? He might have searched the whole city and looked everybody in the face but he would never have found the One who healed him. Jesus did it quietly so that the blind man could not endanger Jesus before his time.

NEIGHBOURS: SENSATION (9:9-12)

The third group are those concerned with sensation, whose interest is purely emotional. Unfortunately, wherever Jesus heals, there are those who are interested in pure sensation. If I asked how many of you have been healed by Jesus from some affliction, including blindness, I think you would be amazed at how large a number that would be. But the interest is often purely sensational. The neighbours and the friends said, "Isn't this the man? How marvellous!", and they came. Some said, "No it's not him; it can't be. It looks like him, but it's probably his brother." Do you realize why they didn't recognize him? The eyes are so much part of a person's face: they are the windows of the soul. They had seen this man with closed eyes all his life; now they see him with open eyes. It must have been shattering: he looked so different.

It is like someone who starts wearing glasses or who stops wearing them: it changes them. They said, "It's not the man," but he replied, "I am the man. You've seen me sitting begging. Well, look at me now." The neighbours were amazed at what had happened: nothing like this had ever happened before.

But they straightaway lost interest in the poor man and said, "We must go and see the man who's done this. Where is he?" They switched from what had been done to who had done it. Here were all the makings of a personality cult. If the blind man had been able to find Jesus, Jesus would have had a tremendous crowd following him around to see the next thing that he did, but it was only sensational. It was a passing emotional interest. Maybe the healing was reported in the *Jerusalem Evening Chronicle* but eight days later it would have been forgotten.

PHARISEES: SCRUPLES (9:13-17)

The Pharisees are the next group: their interest is in scruples, which are good servants but bad masters. There are two great dangers in the Christian religion and in the Jewish religion before it. On the one hand are those who have no standards saying, "As long as I believe in Jesus, it doesn't matter how I live." On the other hand are those who with many scruples who say, "You mustn't do this and can't do that," and you end up with a long list of things you can't do on a Sunday, for example.

The Pharisees had many scruples: they had got a long list of commandments you couldn't do on the Sabbath. One of them was making ointment. Jesus had just made some ointment: he had "manufactured something". Spitting in the dust and mixing it a bit was, in their eyes, manufacturing on the Sabbath. Then he had opened a clinic on the Sabbath and healed a blind man. That could have waited until the next day! The man had been born that way. These Pharisees had the closed mind of an over scrupulous religion. Those with scruples cut down on enjoyments and become a misery. Unfortunately, we have all met them.

The Pharisees with their closed mind said, "There's a

contradiction here. We've got a miracle worker and a Sabbath breaker in one person and those two things can't go together. He's broken the Sabbath – he can't possibly be a miracle worker." They were trapped in their own logic and narrow attitude: secondary things crowded out primary things. The big thing was a blind man could see! But they were so full of scruples about the Sabbath that they could not rejoice. They could not shout, "Hallelujah! That's wonderful!" because they were bothered about their own traditions. They said, "He can't be a good man or he wouldn't break the Sabbath." Somebody else said, "Well, he can't be a bad man because bad men can't make the blind see."

What a dilemma! So they asked the man himself, who said, "I think he's a man of God." But the Pharisees wouldn't accept this. Like many sceptics today, they'll find any possible explanation to explain away a miracle. They try the explanation of mistaken identity, saying, "Bring the parents. It can't be him. We'll prove that a man can't be a Sabbath breaker and a miracle worker; it's a case of mistaken identity."

PARENTS: SAFETY (9:18-23)

So we come to the parents. What was their interest? Safety. It's embarrassing to be parents of someone Jesus has changed. There are many embarrassed parents nowadays because their young people have been touched by the Lord and changed. Suddenly you find yourself engaged in controversy, being asked questions that you don't want to answer. "Yes, he's my son, but I don't know what's happened to him. He got religious mania somewhere. It's the Christian Union or the church or something happened to him." Parents can get embarrassed because Christ has changed their children. These parents were embarrassed and they said, "Yes, that's our boy. Yes, he was born blind, but that's all we're saying. We don't want to get involved. Don't ask us any more questions" – they were playing for safety.

We get the feeling they did not want to know anything more: they were disowning their son. They said, "Ask him, he's grown up now, he's not our responsibility. He lives his own life now. We're not responsible." Do you get the impression they didn't want to know because it might have prejudiced their safety? They might even be frowned on in the local synagogue. If they got too involved, they might even be excommunicated.

What was their basic trouble? Fear. Fear makes you do silly things. Fear makes you say, "I'm not going to get involved. Don't ask me any more questions. I'll give you the facts but I don't know anything else."

LEADERS: STATUS (9:24-34)

We come back to the leaders, who are angry. Angry people pass through various stages: denial, insult, abuse, violence. Notice how they progress through these stages: they try to teach this man; they swear him to tell the truth and then they tell an outrageous lie.

It's incredible but they said, "Swear by God to tell us the truth. This man is a sinner." But that's an outright lie. However, in their eyes he was. But we find that this blind man who can now see has lost all fear of people. He was even sarcastic with them, angry though they were: "I've told you more than once what happened. Do you want to be his disciples? Really? Are you really interested in him?" He could have paid for his life with what he said. Thank God that when Jesus has really touched you, you lose your fear of people. You are prepared to say what he has done for you.

"Notice that this man's testimony is up to date. He doesn't say, 'Once....' I have heard too many testimonies that talk about once ... twenty years ago. But he says, 'Now, right at this moment. While I stand before you now. Now I can do somcthing I could never do before because Jesus touched me.'"

In the whole of this chapter there is not one word about the blind man's feelings. Did you notice that? We don't know if he was happy or sad that he could see. We presume he was happy, but it doesn't say. Thank God that in his testimony he stuck to facts. If we're going to witness to Jesus let's stick to facts. Let's not talk about our feelings. It is not a testimony to say we feel great – so does the chap down the road who has just had a 'fix'.

Feelings are no testimony. There are many things you don't know when Jesus first touched your life and you have to say, "I don't know." Say that; it doesn't spoil your testimony to admit you don't know something. What you can say is: "I can't answer your questions. There are some things I don't know. But one thing I do know, once I was, now I am. Once I was blind, and now I can see." Once ... but *now*. Notice too that his testimony is up to date. He doesn't just say, "Once ..." I've heard too many testimonies that talk about once ... twenty years ago. But he says, "Now, right at this moment. While I stand before you now. Now I can do something I could never do before because Jesus touched me." They argued and finally threw him out.

JESUS: SALVATION (9:35-41)

We come now to the loveliest part of this story. The blind man went out but he would not have recognized Jesus if he had met him in the street. But Jesus knew him.

The blind man might have looked all round Jerusalem for the wonderful person who had given him sight, but he did not need to. Jesus was waiting outside for him. Why? No matter how many friendships or relationships you lose because of Jesus, there is one compensation for it all: Jesus himself is there for you. The blind man had been thrown out of the synagogue. Maybe his parents would never talk to him again; certainly the Pharisees wouldn't ever have. He had lost a whole lot of acquaintances but Jesus found him.

If you have got Jesus, you can manage without anybody else. Jesus found him and said something like this: "I'm concerned about something deeper than your physical health. You can see now with your physical eyes, but I'm concerned about salvation too, about your spiritual health. Do you believe in the Son of Man?" The man replied, "I don't know him; how can I believe?"

Do you know, he still had not recognized the voice? So, reminding him of the voice, Jesus said, "I'm talking to you now."

It was as much as to say, "Don't you recognize my voice? And he did: he said, "I believe," and he fell down and worshipped. Isn't it glorious when a man is completely healed, not just in body – that's wonderful! – but when he believes in Jesus and says, "Now I know you. I believe in you," and falls down and worships. That's real health!

You may have perfect physical health but until you've said, "I believe," and knelt before Jesus, you're not healthy or whole. Jesus then said, "I came so that everybody who is blind could see." That covers every person on earth, because everybody is born blind, not physically but spiritually. You're born that way. You can walk through God's world and never see God. You can be blind but Jesus said, "I came to bring light: mental light, moral light, physical light, but while I'm in the world, I'm light for the world."

Once I was spiritually blind. I read my Bible but didn't see anything in it. I just didn't see, but now I see. Once I thought all Christians were miserable hypocrites. Now I see. I was blind. Once I couldn't see into the future at all; I didn't know what was going to happen in the future. I was blind but now I see.

There's another side to this: Jesus said, "I came into the world to judge, to separate people. The blind would see, but those who see would go blind." How can this be? Light has a double effect: it enables some people to see and it turns others blind. Let me illustrate this. A car with strong headlights is going along a road at night. If you are travelling with the car you will see, but if you're travelling against the car you'll be blinded. Many accidents take place because people have been blinded. Before the light came, they could see in their stretch of road but when the light came, they were blinded, because they were travelling in the opposite direction. If you are travelling with Jesus, you'll see. You're in the light: he is the light of the world and you don't walk in darkness. But if you're travelling against Jesus, you're blinded: you won't see.

The Pharisees heard Jesus say this and asked, "Are you saying we can't see?" Jesus replied, "No, I'm not saying that exactly because if you couldn't see you wouldn't be to blame, but you claim to know God. You teach other people and claim you can see, so you're not in the category of those who *can't* see ... you're in the category of those who *won't* see." If there's something more tragic than someone who can't see it's someone who won't, who closes their mind.

The chapter begins and ends with the same question. "Who was guilty for this blindness?" the disciples asked about the blind man. Jesus replied, "Neither that man nor the parents. We'll not discuss the guilt of this blindness." But at the end of the chapter, Jesus says to the Pharisees, "You are guilty for your blindness, because you've closed your eyes to the truth."

So we conclude: the heart of this chapter is Jesus healed the man; he touched his body and put it right. Right now, Jesus isn't dead. He's still alive and here. I want you to claim Jesus for yourself. Come to him by faith and say, "Jesus, you're still the same. You're still the light of the world. Touch me and heal me."

20

"I AM THE GOOD SHEPHERD"
John 10:1-18

PARABLE OF THE SHEEPFOLD (10:1-6)

Danger: the villain revealed
Safety: the voice recognized

PORTRAIT OF THE SHEPHERD (10:7-18)

Life: the flock saved
Death: the Father satisfied

One of the ways of understanding a Bible passage is to look at its setting. First of all, let's consider the general setting of this passage. It could only have been written in the country, not the town. It has a rural pastoral setting. In our urban society we are far from the setting of this passage, so we need to use our imagination. We get milk from cartons, not cows. We tend to forget the pastoral setting in which much of our life support is produced.

When you have been to Israel, you realize that even in the towns you are in a rural country. The hills and fields are all round you. It is a pastoral land. In fact, much of the Bible is written against this agricultural background. Many of the greatest leaders of God's people served their apprenticeship in shepherding sheep. For example, Moses and David: in looking after sheep, they learned how to look after people. People are like sheep. It is this shepherding background of country which helps us understand this passage.

But it is the shepherding background of the East not the West. I used to be a shepherd but my task was different from a Palestinian shepherd. My task was not dangerous except in the bad winter snow when there were risks on sheep's behalf. But generally, a shepherd's life in this country is not dangerous. Neither is it particularly difficult, although it requires skill. There is always grass here; you don't need to look for it. Generally, you don't need to go looking for water. It's comparatively easy to see that the sheep are well fed and watered.

Things are different in the Middle East, however. The shepherd has to be a fighter. It is a dangerous and difficult life. He has got to go by himself looking for some grass, and for some still water, because a sheep can't drink 'troubled', running water. Its nostrils are too near its nose. It gets water up its nose so a shepherd has to look for still water and green pasture, then he has to return and lead the sheep; a sheep can only walk so far and the shepherd has to know when to make them lie down and when to take them further.

There is also the particular setting of this passage. When John wrote his Gospel, he didn't divide it up into chapters. Doing that tends to split a passage from what goes before it but you can only understand this chapter in the light of the previous chapters. In chapter 8, we read of a black sheep they wanted to destroy: they wanted to stone the woman taken in adultery. She was a black sheep in Israel and the shepherds should have dealt with her better than they did. In chapter 9, they threw the blind sheep out of the fold because he could see. Both are examples of bad shepherding: the people who should have shepherded those sheep were bad.

It is against the background of the bad shepherds in those chapters that Jesus says, "I am the good shepherd." By implication they are the bad ones, who are no help to sheep in trouble or need. "I am the good shepherd."

PARABLE OF THE SHEEPFOLD (10:1-6)

This is the only real parable in John's Gospel. The other three Gospels, Matthew, Mark and Luke, are full of parables, lovely little stories. Why did Jesus tell parables? Just to get people's interest because the world loves a story? No, more than that. Was it to plant the truth in someone's mind before they resisted it? Possibly. If you tell a story, people will listen to the end of the story. Even though they might not get the point, you have planted the truth in their minds. Then when you point out the meaning of the story they cannot evade the truth, whereas if you face them immediately with the truth they might close their minds and stop listening. Telling a parable is a wonderful way to plant the truth before people realize that is what is happening. Did he do it that way for that reason?

Another possible reason is that a parable is a marvellous way to stab the conscience. You tell a story so that people become emotionally involved in it, and then ask, "Where do you come in this story?" Do you remember one prophet who went to King David and told a parable about a shepherd (2 Samuel 12:1-14)? The shepherd had a large flock, but he noticed another shepherd with a little ewe lamb. He wanted it so badly and this shepherd took that lamb and killed the other shepherd who had it, taking the lamb for himself. The prophet told David this story and David was furious. He got emotionally involved and asked, "Has that actually happened? Bring the man – we'll punish him." The prophet said, "David, you are the man! I've been telling you a story about yourself. You had everything you wanted except Bathsheba and you killed Uriah to get her. You sent him to his death so you could pinch his wife. I've told you the story to stab your conscience."

That's why Jesus used parables. They aren't just nice little children's stories. They are not just to generate interest or even to plant the truth before people realized what he was doing. Primarily, they are to stab their conscience, make them think about themselves and about him and repent. So he tells a parable from verses 1-6. It is only a parable, a short story about shepherding. It isn't personal. He talks about the shepherd as "He" and the sheepfold as "It."

Danger: the villain revealed

Here's a contrast between goodies and baddies. The goodies mean safety and the baddies mean danger. He deals with the baddies first. In the Middle East, they don't leave sheep out at night as that is dangerous. There are no fields or fences, so at night they bring the sheep back to an enclosed area, usually just a wall with a wooden gate. Many shepherds share one fold and they bring their flocks all inside the same fold and then go off for the night and leave it to the night watchman (the gatekeeper), who sits all night outside the gate. He won't let anybody in except one of the real shepherds. That is the scene.

Sometimes at night under the shadows you see a figure creeping round the back of the wall, coming over the side. He doesn't want to be seen. You can tell he is up to no good by how he approaches the sheep. A true shepherd comes straightforwardly and openly, in a way others can see, not ashamed or afraid. But a man who is after something for himself and who will be dangerous and cause damage to the sheep comes in a secretive roundabout way. He is a thief who has come to kill.

Getting live sheep out of a fold without the gatekeeper noticing isn't easy. It's easier to kill them and take the carcass, to take the meat or the wool. That is why they came to kill, destroy and plunder. The sheep would sense danger and they would run to the other side of the fold.

Safety: the voice recognized

In contrast to that, there is safety with the shepherd. In the morning, the shepherd wakes up and comes to the gate of the sheepfold. He is confronted with about 100 sheep, of which 25 may be his. How on earth is he going to sort them out?

I used to lead sheep to market and once got them mixed with another flock; it was a nightmare sorting them out! But the shepherd in the Middle East is not the slightest worried. I have seen two flocks of sheep mix on the road and the two shepherds, who were walking in opposite directions simply passed each other and walked on and called. One by one, the sheep just sorted themselves out and followed.

"The relationship between sheep and shepherd is a glorious picture of mutual trust, knowledge, care and love ... the real security of a flock lies in the relationship with their shepherd."

In the Middle East, a shepherd doesn't need a sheepdog. He has got a better relationship with the sheep than we have here. You live with the sheep for up to ten years because you keep them primarily for wool, not for meat. You have only up to 25 sheep to look after so you get to know them all as well as I knew my sheepdog. In the Middle East, the shepherd knows his sheep and simply calls them and they come. He gives them each a name, e.g. "Black ears," "Short legs". In the morning, he calls them and leads them out, leaving the safety of the walls of the fold. They are safe because the walls have been replaced by the man himself walking in front: he is their fold, wall, guardian and protector. He leads them out and finds pasture. In the heat of the midday sun, he leads them to a quiet, shady place and makes them lie down. He himself lies down with them, just as Jesus once said to his disciples, "Come with me and rest a while" (Mark 6:31).

When they come back at night, they face a crisis. The sun is going down and in the deep limestone cleft hills of Palestine they must go through the Valley of Deep Shadows to reach home.

Jackals, hyenas and wolves are lurking there – and in Bible days lions and bears – and the shepherd must be able to fight such animals with his cudgel, his rod. The sheep remain safe because the shepherd is there.

Notice the shepherd walks in front of the sheep. He leads them; he doesn't push or chase them. He leads them from in front and that is one of the keys to the relationship.

This is the picture. It is a glorious picture of mutual trust, knowledge, care and love. It's a relationship that is right. You can have the security of a structure or the security of a relationship: the fold is the security of a structure, but the shepherd is the security of a relationship. The real security of a flock lies in the relationship: a person rather than a thing.

.

PORTRAIT OF THE SHEPHERD (10:7-18)

Life: the flock saved

Jesus told this parable and they might have said, "Well, we know all that. We are not ignorant about shepherds. We have heard all that before. There is nothing interesting or striking there," and Jesus realized they had not understood why he told them a simple story. So he turned to being more personal, from the parable of the sheepfold to the portrait of the shepherd. Instead of talking of the sheepfold as "It," he now says, "I am the door." Instead of talking of the shepherd as "He," he now says, "I am the good shepherd." Once again there is a contrast, here between life and death: life for the sheep, but death for the shepherd. Jesus makes it clear this story is an allegory, a picture of the people around him.

He states that everybody who has tried to be a messiah before him is a thief and a robber, not a shepherd. Israel suffered greatly because there were high hopes of a messiah and many false messiahs. People came and said, "I'm the one you're looking for," and they tried to exploit the expectancy of the people, just as today people exploit the hopes and dreams of many ordinary people. Jesus says that none of them was a shepherd. "Many people have come to you and said, 'I'll lead you into freedom. I'll lead you into pasture. I'll give you what you're asking. I'll give you safety. I'll give you peace,' but they were thieves and robbers, after position, status and possessions."

"There is no other door to safety except through Jesus. There is no other door to salvation. 'I am the door for the sheep. The sheep will come in through me and be saved.'"

Before Jesus there was no door but now there is a door and, mixing his metaphors, he says, "I'm not only the door for the shepherd, I am also the door for the sheep. Sheep start outside my fold. They need to come into my fold and come in through me." There is no other way to heaven except through Jesus. He is the door. He is the way. There is no other door to safety except through Jesus. There is no other door to salvation. "I am the door. The sheep will come in through me and be saved."

Notice also that he says, "they will not only come in through me, they'll go out through me as well." It's too easy for us to come in through Christ to safety and forget he wants to lead (thrust) us out. You will find your pasture in the world. If you really want to feed and live, then don't just come into the church through Christ: go out into the world with Christ. Go in and out through Christ. "The thief comes to take your life away, to destroy. I came that you might live: have real, abundant, full life." You won't have full life if you stay within the church all the time. For full life, you need to be out in the world with Jesus. Abundant life. That is what he wants to give: a rich, full, free life, lived by coming in and going out through Jesus Christ.

Death: the Father satisfied

How far is the shepherd prepared to go to see that the sheep get this life? To the uttermost limit of sacrifice. It was not uncommon in the 20th century for shepherds in the Middle East to die looking after the sheep, e.g. fighting wild animals. H V Morton in *In The Steps of the Master* tells of one such incident while he was visiting the Holy Land: they found a shepherd torn to pieces. The sheep were safe but the shepherd was torn to pieces and lay dead in the hills. A shepherd was often in danger of his life. David fought with a lion and a bear: that's where he developed his skill with the sling, which was useful later with human enemies. But he developed it with wild animals.

Jesus said, "A good shepherd is willing to die." That's a strong statement. The word *good* here doesn't mean morally good; it means aesthetically good, attractive, beautiful. It is an intriguing adjective. Why is he beautiful? Why is he attractive? Why is he the good shepherd? Because he's willing to go to that length.

Now many shepherds in the Middle East are unwilling to go to that length and the reason is simple. You are only prepared to go that far if the sheep are yours. If they are somebody else's and you're in it for a job, primarily for the money you earn, then there comes a point beyond which you will not go in sacrifice. You may be a good shepherd so far but if you regard it simply as a job, from then on you won't be prepared to make any further sacrifices.

The hired servant stops at a certain point because he is more concerned with his own life than the sheep's life beyond that point. Likening the Pharisees to hired servants is a damning indictment of the Pharisees. Jesus is saying, "You'll care for people to a point but beyond that you're more concerned about yourself than them." It is a serious word for clergy and pastors if I think of this calling as simply a job and start thinking I can draw a line beyond which I am not prepared to sacrifice. But the good shepherd says, "I will make as great a sacrifice as the needs of the sheep demand. No line will be drawn. I will give whatever is required by a sheep even to the point of giving up my life."

Jesus then describes the good shepherd in terms of knowing the sheep and caring for them: a good shepherd knows the sheep and cares for the sheep. Good sheep know the shepherd. We are also told, "I know my Father and he knows me. I know my sheep; they know me." Knowledge is a two-way relationship. You can never have full knowledge if it is only one person knowing a lot about the other: it needs to be mutual. Shepherds have a duty to know the sheep. But sheep also have a duty to know the shepherds.

In thinking about his death, Jesus is thinking of all his sheep, not just a few of them. Talking to the Jewish sheep of the house of Israel, he says, "You're not the only sheep I'm going to die for. I look beyond this fold and see other sheep. I'm going to bring them and I'm going to join them to you." It is a clear reference to Gentiles, as most of us are. Thank God Jesus had other sheep to bring, or we would never be in the fold.

Here is the glorious truth: my future is bound up with the future of the Jews because there is going to be one flock, one shepherd. This is important. When you realize this, your attitude to the Jews changes. My future is bound up with them. There is only going to be one flock. I'm being brought into their flock by their shepherd because Jesus was born a Jew, still is a Jew and always will be a Jew.

So thank God that Gentiles have been brought in. Notice Jesus never says there would be one fold. One of mistakes in talking about unity is that people are anxious to create one fold, with its structures and organization. We've seen a lot of futile energy spent on trying to create one fold. Jesus puts the emphasis on the *relationship* not the *structures*. He says one *flock* (not fold) and one *shepherd*. It is the shepherd who will bring about one flock; people can only build bigger folds. It's the shepherd who draws the flock into one through himself.

Jesus makes one final point. The shepherd is willing to die: it is his voluntary choice. There must be no imposed pattern on the good shepherd. The good shepherd is willing to lay down his life: he does it entirely himself. He is saying, "I make this decision. I choose to die," and Jesus did. We sometimes talk about Jesus being put to death, but nobody could put Jesus to death. There were at least five different attempts to assassinate him during his lifetime. None of them succeeded because Jesus didn't let them, and he would never have been crucified unless he let them. "I choose to lay down my life."

"We have a shepherd [Jesus Christ] who has died and is alive for evermore. We have a shepherd who went to the absolute limit and who then came back to look after us."

A dead shepherd is of no use to the flock. Once the shepherd has died for the sheep in the Middle East, that is the end of that flock. It must be given to other shepherds. So it was necessary in Jesus' case, having laid down his life for the sheep, for God to give life back to the shepherd. It was necessary for him to be willing to take it up again. That is why Jesus said, "I'm the good shepherd. I lay down my life of my own free will. I have the right to lay it down. And I have the right to receive it back again and I will do," so we don't have a dead shepherd. We have a shepherd who has died and is alive for evermore. We have a shepherd who went to the absolute limit and who then came back to look after us.

In all this, what is Jesus doing? He is saying, "I want you to put your trust in me. If you put your trust in others to be your saviour they will disappoint you. In the world are thieves, wolves and hired servants. They vary in their qualities. A thief and a wolf are wholly bad. A hired servant is partly good. But the effect of hired servants is the same as the effect of thieves and wolves because if at the point when the shepherd is needed to sacrifice he runs away, then the effect is the same: the sheep die.

Whatever their varying qualities, thieves, wolves and hired servants are no use to the sheep. You must be on your guard against them. But Jesus says, "I am the good shepherd. Look to me. I know; I care. I die and the good shepherd rises again and returns."

21

WHO IS JESUS?
John 10:19-42

JERUSALEM: BEWILDERED CITY (10:19-39)

     Maniac: division
     Messiah: doubt
     Man: distortion

JORDAN: BELIEVING COUNTRY (10:40-42)

     Bearer: sin
     Baptizer: Spirit
     Bridegroom: Son

There is no point studying the Bible unless you are looking for a person. Otherwise, it is only words, because the most important question about Jesus is not what he did, or what he said, but who he was. As we read John's Gospel we face this question again and again, as people did in the days of his flesh. Who is Jesus?

JERUSALEM: BEWILDERED CITY (10:19-39)

Maniac: division

We're looking at one occasion when the debate raged as to who he was. The result of him claiming to be the good shepherd was that people said he was mad or demented. *Demented* takes us further than mental insanity, because it includes the word *demon*. A demented person is someone (they thought) mentally insane because demons had made them so. "The demons must have turned his intellect." Why would they say that? First, he talked about laying down his life – that could be considered a sign of imbalance. Second, he had this delusion that if he lay down his life he could pick it up again. Only a demented person talks about that, of throwing their life away and then picking it up again as easily as that.

"You could never get a whole group of people to agree that Jesus was mad, because you can't ignore one simple fact: crazy demented people don't go round helping people with problems. They are destructive. So when people said, 'He's demented,' others said, 'How could a crazy man help a blind man see? Crazy people don't behave like that.'"

Or thirdly, maybe they said he was demented because of what he said about them. They responded to criticism by saying he was demented. Maybe they said he was demented because they did not like being called a wolf, thief, robber, or hired hand. If you don't like somebody's arguments you can always say the person making them is crazy as a defence.

Whatever reason they said it, it is interesting that they could never get a unanimous opinion that Jesus was mad. Many people (including even his own brothers and sisters) thought he was crazy. A time came when they said they had come to lock him up, restrain him and take him home for his own good.

But you could never get a whole group of people to agree on this, because you can't ignore one simple fact: crazy demented people don't go round helping people with problems. They are destructive. So when people said, "He's demented," others said, "How could a crazy man help a blind man see? Crazy people don't behave like that."

Messiah: doubt

Between verses 21 and 22 some months have elapsed. It is now December in AD 29. It's not the Christian Christmas, but the pagan festival we call Christmas, which started long before Jesus came. It is the festival of lights, in which you illuminate your houses with little lights. This happened before Jesus came: it is not connected with Jesus but with the winter solstice. Throughout the world for a very long time people have had a festival of lights at the end of December. The Jews did, and they called it the feast of lights.

To the Jews it meant more than simply the pagan festival of the returning sun. As well as celebrating the return of spring, they called it the Feast of Dedication and their minds went back 165 years to a great moment in their history. They had been occupied by the Greek armies and the evil Antiochus Epiphanes had deliberately defiled their temple, making it no longer a clean place to worship. For three years they laboured under this dreadful invasion from the Greek armies. Then the Maccabean family fought against this invader and won. Judas Maccabees in December 165 BC went back into the temple and cleansed the altar, restoring the worship of God. They found one bottle of oil intact and used it to light the lamp again.

However, it wasn't long before the Romans followed the

Greeks. The Roman occupation was in full swing by the time of John 10. The people had a frustrated hope; they longed for someone to do for them what Judas Maccabeus had done. They looked for someone greater than Judas Maccabeus who had set them free not just for a few years but for the rest of time. All this hope centred on one human figure: a messiah.

As they remembered how Judas Maccabeus set them free and cleansed the temple at the Feast of Dedication, Jesus came to the temple. It was winter; it was probably raining as we see Jesus walked in the covered porch. They came to him, saying, "Tell us plainly. We want to know once and for all. We are fed up with these parables and hints. Are you the Messiah, the one we're waiting for?"

It was a direct question but it did not receive a direct answer, because it was the Feast of Dedication, when political nationalistic hopes were riding high. If Jesus had said, "Yes, I am," it would have been true and it would have been tragedy. He would have immediately been hailed as a political rebel and a leader to free them from the Romans. Jesus came to free them from sin; it's the one thing they could not seem to grasp. They wanted to be free from evil in other people. This is the besetting temptation of human thought. But God was saying, "It's you to blame." You only begin to realize the world could be put right when you begin to realize you are wrong and that you need putting right. So Jesus would not answer them directly. However, he said, "I have told you the answer time and time again, but you wouldn't listen. You ask me for plain speaking. The fault is not in my speaking, it's in your listening." That's a profound truth. If you have difficulty understanding the word of God it may not be because God is speaking in an obscure and puzzling way. It may be that you're not listening properly.

Jesus said, "My miracles are enough proof. You ask me plainly am I the Messiah; what more evidence can I give you? I've told you often enough and if you looked at my miracles you'd know. But you will never believe." He's saying: "When I talk to you and do miracles among you, there's no response, because there is no relationship." It seems puzzling to many young Christians as to why, when you tell people about Jesus, you might as well be talking to a brick wall. You can give them all the evidence there is – and there is a lot – and you are talking to a wall. The answer is there is no response because there is no relationship. In other words, people who are not interested in relating to Jesus as a person will make no response, no matter how much you talk to them, no matter how much evidence you give them. So Jesus says, "I've talked to you, I've given you miracles as proof but you're not my sheep. You recognize no relationship. This relationship must be two-way."

Notice Jesus describes this relationship in terms from both sides. He alternates between *they* and *I*: "They listen; I know them; they follow; I give them eternal life. They will never die; no one will snatch them out of my hand." It's a lovely, interwoven, interlocking relationship. Where there is that relationship, I guarantee that as soon as God talks, you hear and understand. You know who Jesus is. You hear a voice and recognize that voice as the shepherd's.

"Sheep do three things. They listen – the relationship begins by listening. They follow: they are not just hearers but doers of the word. And it is a relationship that can last for ever because Jesus will never die, neither need his sheep. So when you have got a relationship with Jesus, when you have listened to him, when you have followed him you have started something that need never end."

Here are three things that sheep do. They listen – the relationship begins by listening. They follow: they are not just hearers but doers of the word. And it is a relationship that can last for ever because Jesus will never die, neither need his sheep. So when you have got a relationship with Jesus, when you have listened to him, when you have followed him you have started something that need never end. That is our side of the relationship.

Now look at his side, "I know my sheep." He knows every single one. He gives to his sheep. Abiding in him they can find eternal life. He says: "No one will ever snatch them out of my hand." You can be a sheep that does silly things and wanders away but there is a shepherd who goes on looking for you. I have known Christians who have gone away from the Lord and been away for some years, maybe many years, and are drawn back to him. Maybe the sound of a hymn coming out of a church door; maybe a sunset, maybe a memory of their first altar in life, their mother's knee; maybe a chance meeting with an old Christian friend; but somehow, somewhere the shepherd pulls them back, though they are ashamed of the years that have been wasted.

Tom Rees tells in one of his books of a boys' camp that he was speaking at before the war. One lad from East London asked him, "Mr Rees, I'd like to be a Christian, but where I come from you couldn't keep it up. If you knew my home and where I have to live, you'd know, it's too tough to be a Christian." Tom Rees told him, "Put out your hands." Tom Rees got hold of this lad's thin wrists, gripped and said, "Now you get away from me if you can." He struggled and pulled but he couldn't. Now Tom said, "You hold my wrists." Those little hands got hold of Tom who was well built and Tom easily broke the grip. Tom then asked, "Why do you think the hold didn't break the first time but did the second?" The lad replied, "That's easy, the first time you were holding me, the second time I was holding you." Do you get the point? The devil isn't tough enough; the people you work with who ridicule you aren't tough enough. There is somebody holding on to you. It's isn't "I can't keep it up; I could never face up to the demands."

We must realize the statement "My Father and I are one" is deliberately ambiguous. It doesn't mean – and Jesus didn't say what the Jews thought he said and tried to stone him for – "I and the Father are one person." He said, "I and the Father": two persons. He then used a plural verb: "I and the Father are one." The word *one* in the Greek is not a masculine word but a neuter word, meaning not one person but one function, doing one thing together. It comes when Paul says in 1 Corinthians 3:8 "he that plants and he that waters are one." He's not making a profound philosophical statement, he is simply saying, "My sheep will never get lost, because I hold onto them and my Father holds on to them and I and my Father are working together. We are one team."

Man: distortion

Unfortunately, the Jews misunderstood this, and soon Jesus was in danger of his life. The temple was still being built: blocks of stones were scattered around the floor. They ran and picked up these stones to put him to death. They quoted their own law, Leviticus 24:16, which said that anyone who blasphemes the name of the Lord must be stoned to death. They jumped to an awful conclusion: "Jesus, you deserve death by stoning." Here is a critical moment: Jesus knew he must not die for another three months, but he was within an inch of losing his life. Skilfully he plays for time; he could have called ten thousand angels to come and wipe them out but he prefers to deal with it at a human level.

He uses no resources but words. As they lifted the stones to throw, he asked, "What have I done to deserve this? What evil deed do you charge me with? Of all the things I've done in Jerusalem which of them deserves death?" It got them talking and made them think. They replied, "It's not for what you've done; it's for what you say. You call yourself God and you're just a man. You're trying to make yourself someone you're not."

Jesus dealt with this most unusually, in a way that has caused many questions. He said, "It is written in your own law that God said you are gods." He's saying you can't object to me being called God when in your own Bible people are called gods and you accept it and make no objection." He quotes from Psalm 82, concerning the judges in court in Israel. God is speaking to these judges, warning them about false judgments and says, "You are gods." What does he mean? He means that a judge sitting at the bench with the power of a man's life or death in his hands is the representative of divine justice. He is god to that man in the dock, because only God has the right to decide if a man lives or dies. He literally has the power of God over his life and can take it or leave it.

Jesus lays down a simple principle that if a person on earth who has been appointed by God to do a particular job does it as God has directed him, then he becomes god for the people. It doesn't mean he is God as a person. He is acting as god and a judge in a court has to act as god. If God appoints his representative as a judge, that man is not God as a person, but is God's representative and must do the will of God in that situation.

Jesus said, "You never objected when your judges are called gods. Why do you object in my case, since God chose me and sent me and I am simply doing his works? You have no right to say that's blasphemy. Even if I'm just a human being, if I'm doing the Father's works, then according to your own principles and Scriptures, you can call me God. I'm his representative, doing his works." It's a human argument; Jesus is talking to unbelievers; he will not therefore talk as he does to his sheep.

He succeeded: they dropped their stones and decided simply to try and arrest him pending further trial and examination. The crisis was averted. And Jesus slipped away in the crowd during their consternation. But they were all wrong. He wasn't a maniac, he was the Messiah and he was more than man. But they did not believe.

We still find people who believe Jesus was mad, people who wonder whether he was simply a political figure, the first revolutionary, the first dropout hippy leader, and those who wonder whether he was simply a man and no more. They are all wrong. He was not mad, he was the Messiah and he was much more than man.

JORDAN: BELIEVING COUNTRY (10:40-42)

As we look at these last few verses, it is like leaving the city with its priestly leaders, and going out into the fresh air fifteen miles down through the hills, below sea level, right down 1600 feet to the little river where it all began. It's moving back to where it all began. Jesus went back to the place where, three years before, he had gone into a muddy river, where God had said, "You are my beloved Son." Three years had passed, he had been wandering north and south, preaching, teaching, healing, and now the big question was "Who is he?"

The people in the country were simpler than the people in the city. The best place to find sheep is in the country, and Jesus found many sheep there. He came to the country where John the Baptist had been such a power for good. So they look over three years, and the people living there remembered John's ministry over the three years of Jesus in history. They then gave a lovely tribute to John. "He did no miracle but everything he said about Jesus was true." What a glorious epitaph for a servant of God! You don't need to do miracles to be a great person. All you need do is talk about Jesus truthfully, as John did. John did no miracles, no lame man walked because of John, no blind man saw because of John, no deaf heard because of John. He never walked on the water, stilled a storm or fed a multitude from a few loaves and fishes. But Jesus said, "My cousin John is the greatest man who ever lived." Why? Because John said "I'm just a voice. I'm talking to you about Jesus." That's all God wants. He may choose you to do miracles and give you supernatural powers but what he wants from everybody is what he got from John, a voice who says, "Look at him, think about him."

Let me finish by reminding you of the three things John said about Jesus. None of them had come true by this time; they all were still to be fulfilled.

Bearer: sin

First, Jesus is the bearer of sin. John the Baptist said, "I can deal with your past; I can wash away the past, I can remove the guilt, be baptized. But Jesus will take the future sin away. He will take it right away." It's one thing to leave people to repent, it is another thing to remove their sin. God has removed our sins from us as far as the east is from the west. Jesus has taken them away. John said, "I call you to repent. Look, the lamb of God who bears the sin of the world."

Baptizer: Spirit

John said, "I baptize you in water: that is an emptying, an external washing, water outside you. But somebody is coming after me who is another kind of Baptist. He baptizes in the Holy Spirit and fills you with living water inside." What a difference in ministry. John said, "I tell you to empty your life, but he will fill it. I talk to you about this water of the Jordan River; he gives you living water."

Bridegroom: Son

The third thing John said about Jesus was "He is the bridegroom, because he is the Son." The best man is only temporarily on the scene, and then his job is done. His job is to do all the things so that the bride and the groom go away happily. So John the best man pointed to Jesus and said: "I'm just a servant; he is the Son of God. He's the bridegroom, the One coming for you. Your lasting and loving relationship is with him, not with me."

John said these three lovely things that are still true about Jesus. Jesus can do for you what John cannot do, and what I cannot do, what no man can ever do. Jesus is your bearer, to take away your sins. Jesus is your baptizer to fill you with his Holy Spirit. Jesus is your bridegroom coming for you to consummate the relationship for ever in glory. Everything John said was true. And many there believed (v. 42).

There is a line running through the world. On one side of the line are those who will not believe, even if they see miracles. On the other side are those who have believed even if they have not seen miracles. In Jerusalem, the sophisticated city, people kept saying, "Tell us plainly. Give us proof," and Jesus said, "I've given you all the proof you could ask for. But you don't believe, you don't believe what you hear; you don't believe what you see." But he went to the Jordan River where it all began, there many believed. John did no miracle, but everything he said about this man is true. That's faith.

This is what separates the sheep from the goats finally. The sheep are those who hear and who follow and who never die. And the goats are those who have no shepherd, who don't follow and won't believe, and die for ever.

22

"I AM THE RESURRECTION AND THE LIFE"
John 11:1-44

SUFFERING OF DISEASE (11:1-16)

Family: hope delayed
Followers: hope dashed

THE SORROW OF DEATH (11:17-37)

Martha: faith strengthened
Mary: feeling shared

SQUALOR OF DECAY (11:38-44)

Cave: people afraid
Corpse: prayer answered

The acid test of someone's religion is how much help will it give when the time comes to die. Job cried out, "If a man dies, shall he live again?" (Job 14:14): not will his memory live on, will his children survive, will his influence live on, will his books be read, but will he as a person live again? That is the big question before us. Does death have the last word?

This story is packed with emotion: fear, sorrow, joy, excitement. It is the last great miracle in John's Gospel, the seventh of seven miracles. The first miracle, like the last, began in a domestic situation: the first began at a wedding; this at a funeral. But both were designed to meet the needs of a family.

Jesus did not own a home on earth, but there were a few homes where he was welcome and where he loved to go. One of those was lived in by two sisters and one brother: Martha, Mary and Lazarus. No one was more welcome there than Jesus. It was two miles from Jerusalem, within easy reach to slip into the city but quiet enough to leave the city at night. It was just over the brow of the Mount of Olives, east towards Jericho.

Mary and Martha seem to be prominent in this household but Lazarus is there and he is loved. He is part of the scene and Jesus loved him as he loved the two. Into this home came disease, death and decay – and Jesus.

Suffering of disease (11:1-16)

There are two naive ideas which we must deal with first concerning suffering. First, the idea that only bad people fall sick, that a godly person will not be sick. It was the view of Eliphaz, Bildad and Zophar, "Job's comforters." They told Job (who was a godly man whom God allowed to suffer sickness), "You can't be really godly or you wouldn't be sick." But this is too naive; it doesn't fit the facts or our experience of life.

The other idea is that as soon as a person believes sufficiently, Jesus will heal their sickness. That is another idea that does not fit the facts and it does not fit this story. Martha and Mary were sure Jesus would heal if he had been there and could do something about it. Deliberately, however, Jesus leaves a man in sickness, the family in anxiety and despair, and then pain, fever and sleeplessness pass into death. He deliberately let it continue.

I have said both those things because I am the first to say I believe Jesus can heal. But I do not want us to swing from the church's neglect of the healing ministry to this naive teaching which causes much mental and spiritual pain, that only ungodly people are sick and that if only they have enough faith they would be healed immediately. Jesus can deal with every physical affliction, not just disease, but also death and not just death but the decay that follows death. No physical condition is beyond Jesus' power. But it is within Jesus' will to use these things and to use the curer of these things for God's glory. The health and happiness of human beings is not Christ's first concern. His first concern in any situation is what action will bring glory to the Father and help his children develop their faith.

Family: hope delayed

When the family sent the urgent message, "Your dear friend is ill," they sent it simply as information. They didn't say, "You must come." They said, "Your dear friend is sick." They left it to him to decide what to do. Why did they tell him? Because he was a close friend, but also because he was the best doctor, since he could cure every disease. No other doctor has ever been able to claim that. No wonder they sent for him; wouldn't you?

But Jesus delayed two days and it would take him another few days to get there if he went. This is extraordinary. Here is Jesus who is told one of his dearest friends is sick, and instead of immediately going to relieve the pain and the anxiety with his godly power, he deliberately stayed where he was. Furthermore, we know that Jesus had the power to heal at a distance: that's what happened to Jairus' daughter. He would only need to say the word, without even going, and he could have healed Lazarus and raised him from that bed. But he didn't. I believe there are times today when Jesus does not heal straightaway. The delay was deliberate. Why? Some things in life are even more important than physical health. What is more important? That what happens should bring glory to God; that is the fundamental purpose of our existence.

He had a higher aim and also had a longer view. He said, "Let's think of what this is all going to lead to ultimately." That's important: not that I should think what will immediately make me comfortable or happier, but what is it all going to lead to? What is the outcome? He says, "The final outcome will not be death, but life. I'm delaying so that God may be glorified and his Son receive glory too." That is the purpose of your life – sick or well; healed or not healed: to glorify God and his Son. That is big enough to encompass every experience of life, welcome or unwelcome experiences.

Followers: hope dashed

I am sure the disciples were relieved, because if Jesus had gone to Jerusalem it would have been like a man putting his head into a wild lion's mouth. The situation in Jerusalem was such that if Jesus had stepped back into the city it would have been his last visit. He had only three months to live; it was dangerous to go near the city and the disciples were relieved. They were shattered when a few days later Jesus said, "Let's go to Judea." They replied, "Lord, do you realize what you're doing? Do you realize your life and ministry could come to a premature end?" Jesus answered rather enigmatically: "Are there not twelve hours in the day?" In other words, "The day of my life is decided by God and it will run through to the end of the day to my sunset." Jesus had such faith and said, "If I go to Jerusalem, if it's not the end of my day, it won't come to death. But if I've reached my twelve hours, if my sunset has come, then that's all right."

Jesus said, "Not only is the day going to be long enough but it will only be long enough if you walk in the daylight. If you're walking in the darkness then this doesn't work. But if you're doing what God wants, then your day will have twelve hours." That's its condition. Walk in God's light. Let him guide you, and you won't stumble. You will walk to your sunset. You won't fall before you get there.

So he said, "Let's go to Judea. I'm walking in the daylight of God's love. He's shown me to do this and if I go, it will be all right,

I won't die before my sunset. We've got to go because Lazarus has fallen asleep." They thought he had a fever, probably typhoid or something similar that sleep would heal and soothe, so "You don't need to go now, he's getting better, he's fallen into a lovely healing sleep, the crisis was over and he was resting." But Jesus said, "No, I mean he's dead." Why did Jesus say "fallen asleep"? Was he speaking euphemistically about death, as we say "passed away" or "passed on"? No; he wasn't evading the fact. I have noticed that Christians freely use the word *died* and then add something like "gone to be with the Lord" or "gone to glory." They are not evading the fact of death. What was he saying? He was saying, "Death to me is like someone asleep because it's someone you can go and wake up." "Fallen asleep" is a lovely phrase because it implies you can shake them awake. So Jesus used this phrase, as did the early Christians, e.g. in 1 Thessalonians.

Jesus said, "Lazarus is dead; we've got to go." Thomas, the pessimist, added, "If he's determined to add one corpse to another, we'll add ours too: let's have a big funeral! Let's all go and die with him if he's determined to play the fool." There is a kind of dogged loyalty in pessimists like Thomas. They look on the black side but they will be with you till the last ditch. And so they went.

The sorrow of death (11:17-37)

The two sisters then met Jesus. Each has the same words on their lips but there the similarity ends. Each said, "Lord, if you'd been here, he wouldn't have died," but then Martha and Mary are different. They represent two reactions to bereavement: those who talk a lot and those who say nothing but weep; those who think about it and those who feel it; those who are confused in their mind about what has happened and those who are overwhelmed in their heart. I praise Jesus for his sensitivity to deal with them differently. He talks a lot to Martha; he doesn't say anything to Mary, he just weeps.

Martha: faith strengthened

Martha was confused in her mind and full of questions and doubts. She was practical. "Lord, if you'd been here ...," showing Martha has the stronger faith, "he wouldn't have died. But even now, I know you've only got to ask God..." What does she mean by "even now"? What could he ask of God for the family? "I know you're not helpless, you could obtain something from God, your Father, for us, even now." When Jesus sees she has a faith to be developed, he draws it out, challenges her, presses her, saying "Do you really believe this? Let's see what you really mean."

Jesus said, "I'm going to ask my Father to raise your brother from the dead: what's your reaction to that, Martha?" Martha replied, "I've heard all this from our preacher, that we're all going to be raised up at the last day. I know of something in the future, but Jesus, I expected more from you. I expected you to be able to do more than give me the conventional condolences. I know there's this promise of future life but I've got to live now; can you do anything for me now?"

"Jesus said, 'I am the resurrection. Not only can I raise a person from the dead but I am also the life they live afterwards. Not only can I raise a man from the dead, I can also give him life. Do you believe that a person who lives and believes in me will never die? Do you really believe that?'"

Jesus answered Martha, "Who do you think is going to raise up the dead at the last day? I am the resurrection. Not only can I raise a person from the dead but I am also the life they live afterwards. I am the resurrection and the life, the resurrection, an event in a moment; the life a continuing experience. I am both. Not only can I raise a man from the dead, I can also give him life. It isn't just I raise him from the dead and give him life: *I am* the resurrection, so if he believes in me, if he's related to me, he rises and lives. Do you believe this? Do you believe that even though a man dies yet shall he live? Do you believe that a person who lives and believes in me will never die? You've heard it preached; do you really believe it?"

Martha expressed the fullest and most wonderful statement of faith yet given: "I believe you are the Messiah, the Son of God, the One coming into the world." What tremendous faith Martha has.

Mary: feeling shared

Realizing Martha had the faith, Jesus said, "Go and bring Mary. Go and tell your sister." She did. Mary came but was overwhelmed, blurting out, "Lord, if you'd been here, my brother wouldn't have died." Maybe she picked that up from Martha, and then she just cracked up. She couldn't say anything more. Jesus said nothing too: it's better not to. But here we have a description of Jesus' emotions which at least tells us Jesus was a real human being.

Two emotions are spoken of in Jesus. The first is very unusual. Literally the Greek says, "he snorted like a horse." It's a word translated in v. 33 as "deeply moved", which implies great anger. He didn't weep at first: he was indignant and disgusted. It's a strange emotion but let us think why he is like this. The Son of God is angry, because this kind of scene need never have existed. He is angry with the devil for introducing death into the world. He is furious that family life should be broken up in this way. This is his first reaction, as he sees its unhappiness. He is deeply moved with indignation and disgust.

We look forward to a day when God recreates the whole universe as it was intended. In that new heaven and new earth, "God will wipe away all tears from their eyes. No more pain or sorrow" (Revelation 21:4). Jesus was angry that it was happening, not with the people but with the devil himself for ever doing it. God never intended any of his good earth to be used as a cemetery, and so his first reaction was that he shuddered.

His second reaction of weeping came later. They walked to the cemetery; they buried corpses in caves and put a great stone over the entrance. When Jesus reached there, he sobbed. Why? Some have said he wept out of sympathy for Mary and the others.

But if that was the reason, he should have wept in the house: it's a bit late for this to happen. The second reason given is that it was sympathy for himself at losing Lazarus. That's how the Jews interpreted it: "See how he loved him." It's the weeping of sympathy with himself.

The third reason is I wonder if he wept out of sympathy for Lazarus. We look at it from a human point of view. We think it must be lovely to call someone back from the grave into their family's circle, that it must be good to complete what has been broken. We want this to happen at every funeral. But let's consider it from the point of view of the Son of God. He is going to call back a person into this world to die again. He is going to call back a person into this world of sin, sickness and suffering. Lazarus is a man of God – his name means "lover of God," and Lazarus certainly loved God. He's safely out of that now. Jesus has got to bring him back into it, so I think he's weeping for Lazarus. It is terrible to bring someone back into this world.

We know from the rest of the chapter that in bringing Lazarus back, he was signing his death warrant because 12:10 says that Jesus' enemies decided to kill Lazarus also, because he was the greatest exhibit of the Lord's power. Jesus saw all this, and yet God had told him to do this. He wept because he had to bring a man back to life, put him back into the earth, to go through it all again, to die again. Jesus wept.

SQUALOR OF DECAY (11:38-44)

Cave: people afraid

Jesus now came to the tomb. One of the sad things we have to face is our bodies will one day be a stinking, rotten mess. That is the end of human life: we will decay and smell. But Jesus has the last word, not just over disease and death, but also decay. "Change and decay in all around I see – / O thou who changest not abide with me" (Henry Francis Lyte). Here we see Jesus facing decay, but he has changed the whole picture.

"Take away the stone" is Jesus' ringing command; he could have called an angel to roll away the stone. An angel would roll his own away a few weeks later. He could have pushed it himself; he could even have told the stone to roll itself away. But Jesus was constantly calling people to cooperate and he said, "You take part in this with me. You do what you can, you roll the stone away," as he told a man to take up his bed and walk and a blind man to go and wash in a pool.

At this point Martha's faith failed. Marvellous though it was as a creed, when it came to the crunch she couldn't believe. Isn't that like many of us? We believe God can do anything, but when it comes to a particular situation that we have to believe, all our common sense, logic and past experience swamp our faith and we can't believe. She said, "Lord do you realize what you're doing?" Jesus replied, "Whose word are we going to take: yours or mine? Did I not tell you that you would see God's glory if you believed? All right, whose word, yours or mine?" They took away the stone: Jesus' word, not Mary's.

Corpse: prayer answered

Now Jesus spoke to two other people. A God in heaven and a man in Hades. The voice of Jesus can penetrate the whole universe. First, his voice reaches heaven. Jesus prayed standing with his face uplifted and his eyes opened. (There's nothing in the Bible about kneeling, putting your hands together and shutting your eyes.) Jesus looked up to heaven, saying, "Father, thank you that you've heard my prayer," which means he'd already uttered it before and that he was thanking God for the answer before it came. This is living prayer. Even while he was talking to Mary and Martha, he had already been praying.

"Now," he said, "Father, I want these people here to know that you heard me. I'm speaking aloud for their sakes. It's you, Father, that's doing this, isn't it? You've heard my prayer." Jesus' aim was twofold: God's glory and people's faith. He was concerned that God should be glorified and that people should believe. So he does everything he can to glorify his Father and help people to believe.

And now, "Lazarus, come out!" Jesus' voice went not only to a corpse, it also went down into the world of departed spirits and called a spirit back into a body; he reunited the two. I can't imagine what happened next. As they peered into that dark, gloomy entrance, they would first of all have seen a movement. Then they would have seen a bandaged figure with blinking eyes in the light, clambering out of that opening. What a dreadful, frightening, wonderful moment!

They recognized the eyes; the rest was all bandaged up. Lazarus stood there. They never thought they would see him again. And Jesus said, "Untie him. Let him go home." That brings out the full flavour of what he said: "Don't treat him as an exhibit, don't exhaust him with questions. Don't make him a seven-day wonder, just let him go." How thoughtful. Lazarus became the talking point of Jerusalem; you can imagine today all the TV cameras would be there, with reporters queuing outside the little house in Bethany. Because Jesus had said, "Let him go," even if one rises from the dead, people will still not believe what he says. And they wouldn't. It would simply be a nine days' wonder and then people would start explaining away how it happened.

Did Lazarus tell them what it was like to die, what was beyond death? We don't know. The Bible always discourages communication with the dead. It says, "Put your trust in Jesus. He is the resurrection and the life. Don't try and find out from anyone else." When Paul visited heaven and returned to earth he said, "I saw things that can't be uttered, don't ask me. I can't speak about these things," and we haven't a word from Lazarus. So my first conclusion is that it's sufficient to know that Jesus is the resurrection and the life. We don't need to try to find out more; that is enough.

"When I get to glory and enjoy life for evermore, it will be because of Jesus' death. He died ... that I might live. What a cost! Jesus knew that in God's purposes eternal life would have to be paid for by his own death."

My final thought is to ask, "What were Jesus' feelings as he stood at the empty tomb with the stone rolled away?" Here I am guessing. As he looked into that empty tomb I wonder if he thought that a few weeks later they would be putting him in a tomb like that and rolling a stone over him, because of what he had done just then.

The truth is that when Jesus brought Lazarus back to life, he sealed his own death. This event finally caused the Jews to make definite plans about Jesus' assassination. Jesus only gave Lazarus life at the cost of his own. He had come to Jerusalem and raised Lazarus, which was the last straw. The Jews now said, "The whole world will go after him. We've got to kill him" (12:10, 19). They made their plans but here is the most glorious truth. When I get to glory and enjoy life for evermore, it will be because of Jesus' death. He died ... that I might live. What a cost! Jesus knew that in God's purposes eternal life would have to be paid for by his own death.

23

DO YOU KNOW WHAT YOU ARE SAYING?
John 11:45-12:19

JESUS' DEATH PREDICTED
— BY A PRIEST
(11:45-57)

JESUS' BURIAL PREPARED
— WITH A PERFUME
(12:1-11)

JESUS' RESURRECTION PREFIGURED
— BY A PROCESSION
(12:12-19)

Someone has said that the gospel story is like an express train slowing up at a station. You dash through the years of the first part of the story and then slow up a bit and look at the months. Then you slow up further and look at the weeks, then even more, you look at the days, then the hours and finally you come to a halt at the cross. If that is a good picture, then there is no doubt as to when the brakes were applied: the raising of Lazarus was the crisis of Jesus' ministry.

Repercussions of this one miracle led to the final plot to assassinate Jesus Christ, and so Lazarus is often mentioned throughout this passage. The council meets to plot Jesus' death and they discuss Lazarus. There is a supper at Bethany and crowds come to see Lazarus. The high priests decide to kill Lazarus too. Then we have the triumphal entry into Jerusalem but John tells us the crowd was large because of Lazarus. Lazarus was the key figure in what happened the week before Jesus died. It is tragic that such a lovely act should produce such terrible consequences. But we are going to see that unredeemed human nature can take the loveliest acts and spoil them; even such a lovely act as Mary's anointing of our Lord is ruined by greedy Judas.

This passage is an in-between passage. At first sight it may be familiar: three themes, one in a courtroom, one in a dining room and one on the Mount of Olives. As we look at these three scenes leading up to the climax, we see that in the first our Lord's death is mentioned (11:50), in the second our Lord's burial is mentioned (12:7) and in the third our Lord's resurrection is mentioned (12:16). The shadow of these three major events is already casting itself before they take place. This is the theme of the gospel: "When I came to you, the fundamental things I preached were Christ died, was buried and was raised" (1 Corinthians 15:3-4). These are the three dimensions of a full gospel: *Jesus dead, buried, raised*.

JESUS' DEATH PREDICTED — BY A PRIEST (11:45-57)

The first event is in the courtroom. As usual a miracle had a double effect: many believed, but others did not. The high priests did not believe in the resurrection, and it was a real embarrassment to them that Lazarus was walking around. Their theology and the facts didn't fit. Which was going to give way? The facts. So they plotted to kill him. It is embarrassing to preach there is no resurrection when there is a man walking round who has been dead four days. They are so blind that they say, "The facts must be wrong; our theology must be right. Our views must be right whatever happens." That's the kind of perverse, stubborn outlook we can adopt. All the evidence stands before us, but we still say, "I don't believe it." So they were divided by this miracle. Some believed, some didn't.

Some were afraid. What were they afraid of? In the time of soviet communism there were tensions among Christians. The problem was that the communist states recognized the churches registered with them. Certain limitations were imposed on their activities. Some Christians felt that for the sake of peace, spreading the gospel and keeping the church alive, the right course was to register, to be acknowledged and to work within the limitations allowed. On the other hand there was the underground church that recognized no limits, would not compromise with the authorities, and would do everything they felt they should, and they suffered the consequences. And in some countries they do today.

A tension arises between these two groups: you can understand why. Those who have officially cooperated to some degree with the "occupying power" and have accepted limits for the sake of survival and those who say no limits, no compromise, no agreement: "We will go ahead even if it means wiping us out all together." Now Caiaphas was in precisely this position. He had come to a compromise agreement with the Romans that provided there was no civil disturbance and no underground movement in Judea, he could be the high priest, the temple could stay and Israel could keep its nationality. But at the first hint of trouble, the nationality would be removed, the temple would be removed, Caiaphas would be removed. He had accepted the compromise for the sake of survival. That was his position.

The fear that comes is that Jesus is going to lead a rebellion, an underground movement that is not going to accept the Roman limitations. They fear Rome will do what it did ruthlessly and mercilessly to many other satellite countries. As soon as there was a hint of trouble, the Roman legions moved in and did what Communists did in Hungary (1956) and Czechoslovakia (1968). Now Caiaphas could have argued logically that he was in the right position; he had been allowed this position by the Roman authorities. But he was faced with this problem, that the temple could close, the nation of Israel could be obliterated, the Roman forces could march in powerfully and take over the entire responsibility for governing the land. I am not trying to paint Caiaphas as a person to be pitied; I'm simply putting you in the picture: what would you have done?

It is so easy for us to condemn all those who were against Jesus in the last week. I am saying to you they – and we – were involved. The decisions we make today are the same decisions they made then. They were not ogres; they were ordinary people, caught in the cleft stick of a dilemma forced on them by political circumstances.

"Caiaphas said, 'It is expedient that one man should die rather than a lot of people.' Glory to God: that is the gospel! That's the meaning of Christ's death and Caiaphas was the first one to tell us what the cross would do, apart from our Lord himself. Isn't that amazing? His death is already predicted here."

Caiaphas was caught in this cleft stick and he said something that goes down in history as a ruthless statement, devoid of principle, a pure political expedient. He said, "Looking at the situation, we're in for a bloodbath. It's better that one man should shed his blood rather than all the people." Politically, he could have been right. But we know that Caiaphas was a scheming manipulator, a calculating politician who would not be troubled that the life of an innocent man was the cost of maintaining political peace in his country.

But here comes something wonderful. When Caiaphas said that, God was speaking through him. God can speak through anyone; he can speak through a donkey. God can speak through someone who doesn't intend to be God's spokesman. Caiaphas was speaking purely as a politician, but God can use a politician's mouth even if the politician doesn't realize it. Caiaphas said, "It is expedient that one man should die for the people, that one man should be sacrificed for the sake of peace." The Bible tells us that's exactly how God was thinking at that moment. Isn't that amazing?

You can say something and you don't realize what you're saying. Caiaphas didn't. He was high priest and therefore God's representative, so God could use him. A bad man said a good thing. Caiaphas said, "It is expedient that one man should die rather than a lot of people." Glory to God: that is the gospel! That's the meaning of Christ's death and Caiaphas was the first one to tell us what the cross would do, apart from our Lord himself. Isn't that amazing? His death is already predicted here.

Unfortunately, Caiaphas meant it purely as a political statement and they now agreed on the sentence before the trial. It was a gross miscarriage of justice, because the judge decided on the sentence even before the trial was held, that the man was going to receive the sentence of death even though he was innocent. The whole council had already decided this innocent man must be sacrificed to stop bloodshed in the nation. So it was only a matter of time until the mock trial was held and the unjust verdict given.

JESUS' BURIAL PREPARED —
WITH A PERFUME (12:1-11)

The Passover feast had come and what an appropriate time for Jesus to come to Jerusalem for the last time. It was the occasion when they remembered that the first-born son of every Egyptian family died, when they remembered that in their own homes the angel of death passed over their homes because in their home a lamb lay dead. It was God's hour and Jesus knew he was going to be the lamb that would die so that angel of death might pass over thousands of other people. So Jesus came for his last stay in the home of Martha, Lazarus and Mary, which meant so much to him.

It is a normal custom in the Middle East, when you show honour to an honoured guest, that you wash his feet, anoint his head and put perfume on him because the heat – the perspiration – from the journey mean that his body smells. It is a courtesy.

Martha is in the kitchen again, getting a meal ready, but where is Mary? She is rummaging in a chest that contains her belongings.

Inside it is something that cost nearly a year's wages. I don't know how she got it: whether she was left it by someone else, or whether she had saved up and bought it. But in her chest of belongings was a little jar made of fine-grain gypsum and inside just twelve ounces of nard, which had come from Tibet on a camel's back. Nard comes from an aromatic herb that grows on the Himalayan mountains. It was worth three hundred days' wages. What was she going to do with it? She comes, smashes it on the ground and then scooping up the ointment on her fingers, puts it on Jesus and his feet.

"Do you realize wherever Jesus would go for the next few days people would smell that rare perfume? Do you realize when they spat on him, his body would still have smelt beautiful? When they nailed him to the cross, you could probably still have caught the aroma? When they laid him in the tomb, that aroma would still have been hanging around?"

Then horrifically, breaking all rules of public propriety, she let her hair down in public and washed and wiped Jesus' feet. What an extravagant thing to do! Love is lavish. Let us realize this love is not niggardly; it is generous and lavish. If you love someone, you want the best for them. If you really love someone you will go beyond what is needed. If you are buying a present for someone you love, you don't just ask what they need. You want to buy something more than that. Love is lavish.

Mary went rummaging for this little box of ointment, smashed it and spread it on Jesus. How long do you think that perfume would last? Do you realize wherever Jesus would go for the next few days people would smell that rare perfume? Do you realize that when they spat on him, his body would still have smelt beautiful? That when they nailed him to the cross, you could probably still have caught the aroma? That when they laid him in the tomb, that aroma would still have been hanging around? This rare herb from Tibet is one of the most pungent and sweet smells in the world. She did it because she loved.

Jesus said, "You see what she's done? Do you know what she's done? She's kept it for me, for my burial." This means that out of all the people who knew Jesus only Mary realized what was about to happen. Mary knew that he would die and that she would not have the opportunity to anoint his body properly. So she had kept it for him and now was the opportunity to anoint him. She realized the aroma would last until he was buried and she was simply doing it as part of her love.

Now comes the horrible moment. Against the background of generosity, we see greed: Judas. He sounds sensible, humanitarian, concerned and generous, but in fact he is the opposite. He is calculating because he has already weighed up exactly how much that was worth. Can't you see him? He has weighed up the size of the jar and the weight of the ointment. He has done his mental calculation. He couldn't calculate love, but only money. He is the materialist of his day.

He was also concealing. He sounded concerned about the poor, but he wasn't. Jesus told him, "You can go and help the poor any time you want, Judas. Why don't you?" It wasn't that he wanted to help the poor; what was the real reason? We are told that Judas' trouble was simple: he was greedy. He liked to get as much money as possible. Since he was the disciples' treasurer, he dipped his hand into the bag when he needed.

Many sermons and many books on Judas have involved explanations as to how he had political dreams and his conception of the Messiah was disappointed, that he was trying to force Jesus to take the kingdom by betraying him. The Bible does not allow any of these. It simply says Judas was greedy. We like to think it was a complicated political reason because that would remove it from us. But Judas was greedy, and it went against the grain to see something, as he thought, being thrown away. He was niggardly. He counted every penny, especially those that came his way. So he objected; "What a waste!" Do you know the world cannot understand anything spent for the Lord? They just cannot understand it. They cannot understand your spending time in church. You are not there for your own good; primarily, we are in church to let God enjoy our company, to let him hear our praises. People say, "You're wasting your time singing; why don't you get out and do some good for people?" They say that because they don't love the Lord. They don't understand that the Lord likes to have time spent on him, as well as money.

People say why spend money on this and that when you could be doing good with this and relieving needs with it? There is a place for Christians to spend money for the Lord and to tell him only the best is good enough for him. There is a place for love to be lavish. But the Judases of this world don't understand you can love the Lord and want to give him something for his own sake. There is a time and place to share, but Mary was saying, "I've kept this for you."

If this had been a funeral service and Mary had been anointing a dead body, no one would have complained: this would be regarded as normal expenditure for a funeral. But Judas did not see what was happening. So Jesus said, "Judas, have you forgotten that people can do things for me as well as for the poor? You've got many opportunities to help the poor if you really want to. But she wanted to do something just for me. She's not been doing it extravagantly; I am going to be buried. She's done something for my burial that you really shouldn't argue about." Isn't it terrible when human greed spoils something lovely for the Lord? When someone who lives at a materialist level, who can only see human factors and money and can just calculate, instead of seeing that love doesn't calculate? There is recklessness in love.

Let us not be put off. Jesus said about Mary, "I am going to reward her for this. Everywhere the gospel goes in the whole world people will talk about this act." Here we are doing so two thousand years later! The reward is hers.

JESUS' RESURRECTION PREFIGURED —
BY A PROCESSION (12:12-19)

It was a Sunday (then a working day), but about two million people were on holiday camping on the Mount of Olives near Jerusalem for the Passover. The excitement was intense: they would sing on the hills, playing their stringed instruments. They lived in tents; it was a great festival. They would sing in groups and they would sing Psalm 118 – a psalm especially for Passover, a cry to God to be delivered from enemies. The cry included *Hosanna*, which doesn't mean "hooray," but "save us now." Every year there was the expectancy, "Save us now; we want to be free."

Now at last they believed they had the leader to release them. News spread around the camp: "Jesus is coming!" The whole crowd turned out; what a sight it must have been! The pent-up feelings of years were going to be released. All their hopes for centuries were centred in one person. And as usually they had done it for Simon Maccabeus, they had done for Judas Maccabeus, they ripped off the palm branches, instant flags, and went out to the Mount of Olives to meet the procession.

But they misunderstood Jesus. The tragedy of this scene is that he had something to say to them which they did not want to hear, and they never heard. With the size of the crowd Jesus could not have spoken to them all. So he spoke to their eyes rather than their ears. He did it through a donkey but they missed the message. They had eyes only for the One who sat on the donkey.

The crowd on Palm Sunday got it wrong. They said, "Look who's sitting on that donkey," when they should have been looking at the donkey, because in that donkey Jesus was teaching a profound lesson. But because they missed it, the result of this procession was complete disappointment. There was such disillusion that a few days later they stood by without lifting a finger while he was crucified. They missed the donkey. Why? What was this about? The enthusiasm was there: they were keen to welcome Jesus. But in their minds they were saying, "We want Jesus to set us free from other people and then we can have peace." That involves a military uprising: a revolution, and by nature people easily respond to the message of revolution. It's easy to blame others and say, "If we were free from them, we'd be free and we'd have peace." This is why the message of revolution and violence goes round the world today. People fall for it, thinking, "If we could be free from them, if we could have a revolution and put them out of power, we'd be free and have peace."

Jesus came on a donkey, fulfilling a prediction made hundreds of years before by the prophet Zechariah. "See your king comes to you, meek, lowly, riding on a donkey" (Zechariah 9:9). He has come to bring peace. He is not a revolutionary or a political rebel, because he does not believe peace comes from being set free from others. How does real peace come? When you are set free from yourself: that is real freedom. Everybody wants to be free. "If only I could be free from them I'd be free," and Jesus says, "I have come to set you free from yourself."

They missed the donkey; even the disciples who had brought the donkey to him didn't understand it. But after the resurrection he came back and every time he met them he said, "Shalom. Peace." It means "harmony, with yourself, with other people, with your God; health; salvation; victory." When Jesus rose from the dead, they realized he had come to bring the kind of peace the world may not even be interested in, but certainly a peace the world cannot give and a peace the world cannot take away. It is a peace that is free from self. That is real peace: it was all there in the donkey.

"What are we saying? We're saying that behind the human story, behind all these events God is active, working out his plan and filling it all with eternal significance."

Some people in the crowd were standing at the back, not waving palms, but standing, I think with their arms folded, and muttering to each other, "Look! We've failed; the whole world's gone after him." Do you know one of the worst things in human nature? Envy. It came into the hearts of a few Pharisees there. They said, "Look! We're not succeeding; they're all going after him!" Envy was responsible for the first murder in history. Cain killed Abel out of envy. It was to be responsible for the worst murder in history. Pontius Pilate knew "it was out of envy that they had handed him over" (Matthew 27:18). It is tragic that with the crowd shouting, "Hosanna", men in the crowd were filled with envy at Jesus' popularity. Envy can also come into Christian service; you can envy another Christian who is more successful in Christian work than yourself. You can envy another church with a bigger congregation.

But they too said something whose meaning they did not know. "The whole world is going after him." That's true too. Isn't it amazing? These people are doing and saying things whose significance they didn't realize. Caiaphas saying, "One man should die for the people," which was exactly what God was saying at the same time, and that is the truth of the cross. A woman was breaking her most precious ointment over Jesus and Jesus said, "She's done it for my burial." Envious men said, "The whole world is following him," and that is gloriously true. Today throughout the world people are praising the Lord through Jesus Christ. Millions follow him and all the world's envy cannot stop it.

What are we saying? We are saying that behind the human story, behind all these events God is active, working out his plan and filling it all with eternal significance.

24

THE CHALLENGES OF DISCIPLESHIP
John 12:20-50

RENUNCIATION (12:20-26)

REDEMPTION (12:27-36a)

REJECTION (12:36b-43)

RETRIBUTION (12:44-50)

This study is the last public sermon of our Lord Jesus Christ. The end of Jesus' life was coming: the time that was to split history, to be the pivot of human affairs. Gone are the simple parables, those lovely stories we remember so well. Instead come the deep principles of discipleship: he goes very deep at the end. He faces people with his last word, his ultimatum, "What I say is what God says. If you don't listen to what I say and obey what I say, then I won't need to judge you on Judgment Day. The words you've heard from me will be your judge." Jesus talks about four principles in his final challenge.

RENUNCIATION (12:20-26)

The passage starts with a request (v. 21), "Sir, we want to see Jesus." Your first reaction is what a lovely request! I have seen it in many pulpits, usually on a brass plate. But it is only valid if you take it out of context and give it a different meaning. Jesus saw this request as a temptation, a diversion, an invitation to depart from his Father's way. It's not a request that should be made. I can understand how it came to be made; it didn't come from Jews, but from Greeks.

Just as in Ethiopia today you will find Italian families as living remnants of the Italian invaders of Abyssinia in the 1930s, so in Israel in those days lived Greek families who were the remnants of the Greek invaders under Alexander the Great. They had settled down in ten cities to the southeast of the Sea of Galilee. (The Greek for ten cities is *Deca* ["ten"] *polis* "city": the Decapolis.) Jesus had already visited that Greek area. He had cured a demoniac, a naked man of whom everybody was frightened, and the man was clothed and in his right mind. Jesus had fed 4,000 people among the Greeks with a few loaves and fishes, as well as feeding 5,000 Jews. They had already seen something of Jesus. Now these tourists maybe came to see the fun at the Passover and asked,

"We want to see Jesus."

"This is a fundamental principle of Christian discipleship. It is not just enough to see Jesus, to want to have a vision or an experience of Jesus, a death is involved. Jesus said, 'Take the road of personal sacrifice, which I must take. If I am going to multiply myself, I must die.'"

The significance of this is that they realize that Jesus is not being appreciated by his own people. It is the offer of another tour. They are saying, "You're not appreciated here, but we'd love to see you in our country. Come and see us." Jesus replied, "There's no use in my coming to see you until I've died first."

This is a fundamental principle of Christian discipleship. It is not just enough to see Jesus, to want to have a vision or an experience of Jesus, a death is involved. The Greeks have had perhaps more influence on the culture of other countries than any other ancient nation. In architecture, sport and many other ways they have contributed greatly to human affairs. Yet they had a hollow in their soul that their achievements could not fill. They tried to pack it with gods and they couldn't. Perhaps these Greeks were coming because they were hungry: their achievements left them empty, and they wanted more. They said, "We want Jesus. We can fix a great tour for him. Come over, we'll welcome you. We won't grumble, we won't plan your death. Come to us." That's how Jesus saw it. He never granted their request and because it's not the right request.

Jesus told them, "I will tell you the right way. Take the road of personal sacrifice, which I must take. If I am going to multiply myself, I must die. If I come to you Greeks now and come on a tour, I come alone. I'm the only One who can come to you, but if I die here in Jerusalem, the law that applies universally in the natural world will apply in the spiritual world." Every potato or seed you plant in your garden must die or it remains a single potato or a single seed. But if it dies, it produces more potatoes, more seeds.

Jesus said, "It's a short-term policy for me to come. If I die here, I will multiply myself, and one day many people will come." Jesus was going to multiply himself by death. It is a principle he laid down that if you really love yourself that is the way to destroy yourself. If you want to hang on to life, if you are just interested in experiences and want to pack life with every possible excitement, that is the way to destroy your life. Whoever is going to hang on to life and just wants to add to their experience, then that person will destroy themselves.

Unfortunately there is a demand today to see Jesus. Many people want to see Jesus, that's why the box office has discovered that Jesus is money. If you stage a play about Jesus or write a song about him, people want to see him. They want to sit in a theatre and have a good evening, sing the songs and see Jesus on stage. But Jesus is waiting for people to say, "Sir, we want to sacrifice for Jesus." Or: "Sir, we want to serve Jesus." He says, "If you really want me, then you'll have to stay with me because you're no use to me unless you're where I am. If you want to serve me, then stay with me, follow me. I need a servant who'll stay right where I am, so that I can say to him do this and he'll do it."

Jesus is not interested in showing himself to people. He is looking for people who are ready to serve and sacrifice, not just come and have a nice time in church. "Sir, we want to be told how to get on with the job. We want to go out and tell. We've come not to just to see, but to serve and if need be to sacrifice." This is the principle of renunciation.

Jesus replied to the Greeks, indirectly, through Philip who brought the request, "Go and tell them. I'm not coming with you; you come with me." Do you see the difference? I'm not coming to the Decapolis; I'm not coming to you. You come with me and serve me." That is how it must be.

You may miss out on many experiences that others have, but you will have one thing they don't have. "My Father honours those who serve me" (v. 26). What kind of honour would you like? What kind of life would you like to have lived? Would you like to get to the end of the road and say, "I've had every experience I wanted. I've even seen Jesus!"? Or would you rather have the Father say, "This person is a good and faithful servant"?

"The One who was going to say a few days later to his disciples, 'Let not your hearts be troubled,' was prepared to admit his own heart was troubled. 'My soul is troubled, what shall I say?' Do you know the best thing to say when you're troubled? 'Father, Father. My soul is troubled, what shall I say? Father.'"

REDEMPTION (12:27-36a)

Secondly, Jesus talks about redemption. Speaking about the death of the grain of wheat made him realize his death was only a few hours away. Thank God Jesus was a real human being who shrank from death. Death was real to him; it wasn't a charade. He didn't want to die, especially not how he had to. Thank God his Son tasted real human experience, that he was a human being. He shrank from death; his soul was troubled (v. 27). The One who was going to say a few days later to his disciples, "Let not your hearts be troubled," (14:1) was prepared to admit his own heart was troubled.

He was going to bring peace to others, but he didn't have it himself at this point. "My soul is troubled, what shall I say?" Do you know the best thing to say when you're troubled? "Father, Father. My soul is troubled, what shall I say? Father." That is the best point to begin when you are in trouble. "Shall I say, 'Father, save me from this hour'? Lord, I'm willing to do anything but this." That's what Jesus was tempted to say. You could say to the Lord, "Lord, I'm willing to do anything except this or that."

Jesus had reached a crossroads which you may reach now and which all of us reach sooner or later in our Christian life. Which is going to be the deciding factor: my happiness, my safety, my comfort, my ease or his glory? That is the important point. Jesus reached it at this point. Praise God that after a struggle – a mighty struggle with its climax in Gethsemane – Jesus said, "No, Father, glorify your name. Not save me, but glorify yourself," was the prayer Jesus prayed and the prayer we are to pray. "Lord, I'd like to be happy, comfortable, safe, healthy. No, Lord I shouldn't be praying like that, should I? Father, glorify your name."

God answered that prayer and spoke. I have never heard God speak in a voice from the sky like thunder (v. 29). I think I would be scared stiff if he did. God said, "I have glorified it and will glorify it again." When God has a person who says, "Glorify your name even if it costs suffering for me," then God can glorify his name, and he will do so again. So Jesus faced up to this death.

Let us consider the atoning death of Jesus, what his death achieved: this is why God's name has been glorified ever since. This tragic event achieved so much; it achieved the exact opposite of every appearance.

First, it looked as if Jesus was on trial and being judged. But in fact the world was being judged. Everything that appeared to be happening wasn't happening: the opposite was happening. It wasn't really Jesus who was on trial. It was the world that was judged. Pontius Pilate, Annas and Caiaphas were judged. The world of human opinion has given its verdict against these men. But it wasn't the Jews or the Romans that were judged, it was the world. You and I were judged at the cross. This is what our world is really like when Jesus really faced the world with God. Our world, our human nature, our sort of people did that.

When someone once sang the spiritual, "Were you there when they crucified my Lord?" a deep hush settled on the crowd and one person cried out, "Yes, we were all there." It was not Jesus that was judged. He said, "Now is the world judged." The human race stands guilty at the bar of God for overthrowing his own Son.

Secondly, it looked as if Jesus was being overthrown and driven out. But in fact the devil was being overthrown and driven out. It was a triumph, not a tragedy. The glory is that the devil was overthrown this day; Satan's power was broken. You can prove it in your own experience by claiming the power and victory of the cross when the devil is after you.

Thirdly, it looked as if the cross was the end of the road: every follower abandoned him and he was left alone. They thought it was failure when even the last eleven men ran for their lives. But was it? "I will draw all people to myself if I'm lifted up" (v. 32). The death of Christ has drawn people from every nation: everywhere the story of the cross is told people are drawn. They realize there is life through his death.

The Jews cannot accept this idea of being lifted up. It is still their biggest problem that their Messiah should be crucified and their problem is mentioned here. "This lifting up," they said, "who is this Son of Man, how can you say the Messiah is to live for ever, how can you say he's to be lifted up on a cross? We don't understand it."

Jesus didn't answer the question. He pointed out that this intellectual problem was secondary to the practical issue: "While the light shines, seize your opportunity to live in it, or you'll find yourself in darkness." Do you know that the natural state inside a room is pitch darkness? The light comes from the sun; if there were no sun you would be in darkness. One of the shocks when the astronauts went into space was to see that the sky was black, not blue. The natural state of things is darkness. When God created the earth, "darkness was over the surface of the deep." He had to penetrate that darkness with light: on the first day, he said, "Let there be light" (Genesis 1:2-3). But if you put out the light, the natural state to which everything reverts is pitch darkness. Humanity's natural state is darkness. If the light is put out in a person's life, they will go dark. You cannot avoid this. You cannot choose between light and darkness. You can seize the opportunity of having a light when there is one offered you. But if you don't take the opportunity, you revert to darkness. This is true physically, and Jesus said, "I want to warn you that I'm not here much longer. The light is shining only briefly, and when it goes you revert to darkness."

Do you remember that when they nailed him to the cross even the sun went out (Matthew 27:45)? Do you realize that sun is shining today only because of Jesus? If Jesus were not upholding all things by the word of his power we would not see anything here; we would be in darkness. When Jesus died, even the sun went out. It was not an eclipse because it lasted three hours and eclipses don't do that. It was because he is the light of the world and the light was being extinguished by evildoers. What was true physically on Good Friday is true spiritually of men and women. If they do not seize the light of Jesus, then they finish in mental and moral darkness. That is their natural state. It is also true eternally.

I think the most horrible thing the Bible says about hell is that you have to live in pitch darkness if you go there. Heaven is so full of light there's no need of sun, moon or street lamps. But hell is pitch black; Jesus calls it "outer darkness", because where he is not, light is not. He said, "You've got the light shining – seize it. While it's shining onto your mind and heart live in it, believe in it, or else the enveloping darkness will come back in on you."

REJECTION (12:36b-43)

Why do people reject the light? Why do they shut their eyes to the light? Why don't they believe? It seems impossible to persuade people to accept the light. Why is it that you can talk to so many and they don't respond? It's the biggest question that a Christian has to face. You came to Christ and found the way, the truth, and the life and you want to tell everybody. You tell them. They say, "The way? There are plenty of other ways. The truth? How do you know, what proof have you? The life? Why, you're missing out on life!"

Why won't they believe? Isaiah gave the answer seven hundred years before it happened. Talking about Jesus in the same chapter in which he said, "He was wounded for our transgressions," Isaiah asked, "Who has believed our message?" (53:1, 5). "We tell them, but who believes?" Why don't they believe? The terrible answer Jesus gave here, which may well have puzzled you is: God has blinded their eyes; he has closed their mind.

"It's a solemn word but Jesus is saying there can be no neutrality: when you hear the word of God you're either open to it and accept, responding to the light as a flower reaches for the sun – or like some little insect you run for the darkness under a stone."

Would a God of love do that? Why would God close a human mind? Isaiah was told by God, "The more you preach, the less people will believe. The more you give them the truth, the more their minds will close to the truth, because they have already rejected me." We come to the solemn truth that every sermon you hear either gives you more truth or takes away from you what you have got. Every sermon you hear either makes your mind harder and more closed, or softer and more open to the truth. You cannot remain neutral when you hear the word of God. If you have decided it is not true, then your mind will close tighter the more you hear. It is one of those laws of God's universe and unfortunately it is true. Walk while you have the light, believe in it while it is shining, or else God will close your mind. It is God's punishment for those who reject. God is saying: "I will help you along whatever path you choose, if you choose to be open to the truth I'll give you more and more of it. If you choose to be closed to the truth I'll help you to close up."

It is a solemn word but we cannot water down the word of God. He is saying there can be no neutrality: when you hear the word of God you're either open to it and accept it and grow and walk in the light, responding to the light as a flower reaches for the sun – or like some horrid little insect you run for the darkness under a stone.

Jesus mentions another sort of rejection: the closed mouth. The people who believe it inside but do not let it come out. "Many Jews believed in him but because of the Pharisees they didn't talk about it openly" (v. 42). Letting the truth out of your mind is as important as letting it into your mind, out of your mouth. Unfortunately, this is where the blockage occurs. The word of God says: "If you believe in your heart [letting the faith in] and confess with your mouth, [letting it out] ..." (Romans 10:9). Faith cannot be real unless you let it out. Jesus said, "If you disown me before others – if you're ashamed to confess me – I'll disown you before God" (Matthew 10:32-33). Confession is a vital part of faith. You are not really a believer unless you have let it out.

You may accept the word of God intellectually and believe it is true, but do you let it out? If you don't, then you're in the same boat as these people mentioned here. The practical effect on the world of the closed mind on the one hand or the closed mouth on the other is the same: the world will never hear the truth.

So here are two groups of people who reject the truth: those who close their minds to it and don't let it in; and those who let it in but close their mouths and don't let it out. Why don't they?

Because they are more afraid of people than of God, because they are more anxious about what people think of them than about what God thinks. Why should they be so? Because human approval is immediately apparent and felt, but God's approval waits till the end of the day. We are frightened of upsetting people, of offending them. A real believer is not only one who has let the truth in to his mind but also one who has let it out of his mouth.

FINALLY, RETRIBUTION (12:44-50)

This is the last principle in Jesus' last public sermon, which can be summed up in two points. First, to meet Jesus is to meet God, to see Jesus is to see God; to listen to Jesus is to listen to God. Your attitude to Jesus is your attitude to God. If you listen to him and believe in Jesus, you'll walk in the light and you will no more be in the darkness. He came to save people, not to judge them. But that does not mean there isn't going to be a judgment.

Secondly, there comes the final terrible warning. Jesus said, "I came to save people, not judge them, but one day there will be a day of reckoning when a person will be judged by what they heard of my words but did nothing about." Dare we open God's word, knowing that one day God will say to us, "You heard that in church," but hearing by itself is no good; it doesn't do anything? God says, "You have heard my word," and he will ask: "What did you do about it, what did you do?" Are we hearers only or doers?

So we finish Jesus' last sermon. We began this study with those who said, "We want to see Jesus," and Jesus finishes by saying, "It's not what you see, it's what you hear and do." He says, "You've had a visual communication from God. If you've seen me, you've seen the Father. But you will receive a verbal condemnation from him: what you've heard – not what you've seen – but what you've heard will judge you if you didn't do it.

25

WHAT IS TRUE HUMILITY?
John 13:1-17

JESUS' HEAVENLY EXALTATION (13:1-3)

JESUS' HUMBLE EXERCISE (13:4-11)

JESUS' HAPPY EXAMPLE (13:12-17)

This study is first a picture of Jesus as a unique person, then a picture of what he is able and wants to do for people, and finally a picture of what he wants us to do for each other.

JESUS' HEAVENLY EXALTATION (13:1-3)

First, let's look at Jesus, the unique Son of God. Several things are said here which could not be said about anyone else in the same way. First, he knew when and how he was going to die. I don't know that and I don't suppose you do. But Jesus knew his hour had come; he knew he was going to die; he knew how he was going to die, and he knew where he was going to die.

He also knew where he was going after death: perhaps that is true of you. But it was true of Jesus in a unique way; he knew that he was going home to the Father. He felt about going home in a way that we could never feel, because even though we call heaven "home" it is a place we have never been to. It is therefore strange and even Christians become apprehensive about the unknown, but not Jesus. He not only knew he was going to die and that he was going to the Father in heaven, he also knew he had come from there, and that is not true of another soul.

It felt like going home; can you imagine that? From all eternity he had lived with the Father in glory, he came to this planet for thirty-three years, and now he is going home again. Already his mind is thinking of the glory and everything that is waiting there. If you are going home, you can get so excited that you forget other people's needs. If you are a few days from travelling back to someone and somewhere you love, then you can easily overlook the needs around you, but not so with Jesus. Knowing he had come from the Father and that he was going back to the Father, what did he do?

"Jesus knew that one of his friends would sell him for hard cash; he knew another of his friends would deny him; he knew the others would reach the limit of their loyalty and run away, but he still loved them to the end."

"Having loved his own who were in the world, he loved them to the very end" – in spite of what he knew about them. He not only knew that he had come from the Father in heaven and was going back to the Father, he also knew that one of the people sitting at the table with him was going to hell and he knew why. He knew that one of his friends before that night was over would sell him for hard cash; he knew that another of his friends would deny him; he knew that the others would reach the limit of their loyalty and run away. He knew all that, but he still loved them to the end.

We are also told that he has unlimited power. He knew that all authority was being given to him by the Father. One of the things that corrupts human nature is power: as soon as we get power, we show the worst side of our nature. As Lord Acton said, "Power tends to corrupt and absolute power tends to corrupt absolutely." We have seen people with power over nations who have plunged the world into suffering. We have blamed them for their abuse of power and yet maybe within our own family circle or at work, we have had someone we push around, maybe our children – and we have shown that power doesn't do us any good either.

In Jesus himself, perfect love and power go together.

JESUS' HUMBLE EXERCISE (13:4-11)

Love without power produces only sympathy. Power without love produces selfishness, but love with power equals service. We are now going to see what a person does who has unlimited power backed by unlimited love, and this is precisely what the world is crying out for. We need both in perfect combination. So we turn from this tremendous background to see what Jesus did with all that love and power. Only John's Gospel tells us. He came down from heaven. Paul says it like this "being in very nature God, Jesus did not consider equality with God something to be used to his own advantage but took the form of a servant" (Philippians 2:6). That's how love and power operate. Power tries to climb; love gets down on its knees. Power is interested in exaltation; love is interested in humility.

What Jesus did was ordinary and unsurprising, nothing in itself that causes any attention. However, it was who did it that made it extraordinary, because it happened at every public meal. If you invited guests to come to a banquet, and this still happens in the Middle East, you send the invitation, and on that day they would have a bath before coming. But on the journey walking in their sandals along dusty roads that were not made up with tarmac in the hot Palestine climate, their feet would become caked with mud, dust and dirt. So every host, having set the table, would put by the door a basin full of water and a towel. As the guests came in, two slaves were stationed at the door. The second lowest slave undid the sandal and took the sandals off, and the lowest slave washed the feet. It is interesting that John the Baptist said, "I'm not worthy to loose the sandal. I'm not worthy to be the second bottom slave." He didn't mention the bottom one.

"Humility is positive, not negative: it's not what you don't do, it's what you do and how you do it that shows."

The disciples came that night; the meal had been secretly arranged because Jesus wanted this last night to himself and the disciples. Nobody knew where it was, so no slaves were at the door. The disciples came in, looking around for someone to do it but nobody was there, so they sat down with their hot, smelly feet at the table. Nobody would do it for anybody else.

Imagine the scene: a perfectly normal situation, yet something is going to happen which lifts it into the supernatural, but it is not a miracle, but something ordinary. Here is a picture of complete humility.

Let me say something you may misunderstand at first. Some people think humility means getting out of the limelight, becoming a person who imitates the wallpaper that people never notice in the background. They think that is humility, but I want you to think again. Humility may mean you have to put yourself right in the centre of attention, but it is how you put yourself there that tells whether you are really humble. Humility may not keep in the background, humility may step right into the foreground: that's what Jesus did, humbly doing something that made him the centre of attention. It was how he did it that showed his humility. Humility is positive, not negative: it is not what you don't do, it is what you do and how you do it that shows.

Jesus stripped his body. They were going to strip it again a few hours later to humiliate him. Jesus stripped himself first; he humbled himself long before anybody else did. He took off his coat and was clothed simply in a loin cloth: that's how a slave dressed. Then he took the towel and fastened it round his waist. Can you imagine what the disciples felt? "I wish I'd have done that. I wish I'd thought of that first, and now he's had to do it."

Do you know we don't mind humbling ourselves before the Lord but we can't stand the Lord humbling himself before us? It hurts. It's the wrong kind of relationship. For the King of kings to be kneeling to me cuts right across our sense of etiquette or protocol. It doesn't seem to fit; it is too humble. Yet here is a glimpse of how Jesus saw himself: with all the power in the universe, in his love he was prepared to go down on his knees in front of others. What humility! It's one of those glimpses that tells you what kind of a person Jesus was and is. In a sense, he is still that humble. He still comes into your life gently. He still

comes to you and says, "Will you let me do something for you?"
He doesn't start by asking us to do something for him; that's the
wrong place to start. That would allow us to keep our pride. But
he says, "Would you let me do something for you?" That's where
he begins.

It is against the humility of Jesus that we see how terrible the
disciples' pride is. Notice how Peter reacted. Clearly, Jesus didn't
start with Peter; he came round the table and Peter didn't like to
be treated like the others. He was going to be different. There is
something in us that likes to be treated differently. So he came
to Peter, who swung from one extreme to another: a typical sign
of immaturity. When you swing from one extreme to the other,
it is difficult to get a balance in the Christian life. So Peter said,
"You'll never wash any part of me or you'll wash every part of
me. Nothing or everything." He swung from one extreme to the
other; he had not learned that obedience brings balance. Being too
proud to serve others, Peter is now too proud to be served. There
is a connection here: pride can invert itself. Peter would not take
up the basin and towel himself: he was too proud, as the others
were. But similarly, he was now too proud to let somebody else
take it up and wash his feet.

**"Jesus may not want to do a miracle, but ordinary things,
in your life. You would love him to do something big and
spectacular, but he may say, 'Just let me do what I want to
do with you. Then we'll have fellowship and walk through
life as partners.'"**

Jesus says something startling and terrible, and it applies to
everyone: "Unless I wash you, we can't have fellowship together.
We can't belong. We can't be friends. We can't go any further
together unless I wash you." The solemn truth is what makes you
a Christian is nothing you do for Jesus, but what Jesus does for
you. Jesus said, "We can't go any further together unless you will
let me clean up your life. If you let me do that, we can continue
in partnership, have fellowship, walk together and talk together.
But that's where it's got to begin. Unless I wash you, Peter, we

can't go on together." So dear old Peter swung to the opposite extreme and makes the grand gesture. There is something in us that would love to do something great, to be different from all the other Christians. Peter said, "You've washed their feet, but Lord I want to go the whole way with you. I want to be washed from head to toe. Lord, I'm special." Poor Peter reveals again that he doesn't like submitting to Jesus. It is painful; it is humiliating to him to submit to what Jesus wants to do.

Jesus may not want to do a miracle, but ordinary things, in your life. You would love him to do something big and spectacular, but he may say, "Just let me do what I want to do with you. Then we can have fellowship together and can continue walking through life as partners."

There is a deeper lesson to be learned here, which Peter is taught: once you have been bathed, you don't need ever a total bath again. That's why baptism is never repeated; it is only once. When you're baptized totally in water, that will never happen to you again. It is a total bath, which symbolizes the fact that when you came to Christ you had a total bath. All your sins were washed away; you were made totally clean in God's sight. He didn't half-do the job; you were clean in God's sight.

But you and I know that as we walk through life, we pick up dirt. You will never need a total washing again, but you will need a daily washing. You will need Jesus to come and wash away the dirt that you picked up as you walk through life. You have had a bath, but you will need your feet washed. "Peter, you've got it all wrong. You're already totally clean: it's just this dirt on your feet I'm concerned about. I want to keep you clean." This is a secret of the Christian life: Jesus washes us totally at the beginning of our Christian life and then he wants to keep us clean and wash away the dirt we pick up.

Jesus added: "Peter, there's someone here, I'm going to wash his feet, but he's not totally clean, so washing his feet won't do much good. He's got a dirty heart and a dirty head." Jesus knew his name: it was Judas. He was one of those at that table who was not totally clean, who had not had a bath, who had not really come to Jesus and had a total cleansing. Even though he was going to have his feet washed, it would not stop him going to hell or his own place. This is the pattern. You cannot have the daily forgiveness and daily cleansing until you have had the total bath. That is why the Lord's Prayer is only for Christians. It is a daily prayer asking for daily cleansing, "Forgive us our trespasses." But you can only pray that after you have had a total cleansing through Jesus Christ. It is a daily prayer for those who have had a bath and have picked up some dirt as they walked through life. That's the picture.

JESUS' HAPPY EXAMPLE (13:12-17)

After Jesus had finished washing their feet, he said, "Now let's talk about what I've done, do you understand it?" They thought they had but they hadn't. He said, "I'm going to change your way of thinking through this. It's the last night I'm with you. I've taught you an important lesson. I want you to learn what lordship is. You call me Lord and master, and that's good and right. But it's shaken you, hasn't it, that a Lord and Master does this for you, but that's what lordship is. If you want lordship, then this is how you achieve it. If you want to be great, then get on your knees."

It revolutionizes human thought, when parents talk to me proudly about their offspring and say they have done very well and have got on. I ask, "What do you mean?" And they tell me, "Johnny's gone up the ladder, earns a bigger salary with more responsibility and more people to tell what to do." Jesus didn't think like that. Jesus said, "You rightly call me Lord and Master, but did you see what I did as Lord and Master? That's what lordship is."

That is what it is to make progress in life. If you really want success, you'll find it through service. If you really want to get on, you will find it by bowing before others in their need. What a different place the world would be if this were to be practised.

Jesus said, "Look at what I do with my love and power. I love, and look at what I do. I have all power, and look at what I do. I am the Lord, and look at what I do. I am your master with every right to tell you to wash my feet." Do you know if he had asked them to do that, they would have done it like a shot? If Jesus had sat down at that table and asked, "Would one of you wash my feet?" they would have been scrambling for the privilege because I know what they were talking about as they came through the streets to that upper room. It is mentioned in Luke 22:24-30 (see also Matthew 20:23-28; Mark 10:35-45). Who should sit next to Jesus? Who would have the chief seat? Who would have the main place? Jesus had been listening as he walked along and he had heard them and Peter was saying to John, "I ought to sit on the right hand of Jesus," and John said, "No, I ought to," and they were arguing. Jesus had heard it all.

So he did not ask them to wash his feet. He said, "I am your Lord and Master and I am going to wash you. Therefore I have given you an example." I don't think he meant the ceremony of foot washing. What he did mean is that if you walked to our church today in your bare feet and your feet were dirty and needed washing, that we should be ready to do that. It means that no task is too menial for the Christian to perform. It means that what he did for us he wants us to do for each other, namely to meet any little need there may be.

That is a big thing to do; it's not just something to do on Maundy Thursday. It's not just something to do with feet; it's something to do with every need you meet. That's how he wants Christians to behave to each other: to look around and see if someone needs anything. Does someone need showing to the cloakroom after the service? Then that would be the equivalent for you. Just to take them. Does someone need to be shown where to hang their coat up when they arrive? Then that is your privilege. "You call me Lord and Master, then you do it for each other. Whatever is needed as you arrive together, to have a meal together, do it for each other." It is as simple and down to earth as that. He doesn't want a ritual, he wants reality: simple acts of kindness. He wants people who are looking round to see if there's a basin and a towel not being used, and somebody who needs to have it used. That is a simple picture of the Christian life: "I've done it for you, you do it for each other."

Jesus is really interested in what we do to one another rather than what we do for him. He says, "I do it for you; you do it for one another." It flows from him to us and through us to each other. "I've given you an example."

But I'm going to add something. We should never be ashamed of doing anything that Christ did, even washing feet. But I think he had a spiritual meaning: it means not only caring for each other's physical fitness and needs but also caring for each other spiritually, helping keep each other remain clean spiritually, helping meet others' spiritual, emotional and mental needs. Seeing that someone is lonely and going to talk to them, seeing that someone is losing the joy they once had in the Lord and going to see them and asking them if you can help them find their way back. Seeing that someone is slipping out of the fellowship and stretching out a loving hand and pulling them back in. All this is involved. Jesus is saying, "Whatever I have done for you and your need, then you go and do for one of your brothers or sisters in their need."

26

WHAT IS IN YOUR HEART?
John 13:18-38

JUDAS: GREEDY (13:18-30)

JESUS: GLORIOUS (13:31-35)

PETER: GLIB (13:36-38)

It is extraordinary that half of John's Gospel is written about one weekend, about Jesus' last few days, death and resurrection. Chapters 13 to 17 concern the last evening of Jesus' life and what he said. Chapter 13 gives us a poor picture of the disciples; but we finish in that matchless prayer of Jesus in chapter 17. There is an ascending spirituality in these chapters. You begin with the disciples squabbling for the chief places, refusing to wash each others' feet, with predictions of betrayal and denial, and you finish with the Lord praying for them. It is tremendous.

I have divided this study into three sections, each concerned with one person: first Judas, second Jesus and third Peter. In each of these three Jesus makes a general statement about the situation, a specific prediction about something that's going to happen and a direct command telling one or all of the disciples what to do.

JUDAS: GREEDY (13:18-30)

I tremble when I read this story, but one of these twelve apostles never reached heaven. He had lived for three years with Jesus, gone preaching and teaching in Jesus' name, healed people and driven out demons in Jesus' name. He had kept the money given to the disciples and used it to buy the necessities of life and give alms to the poor. He had been the first Christian treasurer. He had been all that but he never reached heaven.

This man gives a profound warning to all professing Christians: you can actually get as near to Jesus as that but still be lost. We have got to ask why and look deeply into this man's heart, because Judas was not an ogre; he was not someone who was just evil through and through from his mother's womb but was an ordinary man who allowed the devil to get hold of him. He was one of the twelve disciples who allowed Satan to suggest things to him.

First of all, Jesus makes a general statement. He expects treachery. He has already warned the disciples there are going to be enemies outside their group who are going to attack and kill him. Now he says something far worse, "We have a traitor inside." Throughout the last two thousand years, the church of Christ has suffered more from traitors inside than from enemies outside. That is always more difficult to face.

Jesus quoted Scripture: Psalm 41:9, a psalm born out of a difficult experience when King David learned that one of his close followers had gone over to the enemy and was a traitor. In his anguish in the psalm David says, "The one who's been eating bread with me has lifted up his foot against me, he's kicked me." It's a treacherous act. Jesus said, "Not only did David have that experience, that Scripture also tells us that the Son of David will have the same experience. "The same thing that happened to my ancestor is going to happen to me, the man who has been eating bread with me has lifted up his foot against me, he has kicked me from the back. Not the enemy in front, but someone from behind who should have been supporting me."

It's a terrible thing to say. But Jesus knows that the most important thing is the confidence of the other eleven when they discover this. There is nothing that destroys morale so quickly as finding you have a traitor in your midst. So Jesus seeks to lift their confidence and says, "I'm telling you now, so you won't be upset when you realize what's happening. I want you to know that I am who I am [that's a divine title: Jesus is saying, 'I am God']. You will be surprised and shattered, but I'm not. I want you to keep your confidence in yourselves; you are still royal ambassadors. If anyone receives you, they receive me and if they receive me, they receive the One who sent me. Don't let this dreadful thing that's going to happen shake your confidence in your apostleship. Keep your morale."

It is lovely how Jesus, facing all these problems, spends so much time preparing the disciples to face them. So he says, "When it happens and you realize one you have lived with for three years is a traitor, you don't need to lose confidence in me, I knew it all along. Don't lose confidence in yourselves, you're still my ambassadors and wherever you go, whoever receives you will receive me."

Then comes the moment of a specific prediction. It is a verse that describes Jesus' feelings: he was terribly upset. I don't know how he looked but they could see he was deeply troubled. He repeats it: "I can see you don't believe it, I tell you the truth. One of you is going to betray me." This is an eyewitness account of what happened. It must be an eyewitness account because what happened next is just what people would do: the first thing they did was that everybody looked at everybody else. They all looked around at one another. "Who is it?" We know from this passage they were lying at table, reclining on couches, with their feet out and their heads towards the table. Jesus was in the centre; John was on his right hand, closest to his face, since they always leaned on their left arm and ate with their right hand. So John was here; then came Peter. Interestingly, Judas was on Jesus' left, so just behind his back, where he literally could kick Jesus and lift up his foot against him.

Peter is curious – he could never keep his thoughts inside so he said, "John, ask him who it is." John leaned up against Jesus and whispered, "Lord who is it?" With an amazing touch, Jesus was going to tell John the truth but in such a way that the name was not spoken aloud so that the others didn't get upset. He whispered back, "Watch who I give the bread to next." He answered the question to his beloved apostle, took some bread and passed it behind his back to Judas. So John knew. We don't know if John told Peter. There was a stunned silence maybe, perhaps John was so shattered that he was struck dumb.

In that moment Jesus did something so quickly that it was done before they realized; he said, "Judas, get on with it quickly. Get out!" Judas went out. That was the direct command in this scene: "Move. Hurry. Get on with it."

Why did Jesus say that? Some people have thought that Jesus was impatient to get to the cross. I don't think so. Others have said that if Judas had stayed there and the word had gone round the table, Judas would never have left that room alive. Peter had a sword with him and was prepared to use it, because he used it later that night. Perhaps Jesus was getting Judas on with it to set the whole train of events in motion before the other disciples recovered from their shock.

I think there's another reason, however: Jesus couldn't talk freely with Judas present, and he desperately wanted time with the other eleven to talk about the Father, the future, the Holy Spirit and so many things. He was being hampered by Judas' presence, so he wanted to get Judas out and then he could talk to the others as one family. He didn't use the word "Father" while Judas was with them, but as soon as Judas left, he used it in almost every sentence.

So he said, "Judas, get on with it." The other disciples thought that because Judas was the treasurer, he was going to give some money away or buy something they needed, and they let him go.

Only John knew, and he wrote just three or four terrible words. They had come to the upper room in daylight and eaten a full meal. The sun had gone down and when Judas opened the door, John noticed that outside it was black. The last glimpse he had of Judas was of a man shutting himself out into the darkness. That memory stayed with John for sixty years as later he wrote, "It was night."

"Was Judas simply a robot? No. As a human being I know certain actions before they happen, but my knowing them doesn't make the actions happen. In the same way, but in an infinite degree, God knows the future as well as the past. He knows what we're going to do. He holds us responsible for the choices we've made and the habits we've formed."

Let's ask two questions. First, the mental problem. Jesus said, "Do what you must." This raises the big question of predestination or free will. Was Judas predestined to do that? Was he simply a tool in God's hands? Was he really to blame for what he did, because it is clear that Jesus had known all about Judas for a long time? At the end of the feeding of the 5,000, Jesus said when everybody left him except the twelve, "Are you going away too?" They answered, "No, we're staying," and Jesus replied, "You're staying are you? Even one of you is a devil." Earlier that night he had said at the supper when he washed their feet, "I've washed your feet but I haven't got you all clean. One of you isn't clean, even now." He had known from the beginning who would betray him; he had known when he chose the twelve disciples. Jesus knew when he chose Judas that he was choosing the man who would betray him. He prayed about the choice; he had spent all night in prayer and God said, "Choose Peter, James and John and Judas Iscariot." But Jesus chose him and said, "I know whom I chose." It looks like a put-up job, doesn't it? Furthermore, even the Old Testament knew about it and had predicted it. God knew a thousand years earlier it would happen. Jesus once said, "The Son of Man must be betrayed. It's God's plan and purpose," and he said to Judas, "Go and do what you must."

Does this mean Judas was simply a robot? No. I want to tell you that foreknowledge doesn't make a person do something. Let me give you a simple illustration. If a squirrel appears in our garden, I know what our dog will do, because she's done it often. There's a conditioned reflex, an ingrained habit. When she sees that squirrel, she'll go crazy and go after it. However, my knowing she'll do that doesn't make her do it. She got the idea herself, then because she went down that path again and again, I know what she is going to do. Now even I as a human being can know certain actions before they happen, but my knowing them doesn't make the actions happen. I simply know they are going to happen. In the same way, but in an infinite degree, God knows the future as well as the past. He knows what you're going to do tomorrow but his knowing it doesn't make you do it. He holds you responsible for the choices you have made and the habits you have formed. God knew beforehand what Judas himself would choose and be responsible for and was able to weave Judas into his plan. He can make even human wrath praise him. But he still holds people responsible. Jesus said, "The Son of Man must be betrayed but woe to the one by whom he is betrayed." In other words God has planned it, but the man is still responsible for it.

That brings us to the second question, the moral problem: if Judas was free and responsible, how could he live with Jesus for three years and do such a thing? It wasn't one wrong decision; it was the climax of a series of wrong decisions. Judas had a weakness: greed. He never dealt with that weakness or shared it with others. When they received a little money from gifts given to the disciples and needed a treasurer Judas never said, "Don't give me money; I've got a weakness with money." He said, "I'll look after it," and gradually this got hold of him and he was even stealing money from Jesus and using it on himself. This is a shattering downhill slide. A stage came where Jesus said, "One of you is a devil," meaning "one of you is an antagonist to me; one of you is against me." Later, it says Satan put a thought into the heart of Judas: "You could make a lot of money tonight if you betray Jesus." All the years had opened Judas' mind to such a thought and the devil had already put it into Judas' heart. The thought was there, and when Jesus finally gave him the bread, the last fork in the road appeared. I believe that at that point Judas could still have confessed his sin. I believe he was free to turn to Jesus, because to give a morsel of bread at a feast is a token of love in the Middle East, and it was the last appeal to Judas. But far from responding, it says Judas took the wrong decision, and Satan entered him. That's the climax. A weakness indulged in, Satan suggesting and finally Satan entered Judas.

Jesus realized he had reached the end of the moral road and said, "Get out, hurry. Go and do it. My last appeal to you has failed; you've chosen, go and do it." That's the warning; it could happen to any of us, so we need to stay close to the Lord not just physically, but in other ways too. Remember Judas. He actually shared in the Lord's Supper, he came to the Lord's Table, took bread and wine and then went out, "and it was night."

JESUS: GLORIOUS (13:31-35)

After Judas had left, the atmosphere lifted. Humanly speaking, the events that Judas was starting were a disgrace and humiliation. But Jesus said, "I'll bring glory to the Father; the Father will bring glory to me." Now that Judas had gone and Jesus had started on his way to the cross, the Father was going to be glorified: the wonderful thing is that when Jesus died on the cross, it brought glory to God.

We now know what God's love, justice and wrath are like. Jesus glorified God; he brought glory to the Father. Jesus said, "If I bring glory to the Father, he will bring glory to me now, at once." The glory of Jesus is the cross. The glory of his love is that he died. The glory of his obedience is that he was obedient to death.

Jesus then thought of his disciples and made a specific prediction. Very tenderly Jesus told them: "My children, I won't be with you much longer. The event that Judas has started not only means my glory, it also means our separation. I'm going to leave you. You'll want to be where I am but you can't come. This is the end of our three years together, but now we must say goodbye. Little children, you must be brave. We've been together these three years. You've seen me and I've seen you. We've walked, talked and eaten together, we've slept in the same room. That's going to finish soon. A little while longer and that's got to end. I told the Jews they couldn't come where I was going; now I've got to tell you the same."

He added, "I've got one supreme concern: that after I have gone, you eleven are to remain together." They had all stayed together because they had Jesus with them. If Jesus had left them any time during the three years, they would have split up quickly. Jesus' physical presence kept them together. But they were so mixed temperamentally and by their different backgrounds that without Jesus' presence they could easily split up.

So Jesus said, "I've got one important thing to say to you. My little children, after I've gone, I want you to stick together. Love one another. It's a new commandment." It's not in the Old Testament, which has "Love the Lord your God with all your heart and soul and mind and strength" and "Love your neighbour" but not "Love one another." This is a special love Jesus' followers are to have. It's not a love for God, not even a love for your neighbour and the world, but your attitude to your fellow Christians.

"The command to love one another is a commandment. He isn't talking about sentimental feelings, but about loyalty."

Notice it's a commandment. That is why some people call it the eleventh commandment added to the ten. Some people think that love can't be commanded, that it is something you feel, that you either feel it or you don't. But Jesus said, "Love one another, I command you." The kind of love Jesus is talking about can be commanded. He is not talking about sentimental feelings, but about loyalty, the kind that is at the heart of the marriage service where a man doesn't say when I ask him, "Will you have this woman to be your lawful wedded wife, for better for worse, for richer for poorer, etc.", "When I feel like it, I think I will"; he says, "I will." God expects that man to be loyal until death parts them, and he expects the same of all Christians, to love one another.

Jesus commands it, because it is the one thing that will convince the world that we belong to him. For Jews the badge was circumcision and Sabbath keeping, but for Christians the badge is not what you do or don't do on Sunday, not that you go to church or that you read your Bible. The badge of being a Christian is that you love Christians. It's the only sign he gave us that would convince the world that Christ is our Lord.

Do you know, when the world comes into a fellowship of Christians who love each other, they really are convinced: there is no argument like it, when they see a group of people who are so mixed in temperament and in every other way, who really love each other and are loyal to each other in the way that Christ was?

We are to love one another as he loved us. How did he love them? Let me be practical: he never criticized them to anyone else. If you talk about Christians to the world and criticize them to other people, that is not love. He was loyal to them to the end; he was so loyal that he rebuked them in love: he told them their faults to their face but never told their faults to anyone else. That's love. His love was patient; for three years he tried to teach them things, which even at the end of three years they still had not learned. He didn't write them off, however; he didn't say I'm going to try another bunch. Christians who move from church to church need to seriously ask themselves, "Am I being loyal to my fellow Christians?" "As I have loved you, be loyal to one another and people will know that you belong to me."

PETER: GLIB (13:36-38)

Peter missed all this last bit; he was still thinking about what Jesus said about being separated. So he never asked about loving one another. He said, "Lord, can I just go back a few moments; you said something about being separated from us. Where do you think you're going that we won't come with you?"

Jesus makes a general statement, not about the place he's going to, but about Peter's inability to follow. He said, "Peter, where I'm going you are not able to come at the moment; you're not ready to come. Later you will follow me but you're not ready yet." Peter takes this as a personal insult. He says, "I'm not ready? I would die for you." Peter reveals a weakness most of us possess: our words run ahead of our deeds. What we sing to the Lord in a hymn or song is not always followed up in life. Peter said, "Lord, I'm ready to follow you. I know you're hinting we wouldn't be prepared to die for you. But we would. If it's death you're going to, I'm your man." There's a subtle implication in what he said; "The others may not be there, but I will be. I'll follow you. I'm ready to go anywhere with you, even to die."

Jesus then made a specific prediction and said, "Peter, I know you better than you know yourself. Are you really ready? Let me tell you what the real situation is. The first sign of trouble and you'll be off. Even before the cock crows tomorrow morning you will be saying you don't know me."

Peter was always speaking but notice that for the rest of that evening he was silent: this shut him up. He was shattered and never said another word. Philip, Thomas and the others spoke but Peter didn't. Peter said, "I'll go to the death with you," but the fact was that a little servant girl would have Peter running for his life. You don't know what you're really like until the crunch comes. He was deeply upset and his heart was troubled. So Jesus gave him a direct command, "Let not your heart be troubled; believe" (14:1). All that Jesus said about heaven was to strengthen Peter when he discovered how weak he was.

John 13 presents a poor picture of the apostles, doesn't it? We see them as ordinary and weak; some were so weak they were lost. Studying this chapter could be disturbing but I found it encouraging. "Lord, if you could start with a group of people like that and start the church with them, then you could do something with me. If you could make Peter a rock, then you could take me as someone who is frightened to speak about Jesus." When you think of the people Jesus worked with and what he was able to make of them, then let's be encouraged and say, "Lord, tell me if I'm a Judas. Tell me if I need to take a right decision that will get me off that track. Tell me if I am a Peter, tell me if I'm weak, but Lord do something with me and make me one of your disciples."

27

"DON'T LET YOUR HEARTS BE TROUBLED"
John 14:1-11

PETER: WHERE? (14:1-4)

THOMAS: HOW? (14:5-7)

PHILIP: WHO? (14:8-11)

John 14 is one of the most precious parts of the Bible for many people, because it deals with one of the commonest human diseases – heart trouble. The heart is one of those parts of the body that seems to reflect most quickly the state of the mind and soul. Heart trouble is often caused by dread of the future, an uncertainty that doesn't know what is going to happen next.

This is precisely what lay behind this chapter: the disciples' hearts were troubled. Death was approaching. They were going to be bereaved and were afraid, upset and anxious. The cure for this disease is given in one word: "believe". Faith (trust) is the answer to this kind of heart trouble. Worry and trust are incompatible: if you trust you cannot worry; it you worry you cannot trust. That's why Jesus said, "Don't let your hearts be troubled; the cure for this condition is believe."

"Most people say there must be something or someone up there, some power beyond all we can see. In a public debate I had with a agnostic, he finished by saying, 'I believe man can get us out of our troubles, and if we can't get ourselves out then God help us!' The students cheered and clapped."

But believe in what? You can believe in anything or anyone. There is a certain kind of faith that cures heart trouble. It's not simply belief in God. Most people believe in God but they still get this kind of heart trouble. Jesus says, "Trust in God; trust also in me." This second dimension gives faith a new quality. Most people believe in God; I've met very few convinced atheists and some agnostics, but most people say there must be something or someone up there, some power beyond all we can see. In one public debate I had with a declared agnostic and almost an atheist, he finished his speech by saying, "I believe man can get us out of our troubles, and if we can't get ourselves out then God help us!" The students cheered and clapped.

Most people instinctively have some kind of belief in God but that doesn't cure heart trouble. Jesus said, "Don't let your hearts be troubled. You believe in God, believe in me too. Trust me. Accept my word as true. I'm not the kind of person who would leave you with false hopes. I'm not the kind of person who encourages wishful thinking, who would tell you something if it weren't true. I'd never deceive you. If it were not so, I would tell you. Trust someone who always told the truth, who never let people live under delusion." In fact he disillusioned many people: that was one of the reasons they put him to death. He would not let people live with false ideas about themselves, God or the future. So he said, "If it were not so, I would have told you. Trust me."

It is interesting that the disciples' questions have given us some of the loveliest teaching of Jesus about heaven. Continue to ask questions; don't keep them in. If you have got doubts or don't understand, then ask. Do you realize that if the disciples hadn't come out with their questions, we'd never have had John 14? Peter asked the first question, Thomas the second and Philip the third. Jesus gave much of his greatest teaching in response to questions. The parable of the Good Samaritan is a perfect example. He only told that because someone asked, "Who is my neighbour?"

The key words here are *Father* and *I*. Every time Jesus answered a question, he replied with *Father* and *I*: Father and Son together – he's saying, "Trust us. Trust my Father, trust his Son. Trust us, and you won't be upset and anxious about the future." When you look at Jesus' comforting words and consider them with the comfort the world offers, there is no comparison. When you are anxious and troubled, the world says, "Don't worry; it may never happen." But if you are worried about death it is going to happen. Then the world says, "There's always someone worse off than you." Well maybe there is, but that doesn't help me. Maybe there isn't, and then the world says, "Live with your memories." Jesus doesn't give us such shallow comfort. He has got deeper comfort: he says, "Don't let your hearts be troubled. I'll tell you the truth. I'll tell you the real acts about the future. I won't leave you in any doubt, and then your heart can be at peace and rest."

PETER: WHERE? (14:1-4)

Peter was concerned with where: where the future life is going to be, where was Jesus going that he couldn't follow, where? He is concerned with the place we call heaven. Peter was disturbed by the possibility of bereavement, that the person he had come to love the most was going to leave him and they would be separated. Jesus had already assured him the separation was not for ever, that there would be a reunion, that Peter could follow along later. But this was not enough to reassure Peter's heart. He was worried about the future. "I don't know where you're going, and I don't know where you'll be. I feel I'm losing you." He was upset because Jesus had told him he was not ready to follow right then.

So, with wonderful compassion, Jesus heals the trouble and takes away the worry. Here is a man who's going to die within twenty-four hours comforting those who are going to be bereaved! He is going to face pain himself and he is comforting others. He himself had a troubled heart, as we have seen. But he says to them, "Don't be troubled." He then told them two lovely things: first, "I'm going to prepare the Father's house for you." Secondly, "I'm going to come back and take you to the Father's house. You don't need to worry about the future separation. It has a purpose: I'll take you from this world to live with me for ever. I'm going ahead to prepare the place for you." The two things Jesus is doing right now are that he is preparing a place for people and he is preparing people for the place.

Let us consider this. Let us remove the word *mansions* ["In my Father's house are many mansions," (14:2, KJV)] that implies we'll all be living separately. There is far too much of that here: too many privet hedges and lace curtains! We are not going to live in separate mansions a mile from one another. There is only one house; you cannot have many mansions in one house. "In the Father's house are many rooms."

It is interesting that the word Jesus uses is the word used at the beginning of Luke's Gospel to describe our Lord coming to earth when there was no room for him.

I always picture an eastern inn with a large courtyard; round

347

the courtyard on two storeys are little archways and inside each is a room. In the middle is a drinking trough and a manger where camels can stay. Then the families go to their resting place, their rooms, protected. There is a gateway, which is shut at night. There is a room, but when Jesus was born there was no room, so he was born in the courtyard and put in the manger. He was not born in a stable, but in the open air with a star looking down on him.

There was no room for him. But at the end of his life Jesus said, "There's plenty of room for you. There may have been no room for me but my Father's house has plenty of rooms. No shortage of accommodation there: plenty of room. I'm going to get the place ready for you."

My wife Enid and I were separated seven months after we got married. I was in the Royal Air Force, and they posted me overseas. I went halfway round the world, and when I arrived I wrote back, "I'm getting a flat as soon as I can. I'm getting a place ready for you and then you can come and be with me." And after about three months, Enid came out and we were together again. We could bear the separation because I was going to prepare a place as soon as possible and then we could be together.

Jesus said to Peter, "Don't be worried and upset. I'm going ahead to prepare a place for you." That's precisely what Jesus is doing now. Jesus isn't the kind of person to have said that unless he meant it. So let others ridicule heaven and say it is a dream world, a fantasy or drug. But I know Jesus better than that and he would not give me a drug or fantasy. "I'm going to prepare a place."

Jesus then said. "I'm not going to leave you to find your own way there. I'm going to come back and take you." An old lady I visited regularly some years ago was out once when I went. Later she told me where she had been. Her nephew from Kent arrived one day with his car and told her, "We're taking you down to Kent for a holiday." She replied, "I'm not ready," to which he answered, "Come on, get packed and come. If we'd written to you and told you, you'd have written back and said you couldn't come. So we've come for you and you've got to come." This dear old lady packed her bag and went. She said, "I arrived there and they had the loveliest little bedroom all ready for me looking out over an orchard. It was just glorious: they'd got it all ready for me!" Then each of us remembered this passage. One day quite unexpectedly,

Jesus may suddenly say, "Right, it's ready for you. Come on, come with me," and we are there: it is all prepared. It will be wonderful to get to heaven and find that it is ready.

Jesus has been there already, and he is going to come back again. His second coming is promised three hundred times in the New Testament. "I'll come back. It's all right; I'll take you. I'll look after you. Peter, you don't need to worry about anything," and so the believer looks forward to going home.

THOMAS: HOW? (14:5-7)

Thomas was worried now. These disciples were like us, full of questions. Thomas was slow to grasp and still had not got the message. I am glad he spoke out because we would never have had Jesus' great saying if he hadn't: "I'm the way, the truth and the life." Thomas said, "All right, you've told us there's a Father's house and that there are rooms for us. But I still don't believe you've told us what we need to know." He dared contradict the Lord. The Lord had said, "You know how to get there," but Thomas replied, "We don't know how to get there." Who was right? Jesus.

Christians have this common fault; we underestimate our knowledge. Somebody says, "I could never witness, I don't know enough." But you know enough if you know Jesus! "They might tie me in knots." Well, try! You may know more than you realize. Thomas said, "I don't know how to get to heaven." Jesus replied, "You do, because you know me." Jesus then made a statement that is without parallel in any religion or in the teachings of any other great person. Other great people have said, "I will tell you the way," "I will show you the way," "I will tell you the truth," "I will give you the life," but Jesus went far further than all these. He said, "I am the way. I am the truth. I am the life." Do you want to know the way to heaven? Then all you need to do is get to know Jesus. Do you want to know the truth, reality, truth about God, yourself, the universe? All you need do is to get to know Jesus. Do you want real life, life of eternal quantity and life of full quality? Then all you need do is know Jesus and you have the way, the truth and the life. You don't need to be shown the way or told the truth or given the life. You have them. That was Jesus' answer to

Thomas. He began each little phrase with the name of God: "I am" – the name of God.

"Notice the little word *the* Jesus uses. He is not *a* way. That is why there have got to be missionaries: he is *the* way. That is why we have got to tell the whole world about Jesus because he is *the* truth, not a truth. That is why somehow we have got to get across to everybody that Jesus loves them because he is *the* life, not *a* life."

Jesus said, "I am the way, you know the way. Thomas, you know me, so you know the way. "I am the way to the Father." "You know the truth." It is not just truth about Jesus that saves. It is the person of Jesus who is the truth, the reality and the life. You have got everything in Jesus.

I want you to notice the little word of three letters *the* that Jesus uses three times. He is not *a* way. That's why there have got to be missionaries: he is *the* way. That is why we have got to tell the whole world about Jesus because he is *the* truth, not a truth. That is why somehow we have got to get across to everybody that Jesus loves them because he is *the* life, not *a* life.

Some people think we are just Christians because we like this kind of life and they like another kind of life, that everyone should choose their own kind of life. But there is only one life: the life. Every other life is death and will end. Jesus is *the* life and so he makes the most exclusive statement that has ever been made. "No one can get to the Father except by me." *No one*: this is the death blow to all the ideas the devil has planted in the human mind, deluding us into thinking that as long as we are sincere we will go to heaven. I tell you: sincerity cannot wipe away sin; only Jesus can. The devil makes us think that all religions somehow head for the same point, that "we're all rivers going to the same sea." Jesus said, "I am the way, the only way. No one can get to Father except by me." It is because we don't believe this that we lose interest in the mission Jesus gave us. If you really believe that

Jesus is the way, you have got to be concerned with spreading the truth and offering the life in Jesus' name.

Someone may be clever, kind, nice and friendly. He may be many things and think he is going to heaven. But all these things are of no use when he comes to die. If Jesus was right in saying this, then if you have Jesus, you have everything you need for the future. But if you don't have him, you have nothing to help you.

PHILIP: WHO? (14:8-11)

Philip now says: "We don't mind coming to live with you for ever, but what's the Father like? It's nice to know you and it'll be lovely to come and live with you for ever, but Father ... who's Father? Look, just show us Father and that would really clear up the last fears we've got." A human need is being expressed here by Philip, which is deep in every heart: "If only we could know God, if only we could see him as he is, if we just had a good idea what he's like." Philip expressed this desire. "Lord, show us the Father, that's all we need now. You've told us about the place and the path, how to get there ... well, it's the person I'm concerned about. What's he like? Show us what he's like, and then we're ready for heaven." Jesus answered, "Philip, you've been living with him for three years. Philip, you want to see him; well, you've been looking at him and listening to him for three years. Do you still ask this question?" Again, Philip had underestimated his knowledge; he thought he didn't know but he did.

The glory of it is that when you know Jesus you know exactly what God is like. You know what it feels like to talk to God, if you talk to Jesus, because Jesus said, "The Father and I are so close that we are inside each other. The Father is in me and I am in him. We are closer together than two human beings could possibly be. We are in each other. We are two persons but we are in each other. So everything I say is what he would say. Everything I do is what he would do. Did you think the words I have spoken to you were my words? They weren't; they were his. If you find that difficult to believe, then surely you will see the miracles I did were his works."

How do you get to know what a person is like? Their words and their actions tell you. Jesus said, "If you listen to what I've

351

said and look at what I've done, you know him. You know exactly who you're going to live with because you've been living with him for three years; it won't feel any different. A Son and a Father together. Everything I say and do is the Father's." That makes the relationship with God so intimate, close and dear. It solves many problems: the remote impersonal God some people seem to believe in, whom they never talk to because they don't know him and don't feel he is interested in them – that sort of God evaporates when you meet Jesus and discover a God who is concerned, knows and cares. He loves, rebukes and chastises. He is a real God, the Father of Jesus. That deals with the last question: "What's it going to feel like to be in the Father's house?" Answer: it's going to feel like being with Jesus, and if you know Jesus now, you already know what it feels like.

"Don't let your hearts be troubled. There is a place called heaven: let no one deny that." Everybody else may be proved a liar but Jesus is not the kind of person to tell us something untrue. "Peter, you don't need to worry, heaven is a real place, and you're going to live there with me. Thomas, you don't need to be troubled because you know how to get there if you know me. It's not hard to get to heaven. It's not a complex mystical route that somehow you'll have to search for. Just get to know me. Philip, you don't need to worry what it feels like to live with God: you've lived with me. It's just the same. Don't let your hearts be upset, don't get worried, don't fear for the future, don't dread it."

There's a phrase in the New Testament about death that applies to you if you are a believer. All these words were said to the believers, not the crowd. If you are a believer when you die there is a phrase in the New Testament that says "you will simply be at home with the Lord." If you know him well here, you'll feel very much at home there. Lord Baden-Powell, the founder of the Scout movement, was a Christian. On his gravestone is a simple inscription: a circle with a dot in the middle and Scouts know its meaning. It is a tracking sign that simply means "gone home." That was what he wanted on his tomb: "gone home." That is true if you know Jesus Christ.

28

"I WILL NOT LEAVE
YOU ALONE"
John 14:12-31

JESUS' POWER WILL BE THEIRS (14:12-14)

JESUS' PRESENCE WILL BE THEIRS (14:15-26)

JESUS' PEACE WILL BE THEIRS (14:27-31)

Loneliness is terrible. It is dreadful to be all alone, to be left by yourself with no one else. You can feel that way spiritually too: an old Negro spiritual runs: "Sometimes I feel like a motherless child / A long way from home." That's exactly how the eleven disciples felt at the end of the Last Supper. Jesus had called them "my little children," but they thought of themselves as orphans. He was going to leave them; he had said many things, most of which they had not grasped. But they had understood he was leaving them and they were anxious and afraid.

Jesus set out that night to comfort them and help them cope with the knowledge that he was leaving them. Jesus sensed they were dreading the future, that it seemed empty and hopeless. Here were twelve men sitting round a table and within twenty-four hours their thirty-three-year-old leader would be lying cold, stiff and grey in his tomb. Not only that, but Jesus also knew he would be flogged and mocked before he was put to death. Not one of the other eleven tried to comfort him, however. He had to comfort them; it is an ironic situation, with all that he was going to face, *he* comforted *them*. He desperately needed ministering to himself. He asked them a few hours later to pray for him, but they fell asleep and in fact the only help Jesus received the last night of his life was from the angels. No human being comforted him. But he comforted them.

In this study, we are going to see Jesus said, "I will not leave you alone. There's going to be a gap but you won't be by yourself." Jesus said (verses 18-19), "My little children, I will not leave you as orphans. I'll not leave you alone, wandering around like little children with no one to care for you, no one to belong to. I'm not going to leave you like that. I'll come back, but before I come back I'll not leave you alone. I've got other plans." We are going to look at those plans now.

Jesus could see there were three things the disciples were going to miss badly: his power, his presence and his peace. He dealt with them all by saying, "The power will continue. Another person will take my place. And I'm leaving my peace with you."

JESUS' POWER WILL BE THEIRS (14:12-14)

Before they met Jesus, the disciples could only offer people sympathy. They could say to someone in need or trouble, "I really am sorry": that's all they could do. But when they met Jesus, a complete change took place, because Jesus didn't just sympathize with people, he said, "Satan has bound this person. We're going to set them free." He released divine power into their lives: he made the blind see, the deaf hear and the lame walk; even the dead stepped out of their coffins.

The disciples watched Jesus for three years. Everywhere he went he left people rejoicing. Now if he was going to leave, that would all come to an end and they would go back to the old life of just offering sympathy. They had even been able to share in Jesus' power. He had sent them out two by two and said, "You go to the village in the town where I'm about to come," so they always knew he would back them up and if it didn't work he'd come the next day. It didn't work at times: they came to him saying, "Lord, we've been trying to heal this poor boy but can't do anything for him. Can you help?" And he stepped in: "Yes, I can help. How long are you going to be before you learn how to do this? It takes fasting and prayer." Then he would help them.

All that was going to come to an end, or was it? Listen to Jesus' astonishing promise: "He who believes in me will do the same things I've done. The power is going to continue." I find this verse too big for my faith; I have to bow before the Lord saying, "I believe, help my unbelief. Are ordinary men and women going to continue doing what you did on earth?" Jesus replied, as if that wasn't enough, "I tell you the truth, you've got to believe this: it's going to continue." And as if that wasn't enough, he added, "and he'll do even greater than I've done. When I've gone back to the Father, bigger things will happen. My leaving you is going to increase the work, not decrease it, because through faith people are going to continue what I've been doing."

Scholars have debated what those works include. Some say it can't include the miracles, but it must: those were Jesus' works. Others say it must include all his actions, like washing feet: these would continue. But he's simply saying, "What I've been doing will go on happening." And it did: if you read the book of Acts, you will discover they continued doing what Jesus did, without him. The power continues because Jesus has gone to the Father. Jesus can do much more from heaven than he could on earth. Here is a secret: you have power towards people if you have power towards God. The power towards God is the power of prayer.

"Jesus said, 'If you ask anything, I'll do it so that the Father may be glorified through the Son.' Here's a fundamental condition of prayer, so we don't rush in and pray for something we want desperately. The first question we have to ask is: does it bring glory to God? We could ask for things that would bring glory to us or for things that would be for our own convenience or comfort. But Jesus said it has to be for God's glory."

Jesus now made a second promise, which is even more startling: "I'll do anything, whatever you ask." It means there's no limit to the scope of prayer: there's no situation or need that you should put outside the circle of prayer: "whatever; anything."

Jesus did set two limits to the "anything", however. We must pray out to the limits and within the limits set by this promise. The outer limits are "whatever, anything," but there are two inner limits: first, that it shall be for God's glory. "If you ask anything, I'll do it so that the Father may be glorified through the Son": that's a fundamental condition of prayer, so we don't rush in and pray for something we want desperately. The first question we have to ask is: does it bring glory to God? We could ask for things that would bring glory to us or for things that would be for our own convenience or comfort. But Jesus said it has to be for God's glory.

The second limit is it must be "in my name". That doesn't mean of course simply tacking on a formula at the end of prayer, so what does it mean? That when you pray for something, you are saying, "Father, this is Jesus calling." It's bold: "Father, this isn't me praying: it is Jesus. It is coming from my lips but it is

Jesus your Son speaking, so you've got to answer, haven't you? It's your Son speaking."

Praying in Jesus' name is awe-inspiring. It means that you must first ask Jesus what we are going to pray for, because you can't pray in Jesus' name if he isn't praying with you, if it is not a prayer he's taking part in, if the words aren't his.

That's how God's power is released to continue Jesus' ministry: whatever, or anything, for God's glory and in Jesus' name. The miracles did not stop; the power was not withdrawn. It is becoming greater and greater, and more is happening in the world today than ever happened in Jesus' day.

JESUS' PRESENCE WILL BE THEIRS (14:15-26)

The second thing worrying the disciples was they were going to miss Jesus' presence. They knew he was leaving them, but he said, "I won't leave you alone; I'm going to send you someone else." This was the first time he had specifically talked about a third person. He had mentioned the Holy Spirit incidentally and occasionally, but now for the first time he talked about a third person. They had come to know about the Father and they had known the Son. But now Jesus said someone else, another helper, is going to come along. The word *helper* is difficult to translate. Some people translate it as *comforter*, but that is too soft, as that seems to refer to dealing with sorrow by soothing. Originally *comfort* came from the Latin *fortis*, "brave": it meant to turn a man into a fortress; a comforter was a strengthener who made you a fortress. My translation is *stand-by*: "another stand-by", because the Greek means someone you call beside you: "Come and stand by me; I need you." It was used in the law courts of an advocate, who would stand by you, defend you and stand for you. People sometimes ask me if they should ever pray to the Holy Spirit. If he is literally the One who is called to stand by, you've got to call him. So it is biblical to pray to the Holy Spirit. He's God, so you can pray to God: call on the Holy Spirit to stand by you.

Jesus calls the Holy Spirit "another stand-by." Greek has two words that could have been used here; one means "another, unlike this one"; the other, which is used here, means "another, just like this one." The Holy Spirit will be just like Jesus: the support and encouragement will be the same.

Jesus said, "Whatever I've been to you he will be to you. Someone else will continue to stand by you. He will tell you what to say, he'll protect you, he'll defend you against your adversaries. He'll stand before your accusers. I'm going to send someone else. I wouldn't leave you as orphans; I'm going to send another helper."

Now here of course those who are not Christians are out of their depth because the world cannot recognize the Holy Spirit and so cannot receive him. If you speak to the world about God, you'll find that most people in this country believe there is a God. If you talk about Jesus, most know who you mean: many may simply consider him a human being, while others will say he is the Son of God. But if you mention the Holy Spirit, the world hasn't a clue. The Holy Spirit is moving throughout the world, but the world hasn't a clue about him. In recent times, we have seen a fresh move of the Holy Spirit: I am excited to be alive today. But the world doesn't know who he is. Jesus says, "The world doesn't know the Holy Spirit, but you know him. You know him in a different way from the way you know me. You know me as someone outside you but you know the Holy Spirit is someone in you."

That's the difference for the first disciples: Jesus was very close but always on their outside. But he said, "Haven't you felt the Holy Spirit in you? He's going to remain in you for ever. There'll be no interruption in the relationship as there is with me. He will remain with you for ever as another helper."

Now comes something even more difficult. We must move beyond reason and logic into the realm of experience, where we learn not only that there are three persons in the Godhead to help us – the Father, the Son and the Holy Spirit, we also discover they are so close to each other that you cannot have one without the other. The Holy Spirit is Jesus' other self. He is the Spirit of Jesus and you can't have the Spirit within you without having Jesus within you. This is puzzling. We are in the area of paradox, something that seems impossible but is true.

Look at the paradoxes here: Jesus says, "I'm going to be absent but I will be present. I will be hidden but I will be visible. I will be dead, but because I live you will live also." He's saying, "When the Spirit comes to you, I'll have come back to you. I may be away physically but I'll be with you spiritually." You can't have the Spirit without the Son. Then he says, "You can't have the Son without the Father. So when the Spirit comes in, the Son comes in and the Father comes in. It's one big 'coming in,' and so you'll have all three of us living in you. So why are you worried, you won't be orphans!"

Then Jesus says something amazing. At the beginning of chapter 14 he talked about rooms in heaven for people to go to. He now uses exactly the same word; he says, "My father and I will make our home in you." Here is the double picture: homes in heaven for people, and homes on earth for God. What a picture! "I'm preparing a home for you; you prepare a home for us. You can come and live with me one day but first we want to come and live in you." That's what's going to fill the gap, and until we reach our home in glory, God wants to have a home here. That's what Jesus is saying, and Father, Son and Spirit will come all together and make our home in us.

"We have two problems in relation to God's will. First, ignorance: we don't always know what God wants us to do. Second, forgetfulness: we know but we forget. Jesus said, 'When the Holy Spirit comes, he will deal with these two weaknesses. He will bring you into all truth; he'll teach you everything. And he'll bring it back to your memory when you need it.'"

All this is beyond logic; I've never yet met anybody who can explain the Trinity logically but Jesus said it was in the realm of love. Love understands things that logic doesn't. Love isn't logical sometimes. In the realm of love these things become experience. Because the Spirit lives in me, I know that the Son is in me too. Because the Son is in me, I know the Father is there too: I have become a temple of the living God. It all happens through love, not the kind of sentimental mushy love of songs, but obedient love. Jesus said, "If you want to find out how much you love me, ask how much do you do what I say?" It is the only real test of loving a person. If you love a person, their wish is your command. If you love a person you want to share their life, you want to enter it. He says, "If you love me, you'll keep my commandments. If you love me, I'll love you, and because you love me, my Father loves you, and we all love you and want to enter your life. We'll come right in and you'll no longer be orphans. Now if you're going to obey, you need to hear; the words of God need to come."

We have two problems in relation to God's will. First, ignorance: we don't always know what God wants us to do. Second, forgetfulness: we know but we forget. Jesus says, "When the Holy Spirit comes, he will deal with these two weaknesses. He will bring you into all truth; he'll teach you everything. And he'll bring it back to your memory when you need it. So you'll get the message and obey it, because you love me."

JESUS' PEACE WILL BE THEIRS (14:27-31)

The third thing Jesus talks about his peace. Wherever Jesus went, he brought peace. He said to the storm at sea, "Be still", and the wind and the waves died down and there was peace. Wherever he went, there was peace: why? Because there was safety and security: he was in control of every situation. No matter what was happening around him, he seemed to have an inner poise and serenity. This is the difference between the peace Jesus had and the peace everybody else wants.

In the Middle East *peace* (Hebrew, *shalom*; Arabic, *Salome*) is the word of greeting. Whenever you meet anybody, you wish them peace; whenever you part you say, "Peace." Why? Because they don't have it. Why do you continue saying it because they can't find it? The world always longs for peace, but it's a peace that is dependent on outward circumstances.

What is your idea of peace? Sitting in a deck chair, in a quiet garden with the sun beaming down and all your phones switched off? Is that your idea of peace? Two artists were commissioned to paint a picture of peace. One drew a beautiful woodland scene, with no leaves stirring and the sun's rays coming through the trees onto a bed of bluebells. The other artist drew differently:

storm waves beating against the bottom of a cliff and the wind blowing grass on the top of the cliff, but halfway up a nest and a bird: peace! The peace Jesus gives is not a peace that depends on circumstances around you but on God within you.

The nearest Jesus ever came to making his last will and testament was this last evening. He had nothing tangible to leave; his clothes went to the soldiers, his body went to Joseph of Arimathea; his spirit was given to God and he bequeathed his mother to John. What was he going to leave his disciples? "I'm going to leave you my peace." No one else can leave you that. They can leave you money or property, but only Jesus can make a will and say, "I leave you my peace."

Let us consider Jesus' peace. It has three aspects. First, Jesus' peace depends on a heavenly destination. "I'm going to the Father: that's my peace." He could have said, "I'm going to my death," or "I'm going to suffering," but he didn't; he said: "I'm going home to my Father." Because Jesus has already gone to his heavenly destination, we can have his peace now. He is there preparing a place so we have his peace.

Secondly, it is the peace of moral freedom: the peace of being able to say, "The devil has nothing on me." That's peace, because one of the reasons we lack peace is guilt. There isn't another person in history who has ever been able to say, "The devil has nothing on me." You have seen the temptations of Jesus: the devil tried very hard to get a foothold into Jesus' mind and soul but he couldn't. He couldn't get in. Jesus said, "The devil has nothing on me." Believe me, there is a devil. Jesus believed in the devil, and the devil rules the world. That is why in so many spheres things go wrong even though we try hard to put them right. But the ruler of this world has nothing on Jesus, and if I am in Jesus then I could have that freedom too. That could bring peace of conscience.

The third aspect of Jesus' peace is loving obedience. One of the reasons we lack peace is that there are too many pressures trying to control us: too many loyalties, too many desires, too many alternatives, too many things to do. Jesus, however, had only one authority, which brings peace. He said, "That's why I do everything he tells me. I love him: he's my boss – my Father runs my life and that's peace."

When you have the peace of a heavenly destination, a moral

freedom, and a loving obedience to your heavenly Father, you can say simply, "Rise, let's go, we can face anything now. We can face the cross now. And so he stood up from the Lord's Table at the Last Supper and said, "Let's go." They walked through the night. The conversation continued in the darkened streets, but the meal was over. They left the upper room. He had told them everything they needed to know to face the future unafraid and without anxiety.

Did they grasp it? Did they realize it all? I doubt it. But it all came true. Every promise he made came true. The result was that sixty years later the apostle John wrote it all down word for word as the Holy Spirit brought it all back to his memory.

29

"I AM THE VINE"
John 15:1-17

UNION WITH CHRIST (15:1-11)

Pruned by the vinedresser
Productive in the vine

UNITY WITH CHRISTIANS (15:12-17)

Total love – to death
Trusting love – for destiny

One of the reasons why Jesus was such a good teacher was that he used visual aids. He often used something simple to make a profound statement. He would sit a child on his knee and say, "Unless you become like a little child, you'll never see the kingdom." He could take a fig tree and curse it, giving a wonderful picture of how he saw his people Israel, as those who produce nothing but leaves and no fruit. He did this in parables, including what he said about himself.

In John 15 Jesus paints the last picture in his teaching: a vine. In Israel vines are everywhere; the staple diet in the Middle East is bread and wine. There may be another reason why Jesus then used the picture of the vine. He and his disciples had finished the Last Supper on top of the hill of Zion and were going down to the Kidron Valley and the Garden of Gethsemane. They had already left the upper room (14:31) and to walk from the upper room from Jerusalem down to Kidron they would have to have gone past the main gates into the temple. On those gates were two large six-foot long clusters of grapes hanging from a vine. They weren't real grapes: they were made of pure gold. They would walk right past the gates: maybe the grapes were glinting in the moonlight. They looked at this wonderful golden vine, which was a symbol of Israel (Psalm 80:8,14; 128:3; Isaiah 5:1-7: Jeremiah 2:21; Ezekiel 15; 17:8; 19:10; Hosea 10:1; Joel 2:22; Zechariah 8:12; Malachi 3:11).

That symbol goes back to the Old Testament, to the early part of their history where the children of Israel under Moses were outside the Promised Land. Moses sent spies in, who came to a valley with luscious grapes, which they called the valley of Eshcol (Hebrew for "clusters"; Numbers 13:23-29). They picked the grapes and came back with these clusters, saying, "It's a marvellous land: you should see the grapes! But there are giants in there." When they finally came in, they found it was a land of vineyards, juicy grapes, and so it became the symbol.

Looking at that great temple gate and thinking of the vineyard of Israel, Jesus said, "I'm the real vine. I'm the one who's going to give God the grapes he wants. Everybody else is a false vine. They failed to produce the fruit, but I'm the real one and it's in me that God, the gardener, will be able to pick the grapes he's been looking for for so long."

It is fine to have a lovely garden with juicy grapes but that's not the kind of grapes God wanted. For hundreds of years God had planted his people there and looked to them for justice, caring and righteousness but he had not received it. That's why they've suffered, been out of their land for 2,000 years, lost it again and again: because God said, "Look, I planted you there to be a vineyard, to give me fruit. But I've never had that fruit, so out you go, I'll let my vineyard become barren. I'll let it be trampled on and overgrown because what's the point of gardening if you don't get anything from the garden?"

UNION WITH CHRIST (15:1-11)

Jesus used this picture and said, "I'm the real vine. If you want to give God fruit you will need to remain in me." A vine needs more attention than almost any other plant. The gardener needs two tools: a hoe and a knife. The hoe keeps the ground clear of other plants. But the gardener also needs a sharp knife, which he has to use constantly to get the desired fruit. If God is to obtain from us what he needs he is going to use the knife on us constantly. This is a disturbing thought, but it is a surgeon's knife: it is to make us healthy, able to produce the fruit he wants.

Pruned by the vinedresser

Who likes being cut down to size? No one. It is uncomfortable when God cuts you down and cuts something out. There are two sorts of pruning because there are two sorts of branches in a vine. Some branches produce many leaves but never produce fruit: they must be rigidly cut right out, because they are useless: they draw from the plant but give nothing back in return. They are wasteful, not only not useful but actually wasteful of sap in the vine. They are cut out so that nothing is wasted. That's one sort of branch.

"If you want to get your roses pruned get one of your enemies to do it because it goes against your grain too much to cut them back enough, whereas an enemy will really cut them down. You will then have lovely roses. God is prepared to cut someone down to help them be what they should be: he really must love them."

But we are mainly concerned here with the other sort. Those who produce fruit but not very much: those who have a little sign that they are in Christ but not much – those who do a little for God occasionally: what does God do to them? In his love and tenderness, he cuts them down; he cuts them back. This is done regularly in Palestine between about December and February. If you go there then, you will see the vines, little bleeding stumps in the ground, looking dreadful and dead. But the vinedresser has had to cut them right down to almost nothing.

I was once told if you want to get your roses pruned get one of your enemies to do it because it goes against your grain too much to cut them back enough, whereas an enemy will really cut them down. You will then have lovely roses. It is even more true of the vine, it has got to be cut right back if it is going to produce real good fruit. God is prepared to do that: isn't his love amazing? If you are prepared to cut someone down to help them be what they should be, you really must love them.

How does God do that? Jesus uses the same word *prune*: "You have already been pruned through the word I've spoken to you." Speaking to us through the words of Jesus is God's supreme method of cutting us down. His commands cut us down to size. Don't you find that? God's word cuts us down constantly. It cuts deep, sharper than any two-edged sword, and it hurts. It finds you out: that's how he prunes. It causes us to suffer but those whom the Lord loves he disciplines (Hebrews 12:4-13).

Productive in the vine

Jesus said not only do we need pruning; we also need to keep in a vital relationship with him. The only function of the branch in a vine is to connect the stem and fruit. It is the link between the stock and fruit to transfer from the stock the sap that is rising and take it through itself into fruit. That is its purpose, and that is all our purpose is: simply to be the link between Christ and the fruit.

The branch of a vine is barren by itself. If you go to Hampton Court, you will see a vine with its roots near the River Thames, but it then travels 200 feet through the greenhouse. The branch looks twisted and dead, flaky in its bark. If you take a cutting from a branch of a vine and plant it, it will grow but only produce leaves, not fruit. By itself, the branch cannot produce fruit: it must be in a vine stock and then the sap comes and the fruit grows. It doesn't have the capacity within itself to produce fruit. Neither do we. "Without me," Jesus said, "you can do nothing." By nothing, he means "spiritual fruitfulness". Of course you can drive a car without Jesus, you can have a baby without Jesus, you can do all kinds of things without Jesus, but you can't ever do anything for God. The gardener gets nothing out of all this. The God who made it all does not receive fruit.

"I don't care how real your contact with Christ was years ago, it is your contact with him today that decides how fruitful you are. What is important is whether you have kept up fellowship with him, whether you are always in touch with him; whether you remain in him, make your home in him."

Another aspect of the vine is that the branches are useless for any other purpose. They are wood but if you want to use that wood for anything, you can't: it's too twisted and bendy to use as a stake, it doesn't burn well as firewood and you can't use it for furniture because you can't saw it up. Jesus as a carpenter knew that. The branch of a vine is useless by itself. It might produce leaves as a cutting but that's all show: the wood is useless.

But Jesus says, "If you're really deeply attached to me and in continuous contact with me, then you're useful. You'll do something with your life." It's a simple lesson: I don't care how real your contact with Christ was twenty years ago, it is your contact with him today that decides how fruitful you are. You may have a fine testimony of your conversion years ago but what is important is whether you have kept up fellowship with him, whether you are always in touch with him; whether you remain in him, make your home in him. It is the same word as the word *home* in chapter 14. Jesus says, "Unless you make your home in me, live in me, stay in me and keep in contact with me the whole time, then the branch will go brittle and dry and won't produce any fruit."

Think of the positive side: if we abide in him, look at the things that follow: fruitful lives, a glorified God, complete joy, answered prayer: promise after promise! If you remain in contact with me, all these other things will follow.

Now let us consider a question some ask. The text says that if a branch doesn't abide in Jesus, it's cut out, thrown out, withers and is burned. People have asked me does that really mean that a Christian who has been in Christ can get so out of touch with Christ that they can be eternally lost and go to hell?

There are two possible answers to that question. Many Christians believe what Jesus says here is that if a branch produces no fruit at all, it indicates that the person has never been a real Christian, they are simply a professing Christian, a nominal member of the church, that they are physically or visibly connected to Christ but not spiritually, and that when they are finally thrown into the fire it's because they are an unbeliever and have never been in Christ. Such a position certainly avoids the problem of the text and avoids many other problems contradicting other parts of Scripture. I can only say that I can't see that.

It seems to me that Jesus is talking to branches who have been in the vine and not remained. He is not referring to branches that have never been in the vine but those who have been in but did not stay in. It is about them that he speaks these solemn words: "they are thrown out, wither and burn in the fire" (v. 6). That is the alternative explanation and seems to me to fit better.

This is one of over eighty passages in the New Testament

containing an implicit warning to followers of Christ that they can lose what they have found in him (see, for example, Mark 4:16-17; Romans 11:19-22; Hebrews 10:26-31; 2 Peter 2:20-22; Revelation 21:7-8; the rest are covered in my book *Once Saved, Always Saved?*, Hodder & Stoughton, 1996). Even those who have entered the Kingdom on earth can still find themselves shut out of heaven, in outer darkness with 'weeping and gnashing of teeth' (as we learn from the Gospel of Matthew (25:1-30; cf. 13:47-51). Judgment and its consequent separation will begin with the family of God but must then extend to all who have not responded to the gospel (1 Peter 4:17-18).

These sobering reminders provide a motivation for staying in Christ, held in his hands (from which no-one *else* can snatch you; see John 10:28). They also contain an incentive to store up sufficient resources to see you through a long wait for his return and to show him some profit for all he has invested in you, thus bearing fruit on his vine by drawing life from him. His teaching on himself as the true vine has both positive and negative consequences, as have so many of his words.

But if we do keep the contact what kind of fruit do we produce? Fruit for God and fruit for people. First, the fruit of sanctification: the fruit of holiness, the fruit of the Spirit – love, joy and peace. Whenever you find the expression *good fruit* used in the New Testament, it is invariably the fruit of righteousness. Love and joy are both mentioned in this passage, "that my love may remain in you, that your joy may be complete." Secondly, the fruit of Christian service in winning others. Within every grape there is, or should be, a pip. Within that pip are all the powers of the vine's reproduction. The fruit is therefore not only pleasant to eat but is also capable of reproducing itself.

UNITY WITH CHRISTIANS (15:12-17)

It is a common but mistaken assumption among many Christians, that provided my relationship with Christ is all right everything else will be all right. You may be remaining in the vine, in full contact with Christ, right in the stock and the sap may be flowing, but you may be in a wrong relationship with Christians. "Surely that's not possible?" you ask, but it is or else Christ would never have bothered to tell us. If it follows that if I am right with Christ then everything else will be right, the only thing he needs to tell me is to remain in him. He would never need to tell me to love one another. But unfortunately it is possible for someone to love Christ but not love his fellow Christian.

Go back to Hampton Court and look at the vine. Do you know what the branches do? They are tangled with each other. If that vine is going to bear proper fruit and face the sun properly, you will find that a true vinedresser will untangle the branches, training them to be in line alongside each other.

Total love – to death

Even if the branches are in the vine bearing fruit, they can get all twisted with each other. So Jesus says, "You not only need to remain in me, you also need to love one another. If you're going to bear much fruit that will last, then you need to get untangled and love one another." Such love is a positive relationship. You can come to church and erect a little box round you. "Don't come into my box, this is mine." "I'm just here to worship God." No, that's the vine getting twisted and tangled again. Jesus says, "My love is a love that says, 'My life is not mine, it belongs to my brothers and sisters, it belongs to other people; if they need me then my life is theirs, even to the point of death.'" "Greater love has no one than this that he lays down his life for his friends" (v. 13).

Let us be practical in our own community. It would mean going out of your way to help someone in need when you had planned a quiet evening at home. That is laying down your life. You have got your life planned, but you will sacrifice those plans for the sake of your brother or sister. It is that kind of costly love that says, "My life is yours," that keeps the branches in a right relationship with each other.

Those who only remain in Christ but are not concerned about other branches lead self-centred lives. Jesus says, "You are to be concerned about the life of the other branches. Remain in me but be concerned about them. Love them; let the sap of my love flow to them through you."

Trusting love – for destiny

A trusting love is prepared to confide in people: that is true love. If you really love someone, you will tell them what is on your heart, you will share your plans with them. Jesus said, "I don't call you servants; I could do. I chose you, I'm the master, I could call you servants but I don't. You're my friends; I've told you everything I'm going to do. I've shared things with you." Not only a life that's prepared to lay itself down, but also a life that is prepared to share and talk together, and to be confided in one another.

Jesus then reminded them that the branches did not choose to be in the vine; the vine produced the branches. It is important to realize this: if a man goes to hell, it is his own responsibility and his own decision alone. But if a man goes to heaven it is because the Lord chose him. I can't get round the doctrine of predestination: it's there in Scripture. I thank God for it, even though I don't understand it: God chose me. But Jesus says the one thing that we need to remember with *predestination* is the word *destiny*, which comes in the middle of *predestination*. If you forget the destiny then the predestination will become distorted and false.

We are predestined to a destiny, that we should bear much fruit. Every time the Bible mentions predestination it always mentions destiny. We have been chosen, elected, to be like the first-born, to be made like Jesus. Jesus says, "All this is to fulfil the destiny for which I chose you. Why do you think you're in the vine? Why do you think I planted you? Why do you think you are my disciples? That you may bear much fruit and that your fruit may endure." Grapes go bad easily; they ferment quickly. You can dry them until they become raisins and they keep then, or you can let them ferment and become wine. But to keep them as enduring fruit is impossible.

There has been a progression of thought: fruit, more fruit, much fruit, enduring fruit. It seems as if the one thing that will make our fruit endure is not our remaining in Christ, but our remaining in union with one another. That is what preserves the fruit; the fruit is likely to go bad in a situation in which Christians aren't loving one another. But where Christians are lined up as branches with one another, reaching out to the sun together – lined up to the sunshine of God's love together and loving one another, the fruit will ripen and endure.

Jesus says, "You've got all the resources in me that you need to produce fruit. If you ask anything in my name, you can have it. Draw from me all you need for your love for one another." It is interesting that in the promise "Whatever you wish you can have", the word *you* is plural. It is not a promise to an individual Christian; it is a promise to the vine, to the branches, who together can say, "Lord we wish this." Because they are in mutual love, they can have what they want.

Notice that answered prayer is mentioned twice in chapter 15: once, under the exhortation to remain in Christ (v. 7) and once under the exhortation to love one another (v. 16). Here is another secret of answered prayer: to be in constant fellowship with Christ and in constant fellowship with Christians. Then you can expect your prayers to be answered.

I conclude where I began. What is the whole point of it all? That God should have some fruit. We are his garden, his vineyard. May he have from us what he desires, today and every day.

30

HOW TO LIVE IN
THE WORLD
John 15:18-16:15

SOCIAL HOSTILITY

Why? (15:18-25)
Instinct
Irrationality

How? (16:1-4)

SPIRITUAL HELP

Who? (15:26-27)
Truth
Testimony

What? (16:4-15)

In John 15 Jesus deals with the three relationships every Christian must get right: to his Lord (abiding in the true vine), to his fellow Christians (love one another) and to the world in which he has to live. It is this third relationship that we are concerned with here.

Wouldn't it be lovely when you were converted if you immediately went to glory? All your temptations over; your problems behind you and straight into God's presence. Sometimes we wish it were like that, but we must ask a simple question: if that were so, who would convert anybody else? The task of witnessing would cease. In fact, you would never have heard about Jesus yourself if God had done that, because the first generation would have been the last of Christians. One of our battles is that we have got to learn how to live in a world that doesn't belong to Jesus. That causes great tension. The Lord was so honest he never promised us an easy time. He said, "In this world you're going to have tribulation (trouble)" (16:33). Don't ever suffer from the delusion that the Christian life is comfortable; it's not: it's big trouble. The word translated *tribulation* actually comes from a Greek word meaning "a threshing sledge," made of timber with certain beams running one way and others running another in a lattice work. At each joint was a large metal spike sticking about six inches below the beam. It was dragged by a donkey over unthreshed grain and the spikes would roughen and separate the chaff from the corn. So Jesus is saying that is how we would feel in the world: sometimes as if you're being thrashed.

SOCIAL HOSTILITY

The word *world* in the Bible means the godless society of unbelieving people reigned over by Satan. It covers a wide field of human activity. That is why so much keeps going wrong and why, however hard we try, we can never get it right. It is a world that won't like you at all because you are a Christian. It is a shattering discovery, isn't it? You are full of joy. You have come to know Jesus. Everything seems wonderful, but you are surprised people don't like you anymore. You thought they would welcome you with such good news to share, but they don't. In fact, they may come to hate you.

Why? (15:18-25)

Instinct

Now why does this happen? Somebody who is different will be cold-shouldered. You have different standards, values, desires and ambitions from those around you. It happens on the factory floor, in an office or anywhere. You don't need to cut them off; they will cut you off. Your task is to try and remain there. It is sad when somebody becomes the only Christian in their office or shop and thinks the Lord's will is that they should get into an office where everybody is a Christian. It's not God's will. He called them there that he might have a witness there. It is going to be difficult. They are a social misfit now. But God wants them to stay there and witness.

You do not belong to the world anymore and instinctively they know it. It is very hard for those who come to Christ and have to continue living with an unbeliever as their married partner because that married partner straightaway will recognize that in some deep way their partner no longer belongs to them: this causes great tension. It is one of the reasons why a Christian should never marry someone who is not. If you marry a child of the devil you will have problems with your father-in-law.

Irrationality

The second reason why they will hate those who are different is: there isn't a reason – it is irrational. Sin destroys your thinking powers. The tragedy is that the world's hatred of Christians is irrational. You cannot explain it because they are hating what is good. People don't dislike godly people for what is bad in them but for what is good in them. It is that side that causes them discomfort. They are glad when they discover something bad in a Christian because that reduces their discomfort. It is the good in the Christian that makes them uncomfortable, and that is irrational. Jesus said, "They hate you only because they first hated me and there's no reason for that hatred. You could excuse it if they had not known what I've said and done. Ignorance is an excuse but they can't be excused on that ground. I've done certain things among them and said certain things to them, but they still hate me. I've done good things all around their land and they hate me. I've spoken the truth to them and they hate me for speaking the truth, that it might be fulfilled what is written in their law: 'They hated me without a cause' (15:25; Psalm 35:19; 69:4)." It's difficult to be disliked, when there's no reason for such dislike. Accept Jesus' logic: they hate Christians because they hated Christ, and if they hate Christ they must hate the Father too.

The real state of the world is enmity towards God, and nothing reveals it so much as coming face to face with a godly person. The enmity comes out when you begin to realize that basically man is not indifferent to God – he has declared a unilateral declaration of independence against God: "I don't like him; I don't want him." It is because people are God's enemies that they become Christ's enemies, and so they become enemies of Christians.

How? (16:1-4)

How does this opposition show itself? Here is another shattering teaching of Christ which is true to life: the greatest antagonism will come from religious people and be in God's name. Jesus said, "They will expel you from their fellowships. They will go on praising God themselves but will put you out." That is extraordinary, but through two thousand years, religion has been the great enemy of Christianity. Religious people have disliked Christians. It is those who have gone to church who have been most uncomfortable when they have met a real Christian. It is sad that those who already profess to believe in God provide the greatest opposition. Jesus even said, "Not only will they expel you from their religious places of worship, they will also execute you and think in doing so they're serving God." It takes religion to produce an inquisition; Holy Wars have often been in the name of religion.

Jesus said the sad fact is that religious people persecute Christianity. Why? "They will do these things because they know neither the Father nor me." It is those churchgoers who don't know the Father and don't know Jesus who are most upset by real Christianity. Their religion wants to push out those who love Jesus Christ.

For two thousand years Jesus' words have been true. Everywhere Christians have gone they have been hated. There have been many martyrs for the faith. There is opposition. In some countries, you can count on your hands the number of Christians who remain alive. The rest have paid the price of their faith with their life.

SPIRITUAL HELP

How is it that we can get on so well with our neighbours? How is it that there is not the dislike of Christianity in this country? Is that good or bad? Here are five attitudes that a Christian can adopt towards the world, and four avoid hatred and dislike.

First, retaliation. The world hates you, so all right, you hate the world, you "give as good as you get". The world has a grudging respect for a person who hits back and who doesn't turn the other cheek. In a sense, the world gets on better with someone who descends to its own level, who returns evil for evil and hatred for hatred. That is one way to avoid it. Not many Christians do this, as it is obviously wrong and does not help the situation.

Secondly, isolation: you make sure you never really come into contact with the world even though you have to live in it. For example you spend your lunchtime quietly reading your Bible instead of having lunch with your colleagues. You spend all your spare time with church organizations. You keep your home as a place where only Christian friends come. You isolate yourself so that even though while travelling on a train, others are buried in a newspaper, you're buried in the latest Christian book. You isolate yourself from the world so they don't even know whether you are a Christian or not.

Thirdly, adaptation: when you are with Christians you behave as a Christian, and when you are in the world you behave as a worldly person. What you say and do when you are in the world is exactly the same as they say and do. You laugh at their jokes, talk about their cars, live just as they do when you are with them and you keep your Christianity within Christian circles. You are in the world but now you have become of it when you are in it.

Fourthly, "Christianization": you treat everybody as if they are already Christian. Many people are still buried with a Christian burial, with the words "in sure and certain hope of resurrection to eternal life" read over them. Many babies of unbelievers are still christened. And as long as we Christians go on in this kind of vague Christianization we will never know any dislike. But if a minister has convictions and refuses to christen a baby where the parents have no interest in Christ, that causes difficulty: the world's dislike comes out. We are in a Christianized, but not converted, land. That is a tragedy.

"The basic reason why we find it difficult to talk about Jesus is that we haven't been with him (15:27). You can't learn to witness from a book. You learn to witness by being with Jesus. And if you've been with Jesus you are bound to talk about him because he will mean so much to you."

The fifth attitude is our Lord's attitude: evangelization: "I want you to go into the world and witness. I want you to stay where you are, not pull out of the world. I've chosen you out of the world but I want you to go into it." "Go into all the world and preach the gospel." Our task in the world is not to retaliate, withdraw or adapt: it is to get in there and witness. But that is going to be harder than I can do. We say: "I can't get into the world and witness; I'll get tongue-tied and embarrassed. How am I going to do it?" This is where Jesus says, "I'm going to send you a Helper. The Spirit of Truth is going to come and he will witness and you will witness. You'll both be drawing attention to me together. He'll help you to do it. When the helper comes, he will bear testimony."

Who? (15:26-27)

Truth

Our society is convinced the majority is always right: that's the fundamental principle of democracy. However, that's not the way the Holy Spirit thinks. Because the Holy Spirit is the Spirit of Truth, he says if truth is to be found in only one person, then the rest must be wrong. He doesn't go by a majority vote, but by the truth. And so with a minority of Christians, the Holy Spirit says, "We're going to testify to the truth. I'm the Spirit of Truth. When I come, truth will out. Together we'll bring out the truth about God and humanity: whatever the world thinks, my task is to prove the world wrong and prove Jesus is right."

Testimony

The Holy Spirit will do it through testimony, which means if I'm not prepared to put my lips at the disposal of the Spirit of Truth, the testimony will not be given. Most of the gifts of the Spirit are gifts of the tongue. He wants us to testify by using our tongues: the Holy Spirit wants to fill that tongue with testimony to what is true, that people may know the truth and reality. "The Spirit of Truth who comes from the Father and is sent by the Son will testify of me and you will testify of me," and you can't do that unless you have been with Jesus.

The basic reason why many of us find it difficult to talk about Jesus is that we have not been with him (15:27). It is no use getting a book and getting all the right things from a book and then trying to witness to that. You cannot learn to witness from a handbook. You learn to witness by being with Jesus. And if you have been with Jesus you are bound to talk about him because he will mean so much to you. If you have been actually with Jesus there will be a testimony on your lips. You are bound to say when you meet somebody who is going through a bad patch: I came through an experience like that but I'll tell you who helped me through it. Then the truth will come out and the Holy Spirit, the Comforter, will use you as a witness in the court of the world's judgment and you will stand there and you will say, "I know he lives."

What? (16:4-15)

Here is the other side of the Spirit's help, Jesus' profound teaching about the Holy Spirit. He begins by telling them something extraordinary: "It will be better for you if I go and he replaces me." That is difficult to understand. Imagine I announced that next week Jesus would appear in person here in the pulpit. Can you imagine it? Wouldn't it be wonderful? The answer is no. There is something better: his Spirit is here today and will be here next week and the week after. That's better! "It's better for you that I go because if I don't go he can't come and replace me." It's conditional. "I must return to my Father and then we'll send you someone else."

Why is the Spirit's coming much better? First, because from Jesus' local presence, his Spirit has a universal presence. Second, because from an external presence outside me, he becomes an internal presence inside me. Jesus says, "When you're going out, I know you'd love me to go with you in the flesh." Wouldn't it be lovely to go house-to-house visiting with Jesus in the flesh and just stand slightly behind him and let him knock on the door and speak to the people? You know he'd have just the right word. Wouldn't it be lovely? But there's something better: the two of you go to a door with the Spirit in your hearts and say the right thing. That's much better because there can be another two in the next road with the Spirit in their hearts doing the same thing. Jesus said, "It's better for you in your testimony not to have my physical presence but to have my Spirit, the Comforter, the Spirit of Truth. You'll find he will do three things for the world. He will actually lead them to a conviction that they've been wrong.

I think the hardest thing in the world is to persuade someone they are wrong. When you start talking about Jesus, you run into wrong ideas straightaway, don't you? Somebody says, "I'll tell you what I think." You know what is coming and they tell you and you think: "How am I ever going to get that idea out of their mind. How will they get the right idea?"

There are three things they need to know if they are going to become a Christian: the right idea of sin, righteousness and judgment. But when you meet a natural man, an unbeliever in the world, he has got the wrong ideas about all three.

You ask him for his ideas about sin and he'll say, "Yes, I believe in sin. It's dreadful and there's a lot of it in the world. If we got rid of some people, we'd get rid of sin." People always blame somebody else, e.g. a criminal. "But me, I'm in the Rotary and do a lot of good service. My wife and I have always tried to do our bit and we go to church sometimes." But see what happens if you ask someone, "Did you know you're a sinner?" If they don't cut you dead, see what happens.

You will never convince someone of sin: not until the Holy Spirit is active through your testimony and convinces them that the worst sin of all is not to believe in Jesus.

You may never have committed any other sin but not to respond to the love of God in Jesus is enough to condemn a person to hell. The greatest sin is indifference to Jesus. That is not the kind of sin that others would call sin, but it's what sin is: that God in his great love has sent his only Son to die for everybody and people couldn't care less about it. They say, "Another time, thank you very much," or: "We're not interested." That is sin at its worst: to have such love offered you from the One who made you and to be indifferent to it.

What about righteousness? Righteousness is a word the world doesn't like or use, because they have got the wrong idea, that it's "trying to do your best". That is what someone who is good is: and you say to them, "It's possible for human nature to be perfect," to which they will answer, "I don't believe it." You can tell them there was one person who lived a perfect, righteous life. Christ's goodness is not a matter of whether people think he was righteous. It is God's verdict: he said, "I accept this man into heaven."

The Holy Spirit has to convince someone they will never reach heaven without the righteousness that is required to get in. It is astonishing how many people believe "I've done my best, and the gates of heaven will fling wide open and everybody will shout, 'Hallelujah; he did his best. Here he comes.'" But I tell you: "Who may ascend the hill of the Lord? He who has clean hands and a pure heart" (Psalm 34:4, NIV); "Be perfect as your Father in heaven is perfect" (Matthew 5:48). It takes the Holy Spirit to convince someone they will never see heaven unless they have got righteousness and that there is only one life that has ever been lived that was worthy to step into heaven on its own merits: Jesus. The Holy Spirit will convince people of righteousness because Jesus was accepted into heaven and went to the Father, and he now makes his righteousness available to us to go there too.

You need to be convinced about the gravity of sin and convinced about the possibility of righteousness. Then you need to be convinced that when those two meet, judgment must take place. If you ask people today whether they believe in judgment, whether they believe a day of reckoning will come when they will have to answer for everything they have done, said and thought, they are not convinced. They believe you can do things and get away with them, that if you get away with them in this life you have got away with them for ever. But the cross comes, which shows us not only the gravity of sin and the possibility of righteousness but also the certainty of judgment. At the cross God began to judge this world. What was really happening when they put Jesus to death? That they were judging him? No: God was judging *them*.

The prince of this world was judged at the cross and shown for what he is. God was beginning to put the world right at the cross. That process will continue until the day when he comes to face every person with his responsibilities. The cross tells us that God takes sin seriously, to the point of death. The prince of this world is already defeated and his days are numbered with all the pride, envy and arrogance he has infected into his world that is condemned and judged at the cross. Only the Holy Spirit can convince a person that God doesn't treat sin lightly and that judgment comes.

When people become Christians, the Holy Spirit guides them. He takes the things of Christ and gives them to believers. He brings them into all truth. He teaches them things they were not able to learn before. He guides them into all truth. He does not force them. He leads them into all truth. He speaks of things to come. Have you noticed this? As soon as you come to Jesus, your mind opens wide. It seems as if there were things you never saw before. A new Christian will even say, "I've never heard a preacher say that before." Of course they are wrong. Preachers have been saying it for so long but they couldn't take it in. That was the problem. The Holy Spirit opens the mind and he teaches and brings us into all truth. He glorifies Christ so that Christ is increasingly wonderful in our sight.

The Holy Spirit has a lovely work: not only to help you give your testimony before the world's court, not only to secure a conviction that the world is wrong, but also to teach you that Jesus is right and to open your eyes to his glory. All the resources of the Godhead – Father, Son and Spirit – are available to you. The Father has given everything to Jesus, the Son. The Son has given everything to the Spirit, and the Spirit passes on everything to us. Isn't that a beautiful cooperation? "As the Father has given everything to me I'll give everything to the Spirit. The Spirit will give everything to you."

It is tough in the world. People won't like you if you are a real Christian. They won't love you because you love Jesus. The more you are a true witness, the more uncomfortable other people will be, and the less they will like you. It is tough but possible and you will never have to do it alone. The Spirit of Truth will bring the truth out. He will use the truth from your lips to convince someone else, not that you are right but that Jesus is and that they are wrong.

31

FROM SADNESS TO JOY
John 16:16-33

THAT GLAD DAY

Appearance of the Son
Attendance of the Father

THIS SAD DAY

The weakness of the flesh
The wickedness of the world

It is a miracle that we have these chapters of John's Gospel in our hands. There is no human explanation as to how we got them considering the circumstances in which they were spoken. The fact that anyone remembered any of them is amazing. They were spoken somewhere between the upper room and the Garden of Gethsemane as the disciples walked through the night streets. No one was there with a shorthand notebook taking it all down. They were spoken to a group of eleven disturbed and anxious men. If you have ever tried to leave a message clearly with someone who is disturbed and anxious you will know how difficult it is. The words were not written down until sixty years later but here is every word Jesus said on that lonely last walk on the last night of his life. He had promised that the Holy Spirit would bring back to their memory everything he said, and if that promise had not been fulfilled we would not be reading this chapter.

There are many precious pearls here: many words of wisdom and many of Jesus' greatest promises. But they are all against a background of bereavement. One thing they did understand out of everything Jesus said was that he was going and they were losing him: they would soon not be able to see him. That left them disturbed and anxious.

THAT GLAD DAY

Jesus kept speaking in riddles. They used the word *parable* but it meant "riddle; conundrum." "In a little while you will not see me and then a little while you will see me." They asked, "What on earth does that mean? We don't understand him. Why can't he talk to us plainly? Why can't he spell it out simply? Why does he speak in parables, in riddles?" But Jesus understood them even if they didn't understand him and he knew how their little minds were teased by what he said and so he made it clearer to them.

Appearance of the Son

I expect Jesus was present at the birth of each of his brothers and sisters. They didn't have maternity wards then. The mother had her baby at home with all the other children present. The facts of life were known early to a boy in Jesus' day. Jesus had watched the other brothers and sisters being born and above all he had never forgotten the expression on his mother Mary's face as he watched. He saw the struggle, pain and anguish. Here he calls it a time of suffering. He then adds, "Have you ever noticed the change on the face when a baby is delivered?" Many of you have seen this: suddenly from the anguished strain is light, joy and liberation. A baby has been born into the world.

Jesus said, "I want you to recall that mother's face. I can see in all your eleven faces at this moment the expression I saw on my mother's face when she was struggling to bring another little baby into the world. I'm telling you a day will come, not too far ahead, when your faces will change just as my mother's face changed. A day when you'll change from sad and tense strain to joy, because you'll see life burst into the world.

"Meeting Jesus is to have your face lifted. The joy you'll receive when you meet Jesus is a joy no one can take away."

I am saying this reverently. There is a joy of an empty womb which is a guide to what the joy of an empty tomb is like. This is what Jesus is talking about. His riddle about "a little while you won't see me and a little while you will" refers to the days between his death and resurrection: the days when those men would be broken, when their little world had caved in, when they would not even face another soul. Each would run away home and hide like a wounded animal in the jungle: in those days the expression on their face would be one of pain and anguish. But after a little while they would see Jesus and have a face change.

I saw a notice outside a church: "Come inside and have your faith lifted." Instead of *faith*, you could put *face* and it would work: Jesus says, "Meeting me is to have your face lifted. The joy you'll receive when you meet me is a joy no one can take away." The reason they cannot take it away is that nobody can ever put Jesus back in the tomb. You can't reverse that process any more than you can reverse the process of birth.

People may put Jesus in a tomb, seal the stone and say, "He's there for ever." Jesus said, "The world will be glad." Just think: glad that Jesus is dead. I don't imagine too many gloated over it but I can imagine many people were relieved. Pontius Pilate slept that night for the first time for a while. "It's all over. He's dead, buried. Finished. What a relief! No more trouble from this troublemaker and the world will be glad." "You'll be sad," said Jesus, "but the world will be glad. That will make your sadness worse. They will be relieved you've lost your messiah. They'll ask you, 'Where's your Christ now?' and you'll hide away from other people. Don't worry, you'll see me in a little while, and the joy you'll be given then nobody can take away."

We can apply this promise differently to ourselves because we are going to see Jesus. In the world we will have trouble, tribulation and tension. We are bound to have: we are struggling to bring the life of Christ to birth on earth. Paul said to his own converts, "I am in labour again until Christ be formed within you" (Galatians 4:19). This kind of tension is the daily experience of the Christian here. Don't worry; one day your sadness will be swallowed up in gladness. You are going to see Jesus and when you do, no one will take away your joy.

Attendance of the Father

Not only will that mean joy but Jesus' return would also lead the disciples into something else that would complete their happiness: a new relationship with the Father. When you meet Jesus face to face and have a deeper relationship with him, you will have a new relationship with the Father. This will particularly come out in your prayers.

Jesus said, "Once you've seen me, you'll pray in a freer way to your Father. You'll go straight to him. The things you brought to me you'll take to him now. After you are sure I'm alive and I've defeated death, you'll go to God directly." Notice something Jesus says here. I had the wrong idea of Christian prayer for a long time. I thought that Christian prayer was praying through Jesus to the Father, that when you prayed and used the name of Jesus and said at the end of the prayer, "through Jesus Christ our Lord", it was as if you said, "My prayer is being handed to Jesus, who will then go to the Father and take my prayer along with him and hand it to the Father on my behalf."

But praying in Jesus' name is deeper than that. Jesus says, "I don't say I'll go to the Father on your behalf. I say you go directly to him using my name." Now that's a bolder prayer than praying through Jesus: it is to pray directly to the Father and put Jesus' name in and he'll listen.

Let me illustrate this. Outside Guildford lived a very wealthy man, Mr Paul Getty, the oil millionaire. I want you to imagine that Mr Getty gave me his cheque book with unsigned cheques and that he gave me authority whenever I went to his bank manager to sign "Paul Getty" on a cheque. Can you imagine that? Imagine Mr Getty saying, "Don't come to me for money; just go straight to my bank manager and sign my name on the cheque. You write it. What a bold thing to do. The bank manager would be suspicious if I signed that name. But Jesus said, "I'm not going to go to the Father on your behalf. I want you to go directly to the Father now and use my name. Have the kind of boldness that can say, 'Lord, here is a prayer and it's coming from Jesus. Here's his name in the prayer.' I present it to you directly."

It means a boldness in prayer that only comes to those who have met with Jesus. It takes real courage to go and say, "Father, here is the prayer and here is the name: I've signed it." When we baptize people, we baptize them into the name of Jesus, not into their own name. They are now entitled to use that name. They bear his name. You can go directly to the Father. Jesus is saying, "All the little things you came to me about ... go straight to the Father now because he loves you. He loves you because you love me."

Whenever Dr W E Sangster was introduced to a new baby by a proud mother, he would look at it and say, "What a baby!" That's the perfect remark: it didn't say anything specific but it always opened the mother's heart to him and he could then say anything to the mother. "Love my child, love me," and the Father says, "Love my Jesus, I love you. You can come straight to me and use that name. If you love him and believe in him, then prayer is wide open to you. Come straight to me with every need you've got and just sign it 'Jesus,' and you can draw on the bank of heaven."

You see I am in a better position than if Paul Getty gave me his cheque book, because with that cheque book I could only get things you can buy with money, and that's not much. Another wealthy man, John D Rockefeller, once said, "The poorest man I know is the man who has nothing but money." The richest man I know is the man who has got a blank cheque book on the bank of heaven and who has been told by the Saviour, "Sign my name and go straight to the Father with it. You don't need to go through me; you've got my name. The Father himself loves you."

Here are two discoveries that Christians make that turn their sadness into joy. First, the discovery that Jesus is alive after all and that he has defeated death. Then you complete it because you now have a boldness with the Father. Now you can use the name in prayer. Jesus says, "Those two things will complete your happiness. Meeting me will provide the foundation for it and praying in my name will complete its joy."

THIS SAD DAY

By now the disciples were getting the message. They said, "At last he's not speaking in riddles. We're beginning to understand. He's beginning to speak plainly." Jesus then made a statement that was so plain that they actually understood the message: "Listen to me. Let me sum up everything I've been saying. I came from the Father into the world. I'm going out of the world to the Father." That's not a riddle, but a plain statement. Do you realize there is only one of those phrases that any other human being could use, which is "I'm going out of the world."

I didn't come into the world. I started in the world. I began in my mother's womb, and humanity began in the dust of the earth. We didn't come into the world; we always were in it from the beginning so we can't say, "I come into the world." Nor did we come from the Father. We came from an earthly father not a heavenly one. So we cannot say either of those two things.

Then Jesus said, "I'm going out of the world": that is certain – everybody is going out of the world. "I'm going back to the Father." You can't say that. You can in Christ but you couldn't otherwise. Jesus said, "This is the statement of my whole existence. I came from the Father into the world. I'm going out of the world to the Father."

The disciples answered, "Now at last you're speaking plainly. We're ready to believe you. We understand now. We know you know all about our questions. You've answered our question even though you didn't hear us ask it of you and so we believe you came from the Father. Yes, this is fine." What a patronizing attitude! "We are prepared to believe you, Jesus, because you tell us plainly. If only you hadn't used all those parables before. You know, if only you had just put it simply, we would have been able to understand." How patronizing! Jesus, who was never touched by compliments or flattery, said, "You believe, do you?"

"I know everything, do I? Yes. I know something about you too that you don't know. I not only know your questions, I also know your weakness. I know your cowardice. I know everything, and I'm going to tell you about two more discoveries you're going to make today that will make you sad."

The weakness of the flesh

Every Christian makes two discoveries that make them sad. The first is the weakness of the flesh. It is one thing to tell Jesus you are prepared to believe in him; it's another to be faithful to him. It's one thing to say, "Now you're speaking plainly, I understand," and to have a clear head, but it's another to have a strong heart. It's one thing to profess belief as the disciples did here; it's another to live by it. Jesus mildly rebuked them for this patronizing attitude. "Now you've explained it, I'm prepared to accept it."

Jesus said, "Look, you need more than a clear head. Don't think that now you understand it all, you've got it all. I'll tell you something. This very day you'll all leave me alone and run away to your own homes like ants scuttling under stones. You'll leave me all alone, but I won't be alone. The Father will be with me, but you'll have gone. The very people I want to stay by me will have gone." It is always sad to discover how weak your flesh is: to declare on Sunday, "Lord, I believe. Now the preacher's explained it, I understand it. I've got it all in my head", and then on Monday you discover how weak you are, how easily you run away when it comes to a situation in which you are called to be bold.

"You will not stay with me," Jesus said, "but my Father will." I wonder if he had realized what the Father was going to do, that just a few hours later he would cry out, "My God, my God why have you abandoned me?" Even that was going to happen.

The wickedness of the world

The other sad discovery Christians make is that the world will not comfort you when you are sad. The world will not say, "I'm sorry for you," but will actually make you suffer when you are unhappy. It's one of those things that really knocks you right down. The devil doesn't mind hitting a man when he is already down. When you are having a real struggle and discovered your own weakness, do you expect the world to sympathize with you in your failure to be a good Christian? Far from it; they will gloat over it. They will be delighted, which knocks you even further down.

"What a perfect friend Jesus is! He knows how weak we are. He knows we're going to let him down, but he still says, 'Cheer up. Don't let it get you down if you let me down.' He is a patient, kind Saviour who picks us up again. 'Even if you fail me, I'm still your friend. I'm not washing my hands of you. I'm going to give you the victory.'"

Jesus knew all about the emotions his believers would have: the gladness when they knew he was alive; the gladness of prayer that is powerful with the Father. But he also knew they would discover the sadness of being weak, cowardly people and of having the world knock them even down when they failed.

Jesus, however, never left his disciples on the ground. He always picked them up again, so he said, "Cheer up!" The world says, "Cheer up; it may never happen," but it was going to happen. Jesus said, "Cheer up. The world will never get on top of you because I'm on top of the world. The world will never overcome you because I've overcome it." The world tried its worst against Jesus, but Jesus came through victorious.

You will discover how weak you are. Don't let that lead you to despair. You will discover that the world will take advantage of every depression you have as a Christian. Don't worry; take courage. "We're going to see this thing through together. I've overcome the world. I want you to have peace, not despair or discouragement."

What a perfect friend Jesus is! He knows how weak we are. He knows we don't understand what he says. He knows it is a puzzle and riddle to us. He knows we are going to let him down, but he still says, "Cheer up. Don't let it get you down if you let me down." Isn't that wonderful? He is a patient, kind and tender Saviour who picks us up again. "So don't let it all get on top of you. Even if you fail me, I'm still your friend. I'm not washing my hands of you. I'm not writing you off as bad disciples. You can leave me all alone but I'm still going to try and cheer you up. And I'm going to give you the victory."

This is the kind of patience Jesus has had with every one of his followers, and he has it towards us now. It gives us no excuse to go out and fail him again, but when we do we are not to let it get us down. Come straight back to Jesus and say, "Jesus, you overcame the world. I'm a failure, but overcome the world in me again."

32

JESUS' HIGH PRIESTLY PRAYER
John 17:1-26

JESUS GLORIFIED (17:1-5)

DISCIPLES SANCTIFIED (17:6-19)

BELIEVERS UNIFIED (17:20-26)

It is awe-inspiring to see someone on their knees and hear what they are saying to God. There is something holy about a person's fellowship with their Maker that you don't like to intrude on. There is something even more marvellous when you are listening not just to a man talking to God but a King talking to the King of kings.

We know that Jesus had a rich prayer life but hardly any of his prayers are recorded. Most of them are short sentences, but here is a longer prayer, where he poured out his whole soul. He asked for things which are not the kind of things other people pray. This is the prayer that only Jesus could pray and he asks for three things: that he himself may be glorified, that his apostles may be sanctified and that all believers everywhere may be unified.

Before we look at these three petitions let's consider its setting. It's probably just after midnight on the day when Christ will die. Jesus and his disciples are on the streets near the temple, perhaps walking through the outer courtyard of the temple near where the high priest offered prayers for the people. Every year on the Day of Atonement (Leviticus 16), the high priest of Israel would enter the temple and offer three prayers: for himself, his fellow priests and all the people of God. Then he would come out and kill the sacrifice on the Day of Atonement. It seems as if Jesus is almost deliberately taking over the position of high priest: passing through the temple, offering the three prayers for himself, his immediate helpers and for all God's people. The difference is that instead of going from that prayer to kill an animal, he's going to provide himself as the sacrifice for the people's sins. That is why this chapter is called Jesus' high priestly prayer.

JESUS GLORIFIED (17:1-5)

This request is a surprise: no man would ever dare pray this; only the Son of God could do it. Have you ever prayed, "God, give glory to me"? For us to say that would be selfish: "Honour me; may everybody look up to me. Give glory to me." But Jesus shows he has no selfish motives. He says, "Give glory to me and then I can give more to you." That's the prayer God loves to answer. Have you ever prayed, "Lord, give me more money so I can give more money to someone else"? "For your work"? This is how Jesus prays: "Give this to me and then I can give more to you. Give me more time and I'll give more time to you. Give me more energy and I'll have more energy to give to you."

Jesus was right to pray, "Give glory to me," because for thirty-three years the glory had been hidden. When Jesus came to earth, he left his glory behind. All people could see was a village carpenter, a little baby, a boy growing up or a wandering preacher. The glory was not there. Only once in his lifetime had his disciples caught a glimpse of his glory before he came to earth and then it was so bright that Peter said it was brighter than the midday sun. Now Jesus says, "Lord, give me the glory I used to have, the glory we had before the world began." God answered that prayer. A few months later Saul of Tarsus saw that glory and was blinded physically by it.

But, amazingly, Jesus asks for more: glory in his death. Crucifixion is not only painful; it is also intended to be humiliating. You are strung up naked for everybody to see, throw things at and mock. But Jesus said, "Father, the hour has come. Take this horrible disgrace, take this humiliating act and glorify me." Its glory is that God answered that prayer. When you see a picture of Jesus on the cross, do you see it as humiliation and disgrace? Are you ashamed of him? No, you glory in it.

It's here that God's glory is seen. "Glorify me now the hour is here. The day has come. All the thirty-three years now are coming to a climax. People are going to humiliate me. Father, glorify your Son and I'll hand it all back." Not only was Jesus asking to be glorified by death but he was also asking to be glorified to life so that his death would bring life. That's exactly what it has done. Not only has the cross led to the resurrection and Jesus' life, it's by the cross that eternal life has been given to so many others. It was not a tragedy but a triumph. What could have brought him right down for ever has lifted him up and drawn all people to him.

Jesus goes on from his death to the light that will come to humanity. He says, "Father, you've given me all authority over people." What a statement! Having universal authority has been the dream of world dictators but none could achieve it. Now Jesus, who is quietly going to his assassination, says, "You've given me authority over all people." What do people do when they have such power? They usually bring death to people but when Jesus is given all authority, what does he do? "So I can give eternal life to those you give me." Notice the word *give*, different forms of which occur fifteen times in this prayer. Because Jesus is praying to a God who gives, he's going to give too. The Father gives people to Jesus so that Jesus may give life to them.

"What is real life? Some people say the bigger your bank balance, the more you live. For others, it's the more places you have visited, the more excitement you have had, or in relationships, but Jesus said, 'Life is to have a personal relationship with God and Jesus.' If you don't have that, you are not really living."

If you belong to Jesus, God gave you to Jesus, and Jesus gave you life. But if God had not given you to Jesus, Jesus could not have given you life. The first stirrings of God's Spirit in your heart were the beginning of God giving you to Jesus; then you came to Jesus and he gave you life.

What is real life? Some people say it consists of possessions: the bigger your bank balance or house, the more cars you have, the more you live. Others say life consists of experiences: the more places you have visited, the more excitement you have had, the more you have lived. Others see life in relationships: the more friends you have; if you have got a happy family, this is life. But Jesus said, "Life is to have a personal relationship with God and Jesus." If you don't have that, you are not really living. However, if you do have it, you are alive for ever. It is as simple as that. "This is life to know you, and to know me" (v. 3).

The word *know* is interesting in Scripture: it is used of sexual intimacy: "Adam knew Eve and she conceived and bore a son." It means the closest possible relationship you can have with someone else. Not just to have theology in your head, not to know your Bible and quote chapter and verse, but to know God, to have as deep a relationship with him as you have with a marriage partner and to know Jesus like that.

There is only one true God. There are many other gods that people believe in. You can study world religions with its false gods, which people are convinced exist and worship but real life does not come to them. If you ask them, they are still searching and hoping they will know life but they don't find it for all their searching. Jesus says, "If you come to know the one true God, the one real God and me, that's life." This is what brings glory, so Jesus says, "Bring glory to me in my death, in the life that my death will release for others. I've shown them your glory. I've given them your life. This will bring glory to you."

DISCIPLES SANCTIFIED (17:6-19)

Jesus now turns to his eleven disciples, who are God's gift to him. Every church came from them. Christ thinks of them and tells his Father two things about them. Jesus tells God about a lot that God knows already, so in our prayers let us never be afraid of informing God about a situation. The Son tells the Father two things about the apostles.

First, what he has done for them: "I have introduced them to you. They now know you. I have given them your word, so they know you." Only Jesus does this for you; no one else can. Notice the stress on *words* (verses 6, 8, 14, 17). God's normal way of introducing himself to someone else is through words. That is how you get to know people. If somebody won't talk to you, you don't get to know them, do you? Jesus says, "I've given them your words so they now know you."

Secondly, what have they done with him? Jesus says, "They have received the word. They have believed it and obeyed it. Therefore they know." That is how knowledge comes: not just through hearing God's words through Jesus, but through receiving, believing and obeying. Then you will know God and his will.

Jesus then makes two amazing statements. First: I'm not praying for the world. Realize what Jesus meant when he said that. Why did he deliberately say, "I'm not praying for the world but I'm praying for my disciples"? Because the best thing you can do for the world is to pray for God's people in it. The world doesn't belong to God, so the best thing you can do is pray for the people who do belong. This is what you do in missionary work. When somebody goes overseas with the gospel, do you pray for those to whom they have gone or for the one who has gone? The best thing you can do is to pray for the one who has gone. In seeking to win people, often it is those who are seeking to win who need prayer more for sensitivity, love and patience. So although Jesus had compassion for everyone, he said, "I'm going to focus on those who are going to go to the world. I'm really going to pray for them." That doesn't mean we must never pray for the unconverted. In the rest of the New Testament we are told to pray even for kings who don't acknowledge Christ, that God may use them to bring peace. Nevertheless, I am underlining that when Jesus looked at a world for which he was going to die, he concentrated prayer on those who were going to win that world.

The second amazing thing Jesus says is, "All I have is yours, all you have is mine." Only the Son of God could pray that, but Christians can begin to say these two things too. Notice the order. If everything I have is in God's hands, then everything God has is in mine. Do you see what follows? If you give everything you have got to him, then you can expect to have everything that he has at your disposal. That makes for powerful prayer.

Here again is a fundamental statement. "All I have is yours. Here it is. I'll go to my death. You can have everything of me, so all that is yours is mine and therefore I am able to share it with my disciples." If you want to give a blessing to others, give everything to the Lord and then realize everything that is his is yours and then know you can share it.

Here is the reason for the prayer: Jesus is going out of the world to leave them in it. His concern is that the world is dangerous. Twenty-four hours later, Jesus would be free from the world's pressures and temptations but those eleven would still be there. He's going back to his glory but they won't go to glory until later. It's like parents' concern for their children going to college: "How are they going to manage?" This is Jesus' concern, so he prays, "Lord, I've kept them till now and you take over now. While I was with them in the world I protected them, keeping them safe and secure."

It had been a battle but Jesus kept each one of them. Jesus was honest: "Father, I didn't manage to keep one, but I know now he wasn't meant to be kept. I know now that from the beginning he never belonged to you, so he never really belonged to me. But I've kept all the of rest them. I'm going to have to leave them, so Father, you keep them now. I've kept them through the power of the name you gave me."

It was through the name "Father" that Jesus kept them. That's the name Jesus gives God. So Jesus says, "Now you keep them through your name." The word *father* is not the formal *father*, but the intimate *Dad*, Hebrew *Abba*, which is used six times in this prayer: "Dad, you keep them." Some people say that is being overfamiliar with God. A Hebrew would never have used that: it was too familiar, but Jesus never let it become too familiar. He added adjectives that kept it right: "Holy Dad; Righteous Dad."

"Now, he says, Father, you will have to keep them." He wants them kept in two ways: first, from evil and secondly for good. The world is an evil place. Jesus knows that evil is personal. It is a delusion to think there isn't a personal devil. Evil is not something floating around; it is someone. The Lord's Prayer originally ended with the phrase "Lead us not into temptation but deliver us from the evil one." But unfortunately in our day it's been re-translated as "Deliver us from evil." You should pray about Satan when you pray.

"Lord, I don't want these people to go into a monastery and withdraw from the world." We can withdraw into conferences, spending our time constantly with Christians. It is far easier to be a Christian at a conference than in the office or shop. But Jesus said, "I don't want them out of the world, but right in it. I'm not praying for you to take them out of it. I'm praying that they should be right in it, in full contact with the devil's subjects but not subject to him." We are to be involved in human society, rubbing shoulders with everybody except the evil one.

Not only *from evil* but also *for good*. "I'm not only not praying that they may be taken out of the world, I'm sending them into it, as you sent me into the world: they've got a job to do." No other religion says God sent his own Son into our world. He came and faced temptations, misunderstandings, slander and criticism: look what kind of people he mixed with. He had to come and face all that and if a Christian goes into the world they will have to face all that.

Jesus would have nothing to do with the evil one. He mixed

with everybody else so much that they called him the friend of sinners. He went to places some Christians wouldn't go to today. Pray to God that we would become more concerned to mix with people and get away from the devil than to get away from people and mix with the devil.

Jesus prayed, "I'm sending them, as you sent me, and they've got a job to do in the world, so I'm praying for their sanctification that they may be set apart from the evil one and set apart for the good one to use." The word *sanctify* means to be set apart for God's use. If you are sanctified, God can use all of you; you are set apart *from* evil and *for* good. A person who seeks holiness by withdrawing from all evil but not seeking any positive service is not sanctified biblically. Jesus said, "For their sakes I sanctify myself. I set myself apart. Not just from evil but for good." Sanctification happens through the word of God, which is truth, so it involves those who accept the word of God as truth.

BELIEVERS UNIFIED (17:20-26)

Here is a larger circle now: Jesus now sees millions of people coming to believe in him because of the apostles' word. We have in our hands the apostles' message, through which you come to believe in Jesus. If anybody becomes a Christian it is because they have heard the apostles' message through somebody's lips or read it. Notice Jesus' faith. He never said, "I wonder if these eleven will be able to win anybody. I hope they'll be successful," but: "Father, I pray for those who are going to come. Thank you for those who are going to be converted and come to Christ. Thank you, Lord." They were eleven ordinary, weak men who were going to run away from him a few hours later but he said, "Father, I pray for those who are going to come through them and believe."

What is our Lord's concern for all believers through the ages? In a word, unity. Some people are getting tired of these verses because they have heard "that they all may be one" quoted so often in recent years. But people are beginning to ask questions about unity, whether it may have been confused with uniformity or union.

What we have been seen over recent years is an attempt to organize unity among Christ's people, but we are learning the hard way you cannot organize it. It is true that it is a scandal that we use different labels, but I don't think they're the biggest offence. Neither do I think people look closely at the label outside a church if they find God inside. There is something much deeper.

What is this unity for which our Lord prayed? Is it uniformity? No. Is it union? No, I don't believe so in organizational terms. I think it is unanimity: hearts, minds and wills that act alike spontaneously. That's how Jesus was one with the Father. He prayed, "I want them to be one as you and I are one." That was not a visible unity and nobody organized it outside those two persons. It was a harmony of mind, heart and will, so that whether they were together or separate they acted the same, that whatever one said was what the other would say.

I am longing for the day when there is unanimity among all God's people in this country so it doesn't matter what church you go to: you will hear the same thing, you will feel the same love. It doesn't matter who is trying to decide on the policy, the will of the Holy Spirit is apparent to all. That is unanimity. At the deepest level this is what Jesus had with the Father. "If you listen to my words, you're listening to his. I don't want to do anything different from him. I just do what he sent me to do. It's between us two and it is there." It is not visible, because no one could see the unity between Father and Son, although they could feel its results: in his words and deeds the Father was present. That is the unanimity the world must see.

Were Jesus' prayers answered? Jesus was glorified and the apostles were sanctified but are believers unified? Some people talk as if we must answer this prayer. But Jesus was not praying to us to do it. He told us to love one another but here he is praying that God would do it. I believe that through the ages it has been done and is being done, because I find that wherever there are people who have come through the first part of this prayer they enjoy the unity at its end. Wherever there are those who allow Jesus' glory to shine in their life, wherever there are those who are set apart from the devil for good, you find that God creates a unity of spirit regardless of denomination or label.

"You either know God personally or you don't. It's not those who believe in God and those who don't. It's whether you know the One you believe is there. The world lacks love, joy and glory, because they don't know God. But Jesus has prayed this prayer that his glory may be seen in his followers, that their joy may be complete."

So the third prayer is conditional on the first and the second. Show me a group of Christians in which Jesus' glory is shown, a group of Christians who have severed themselves from the devil and are usable in God's service, a group of Christians who accept the word of God as truth, and I will show you a group of Christians who are thinking, feeling and acting alike.

I believe the prayer is being answered and that we must stop trying to answer it but allow God to answer it by letting Jesus' glory, God's word and the Spirit's sanctification come: then you find it happens and Jesus' prayer is answered. That is the unity of God's people. Nothing convinces the world so much that Jesus is supernatural and that God loves them than to see people of different backgrounds, temperaments and labels living and worshipping together in loving unity. "That they may know that you love them as you love me."

Finally, Jesus says, "Not only on earth but I'm also looking forward to this unity in heaven. Father, I would love to bring them to heaven right now. I want them to be with me where I am that they may see my glory, that they can see what heaven is like." So it is not only a unity on earth, but Jesus also looks forward to the unity we will have in heaven. Five minutes after death you lose your denominational label. There is a unity that will be lost in wonder, love and praise and the glory of God the Father, a unity where he is, a glory where he is and we'll see it.

So Jesus finishes where he began. The world does not know you but these know you. That is the difference. You either know God personally or you don't. It is not those who believe in God and those who don't. It's whether you know the One you believe is there. The world lacks love, joy and glory, because they don't know God. But Jesus has prayed this prayer that his glory may be seen in his followers, that their joy may be complete (v. 13), separated from the evil one.

"Glory be to the Father and to the Son, as it was in the beginning is now and ever shall be, world without end. Amen."

33

JESUS IS BETRAYED
John 18:1-27

JUDAS

ANNAS

PETER

JESUS
He knew all that would happen
He chose to die
His concern for others

Instead of simply going through the events here, we are going to look at the people involved because the real interest of these last hours in Jesus' life is to see the reactions to what is happening. The tragedy is only one life comes through unscathed. In everyone else, something comes out that you would rather not be there: some sin is revealed that causes shame and embarrassment. We are going to look at the four people in this study: Judas, Annas, Peter and Jesus. We are going to look at the first three to see what was wrong with them, although they were ordinary men, the kind of people you meet in the street, the kind of people you see in the mirror. It is easy for us to blame someone else and to look at someone and say, "Wasn't he dreadful?" and to forget that you could have taken his place. As we read through the story of the cross, ask yourself where you would have been. I don't think you'd have been on the cross with Jesus. Neither would I.

JUDAS

It is extraordinary that Judas' betrayal took place in a garden where Jesus had often gone to meditate, pray and have fellowship with his disciples. We have seen previously the downward trail of Judas. He started well: he preached the gospel, healed in Jesus' name, looked after the distribution of money to the poor. However, one thing was wrong with him: greed, which ate like a cancer into his spiritual life until it finally swallowed that up. He had not begun that way, yet his greed began to eat into his soul until finally he could not keep his hands out of the money box. His ambition became not to please the Lord but to gain money. That can happen to anyone.

So the time came when Judas had gone so far down that the devil could take possession of his heart. He could not have done it earlier. But on the night before this happened, the devil entered Judas' heart and from then on he was hardly responsible for his own actions. He had been responsible for putting himself in that position but now the devil had got him and he was going to go ahead with this treachery.

Notice how much Judas misunderstood Jesus, his Lord and

413

Master. We know this, because Judas brought a group of soldiers to arrest Jesus: the word used was normally used for a group of at least two hundred soldiers. How little he knew Jesus! They not only came in numbers but they also came armed with staves, the sort of weapons to capture a wild animal. They came with torches, too, but they were not needed, because it was Passover (full moon): the night would have been like daylight. Torches would only be needed for a man who's hiding in the dark under the roots of a tree. Judas thought Jesus would be crouching in some shadow behind a wall. How little he knew Jesus!

Then Judas came and did that terrible act that is not mentioned in John's Gospel but is in the others. He chose a kiss. When a man kisses another man, he has either got a deep affection for him or something has gone terribly wrong, and it was the latter with Judas.

"Do you know Jesus and Judas are going to meet again? You see, Judas is still a person. It will be a terrible meeting, because Jesus will have to say to the one he lived with, 'Depart from me. Go for ever.' A day of judgment is coming when Judas will stand before the throne and God has appointed Jesus to judge."

We know from the other Gospels that Judas later realized in selling Jesus for thirty pieces of silver that he had in fact sold himself. That's a cheap price for human life. Judas died a few hours before Jesus and a few hundred yards away from where Jesus would die. Whereas Jesus died at the top of the city on a hill above the city, Judas died in the valley at the bottom of the city, in a field so deep in the valley that the sun never hits it. There they were, two young men, dying within hours. But Jesus was going to the Father and Judas went to his own place.

You may feel you don't see Judas in yourself at all but if there is anything in your life that can eat up your spiritual life and continue to do so until you have lost your love for Jesus and your understanding of his mind, then you are doing what Judas did.

Did you know Jesus and Judas are going to meet again? You see, Judas is still a person. It will be a terrible meeting, because

Jesus will have to say to the one he lived with, "Depart from me. Go for ever." A day of judgment is coming when Judas will stand before the throne and God has appointed Jesus to judge.

ANNAS

We know a lot about Annas. From what I have learned about him I would call him "the Godfather." He was high priest of Israel from AD 7 to 15. The Jewish custom was that he would have been high priest for life, but the Romans had occupied the country and they did not like Annas, so they deposed him. Annas then put one of his sons as high priest. The Romans did not like him so he went and another son of Annas came in. He went. A third son came ... and went. Then a fourth son came, who was deposed by the Romans, so Annas was really stuck. He only had four sons. But he had a son-in-law and so he put him (Caiaphas) as fifth.

This family were wealthy, aristocratic and unscrupulous, cunning and smooth in their dealings with people. The nickname for the family was "hissing vipers": the way they had become wealthy was wrong. They had made their money out of religion. They were responsible for the temple courtyard being turned into a den of thieves. They exchanged money for the collection at a high rate of interest. They sold special sacrifices to poor pilgrims and charged exorbitant prices for every sacrifice. They lined their own nest. They made a fortune out of poor people coming to worship God at this temple.

This was Annas and Caiaphas, and nobody dared challenge them because if they had, Annas would have arranged for something to happen. He was "the Godfather": he was the head of a little mafia. He ruled Jerusalem with an iron hand. He was so wealthy and powerful that nobody had ever dared challenge him and although he was not then the high priest, everybody still regarded him as such. He is called that here even though Caiaphas is also called the high priest. He was the power behind the throne.

No one dared challenge Annas until Jesus came into the temple, threw the money changers out and let the sacrifices go free saying, "How dare you turn my Father's house into a den of thieves?" From that day, Annas was Jesus' sworn enemy, because Jesus had touched his pocket and pride, so he began to plot and plan like any mafia chief. He was waiting for a chance to get Jesus. He said, "We'll have to do it quietly and quickly with no one around. How can we do it? We need someone in his disciples, a traitor."

Can you imagine what Annas felt like when Judas knocked at his door and asked, "How much is it worth to you? I'll join your plot." Annas must have rubbed his hands and stayed up all that night. He waited until he heard the tramping footsteps of the soldiers coming back. "Did you get him? At last I've got Jesus in my power! We'll rush the trial through before dawn."

This is Annas, the representative of God to the nation. But again he was a man to whom money had done funny things, who had been corrupted by his own desire for power. No doubt he had his good points. If he had children he was probably kind to them. He now had the Son of God in his grasp.

Some people are puzzled by what Jesus said to him because Annas began to question him about his disciples and his teaching and Jesus appears to have replied rather rudely, "I've said everything I've got to say in public. You ask them." It sounds like a cheeky answer but it isn't. Jesus is quietly telling Annas that the trial is illegal. In Jewish justice, as in our own, a man must not incriminate himself out of his own mouth. It must come from witnesses. He is not allowed to be asked a leading question and Annas had no other purpose than to obtain a confession from Jesus that he was guilty so he could then pass him to Pilate as the man who was stirring up rebellion and insurrection. You can see what he was after and Jesus is saying, "You must find witnesses that I'm a criminal."

There's a rather subtle rebuke of Annas. Jesus is saying, "I don't do things in secret. I don't wait till it's dark before I act. I've said everything in public in the synagogue, in the temple; people hear me. I don't speak in the darkness. Annas, you shouldn't be doing this." It was a rebuke to the high priest but the high priest was God's representative and this was the Son of God in front of him and Annas should have taken note, but he didn't.

Now comes a horrible moment: somebody slapped Jesus across the face. Later, they were going to spit on him, strip him. and flog him. It's dreadful, but Jesus quietly said, "If I've said something wrong, tell me what it is. If I haven't, why do you hit me?" Violence belongs to an evil world, and Jesus calmly put them all in their place.

That is Annas. Once again the trial will be reopened, because Annas will one day stand before Jesus. Jesus will be absolutely fair and just and it will all be done in the open in the day, not at night: Annas will come to Christ's judgment seat.

PETER

Just two hours before this, Peter was swearing his loving loyalty, telling Jesus, "I'm ready to die for you." That was true: he did more than any other disciple for Jesus on that last night, but he did not do enough. This is the tragedy. He went in the wrong direction. Peter was the only one who stuck up for Jesus and fought. The others were clearly thinking primarily, "How do I get out of this? Where's the nearest gate for the Garden of Gethsemane?" But Peter had a little sword inside his coat and pulled it out. He was so nervous he missed by four inches. He certainly was not aiming to cut off an ear. He aimed straight for the man's skull and failed miserably but at least he tried. But it was suicidal to do that with two hundred soldiers. So let's give credit to Peter for having the courage to take out that sword and tackle them. He could not bear to see his Lord being touched. We can applaud Peter for that, but Jesus didn't: he said, "Peter, that's not the way."

Jesus had said so often that violence breeds violence. That is not the way to cure this kind of problem. Jesus had told them this and so he told Peter gently, "Put that sword away. I've got to go through with this." I think Jesus was saying, "Thanks for trying but it wasn't the right way." Poor Peter! He tried hard but didn't go far enough. It was not what God wanted. I see in Peter someone who is impulsive, wanting to do something for God and then finding that was not what God wanted done. It is so easy to have your own ideas as to what will help Jesus and then discover you don't understand what he really wants.

Let's also commend Peter for following Jesus when he was taken away. The other disciples ran to their own homes but Peter and another (nameless) disciple followed. He went as near as he could, to the gate of Annas' house and even inside. Peter had said,

"I'll be loyal to you, even to death," and he meant it. He just didn't realize how far that loyalty could take him and when it would cease, but it took him further than any other.

Peter went a long way and then his courage failed because he had not realized that sometimes it is the little things that get you more than the big things. Little temptations can be more difficult to deal with than big ones. Peter could face two hundred soldiers, but when a little girl asked him, "Are you one of his disciples?" he went to pieces. It is these little occasions when you are suddenly confronted with something unexpected, when you are not ready. He had had that sword prepared in the Garden of Gethsemane and was ready to fight, but suddenly he was caught out, and before he knew what had happened he had said the wrong thing.

Haven't you been caught out like that? If you knew there was a big spiritual fight tomorrow, you would be praying all night. You would come through but maybe tomorrow morning somebody will just catch you off guard and say something that makes you say the wrong thing before you realize what you have said. The trouble is when you have said it once you have got to stand by it, and the next time somebody says it you have got to back up the first time and the third time, and so you sink.

Isn't this true of human nature? Poor Peter said the wrong thing once because he didn't want to say to a girl that he was a disciple. So the next time someone asked him, he replied, "No," and the third time was worst: it was a relative of the man whose ear he had cut off. He could face soldiers but not a relative of someone he had hurt.

Poor Peter fell. The cock crow could have been a cock crowing but it was against Jewish law to keep a cockerel within Jerusalem and the word *cock crow* in Latin and Greek meant "three o'clock in the morning", when they blew the trumpet. I don't know if it was a cockerel or it was a trumpet blowing at 3 a.m., but what is certain is by then all Peter's courage had gone. He had started well but wrongly, and gradually he had lost his courage.

Do you see yourself in Peter, or Peter in yourself? His denial broke his heart. You know, there is something disturbing about seeing a grown man cry. But if you had seen Peter that night, you would have seen a big fisherman with burly shoulders shuddering with sobs. He had let his Lord down. Jesus in the garden had had the courage to say, "I am the One," but Peter said "I'm not his disciple."

Peter was to meet Jesus again, however, three or four days later. Peter returned, because one of the differences between Peter and Judas and Annas was that Peter loved Jesus. He had let him down but he loved him: that's why it hurt. The remorse of Judas that led to suicide was totally different from the remorse of Peter which led to forgiveness and restoration. You can have different kinds of remorse for what you have done but one kind of remorse leads to repentance: godly sorrow.

JESUS

Finally, let's consider Jesus. He dominates the scene, striding across the stage calmly and majestically. I want to say three things about Jesus and ask you whether you can see these things in yourself, because this is really his story, not that of Judas, Peter or Annas.

He knew all that would happen

Jesus was calm, but the rabble weren't. When he said, "I am he," they were so flustered they fell over each other, not to get at him but to get away from him. They fell on the ground, tumbling over each other and tripping up, but Jesus remained calm. Knowing what was going to happen to him could have disturbed him deeply, but when they came for him, he stood there and said, "Here I am."

He chose to die

Jesus stepped out towards them and held his hands out for them to tie. He said, "Come on, let these men go, but here am I. You can tie me up." He was going voluntarily to his death. Jesus didn't die because he had to. He had got two hours between the upper room and Gethsemane. He could have gone back to Galilee. His death was unnecessary from a human point of view.

"This thread of concern for others runs right through Jesus' life to the cross. At the cross Jesus did it infinitely: 'My life for theirs. Take me and let the others go free': that's the meaning of the cross. It's the heart of Jesus' compassion."

Why did he go where Judas would bring the soldiers? Why did he restrain Peter from fighting? Why did he submit to those ropes? Jesus' power could have snapped those ropes, but he didn't: he chose to die, because it was the Father's will. Our human nature is prone to avoid pain, suffering, disgrace and mockery if possible. (We even postpone a visit to the dentist if we can!) But Jesus chose to go through with it. He said, "The Father wills that I drink this cup. You mustn't stop me." He chose to do the Father's will whatever it cost. He could have called 12,000 angels down and followed that up with fire from heaven, but he chose to die.

His concern for others

If you were facing that suffering, wouldn't you be primarily thinking, "What is going to happen next? Will it hurt?" But Jesus' concern was for others. Do you know what Jesus' last miracle was? He healed the ear of the high priest's servant. He put right the damage Peter had done. He lifted up those hands that were soon going to be tied with rope and he staunched the blood and restored the ear. That man was known sixty years later because John mentions his name.

Jesus was concerned for this servant. Nobody else was concerned with him. Why didn't they kill Peter straightaway for doing it? Because he didn't hit a soldier; he hit a servant and servants don't matter. But they do to Jesus. A little later you find Jesus saying, "Look, here I am, you can tie me up, but let these men go." What's he doing? He's saying, "My life for theirs. You can take me but set them free." This is typical of Jesus. This is the thread that runs right through to the cross because at the cross Jesus did it infinitely: "My life for theirs. Take me and let the others go free": that's the meaning of the cross. It's the heart of Jesus' compassion: he was always so concerned for others that he was prepared to give his life for theirs. It's a concern that lasted up to the end of his life, a concern for the soldiers: "Father, forgive them, for they don't know what they are doing." It's a concern for his mother to make provision for her future. It is a concern all the way for other people. Is that your life or when troubles come and disaster strikes are we so wrapped up in ourselves that we have no concern left for other people?

That is the account in a historical setting. Let me put it personally. Do you realize you would never have heard of Judas, Annas or Peter unless they had met Jesus? They would be unknown, but they have become famous. They are talked about all over the world two thousand years later. However, it is Jesus who gives significance to a life, because the one thing that lasts after someone has died is their relationship with Jesus. One day all of us are going to stand before Jesus: each one of us will spend the rest of our existence either with Peter and Jesus or with Judas and Annas.

You are going to meet one couple or the other, because your relationship with Jesus is what will go into eternity. These men had no idea what they were doing. They had no idea that two thousand years later we would be reading about them. Unfortunately, they seem to have had little idea that they would stand before Jesus and the trial would be reopened, but the trial would see them in the dock. This is the real truth: when Jesus went to judgment, it was this world that was judged, not Jesus.

34

WHAT WILL YOU DO WITH JESUS?
John 18:28-19:16

PILATE AND THE JEWS (18:28-32)

PILATE AND JESUS (18:33-38a)

PILATE AND JEWS (18:38b-19:8)

PILATE AND JESUS (19:9-12)

PILATE AND JEWS (19:13-16)

PILATE AND JESUS

Jesus' trial was extraordinary: it took place at an unusual time, in the darkness of early morning, when trials are rarely held for obvious reasons. It took place in two extraordinary places: half was held outside a building and half inside, so the judge was literally on the run from one place to the other. That in itself is significant because Pilate was torn, not just between two places, but between two possible actions. That he kept running in and out of the building showed how uncertain he was and how torn between two loyalties.

The reason why the trial was held in two places and not one is a dreadful indictment of the depths of hypocrisy to which human religion can sink. The Jews made this necessary by saying, "It's the day before the Passover and if we go into a Gentile building the day before, we might become defiled in God's sight because there may be a little scrap of unleavened bread in that home and we shall be ceremonially unclean. We have scruples. We take our religion seriously." So they pushed Jesus inside. Can you imagine a greater irony? They pushed Jesus in, rendering him unclean as a Jew and then they allowed the uncleanness of all the other hatred in their hearts to ruin them. They were defiling themselves with hatred and all kinds of evil plans against Jesus. Here is a warning for us: you can become so over scrupulous in outward matters of religion that you overlook weightier matters. You can be so involved with ritual that you overlook righteousness, so particular about sacraments that you forget sanctification.

Let's look at the trial. We are going to consider it step by step.

PILATE AND THE JEWS (18:28-32)

Pilate was probably in a bad mood, having had to get up so early and start a trial. He had had a bad night: his wife had been dreaming and he was probably irritable. But he came out to the Jews and said, "First, let's be clear what crime are you charging this man with?" That is the right way to begin a trial. He was doing what he should do, beginning by asking simply: "What is the crime?", and then he would try that as judge. It was a legal routine. A formal complaint had to be lodged before the trial could happen. The

Jews answered extraordinarily. "If he hadn't committed a crime, do you think we'd have bothered to bring him to you?" That was virtually saying, "We don't want the trial to take place. We don't want you to reopen the trial. It's all settled. We've just come to you for the sentence, not the trial. Pilate, we're not asking you to try this man. So we don't need to go into the trial and the charge and the crime."

Pilate was annoyed by this and replied to this effect: "If you won't let me share the trial I'm not going to share the sentencing. If you don't have me in at the beginning I'm not coming in at the end. You take him and see the thing through from start to finish according to your own law. If you've tried him by your own law, then see the whole process through." Again, he was perfectly right to say this, because a Roman representative of justice should never cause a man to be sentenced without trying him. He must not accept anybody else's word of innocent or guilty.

The Jews replied, "We can't put him to death. You know that, Pilate. You've kept to the Romans the right for capital punishment." That was hypocrisy because they didn't mind stoning anyone if they could get away with it. They had already tried to stone Jesus on at least three occasions. The simple fact was that at the time of the Passover the Roman Governor was in Jerusalem. Crowds of Galileans were in Jerusalem and to stone Jesus publicly would have been risky, and they saw a golden opportunity to get the Romans to do their dirty work for them and then they could wash their hands and say, "You can see he's a civil criminal: even the Romans see that he's a bad man." It would have discredited as well as destroyed Jesus in the sight of the multitude. The Galileans who were for Jesus would not have dared rise up against the Romans if they did it. So you can see why they wanted the Romans to kill. It was not because they were being dutiful citizens. "We can't put him to death. It's Roman law." They put plenty of people to death if they wanted to. It was a glorious opportunity to blame the Romans and get them to do their dirty work. "We can't impose the death penalty."

In v. 32 John adds Jesus had known all along that he would never die by stoning. The Jews would kill him but he would not die by stoning; he had predicted that the Son of Man would be lifted up as the serpent was lifted up on the pole in the wilderness by Moses, that he would be crucified. John points out that the Jews fulfilled Jesus' own predictions about his own death by insisting that the Romans did it.

So far Pilate was being fair. He did the right thing. So what was he to do? He decided to return to his palace and reopen the trial. Again Pilate as a representative of justice was doing what he should.

PILATE AND JESUS (18:33-38a)

Back inside, Jesus was standing in the dock and Pilate said, "We're going to reopen the trial. The only crime deserving capital punishment is insurrection. Are you a rebel leader? Are you starting a nationalist movement that will fight the Romans? Are you the King of the Jews?" The word *king* is the key word throughout this trial. "Are you going to rise up and try and get the throne for yourself?"

It's interesting to note that the Romans were happy with the puppet king they had appointed. They were unhappy with a man who sprang up from the people claiming to be king. They didn't mind appointing King Herod who was in their hands, but when a new man came saying, "I'm king", then they became worried, so he asked, "Are you one of these kings? Are you going to try and take the throne? Is that what you're after? Is that why they've brought you to me?"

Jesus often answered a question with another question, so he put the ball back into their court, saying, "Who told you to ask me that? Are you really thinking that up in your own heart or did those outside tell you to ask me?" Of course the ones outside had said, "He says he's the King of the Jews." But the important thing that Jesus is pointing out is that he is appealing to Pilate's conscience by saying this. "If you have evidence against me as trying to claim a throne, then you're in order to ask me a leading question like that, but if you have no evidence yourself and this is only hearsay, then you've no right to ask me." Jesus is pleading for justice. He is saying, "Pilate, do I have to teach you your job?" A judge should not ask the accused, "Have you done this?" The judge should listen to the evidence and have the evidence before he asks the question. So Jesus asked Pilate, "Are you saying this from the evidence you've got? Do you have a case against me or are you just repeating what they've said to you outside?"

Pilate had to admit that it was a second-hand question. He was rather annoyed to have been found out, so he answered, roughly admitting he had been put up to it: "I'm not a Jew: it's your people. Your priests out there are saying it." You can almost see him trying to get out of the blunder he has just made as a judge through asking a second-hand question.

Pilate then asked: "Look, I'm trying to help you: let's start from scratch. What have you been doing?" That again is extraordinary to ask someone who has been arrested. You should tell the prisoner what he's arrested for, but Pilate said, "Look, we've got to get some kind of a case. You tell me some crime you've committed and then we can keep everybody happy. What have you been doing to have them all outside like that, passing you over to me?"

Jesus calmly and quietly replied, "Look, I'm not fighting for a kingdom. If I wanted the kind of kingdom you Romans like, I would have fighters. I wouldn't have been arrested. I'd have had enough fighters to stop me even being arrested. My sort of kingdom doesn't belong to this world." In other words, "Pilate, you've nothing to worry about from me. I'm not going to try and take the throne from you Romans. I'm not going to fight any of you. There's no need for you to be afraid of me."

Two wrong deductions have been made from Jesus' statement "My kingdom is not of this world; otherwise my servants would fight." First, that Christians should be pacifists. That is wrong simply because Christians are citizens of two kingdoms according to the New Testament: an earthly kingdom and a heavenly kingdom and they have duties to both. Jesus is only speaking here of the heavenly kingdom. He admits freely that an earthly kingdom has to maintain itself by force. The rest of the New Testament acknowledges that. The *Pax Romana*, the Roman peace, was maintained by the soldiers who are commended in Scripture for doing their duty and maintaining peace, so we mustn't judge this statement in that light.

The other wrong deduction is that Christians are not to have anything to do with the kingdoms of this world. But that is not true either. Christians belong to two kingdoms. I am a double citizen, with a passport showing I'm a United Kingdom citizen and I also have the Spirit's witness to prove I am a citizen of the heavenly kingdom. I have duties to both; that is part of the difficulty of working out our faith in social and political issues. Jesus is saying, "I haven't come to establish a new earthly kingdom. I'm not trying to carve out a bit of land on the map that can be labelled 'Jesus' kingdom.' I'm not after that kind of kingdom, so you don't need to be afraid."

Pilate, with quick perception said, "*Kingdom*: you are a king then? What kind of a king are you?" Jesus replied, "You called me a king. I don't want to use that title; it will be misunderstood. You wouldn't understand me if I used it. If I say so, you'll say, 'Ah, he's a political rebel,' so I'm not saying so. It's on your lips."

Then Jesus said, "I'll tell you why I've come. The only weapon I ever use is truth. I'll establish my kingdom not with a sword but with the truth. Whoever's interested in truth will be interested in me. I've come to bear witness to the truth. Pilate, move from *king* to *truth*. As a judge, you should be concerned with truth." Do you see the impact of this on the judge? Pilate cynically said, "Hmm, what is truth?" because he didn't even wait for an answer. He turned around and went straight outside again.

"What is truth?" He asked that because Pilate was a Roman, not a Greek. The Greeks studied truth, but the Romans were practical. They were not unlike many people today, who aren't interested in abstract discussion of truth but only interested in practical things that work. So when Pilate heard this man talking about truth he realized, "Here's another philosopher. I don't need to spend any longer on this man. Let these Greek philosophers discuss it. I'm a Roman. Someone who is nattering about truth is no danger to Rome." So he asks, "What is truth?"

The answer was standing in front of him: this was the nearest Pilate ever got to truth. Jesus said, "I am the truth. If you want to know what's true about man and God, come to me. If you want to know the truth, I am the truth." You can be so close to the truth and miss it because you are cynical or because you are only interested in down-to-earth practical matters. Pilate went out again and missed it.

PILATE AND JEWS (18:38b-19:8)

Pilate was clear in his own mind that Jesus did not pose a threat to Rome; there was no crime and the sooner he dealt with this the better. It was here Pilate began to weaken. He said, "I can't condemn him; he's innocent," and then made his fatal mistake by saying something like, "You think and say he's guilty. I think and say he's innocent. There's one way in which we could all act and be happy. You could go on thinking he was guilty and I could go on thinking he was innocent. It is the custom at the feast for me to release to you a political prisoner. In that way you see him as guilty and I could see him as innocent. In that way I've released him, so my conscience is clear but you can always regard him as guilty." Everybody would be happy; for the rest of his life he could be labelled "guilty." After all, he was a prisoner even if he was released. It was a subtle and clever suggestion.

The right thing Pilate should have done would have been to have released Jesus then from the back door of his palace. But to make a show and release him as a political prisoner was to allow the label "innocent" to be fastened by Pilate on Jesus and "guilty" to be fastened by the crowd. Pilate was astute and came up with this brilliant compromise. The only difficulty was that they then said, "It's a good idea to have a prisoner released: how about Barabbas?", and the whole compromise collapsed.

What did Pilate do next? Clearly the first compromise had not worked so he thought of another. He said, "I know it's because I would be letting him go without any punishment. So I'll punish him and let him go. And that'll keep us all happy. It'll keep my conscience happy because I've let him go. It'll keep their conscience happy because I've punished him. Take Jesus out and flog him." Notice the downward track: each compromise did something worse. The truth suffered in Jesus, and since Jesus is truth, whenever the truth suffers Jesus suffers.

Jesus began to suffer. The flogging was done with a whip that had a long leather thong with pieces of bone fastened all the way down. A man was flogged until he went mad or died or became unconscious with his back flayed to ribbons. It is a dreadful punishment. Pilate allowed Jesus to be flogged even though he knew he was innocent. Pilate had him flogged; the soldiers had freedom to do what they liked with a prisoner they flogged. They pulled his clothes off, dressed him up and made fun of him. They stood him on a table, saying, "Long live the king", spat on him and slapped his face. Then Pilate brought him out: "Look at him. Now are you satisfied? Now can I let him go free? Now we're all happy. You've seen him punished and I can let him go free. All right? Is that a sufficient compromise for you?" Can you see how Pilate's mind was working? He's still trying to find a way to please everybody and one of the lessons here is that you will never find a way to please everybody, and if you do, Christ suffers.

The Jews shouted out, "More blood! Crucify him! That's not enough. Nail him to the cross: crucify him!" They wanted the extreme penalty; they had got it all planned. So Pilate finally said, "You crucify him. I know you're not allowed to but I'll overlook it here. I'll stretch the law. I can't do it but you crucify him and I won't say anything. I won't bring you to court afterwards for breaking the Roman law. Take him away." That's even worse, isn't it? He's going further down, trying to keep his hands clean but he can't. He said, "I can't find any reason for death," then finally the Jews came out with the real reason. It wasn't political, but religious. They said, "Look, Pilate, there is a reason. We haven't told you before now, but do you know this man says he's the Son of God? And by our law he deserves to die."

That alarmed Pilate who, like most Romans, combined his practical interests with superstition. "The Son of God? I'm out of my depth. I'm dabbling in things I don't understand." He was afraid, not of the Jews because these religious matters got them excited, but of Jesus. Perhaps he was dabbling in something beyond his power, perhaps Jesus was more than human. He was afraid, feeling the trap closing in on him. He wanted to please people but now he was beginning to be afraid of the gods, and Romans were afraid of the gods: they used to erect all kinds of statues to them whenever they could.

PILATE AND JESUS (19:9-12)

Pilate's question was now, "Where do you come from? What kind of person are you? Are you just a man? Could you have come from the gods?" But Jesus was silent. I find this puzzling. Why didn't Jesus reply? Well, would Pilate have understood? Would it have played on his fears and superstition? Jesus wasn't one to do that with people. Or could it be, and this is what I think, that if Jesus had answered that question he would have escaped the cross so easily? If Pilate had got the idea that he might be the Son of God Jesus would never have gone to the cross. I think that here was a temptation to Jesus to take a way out. If he had answered, he would never have been nailed to the cross and it was God's will.

"Before we rule out Pontius Pilate as someone beyond redemption and depraved, let's look into his heart as into a mirror and see an ordinary human being trapped between right and popularity."

Pilate was annoyed Jesus didn't answer. He said, "Look, I'm trying to help you and I'm asking you to help me. Can't you see the dilemma we're both in? Don't you realize in not answering me you're leaving yourself in my hands and I can do anything with you? I can set you free. I can kill you. I've got power over you. Answer me," but Jesus said quietly, "You have no power unless God gave it to you. No one on earth can do anything unless God allows him to and you could have no power over me unless God was willing it. So your power is limited, Pilate, and your guilt is limited."

Jesus showed himself a fair judge. Isn't it interesting that all this time Jesus was judging others fairly? And he said, "Pilate, you've got guilt, but not as much as that man outside (Caiaphas) who pushed me in here. You're guilty, but not as guilty as he is because your power is limited by God."

Jesus' calmness stands out. What could Pilate do? He realized he had compromised and was guilty, that he had innocent blood on his hands and if he wasn't careful there would be more. He already felt he was in the dock. He was clear in his own mind that he had to get out of that situation, and he still could have done so.

PILATE AND JEWS (19:13-16)

If only Pilate had let Jesus have the last word but he didn't. He took the last fatal step and let the Jews have the last word. Pilate was keen to set Jesus free so the Jews used blackmail: "Pilate, you are not Caesar's friend if you let this man go. He's an enemy. We'll report you. We'll complain to Caesar you've not been loyal or patriotic." That hit Pilate hard because he had obtained his position from Caesar's favour and that could easily be lost. The situation was delicate.

Pilate was the only man in the Roman Empire who had been born as a slave and risen to be governor. He had travelled further up the ladder of ambition than anyone. He knew if you climb quickly you can also fall quickly. They said, "Your position will be in jeopardy, Pilate. We're not having this."

Pilate then brought Jesus out, saying, "Here's your king. He's got royalty about him in my eyes." The crowd, which had grown in numbers through the trial, shrieked hysterically for Jesus' blood: "Crucify him!" Pilate asked his question, "Do you really want me to crucify your king: is that what you want?" Notice the word *want*. When a public servant, a public ruler or a representative of justice asks the public what they want, he is finished as a leader. One of the punishments God allows a nation to suffer is to be ruled by people who are only concerned with what people want rather than what is right. That can happen to any nation. Pilate asked, "Is that what you really want?"

Pilate sealed the fate of Jesus and his own when he asked that question. They replied, "That is what we want. If you do this, then we'll be loyal to you. We have no king but Caesar." What a lie: they had wanted a king for centuries. They had lost king after king. But this was the last trump card they played: offering political loyalty to Pilate if he did it. They had said it negatively. "If you let this man go, you are not Caesar's friend." Now it is positive: "If you crucify this man, we'll be Caesar's friends." Pilate listened and said, "Here he is" and handed Jesus over to them to crucify him.

Pilate made one final gesture later. The regimental sergeant major, the centurion, came and said, "We need a label to go on the cross for his crime: what shall we write?" Pilate replied, "Write 'This is the King of the Jews.'" The Jews came and said, "Don't put that; that'll upset many people. Say, 'He said he was the King of the Jews.' That's his crime." But Pilate had by then come to the conclusion that his real crime was that he was the king and in one final, but futile, gesture, to show he was not completely their tool, Pilate said, "I've written that and it stays written."

PILATE AND JESUS

So Pilate has gone down into history. Only two human beings are mentioned in the Christian creeds. Mary, who brought Jesus into the world and the man who sent him out of the world. Everywhere the Christian faith has spread, the name of Pontius Pilate has gone down into history. What was wrong with this man?

The key to a man's behaviour at a time of crisis lies in his past, what he has been up to that moment. Pontius Pilate began life as a slave; astonishingly, he rose to the level of governor by fawning on those in higher office, gaining favours and being ruthless to those beneath him. He was ambitious: the result of his rapid climb was that he made blunder after blunder. When they sent him as governor to Israel, the most notoriously difficult part of the Roman Empire, to deal with the Jews, he was determined to show the Roman Emperor what he could do with difficult people.

He arrived in Jerusalem, marched straight into their temple and erected the Roman standard with the Roman eagle on it and a bust of himself in the place of honour, not even stopping to enquire what they thought about graven images. It started a riot which he put down at the cost of hundreds of lives. Later, he wanted to improve Jerusalem's water supply and he built an aqueduct. However, he didn't have the money to do it so without consulting anyone, he borrowed the resources of the temple treasury, money that had been given to God.

> **"We see Jesus as king here. Notice how he submitted to being whipped, stripped, slapped, mocked, handed over and crucified. Here is his humility, no aggressive response, just a quiet spirit. He strides through this scene as a king. Of all the people he is dignified; the others are degraded."**

Again there was a riot, and the blood of Galileans mingled with sacrifices. Here was a man who in rushing up the ladder had committed blunders but his great ambition was to climb even higher by sacrificing principle to expediency. He never asked what was right but what would help him climb higher. He's not unusual. Many have taken that same line; you can do it even if you are a foreman in a small workshop with three or four workers under you.

This present crisis was the greatest test of his career and character. He failed at the crucial point: through cowardice he gave way to compromise. He knew what was right but was afraid to do it because of public pressure which threatened his position. This is a pressure we have all felt: the pressure of what others think about us and what they can do to us is real.

By letting the Jews have the last word, Pilate made his fatal mistake. In listening to Jesus on one side, who quietly told him what was right, he also listened once too often to those who were demanding wrong. You can see how he fell, in the same way as we fall. He was subject to the same pressure: when we know what is right but don't do it because we listen to others more than listening to Jesus. So before we rule out Pontius Pilate as someone beyond redemption and depraved, let's look into his heart as into a mirror and see an ordinary human being trapped between right and popularity.

Pilate had sacrificed Jesus for his career but he lost his career just a year or two later through another blunder. He became unpopular with Caesar and was sent into exile. He and his wife lived a lonely life away from their home country. They must often have sat miserably, asking, "Where did we go wrong?" I'm sure his wife would answer, "It was Jesus. I dreamt about him, that if you did anything to that man we were finished," and that is what happened. They died in obscurity and in all the Roman records Pontius Pilate is not mentioned. In fact there was no proof he even existed until recently. Although Pilate was mentioned by the historian Tacitus, by Philo of Alexandria and by Josephus, for centuries some people said his name was an invention of the Bible writers. However, in the twentieth century a stone was unearthed at Caesarea, on which was engraved "Pontius Pilatus".

It is not the end of the matter though, because one day Pilate will rise from his grave. Nobody knows where his grave is, but one day he will rise from it and stand before a fair judge. That judge will have to say, "Pilate, you were not as guilty as Caiaphas of my death. But you were guilty." And he will be sentenced by Jesus Christ.

Let us conclude by considering Jesus. The key word in this passage is *king* and if ever you see a king, you see a king in Jesus here. Notice his docility, how he submitted to being whipped, stripped, slapped, mocked, handed over and crucified. This is the Son of God, with 12,000 angels waiting to do whatever he told them, and he submitted. Here is his humility, no self-assertion or aggressive response to his attackers, just a quiet spirit. He didn't even try to defend himself. His dignity is striking. He strides through this scene as a king. Of all the people he is dignified; the others are degraded. Think of his integrity: no wrong word escaped his lips. A concern for the truth is apparent in everything. See his authority: he is telling his judge, "You are guilty." The picture is that of not only the King of the Jews but the King of kings and the Lord of lords.

What a coronation! For a throne: a beam of wood. For a crown: a bit of hedge. For robes: nothing. For a bodyguard: soldiers gambling. For a sceptre: crude nails in his hands. What a coronation! But this is the King. Pilate came face to face with the King of kings, but never submitted to him. The question that Pilate had to cope with was the question that every person now has to cope with: What will you do with Jesus?

35

JESUS' CRUCIFIXION
John 19:17-42

TO THE CROSS (19:17-24)

ON THE CROSS (19:25-30)

"She is your mother"
"I'm thirsty"
"It's finished"

FROM THE CROSS (19:31-42)

TO THE CROSS (19:17-24)

Near Marble Arch in London, some stones are set into the road, which marks Tyburn, where public hangings took place. There was a time where you faced the death penalty for stealing either 25p worth of goods or 5p in money. It was a day out for the family: they would take picnics to watch the hangings. There was a sadistic streak in seeing such things.

The streets of Jerusalem were crowded one morning when a young man of thirty-three staggered under a heavy beam of wood for about a mile and a quarter through the narrow streets. It was Jesus. The little procession that took someone to a cross had the criminal walking in the centre carrying the cross beam. Round him were soldiers to prevent his friends from effecting any rescue. In front of him walked the centurion, the regimental sergeant major in charge of the execution party. Between him and the ring of soldiers around the prisoner was another man holding a placard on which was written the crime for which the man was to die, to deter others. Here, as we have seen previously, Pilate made his last futile gesture of independence by writing "The King of the Jews." He revealed his scorn and hatred for Jews in that act. He revealed his unhappy conscience at what he had done. He was trying to salve his conscience from guilt.

So Jesus took his cross. His hands must have been strong; they were carpenter's hands. You can't work eighteen years with wood, nails and a hammer without getting strong hands. But they were also tender hands that had been used to heal the sick and bless children.

There is debate as to whether they nailed Jesus through the palm or the wrist. Some remains have been found of crucified skeletons and the nails went through their wrists. Wherever it was, those hands that had been used to hammer nails in found themselves pierced by the nails into wood with a hammer.

Jesus was crucified at nine o'clock in the morning. It was a dreadful moment. I don't think many of us would like the sight of seeing a man pinned like a dead butterfly to a board. But he was alive. Have you ever realized what a mess Jesus' body was in by the time he died? His back was in ribbons. Blood was running down his face. His wrists and feet were shattered by these rough blacksmiths' nails and blood was on them too. Before the end of the day, blood and serum would flow down his side. There was dried Roman spittle on his face, and bruises and marks all over him.

They nailed him to the cross and strung him up between two other criminals. It had been said by Isaiah centuries before, "he was numbered with transgressors" (Isaiah 53:12), and the regimental sergeant major filling in his records for his superiors that night numbered Jesus with the transgressors. "Crucified today: three." The notice was nailed above his head, a notice no one believed except Pilate, because deep down he recognized a king. A dying thief alongside Jesus believed that this man was going to come into a kingdom one day. But the rest laughed or they didn't like it. It hurt.

Then they took the clothes. Losing your clothes isn't nice. Have you ever been into hospital? Don't you feel you are losing something of your freedom and independence when you see your clothes taken away? His clothes were gambled over by soldiers, taken away to be used for someone else, a further indignity.

This chapter has a tremendous sense of a plan being unfolded, that all the things that happened had been foreseen. We can read: "They have pierced my hands and my feet and they cast lots for my clothing" (Psalm 22:16, 18). King David wrote that a thousand years previously but that never happened to King David. How could he write about a death that would bring intense thirst and dislocated joints? He had never known that experience. But this is one of the miracles of the Bible: the miracle of prophecy, by which God knows the end from the beginning. He knows the future as well as we know the past. He is a God who reveals his plan, and he shows us what he is going to do long before he does it: that is how we know he knows.

That is how we can face an uncertain future with calm and peace because we know he knows how it is going to end. He has told us what we need to know about the future and so he had revealed they would pierce the hands and feet of his Son, that they would gamble for his clothes, that they would mock him and say, "Let him call on God and we'll believe in God if God saves him from this," and why it is predicted that he would cry out, "My God, my God. Have you gone too? Why have you forsaken me?"

ON THE CROSS (19:25-30)

"She is your mother"

A man's dying words are remembered long after he is dead. You may have sat by the bedside of a relative and you can still remember what they said in their last moments even though it was years ago. You knew they could not say much more. Their time was limited and so you paid careful attention.

"Mary was looking at her son as naked in death as he was at his birth, soon to have that body wrapped in swaddling clothes again, but this time for a grave. A sword was piercing her heart."

When a young man of thirty-three who knows he's dying after an outstanding life speaks, you listen carefully. Every one of Jesus' "Seven Last Words" was caught by someone and passed down to us. The number seven in Scripture is the number of perfection: it is almost as if Jesus was saying, "I'm going to preach a perfect sermon from my cross. I want you to remember these seven things." John singles out three of Jesus' seven sayings from the cross.

The first thing Jesus said is: "Woman, this is your son. Son, this is your mother." He said them at about nine o'clock in the morning. Women were at the cross, which says a lot about the women. Of course they did not have as much to fear from the Romans. But the men ran and the women stayed. Among them were some of Jesus' relatives. Did you realize how many relatives of Jesus play a part in the Gospel story? Out of twelve disciples, five were Jesus' own cousins. Jesus began with his own relatives and family. Maybe that is where the Lord wants you to begin, in your witnessing.

It is lovely to see through the New Testament how those who were closest to Jesus at a human level are those who came to play a part in the gospel. James, his own brother who had once thought Jesus was mad, later became a leader in the church in Jerusalem. One of the acid tests of your Christian faith is the effect it has on your nearest relatives.

But here is Jesus surrounded by some of the women related to him and among them, Mary. Thirty-three years rolled away and the pain she had experienced at his birth came back mentally and emotionally at his death. She remembered the prediction of old Simeon when he saw Jesus in Mary's arms: "A sword will pierce your own heart too. This boy is going to bring great pain into your life."

Now Mary was looking at her son as naked in death as he was at his birth, soon to have that body wrapped in swaddling clothes again, but this time for a grave. A sword was piercing her heart. There was a specially close bond between Mary and Jesus because Joseph was only the foster-father and Mary was his own mother. But during the last three years the relationship between Mary and Jesus had grown apart. He didn't call her mother any more; from the beginning of his public ministry he used a polite, but impersonal, term: "Woman." It had started at the wedding reception at Cana in Galilee, and later they had said, "Your mother is outside asking for you," and he replied, "Who is my mother? Whoever does the will of my Father in heaven is my mother." Somehow it seemed as if Jesus through those years of public life was pulling away from Mary and now he was going to complete the separation.

He had been doing it to prepare her for the future. She was to take her place again among the ordinary women of the world. So he looked down from the cross, and seeing Mary he made arrangements for her. He did not commit her to any of his physical brothers, but to John, the one he loved, who understood him best. He committed his mother to John, saying, "Dear woman, this is your son," and, "John, this is your mother." There must have been something in his voice that told John what he wanted done because John immediately took Mary away from the cross to his own home. That is why he missed some of the sayings from the cross.

Jesus was anxious not just about his mother's future but also the present and he didn't want her to suffer more than necessary, so

John takes her away. This shows us two things about Jesus. First, he honoured his obligations at a human level. This is an example to us, not to be so heavenly-minded that we are of no earthly use but to honour our earthly obligations. Secondly, it tells us that even though Jesus was suffering sorely, his heart remained concerned for others and their suffering. That is astonishing because we usually find that the more we suffer, the more preoccupied we are with ourselves. But Jesus was concerned with others.

"I'm thirsty"

The second thing Jesus said was at about midday, "I'm thirsty." It's the only one of the seven sayings that indicates any suffering in himself. The midday sun had not disappeared. It was about to disappear for three hours, but he had had the blaze of the sun beating down on him. In crucifixion, your mouth dries out. Your tongue cleaves to the roof of your mouth. You are desperate for some liquid. Your whole body dries up.

So Jesus said, "I'm thirsty." That tells us two things about Jesus. First, his humanity. Jesus really was human. He wasn't a heavenly phantom, a visitor to this planet, but a man. As a man, he was thirsty and admitted it. He experienced human passions and pressures. They even mocked his thirst by giving him sour wine, which has an astringent quality. It dries you up even further, making you even thirstier. It is like giving salt water to a thirsty man. They gave him this vinegar: have you ever tried to quench thirst with vinegar? This was the one who had said, "If any man is thirsty let him come to me and drink," and he was left thirsty himself. This is the amazing thing, that the One who came to bring springs of living water to others did it at the cost of his own thirst.

Secondly, this teaches us about his hell. Jesus went to hell on the cross. If you want to know what hell is, then listen: "I'm thirsty." Jesus had portrayed hell in his teaching as a thirsty place. You must take this seriously. Scholars argue as to whether Jesus meant the fires of hell to be taken literally or metaphorically. The trouble is if you take them metaphorically you don't take them seriously.

The heat caused thirst, so Jesus said, "I'm thirsty." He was going through hell. He had talked in a parable about a rich man who had got everything on earth. He even had a good funeral, but he finished up in hell and begged for a drop of water on his tongue. That's how Jesus talked about hell, and now he was going through it himself. Jesus went through hell so that you could go to heaven.

"When Jesus said, 'It's finished', he meant, 'My suffering is over, I've completed what God wanted me to do.' What satisfaction Jesus must have felt when he was able to say, 'It's finished. I've completed it.' "

"It's finished"

This was the third thing Jesus said, at three o'clock that afternoon. He expressed the thought that was on everybody's mind but he gave that simple phrase a different meaning. The soldiers said, "It's finished," meaning their duty for the day. They could go off duty and have a good time in the barracks. The crowd said, "It's finished; the entertainment is over. We can take the kids home now." The women at the cross said, "Our vigil is finished. It's all over; we don't need to stay." The priests said, "It's finished. The crisis is over. We came through that all right, didn't we?" The Governor, Pilate, said, "It's finished. The dilemma is behind me. The decision is made. I'll try and sleep tonight without dreaming." Jesus' mother said, "It's finished." The relationship she had had with her son was over. You don't see her again except as an ordinary member of the congregation waiting to be baptized in the Holy Spirit a few days later. And the disciples said, "It's finished." Three years of dreaming were over. Their hopes and dreams had crashed to the ground and their little world had caved in.

But Jesus didn't mean any of those things. When Jesus said, "It's finished," he meant, "At the age of thirty-three I have done every single thing God wanted me to do." No one else alive has ever been able to say that, even at the end of seventy, eighty or ninety years. You will not be able to say, "It's finished," when you reach the end of your earthly pilgrimage, because this word means "completed," not just ended. "I've finished the work you've given me to do. I've completed it all. Everything that God ever wanted me to do is done." What satisfaction Jesus must have felt when he was able to say, "It's finished. I've completed it."

Of course his ministry was to continue. He is still ministering to people. He is still alive and active. But the work of atonement, the work of pain for your sin and mine, the work of redeeming people, the work of breaking Satan's power over people, was finished. He doesn't need to do anything more to conquer Satan. It is done.

Then it says, "he dismissed his spirit." He dismissed his life. The verb is carefully chosen to tell us Jesus actually decided to die at three o'clock in the afternoon. Normally crucifixion took up to three days, although it was less if they'd been flogged first. It could even last seven days. It is a lingering death that comes about by suffocation.

Why did Jesus die in six hours? Not because he had been flogged, but because it was completed. Jesus said, "It's completed. I've done all you wanted me to do. I've been through hell to save people for heaven," so he gave up his spirit and decided to die.

"No one takes my life from me, I lay it down of myself. I'm deciding to die." Why did he choose three o'clock? Because at that time all around Jerusalem hundreds of lambs were killed. It was the Passover, and at that time the Passover lamb was killed so that the angel of death might pass over those who offered the sacrifice, but that year none was needed but one. Jesus offered it at three o'clock that afternoon.

FROM THE CROSS (19:31-42)

Let us now consider three things that happened after a crucifixion. First, they broke the criminals' legs. They used a big mallet to break the legs, so that the man could no longer support himself and he hung and it pulled on his lungs and he soon choked. It was a way of hastening death; the shock alone could kill a weak man. They broke the legs of the two thieves who were still alive. They came to Jesus but were surprised he had already died. This is interesting: it had been predicted centuries before that not a bone of God's lamb would be broken (Psalm 34:20). With the Passover lambs that were offered they must never break a bone: they had to kill the lamb by shedding its blood. The Lamb of God was treated the same way.

The soldiers hesitating at Jesus' cross had no idea that their hesitation was due to centuries of planning by God. Similarly, people today don't realize the things they do are part of God's plan, that God has the whole situation under control, that he knows what he is doing. People think they are deciding the future, but they are not. God has it all planned: he is in control. The soldiers hesitated and then, to make sure, they pierced his side. John says the person who did this and saw it told us that from his side came blood and water. That was a visual description of what was seen: after death, blood coagulates and separates into the red clots and a more colourless serum. It was proof that Jesus had really died. Some have tried to explain away the resurrection by saying Jesus swooned, was in a coma and recovered consciousness in the tomb. But John says, "The one who was there and saw it told us that you might believe" (v. 35).

Jesus really was dead. His side was pierced; again you look at the Old Testament and find, "They shall look on him whom they pierced" (Zechariah 12:10). It's all coming true. This was not an unexpected tragedy; it wasn't a dreadful turn of events that God had not foreseen, but was God's plan gradually unfolded.

"Let the water and the blood, / from thy riven side which flowed, / be of sin the double cure – / Cleanse me from its guilt and power" [Augustus M Toplady, "Rock of Ages"]. Christ's death in relation to my guilt is that his blood pays for that guilt and in relation to the power of sin acts as water to cleanse.

The final thing that happened was that his body was buried. Normally, when a man was crucified, his body was left dangling on the cross long after death. Birds were allowed to pick at it: it was part of its degradation. Or the body was ripped off the cross, put on a rough cart and trundled through the city to the valley of Gehenna where they tipped all the rubbish, bonfires kept burning it up and the worms and maggots ate what they could.

They tipped criminals' bodies downhill into the valley of Gehenna, the valley Jesus used to describe hell. A body of one of Jesus' own disciples (Judas) lay there then, dangling from a tree and the intestines lying on the ground beneath the body. Jesus' body could easily have been thrown down with Judas, which would have been a terrible thing to happen but God had planned something else.

The women must have wondered, "What can we do with the body? The soldiers are still guarding it. We can't go and ask for it. We haven't the right to ask. What can we do?" But God knew what he was going to do. God had two secret believers in the Jewish Council: Joseph of Arimathea and Nicodemus. Finally, these secret believers had the courage to express openly their connection with Jesus. It was too late to help Jesus alive but they could do something and they could fit in God's plan because Isaiah (53:9) had predicted, "and they made his grave with the rich in his death." That would never have happened to a crucified criminal, but Joseph, a rich man, owned an allotment next to Golgotha hill, the hill of the skull, where he had already hollowed out a tomb for himself.

God laid it on Joseph's heart to give that tomb to Jesus. They took his body down, washed it and wrapped it up. You can't do that with someone who is still alive. If there had been any spark of life they would have done anything to restore his life. But they wrapped him up, poured spices in, and put him in the tomb, maybe the Garden Tomb outside Jerusalem today. One of the most fascinating things in that tomb is that the stone bed is beautifully shaped out of the solid rock but at its foot it has been roughly dug out to give an extra few inches, hastily with a pick. You can see the marks of the pick as if it was suddenly used for a body of someone taller than the person intended. But the tomb is empty. Do you realize that if the Gospel stopped here, Christians throughout the world would want to make a pilgrimage to a cemetery? As Muslims make for Mecca, we would count it the most important thing in life to visit Jesus' last resting place.

Yes, there could have been a following of Jesus to keep the tomb, to make pilgrimages, but Christianity did not end in a cemetery. The Gospel didn't; even the Old Testament tells us what God had planned. He didn't just plan pierced hands and feet, vinegar to drink or garments for gambling. He also planned that on the third day his Holy One would rise again and never see corruption.

36

CHRIST'S GLORIOUS RESURRECTION
John 20:1-18

THE EVIDENCE OF THE GRAVE (20:1-9)
Stone outside
Clothes inside

EXPERIENCE IN THE GARDEN (20:10-18)
Angels inside
Jesus outside

Until Jesus rose from the dead, nobody had ever thought of setting aside Sunday as a day of worship. The Jews worshipped on a Saturday. The Romans used to worship monthly, with two special days a month for worship. It was a revolution to have weekly worship on Sundays. We take it for granted because we have lived in a country under Christian influence where Sunday has been special for centuries. Our week would not seem natural without Sunday worship. This is all because Jesus rose from the dead on this day. To us, it is a holy day, the beginning of a week. We tend to limit resurrection hymns to Easter. That is tragic because every Sunday is Easter Sunday for Christians, when we commemorate the day Jesus "brought life and immortality to life through the gospel" and the last enemy of our lives was conquered once and for all.

Let us go back to the first Sunday, to this unexpected place. Some women came to the tomb while it was still dark, between three and six o'clock in the morning. I have studied carefully everything the Bible says about the times of all this and I conclude Jesus must have risen from the dead between 6 p.m. and midnight on the Saturday evening. I think that's the only period that fits every Scripture reference. It was, of course, the first day of the week because the Jews began their day at 6 p.m. (at sunset, not at midnight as we do). The Romans began at midnight, but because of this overlap, what was the last day of the week for the Romans and the first day of the week for the Jews, I conclude the resurrection took place during those six hours. The puzzling references to the fact that he rose on the third day but was in the tomb three days and three nights fit perfectly. There is no contradiction as some people have tried to point out. Jesus rose from the dead on the first day of the week which was some time after 6 p.m. on what we call Saturday, and by midnight the tomb was empty.

Sometime between midnight and 3 a.m., an angel came and rolled away the stone, pushing it over. Sometime between three and six o'clock on what we call Sunday morning, the women came. They wanted to be ready to start their loving work as daylight broke. It was an eerie time, with a faint, dim light. It was moonlight because it was Passover so the moon would have been full. They could see their way, and they came to the tomb.

This study is in two parts: the evidence of the grave and the experience of the garden. Both dimensions are necessary to understand the resurrection: you need to look at the evidence to convince your mind, but you also you need to experience the risen Lord in your heart. Either without the other becomes one-sided. The perfect combination is mind and heart.

THE EVIDENCE OF THE GRAVE (20:1-9)

The first way they became aware something extraordinary had happened was through evidence. God in his mercy allowed their minds to see it before their hearts felt it. In this way, they were prepared for what would otherwise have been a terrible shock. Their minds had already begun to think.

Stone outside

The stone would have weighed at least a ton and a quarter. It would have been circular and run in a groove, slightly down to the tomb's entrance. The grave would have been fairly easy to close because the stone would run slightly downhill but difficult to open again. You would need a team of people to push it back up the slope. This was to stop graverobbers. Not only was this heavy stone rolled down into its place, it was also sealed, and guarded by soldiers. The women wondered how they were going to get in. Mark tells us that: "Who will roll away the stone for us? How are we going to get in?" (Mark 16:3).

These women loved Jesus, and so wanted to serve him to the last, to take precious ointments and embalm Jesus' body. But how were they going to get in? Imagine their awful shock when they saw not only that the stone had been rolled back but also it was pushed right over, flat. Seals broken, soldiers gone! We know an angel had pushed that stone over. A heavy stone is nothing to an angel with supernatural strength. The angel pushed it over and then sat on it (Matthew 28:2).

Why was the stone removed? Not to let Jesus out, but to let Peter and John in. You see, Jesus' body came out through the graveclothes: it was a body that was later going to go through locked doors. There was no need to roll the stone away to let Jesus out; it was rolled away to let the world in.

Clothes inside

They noticed evidence inside. Mary didn't even bother to look inside, neither did the other women (see Luke 24). They were overcome with terror, thinking that graverobbers had stolen Jesus' body; they didn't even stop, but ran first to where Peter was staying and then to where John was staying. The Greek implies they ran separately. They had all run to some little hidey-hole of their own, to some relative, some home where they would be welcome. They ran round the streets, with Mary running faster than the other women. She went first to one disciple and then another and said, "They've taken him! Come quickly!" Peter and John ran out; John, being younger, could run more quickly and he got there first. You know this must be true: it has got all the evidence of an eyewitness with the little touches that no one would invent. For example, who would invent the fact that John managed to outrun Peter? The only point of putting it there is that it must have been someone who was there who noticed it. The reactions of John and Peter were true to their different temperaments. Peter ran straight in, but John stayed outside. Peter rushed into situations regardless of the outcome. John was the quiet one who would stay around and think about it. So it has got all the marks of an eyewitness account. Peter went in and here is the evidence of the graveclothes.

I think their stomachs must have turned at what they saw. To explain further, when embalmers took a body, they would wrap it in forty yards of linen, a long bandage, starting at the feet and going up until just short of the shoulders. At about that level, they would leave the shoulders, neck and face bare. Then they started a smaller bandage, called a sweatband, just above the eyebrows. As they wound the bandage, they would sprinkle in spices and sweet-smelling myrrh, etc. to stop the smell of decomposition coming too soon.

What did they see when they went in? Peter didn't understand what he saw but John did. John was the first man to believe Jesus had risen from the dead. He saw the bandages still wrapped round and round, but collapsed. The head bandage was still in the shape of a head, rolled up by itself and separated from the bandages by the gap that would have been occupied by the shoulders and the neck. John knew that no human being had rifled that tomb; you couldn't get a body out of the bandages and leave the bandages wrapped up. Humanly speaking, it was impossible. Jesus' body, if I can say it reverently, had evaporated, and that does not happen to dead bodies in graves: they gradually disintegrate.

"The evidence for Jesus' resurrection from the dead is stronger than the evidence for any other historical event 2,000 years ago. If someone studies it with an open mind, they will be convinced. Why aren't people convinced? Because this is the one historical event that can change my life."

"John saw and believed" (v. 8). He knew that that tomb had been "robbed" by God: God is the greatest "tomb robber", he is going to rob every grave one day! John knew this was not a human activity but a supernatural one, and he saw and believed. John saw and believed and then he adds a little remark in brackets. He says something like this: "You know, we had it in our Bibles all the time but we didn't understand it," which is a picture of so many people today who have a Bible at home somewhere. They have got the truth but don't understand it. They don't believe it, so they miss it.

John says, "We still didn't understand the Scripture." A thousand years before, David had said something like this: "If God is good and a good person comes on earth, he cannot possibly let that good person rot in the grave." In Bible language, Psalm 16:10: "You will not let your Holy One see corruption." It is impossible if God is good and if death is the punishment for badness, then if a good person lives on earth, God cannot possibly let him suffer death's decay and corruption. So logically it was bound to happen that Christ would get out of that tomb within three days because the decay and corruption of a body set in on the fourth day. That's what Lazarus' sister said about Lazarus. "We can't open the tomb; he's been dead four days. It will be too unpleasant" (11:39). The corruption will have really set in. So Jesus said, "It's got to be three days. I'll be alive again on the third day."

EXPERIENCE IN THE GARDEN (20:10-18)

The evidence for Jesus' resurrection from the dead is stronger than the evidence for any other historical event 2,000 years ago. If someone studies it with an open mind, they will be convinced. Why aren't people convinced? Because this is the one historical event that can change my life.

I can believe Julius Caesar invaded England in 55 BC. I accept the evidence for that event which is far less than for Jesus' resurrection, but it doesn't really matter to me today whether Julius Caesar invaded England or not. But if Jesus Christ broke out of death 2,000 years ago, then I have got to take notice of him, let him break into my life, let him be Lord of my life. That is why people reject the evidence for Christian truth, why they don't believe in Jesus' resurrection: not because the evidence is inadequate but because if they accept the evidence, certain consequences follow. He must be the Son of God and they must have dealings with him and so they refuse to consider the evidence. But when you consider the evidence, it is so overwhelming that you cannot but do what John did and see and believe.

Now let's change, from emphasizing things to emphasizing people. There is also a change from men to women. I don't think that these two changes are a coincidence. It seems to me that the Lord has made, generally speaking, men to be more concerned with things and women with people. Women have a more personal interest in life than men. So whereas men talk for hours about things, women talk for hours about people. It is interesting that the women didn't come through to belief in the resurrection through things but through people, through relationships. So Mary, having run round telling all the disciples, now ran back. Peter and John ran away to tell the others and she is alone. She so loves Jesus that she stays at the place of her last association with him: at the tomb.

Angels inside

This woman had once been in Satan's grip, possessed by seven demons. That's not an old-fashioned way of saying she had mental illness. Mental illness and possession are two completely different things. It means she must have been dabbling in all kinds of evil, evil spirits, black magic, that kind of thing. She had become thoroughly involved and possessed by evil spirits so she was no longer in charge of what she said and did. Satan had this woman in her grasp, but Jesus had set her free. She never had any trouble with them again. Can you imagine her gratitude and love? No wonder she wanted to stay at that tomb. She was set free and loved him because she had been forgiven much.

This story of Mary Magdalene only appears in John's Gospel. Mary must have told it to John later because she was the only one there when it happened. The first thing is she went into the empty tomb and found it was not empty. We often say the empty tomb is the heart of our faith but you know the tomb was much more populated than when they first put Jesus in there. It was full.

When she went in, or rather when she stooped and looked in, she saw two angels. What amazes me is that she was not surprised about this: she chatted away with them, because she had been used to contact with spirits. She knew there were spirits in the world, intelligent beings other than human beings. She had dabbled in evil spirits. Now she recognized some good spirits so was not surprised. God's angels were sitting there at the foot and the head of the bed where Jesus had lain, as much as to say, "We've been here all along. We've been watching over this body lying in state. One of our compatriots rolled the stone away and we've sat here and watched it all happen." Just as thirty-three years before they had looked down and watched the Son of God become a baby and wondered at it saying, "Glory to God!", now those angels must have watched what happened to a dead body and have sung, "Glory to God" again. The angels said to her, almost surprised, "What are you crying for on a day like this? You should be singing, dancing and shouting if you'd seen what we've seen! Why cry?" Can you hear the tone of surprise? "Why are you weeping?" She replied, "Because they've taken him away."

I think a man would probably have said, "They've taken it, [or the remains] away," but a woman who loved says, "They've taken him away. I'm frustrated I can't do the last loving rites, the one thing I came to do." Without stopping to ask the angels more, she turned around. Why didn't she ask them, "You must have seen them; where did they put him?" Why didn't she continue talking to them? She turned away; she didn't want to meet angels, turning down the opportunity of having a chat with angels about the resurrection.

Jesus outside

Mary then became aware through her tears of somebody standing behind her. The Greek implies she glanced over her shoulder. Maybe that's why she didn't recognize him: she wasn't looking straight into his face and her eyes were full of tears. She saw somebody behind her shoulder and thought, "That's the gardener: he'll know."

"Somebody has said that two-thirds of Christian sorrow is unnecessary: that if we only understood more of God's ways we would be glad not sad. When suffering comes, we would say, 'We rejoice because our momentary light troubles are far outweighed by an eternal glory.' If we only understood God's will better, we wouldn't be so sad. Mary's joy came flooding back."

Jesus asked her the same question. "Why cry?" Then Jesus tenderly did four things for Mary. I want to emphasize them because they are what Jesus wants to do for you if you are going to come through to a joyful Christian life.

First, he took her from feeling to thinking, by facing her with a question. She was caught up in her emotion. Her eyes were full of tears but he wanted her to use the eyes of her mind and so he asked, "Just think why." Jesus knew exactly why, but he asked the question to draw it out of her. Notice he didn't say, "What are you looking for" but "Who...." He understood she was looking for a person. "Who are you looking for?" She had to think. She didn't use a name, because she didn't think the name would mean anything to the gardener, but she presumed the gardener would know about somebody buried in his own garden and so replied, "If you've taken him away, tell me where. I want to do something for him. I'll carry that corpse back myself." What a thing for her to say! She was thinking. Perhaps her tears stopped as she spoke. You can almost see the determination drying her eyes.

Secondly, he took her from ignorance to knowledge. He said, "Mary," but in what tone of voice? Rebuke? Comfort? I don't know. I would give anything to have heard that one word "Mary." Here, John wrote the word *Mary* not in Greek, the language in which he was writing, but in Aramaic, the language they spoke in Galilee. It was a cross between Greek and Hebrew, a kind of cockney Hebrew, a homely language they spoke up north, what Liverpudlian or Geordie language is to BBC English. In Aramaic the word is *Miriam*. She heard her own name! Her native name in her native language: it's obvious that's how Jesus always spoke to her away in Galilee.

A gardener in Jerusalem wouldn't have said, "Miriam": immediately ignorance changed to knowledge and so sorrow changed to joy. Somebody has said that two-thirds of Christian sorrow is unnecessary: that if we only understood more of God's ways we would be glad not sad. When suffering comes, we would say, "We rejoice because our momentary light troubles are far outweighed by an eternal glory." If we only understood God's will better, we wouldn't be so sad. So Mary's joy came flooding back. She replied in an Aramaic form of *rabbi*: "Rabboni," the Galilean rabbi, and so the relationship they had had in Galilee was restored.

Thirdly, Jesus had to change her from sense to faith. Mary made a mistake. She stooped down, looking into the tomb, probably on her knees. She fell at Jesus' feet and seized him by the ankles. She didn't say anything but expressed with the gesture, "I'm never going to let you out of my sight again." It's almost an anxious mother saying, "You're not fit to be trusted. I'm going to hang onto you. I'm going to stay with you for evermore." She held onto his ankles like that. He replied, "Mary, this isn't the way to hold onto me. This is not the way to a permanent relationship, which is going to come when I've ascended to heaven and sent my Spirit and then you can have me always. So stop clinging onto me. If you insist on holding on, I'll have to break that grip. You want to go back to the human relationship with the human Jesus but it's got to be a divine relationship from now on. I'm going to my Father and your Father. You'll have me then for ever. I'm with you always then. My Spirit will be with you, so stop clinging."

We have to learn as Christians not to depend on our senses, but to have a constant relationship with Jesus in the Spirit, whether we can see and touch him or not. We will see him one day but we are to have a relationship that knows every day he is with us, and you won't need to hold onto him. In fact, he will hold onto you by his Spirit. So that's the relationship.

Fourthly, he wanted to move her from self to others. Mary was saying, "I want you all to myself": you can be selfish even in your Christianity. Jesus said, "Go and tell the others. She was to be more concerned that others should know Jesus than that she should. "Go and tell the others who wait and long to know. Don't just hang onto the precious relationship you've got with me since I rose from the dead." And Mary went: the mourner became a missionary.

Notice the last message she was given for the disciples. For the first time Jesus gave them a new title: brothers. He had never given them this title before. He'd called them *friends*, *servants* and *disciples* but never *brothers*. But from now on they were his brothers, and we are his brothers and sisters. Jesus' death and resurrection has made us his brothers and sisters.

To keep it right we must remember there is a distinction between Jesus as the Son of God and ourselves as sons and daughters of God. He was the only-begotten Son. We are adopted sons. That's why Jesus says, "We have the same Father but a different relationship." "He is my Father and your Father" (v. 17) but Jesus never said, "He is our Father." He told *us* to say, "Our Father," but never said it himself. "My Father and your Father": the same God, same Father, but a different relationship. "My God and your God." The same God but a different relationship. But we can say Jesus is my elder brother. He's not ashamed to call us his brothers. What a privilege! This is the Christ's glorious resurrection. Doesn't your heart beat more quickly as you read it?

37

"MY LORD AND MY GOD!"
John 20:19-31

THE DISCIPLES COMMISSIONED (20:19-23)

Their peace
Their power

THE DOUBTER CONVINCED (20:24-31)

His doubts
His declaration

This passage begins with fear but ends with faith which is precisely what the gospel does. It replaces fear by faith in Jesus Christ. Fear leads you to withdraw from people, to closed doors, to exclude others. The disciples were doing this physically but you can do this mentally and emotionally: people with fear in their hearts "lock the doors" of their life saying, "Don't come near me: I want to hide away and be by myself."

The disciples were in the upper room, where many things had happened, where their feet had been washed, where they had eaten bread and wine, but now the furniture was up against the door. They were jumpy, startled at the sound of every foot on the staircase outside, wondering if there would be a peremptory knock at the door and the forces of law and order demand their arrest.

There were only ten now, whereas four days previously there had been thirteen. Their leader had died a horrible death and was now buried in his grave. One of their number had committed suicide and his remains were lying in a field about quarter of a mile away. A third one (Thomas) was missing – we will see why. They were probably wondering how quickly they would decrease in number until no one was left.

Their fear had a cause. They weren't afraid of God, but of people. They were afraid of the Jews because of the cross. If a new movement was going to be stamped out, its leader would be removed and then the followers arrested. Having lost their leader, obviously they were next on the list and so were afraid because of the cross. They were also afraid because of the tomb. Already a rumour had spread around Jerusalem that the disciples had stolen Jesus' body and they were expecting to be charged with this crime.

THE DISCIPLES COMMISSIONED (20:19-23)

Their peace

Doors could keep the Jews out, but they couldn't keep Jesus out. The one thing you can never do is shut Jesus out of your life. You may have cut yourself off from others but Jesus can step right in and have dealings with you. You don't need to be afraid of Jesus when he comes through a door. You don't need to be afraid of a Lord who comes unexpectedly because his first word is *shalom*, "peace". It is the everyday greeting of Jewish people. It means "good health, harmony, happiness, everything you wish for yourself and everything God wants for you." It is a normal wish, but when Jesus says it, it means more. For one thing it was their urgent need at that moment. Jesus came and said, "I've come to give you the one thing you need. Peace. *Shalom*."

"Jesus wanted to convince them he wasn't a hallucination of the Jesus they had known before he died. He was the Jesus who had died and was risen again."

More than that, he is saying: I can now put my will into effect. Imagine somebody telling you they have left you a lot of money but you won't be able to touch it until after they have died and someone says, "Now the will can be executed. The testament can be put into effect. You can have it now." Four days before Jesus died, he had thought, "I'm going to make my will and testament. They'll even take my clothes. I'll have nothing to leave you except my peace." Having died, the will is effective and he returns, saying, "Now you can have my peace."

However, Jesus was concerned not only for their peace, but also that their peace should be based solidly on fact, not feelings. A peace that is only a feeling will sooner or later be lost when it has to face hard facts. Jesus wanted them to base their peace on facts and so he showed them his hands and feet.

Jesus said, "Come and look. I want to give you peace, so look at these wounds." What is the connection? They thought they were seeing things, and you can have hallucinations. If Jesus' resurrection appearance was a hallucination and wishful thinking by the disciples, they would have seen a Jesus without holes in his hands and feet. Many people have hallucinations and think they see someone again who has died because they wanted them but they see them as they were before they died. That's important. Jesus wanted to convince them that he was not a hallucination of the Jesus they had known before he died. He was the Jesus who had died and was risen again. You see, nobody else walked around with holes through their hands and feet because nobody else survived crucifixion. He showed them his hands and feet, saying, "Look, I really did die and I really am alive again. It's not a hallucination. I went through death so you can have peace because I really was dead." When we see Jesus, we will see the marks on his body.

Their power

Jesus was concerned not only that his disciples should have peace but also that others should have peace through them, so he now talks of something else, or rather Someone else.

We come to the difficult verses 21-23. Here are three key words: *sent*, *Spirit*, *sins*. First, "As the Father sent me, so I now send you." In other words, "Get that furniture away from the door! Remove the key from the lock. Open that door and go out into the world. I don't want you to huddle in here even if you have peace. Go and get involved. Be bold, not frightened. I'm sending you into the world as my Father sent me."

It is clear that Jesus was sent into the world where he could be hurt and reviled. The Father wants to send you into the world where you will get hurt. He is going to send you as sheep among wolves. That's how he sent Jesus. He sent Jesus to come preaching, teaching and healing, to individuals and crowds. "You ten are going to continue my mission." This is Jesus' commission. God had only one Son but he sent him as a missionary. Jesus has many brothers and sisters and he is sending each one to be a missionary.

How can I continue doing what Jesus did? You will need the

Holy Spirit. So Jesus moved straight on from the sending to the receiving. He tells them, "You must receive the Holy Spirit. You can't do this any more than I could," because how did the Father send the Son? The Father sent the Son to begin his mission by anointing him with the Holy Spirit, who came as a dove at his baptism. Jesus says, "As the Father sent me, so I'll send you. As I receive the power of the Holy Spirit and began to preach and began to do mighty works, so you receive the Spirit and you'll continue."

You cannot possibly fulfil a mission for Jesus without the Holy Spirit. How could you possibly do what he has done without the Spirit's power? You can talk to people about the church without the power of the Holy Spirit. But the one thing you cannot do is do anything Jesus did. You won't be able to change lives or open them up to the love of God without the Holy Spirit.

So Jesus blew on them and said, "Receive the Holy Spirit." Why did he blow? That's the literal word, the noise. To give them a sign, which would tell them when to receive. The next time Jesus blew on those ten disciples was six or seven weeks later: once again Jesus blew. Then he was blowing from heaven and the sound was like a rushing mighty wind, but they knew. They knew that when Jesus blew on them they must receive.[1]

Ever since the beginning of the Bible, the picture of the Holy Spirit has been the wind, the breath of God. You cannot see, touch or seize breath, but you know when someone has blown on you. Jesus says, "When I blow, you receive." You cannot lay hold of the Holy Spirit and say, "I've got him." You cannot see him coming but you know when Jesus is breathing on you, and you ask him in prayer to breathe on you. Jesus says, "My breathing is no use without your receiving. That's how you'll begin your mission. That's how you'll get out from behind these locked doors."

Some people say it was Jesus' resurrection that turned the disciples from frightened into bold men, but it wasn't. Even the next Sunday, when they knew he was alive, they still kept the doors locked (v. 26). It wasn't the resurrection. It isn't an encounter with the risen Jesus that sends God's people out into the world to mission. It is the breathing of God the Holy Spirit that does this. You may believe Jesus is alive but still keep your doors locked and withdraw from others. But Jesus says, "I blow: you receive. I want to breathe on you. I want to breathe into you the invisible power that enabled me to fulfil my mission in the world." Then you go out and do it.

The key word in v. 23 is *sins*. What is the church's mission to the world? Is to be primarily involved in social service, psychiatric ministry, political outreach? I believe the first thing we are sent to do is to deal with sins. We are to serve people in other needs as the needs arise, to provide furniture and homes for people of different nations, to send food to the hungry, to show our concern for those who have had mental and emotional breakdowns, but this is not our primary mission. It is part of our total expression of God's love, but our primary mission is concerned with the greatest human need: forgiveness. If we fail to bring forgiveness to people when we witness, we will have failed. Our aim is to enable someone to say, "My sins have been forgiven." Jesus makes it clear he was sent into the world by the Father in the power of the Spirit for the forgiveness of sins and God's people are now sent into the world by Jesus in the Spirit's power to bring forgiveness of sins to people.

"If you forgive anyone's sins, their sins are forgiven. If you do not forgive them, they are not forgiven." It almost looks as if Jesus parcelled up forgiveness, gave the parcel to the disciples, saying, "You can choose who gets forgiven. Say to one person, 'I'll forgive you,' and to another, 'I won't forgive you.'" How extraordinary! What did Jesus mean? I am sure he didn't mean that people have the power to forgive sins. Only God can do that. I can forgive you an injury or an insult that you did me, but you can do nothing about the rest of my sins.

What then does Jesus mean? Here is a peculiar verb tense in *forgiven*. Translated literally, it would say, "If you forgive the sins of any, they are having been forgiven." That gives us a clue: it isn't to *dispense*, but to *declare*, forgiveness, because the declaration of forgiveness is based on the Spirit's gift of discernment. When you have received the Holy Spirit and are filled with the Spirit, you know when a person is truly repenting and can give an assurance to that person, "Your sins are forgiven. I know they have been forgiven. So I declare your forgiveness." Similarly, the Holy Spirit shows you when a person is making a false profession of faith and is not truly repenting and has not believed and you can then say, "You may say your sins are forgiven but they're not."

We find the apostles doing this in Acts. They did not go

around choosing people to forgive. They didn't ever say that they dispensed forgiveness. But they said to some, "Your sins are forgiven," but to others they said they're not, for example, Peter to Ananias and Sapphira (Acts 5:1-11), and to Simon the sorcerer (Acts 8:20-23). So ours is the almost holy privilege: if we go into the world as Jesus went into the world, we will have the discernment, sensitivity and authority to say to a person, "I can tell you your sins are forgiven." Sometimes unfortunately we may have to say to someone, "Although you have professed to be a Christian, I know you're not a Christian, so you must call on the Lord until you are forgiven." Our mission is to go into the world in the Spirit's power to bring a reality of forgiveness to people who need forgiving.

THE DOUBTER CONVINCED (20:24-31)

Thomas was a twin, and I wonder what happened to the other twin: did he or she become a Christian? We don't know. You can have twins, one a believer and the other not. Thomas's twin is never mentioned. But Thomas was a disciple.

Why wasn't Thomas with them that first Easter Sunday evening? We can see the answer in his character and temperament. He was a man with a literal mind and loyal heart, quite a common combination. He had a literal mind. When Jesus talked about going to heaven, Thomas said, "Well, I don't know where this is. How do we get there? You bring it down to earth, as it were. Tell me the way." He said to Jesus, "You're not much help to us; I still have doubts," (hence his name "Doubting Thomas"). Thomas wanted everything simple, clear and plain. Many of us are like him in that respect. But he had a loyal heart, as we saw in John 11 where Jesus was determined to go to Jerusalem and Thomas said, "If he's determined to die, we might as well all die with him. I'll go with him." Such a temperament finds it difficult to share its burdens. It's a temperament that led him to go away by himself and brood, which wouldn't want to be troubled by people. "Let me think this out for myself." So, that first Sunday evening, Thomas was brooding somewhere, maybe walking the streets of Jerusalem. He was all alone and missed the blessing. You could miss the blessing through not being with the disciples at the right time. Don't miss out on a blessing from Jesus, especially if you've got a problem and you are brooding alone. It is the worst thing you could do because the answer may lie within the fellowship. If only Thomas had been where the ten were gathered, he would have shared the blessing from the beginning. As it was, he spent another week in misery, loneliness and doubt, because he was not in the fellowship when he should have been. "Let's not give up meeting together as some of you do" (Hebrews 10:25).

His doubts

Thomas was not there and remained with his doubts. What a devastating effect the cross would have had on him. Look at his doubts; everybody else said, "We've seen the Lord!" But he said, "No; I'm sorry, I can't accept that. Clearly you can, but I've got to have evidence. It's not enough to hear from you the Lord is risen. I don't trust my ears. It's not even enough to see the Lord. I wouldn't even trust my eyes because I know you can have hallucinations. I've got to push my finger right through that hole before I'll believe. I've got to push my hand right through that wound." His doubt demanded evidence.

However, I think we have been too hard on Thomas. We can say four good things about Thomas and his doubts. First, he was honest: he didn't believe and he couldn't believe, and said so. Thank God for such honesty! Secondly, Thomas was at least reasonable: he demanded evidence. Christianity is a rational, not irrational, faith. Thirdly, he was discerning. He knew Jesus' physical resurrection was vital or was nothing; either Jesus had risen with a body or was still dead. Fourthly, he was sincere, because he said, "I will never believe unless that happens," but as he says that, he's also saying, "I'd love to believe." A person who says it so emphatically longs to have faith: he was longing to be able to say, "The Lord has risen," but he couldn't: that was his doubt.

His declaration

But now look at the peak of his faith: a week later, same time, same place, same locked doors, same people there, with one exception, Thomas is now also there. It seems like a repetition. Jesus appeared and said, "Peace," and then to Thomas: "Now, Thomas, here's your chance. Come on," and Jesus showed he had been listening to what Thomas had said. He had been in the room all the time, because the other disciples had not told Jesus, "Do you know what Thomas said last Sunday?" Jesus listens to what we say and even think. He said, "Thomas, I know all about your doubts." Here is Jesus' great patience, tenderness and understanding. Jesus said, "Thomas, all right, if that's the only way you'll believe, come. But I must have believing disciples. I must have those who are convinced I'm alive to go out into the world. Thomas, come on, put your finger."

The glory of it is that Thomas never did: there is no record of him touching Jesus. Instead, like a blinding flash of lightning, a revelation burst in on his mind and having been so far behind the other ten he now dashed past them and stood out as the first person in history to say to Jesus, "God!" without any qualification: "My Lord and my God!"

"Note you have to say 'My'. It's not enough to say, 'I believe that Jesus was the Son of God,' you need to say, 'My Lord and my God.' As soon as you put 'my' in, believing changes to living."

"My Lord" was an apology for his unbelief: "Lord, I shouldn't have talked about you like that. I'm your servant. You're my master. I shouldn't have said that." Then he affirmed his belief: "My God." Do you know, for a Jew to say that is a miracle? A Jew is taught from his earliest days there is only one God and he is in heaven: for a Jew to say, "My God" to a human being was a miracle.

Then Jesus said something sad: "Thomas, I'm glad you believe now, but I'm sorry about the way you came to believe. I wish you'd come another way, that you'd believed what you'd heard. Because that's how everybody is going to have to believe. Thomas, you would have been happier if you'd believed what you'd heard. As it is, you're ashamed, embarrassed and unhappy because you doubted for a week when you needn't have. If you'd only believed the word of someone else, you'd be happier. Thomas, how happy are those who've not seen but who've believed the testimony that the Lord is alive." This means that every one of us can be happier now than Thomas was that Sunday. Does that thrill your heart? Because you've not seen but have believed the word and the testimony. One day you will see and be happier because you believed before you saw. Those who wait until they see will, I am afraid, wait until Jesus comes again and then it will be too late.

We have now reached the last and greatest beatitude of Jesus. He said many times, "How happy are the poor, how happy are they that mourn..." but now: "How happy are those who've never seen but who believe." With this beatitude John has reached the climax of his Gospel. He began with the statements "In the beginning was the Word and the Word was God ... and the Word became flesh." Now he has got to the point where one other man has seen that this flesh is God.

That was why he wrote. Imagine John pausing with his pen, wondering about all he had written and looking back through it, and suddenly it struck him how much he had missed out, how much he could have written but hadn't. "There are so many other mighty works Jesus did that aren't written in this book." Will we ever know what these are? I hope so. But the important thing is that although John knows all he has not said, he concludes, "I've said enough." He admits he has been selective, but he tells us why. He had got to the point where a man says to Jesus, "My Lord and my God." He had written so that we can say it too, dear readers.

John wrote so that we may do two things. First, that we may continue to believe that a man called Jesus who lived on earth two thousand years ago and lives now was not only the fulfilment of the Jewish hopes of a thousand years, the Messiah, but is also God's only Son. If you cannot believe that after reading John's Gospel then it can only be because you have locked the doors of your mind.

Note you have to say *My*. It's not enough to say, "I believe that Jesus was the Son of God," you need to say, "*My* Lord and *my* God." As soon as you put *my* in, believing changes to living.

Secondly, believing you have life in his name. You will begin to use Jesus' name. Before you believe who he is, you don't use his name. You might use the title, but unbelievers are often embarrassed to talk about Jesus' name. But now you begin to use Jesus' name in prayer and the prayer is answered. You use Jesus' name in talking to other people and you find what power there is in his name. John wrote his Gospel that you might believe in Jesus, knowing that if you continue to believe, you will really live a new, abundant and eternal life. That real life consists in believing in Jesus. The whole point of reading the John's Gospel is to find a person, believe in him and have life in his name.

---

[1] I expand on this view that this sign (blowing) and the command ("Receive...") are a preparation for Pentecost in my *The Normal Christian Birth* (Hodder & Stoughton, 1997), pp. 125-131 and *Jesus Baptises in One Holy Spirit* (Terra Nova, 2010 edition), pp. 96 ff.

38

"IT IS THE LORD!"
John 21:1-14

THE DARKNESS OF FRUSTRATION (21:1-3)

THE DAWN OF FRUITFULNESS (21:4-8)

THE DAYLIGHT OF FELLOWSHIP (21:9-14)

We can never turn the clock back. Time goes only forwards and we must go forwards with it.

I say that because one of the abiding temptations of Jesus' disciples is to live in the past, to try and recapture what has gone, to long for the "good old days", to go back to methods and strategies that our grandparents used, and to believe in so doing that God's cause is served. We may use out-of-date language and methods to give the impression to the world that we lived centuries ago.

THE DARKNESS OF FRUSTRATION (21:1-3)

In this study, Jesus' disciples are doing exactly this. They tried to go back three years, but it was a miserable failure. It happened in Galilee, the home of all the disciples except one, Judas, who came from the south. It was almost inevitable after the strain and stress of the previous few weeks in Jerusalem that they would make their way back home. More than that, they were right to do so because Jesus had told them to go there. As soon as he appeared, as soon as he rose from the dead, before he said a word the angels had said, "Go and tell the brothers to go to Galilee. He'll see you there" (Matthew 28:7). When he came back to them, he said, "I'll meet you again in Galilee" (Matthew 28:10). Galilee is one of the most beautiful places on earth.

There is something about that little lake, thirteen miles long, eight miles wide, shaped rather like a harp, nestling in the hills of Galilee with the snow-capped Mount Hermon as its backcloth.

They went back home, waiting for Jesus to meet them and tell them what to do next. It was right for them to go back to the old country, but wrong to go back to their old calling, which is what happened. A fisherman who has been away from fishing for three years, who gets within sight of a net, who has not had a tiller in his hands for three years and sees his old boat on the beach, could hardly resist it. So Peter, hanging around the shores of Galilee within sight of those waters and fish, couldn't resist it.

There are many possible reasons why he said, "I'm going fishing." Maybe it was simply the pull of the old calling. Whenever I see somebody sitting on a tractor ploughing a field on a sunny day with the seagulls following, there's something in me that wants to get back on that tractor seat. There is something in all of us that likes to go back with nostalgia and sentiment. Maybe they were in need of money to buy some bread to eat, so they decided to go out for a night's fishing. Maybe it was just that they wanted something to do. They didn't like hanging around doing nothing, waiting for Jesus to come. Or perhaps Peter said it for a deeper reason. Maybe he thought Jesus would never have him back as an apostle after he had denied his Lord, and perhaps he thought, "I'd better go back to a useful occupation. The Lord won't use me as a fisher of men so I'll go back to catching fish."

But notice these were skilled men who knew their job. They chose the right time: fishing in Galilee is undertaken at night. You can still see boats going out at night with a hurricane lamp over the stern: the fish are attracted to the lamp through the water as to a false moon and they come towards the boat – and then they throw the net out. They also went to the right place: Galilee is heavily stocked with fish. Although it is small, it is one of the world's most populated lakes for fish. They went with the right equipment: their nets and boats. But after about eight hours' hard work in the cold darkness, they had nothing to show for it. That is unusual. Fishermen in Galilee always expect some catch.

Why this failure? Only once before, as far as we know in their whole fishing career, had they come back after a night's fishing with nothing.

THE DAWN OF FRUITFULNESS (21:4-8)

They moved out of darkness; the dawn came – it comes fairly quickly in the Middle East. The sun comes up over the hills beyond Galilee about 6 a.m. and a lovely pink glow spreads over the hills. You see the sun on the hilltops first, then it creeps down into the hollow of Galilee to the lake some 600 feet below sea level. Daylight came, and often on Galilee a morning mist lies in the hollow. Through the mist, they spotted someone standing on the shore, about 100 yards away. The human voice carries well on a clear, still morning over water.

Jesus said two things that strike me as unusual. First, look at his question. He calls them "young men" (boys, lads, friends), "have you got anything?" It's an endearing term but it shows something important: none of the disciples was aged over twenty-five – some of them were still in their teens. We often see pictures of bearded old disciples but this isn't so. When Jesus wanted to get something going, he went for young men in their teens and twenties, with mixed-up impulses, misguided zeal at times. This shows us that young people can teach older ones, e.g. about evangelism. I know they may need the wisdom of years and they can benefit from cross-fertilization of a balanced fellowship, but Jesus chose teenagers and men in their twenties. He asked, "Lads, have you got anything?" In fact the form of the question in the Greek is a negative question which expects the answer, no. He knew perfectly well there was nothing in the bottom of that boat. In fact, translated literally, he would make it a statement: "Lads, you haven't got anything, have you?" It is a challenge, which still comes to all God's people down the years, to every church that is not growing as it should, to every Christian who is not bringing others to the Lord: "Friends, you haven't got anything, have you? You've been working so hard, spending so much time and money. You've had so many meetings and have so many programmes. Friends, you haven't got anything."

Then Jesus went further and gave them some advice about how to put it right: as somebody has said, "The biggest miracle in John 21 is that fishermen took advice from a bystander." You can try that out: if you see a man sitting on a riverbank with a rod and line, go and tell him how he should do it! See whether he's thrilled to see you. In fact a fisherman would probably say, "Get away from the shore: the fish can see you." But Jesus gave them advice, and they took it. Why? I think there is an ordinary human explanation.

" 'Throw your nets the other way.' Get away from your traditions. Do something different. Try something new.' The Lord is calling us to do something new, to break out of our traditions and 'this is how we have always done it.' He is constantly opening up new methods of evangelism."

Knowing the circumstances, there are two unusual features of the Sea of Galilee. First, which I can vouch for from experience: I once went swimming off Capernaum and as I swam, I went hot and cold, because the water is hot and cold. Hot springs are down the western shore at Galilee. These caused the hot springs at Tiberias and ill people went there. The fish like the warm water. You can have some warm water full of fish and next to it some cold water without a single fish. The fish are good swimmers too and they go straight for these warm patches. So the fish can be in patches.

The second fact, which I have not personally experienced but H V Morton described in *In The Steps of the Master* how an Arab called Abdul stood on the shore while his companions went out in a boat, about 150 yards, and he stood on the shore to tell them where to throw the net, because from the shore at that angle he could see through the water whereas in the boat they couldn't see into the water because of the reflection of the sky. Abdul stood on the bank and shouted, "Further over on your right side," and so on. If that is so, then the situation is normal so far. The fishermen on the boat are grateful to this man on the shore for telling them where the fish lie, and so they cast the net. Still nothing dawns on them that is extraordinary.

The advice is: "Throw your nets the other way." Fishermen are people of habits: every fisherman has the side of the boat that he likes to throw the net from. He would rather turn the boat round than get out of his habits. Here is a lesson: Jesus is teaching fishers of people something in a way that they will understand: "Get away from your traditions. Do something different. Try something new." I want to underline this because I believe the evangelism of past centuries won't do for now. I believe that the methods God may have blessed in the past are not suited to today. The Lord is always calling us to listen to him and do something new, to break out of our traditions, customs and "this is how we have always done it." Throw the nets the other way. Do something different. Get away from the past. Don't be hidebound to it. The Christians who are going to win people for Christ in our generation are those who are prepared to change, who are prepared to do something differently, who are willing to try something new when the Lord is leading them in a new direction. The Lord is constantly opening up new methods of evangelism.

They took some advice and threw the net out in a new way and it was full of 153 fish, which has led commentators to some fanciful explanations. Somebody has noticed it is the addition of every number from one to seventeen. Some have found that if you take the name Simon Jona (which was Peter's name originally) and replace the letters of the Hebrew alphabet with numbers, e.g. 1 for a and 2 for b, you find that the total of Simon Jona's name is 153. Is that just a coincidence? Others say it means 100 Gentiles plus 50 Jews plus the three persons of the Trinity. Another person has perhaps more realistically pointed out that they believed then there were 153 different species of fish to be caught and eaten and that this is a picture of "all the species" of humanity to be caught by fishers of men. My own understanding of the meaning of the figure 153 is simply that is a lot of fish. It is a fundamental rule of reading your Bible to take the Bible in its plainest sense unless you have a good reason for doing otherwise. The simple plain sense was that was a good catch for one throw.

It was then that something began to happen in their minds and hearts. John, the man of insight, saw it first; Peter was the man of impulse. John sat back and thought about things: he saw and understood. Peter was the one who did something about it. They were like this when they came to the tomb in the garden. John saw the graveclothes and he understood. Peter ran in. Look what happens here. John understood. There was something supernatural about this situation. Why not a single fish all night and 153 suddenly? That's not just the advice from a bystander.

They would have caught a few that way but this is different. Why not one fish all night and now 153? That would have been enough to make for the shore and sell. They could finish fishing: it had taken them one minute to catch enough to sell. Why? John thought there was something extraordinary, something supernatural, happening. Then his memory moved to a former occasion three years previously when almost the identical thing had happened: see Luke 5:4-11. They had worked hard all night but caught nothing. And Jesus came and told them what to do and they caught a net full. And John said here, "It's the Lord. It's the same again. It's Jesus!" There's one difference between the first time then and this time. The first time the net broke and the second time it didn't. What's the significance of that? Three years previously Jesus was saying to those disciples, "I can make you effective fishers. But you aren't yet ready to pull in the catch. You're not yet fully equipped. You're not mature enough." But three years later, the net didn't break. Now he says, "You can pull them in; you can catch them. Now you can draw the net in." And they did. Isn't it lovely how Jesus tells us things through ordinary acts of life and events, and he teaches us profound lessons? Are you ready? Are your nets mended and are they strong enough to witness to others? They drew the net in but it didn't break. "It's the Lord!"

THE DAYLIGHT OF FELLOWSHIP (21:9-14)

I have a picture of this scene at home, of the moment when Peter jumps into the water. In the foreground Jesus is stooping, poking a fire, with fish and bread cooking. The boat is 100 yards out and the disciples are trying to pull the net behind the boat to the shore and Peter is halfway between. Dear old Peter. Impetuous and lovable as ever.

Have you noticed two humorous things in this story? First, that Peter put on all his clothes and jumped into the water. He was wearing nothing but a loincloth. They got so wet and fishy that they would take their clothes off when they went out fishing.

But he was not respectable enough, he was unfit to meet the Lord. He said, "I can't meet the Lord like this." He would rather meet Jesus clothed and wet, so he pulled on all his clothes and jumped into the water. The picture is of impetuous Peter, but at least he loved the Lord.

Notice, secondly, Peter loved the Lord more than the fish. Because the other humorous thing here is that the disciples weren't going to lose such a catch of 153 fish. If they talked about it later nobody would believe them. They were going to bring that to the shore and so they stayed in the boat and brought the fish, but Peter's first love was the Lord.

This shows us you can be too busy fishing to love the Lord, too busy evangelizing to jump into the water and say, "It's the Lord!" Jesus Christ comes first. Love the Lord with all your heart and soul and mind and strength and then go and love your neighbour – that's the order. Peter had got something right.

So they came to the shore and received two things. First, further revelation of Jesus. This was the third time Jesus had revealed himself to the disciples after his resurrection and each time was better than the last. Look at the changed circumstances. It made it so much more real. It's one thing for Jesus to appear at night time in a locked room in a crowded city but here it is broad daylight on the seashore. Not many people have hallucinations at breakfast on the seashore. This is real. They had thought they had seen a ghost in Jerusalem in the upper room and maybe still they were pinching themselves. "Did it really happen? Did we really see Jesus? For just an hour or two in an upper room in Jerusalem? Was it really him?" But ghosts don't cook breakfast ... or start a barbecue!

Even now, the third time they had seen him, they still could hardly believe it. They wanted to ask, "Is it really you?" but they didn't dare because they knew it was (v. 12). This captures the uncertainty they felt so perfectly. It was real, and every resurrection appearance made it even more real. They had a further revelation of Jesus. So if you have been out fishing successfully at Jesus' command, when you come back you will have a fresh revelation of the Lord. You will be closer to him. But if you haven't been out fishing, you'll miss that.

The second thing they received from the Lord was further refreshment. He knew they had been working hard and were tired and hungry. When you give yourselves to others in evangelism, you will come back hungry. You will have given your resources away. You will be tired because you will have given extra time and effort, and Jesus says, "Come and eat." Where did he get the fish? How did he light the fire? We don't know. But it is typical of Jesus to be so thoughtful. In a crisis or need, Jesus always knew what was needed. When he raised a little girl from the dead he said to the mother, "Go and get a cup of tea." He just seemed to know what was needed and here he says, "Come and eat." Sitting on the shores of that lovely little lake, eating with Jesus must have been a foretaste of heaven. Notice there is no wine because Jesus had promised to be teetotal until heaven came. "I will no more drink of the fruit of the vine until I drink it new with you in the kingdom." So there is no wine, but there is still bread and fish.

There is something about a meal that makes for fellowship with Jesus. The first thing we do when we get to heaven is sit down at a banquet, a mixture of breakfast and supper: a wedding breakfast or a marriage supper. On the night before he died, he had supper with them, but here he is having breakfast. Supper ends something but breakfast starts something. They ate breakfast together.

Jesus says, "Follow me and I will send you out to fish for people." Will you follow him?

39

"DO YOU LOVE ME?"
John 21:15-25

PETER: WHO LOVED JESUS (21:15-19)

JOHN: WHOM JESUS LOVED (21:20-25)

God is a God of wonderful variety: no two snowflakes are the same; no two blades of grass are the same; no two grains of sand are the same. The God who made them also made people and no two people are the same; even identical twins have differences. You are unique as a person. God made you different from everybody else. That is not only true of you by creation; it is also wonderfully true of you by salvation. It is wrong to suppose that when people become Christians they all become the same. They become like Jesus, but the amazing thing is that in a true fellowship of believers people do not conform to each other.

God made each of us different because he loved variety within his family. Because we are different in temperament, outlook and experience, he has a different plan for each one of our lives. He deals with us individually, differently from anyone else. Every Christian testimony is different. This is also true of Jesus' twelve disciples. It is encouraging to look at what a mixed bag they were, and how Jesus dealt with each one differently. Here at the end of John's Gospel he talked to two of them, Peter and John, different from each other, and he explained they each had a different future life on earth, a different plan. Each plan is suited to that person, and it is vital to find out God's plan for you, what he wants you to do, not to compare his plan for you with someone else's plan but to look only to Jesus for his plan. That plan will include your life and your death and how you are to live and die. This comes out clearly in the way he dealt with Peter and John.

We are to live in such a way that we glorify God. We are to die in such a way that we glorify God. The manner and place of our life and the manner and place of our death are planned for us by our Lord Jesus Christ. That removes a lot of anxiety from the future. It removes the pressure to try and be like anyone else. You are not supposed to try to copy anyone else. You are to let Jesus fulfil his will in you.

PETER: WHO LOVED JESUS (21:15-19)

In our last study we left Peter, the man who loved Jesus, standing on the seashore on Galilee, fully clothed and thoroughly wet. He had just pulled on all his clothes in a boat, jumped into the sea and swum 100 yards to meet Jesus on the seashore. He was so eager to meet his Saviour. Now, however, something happened. Naturally in the early morning hours, he began to feel chilly and since there was already a charcoal fire on the seashore, Jesus had lit it, and it was natural that Peter would come with his wet clothes and stand near that fire and try to get warm and dry. As he did so, he found himself looking into a charcoal fire. His face dropped and memories of something that had happened three weeks earlier came flooding back. This word for fire (*anthrakia*) is only used twice in the New Testament, once in John 21:9 and previously in John 18:18, where it says Peter was warming himself at the charcoal fire and denied his Lord three times. Jesus hadn't mentioned this incident so far. Jesus and Peter had met on several occasions but Jesus had not yet mentioned Peter's denial. It was heavy on Peter's conscience. Jesus could read Peter's thoughts like a book, just as he can read your thoughts like a book right now. Jesus could see that Peter longed to get that guilt out of his system, to get it put right, to talk it out. Jesus saw it go through Peter's face as he warmed himself by the fire and remembered the last fire at which he had warmed himself.

So Jesus spoke to Peter. Their conversation is brief but moving and it contains a glorious truth: he makes things clean again and white. Peter needed "whitewashing" deep down. Jesus did this tenderly. He didn't say, "Peter, you denied me three times," but he said something three times to make sure that each time he was blotting out one of those denials so that they were all clean. Their conversation doesn't come across well in English. We have one word *love* which covers everything from our noblest emotion to impure emotions. We use the word *love* for the whole range of human emotion, but the Greeks had five different words for love and there's a subtle play on words here.

The word Jesus used is different from the word Peter used and that is significant. I am going to try and put it in English for you. I want you to imagine that a girl and a boy have been going out together, going steady, for a few months. But she is beginning to become anxious because he doesn't seem to get any further and she's beginning to feel, "You know this is going to be a platonic friendship," and not go much further, so one evening she feels she should take the plunge and asks him, "Do you love me?" And he replies, "I'm very fond of you." "But do you love me?" "Oh yes, I'm very fond of you." "Are you just fond of me?" "Yes, I'm fond of you." That's the feel of this conversation. Somehow the answers to the question don't rise to the heights of the question. This is what happened with Jesus and Peter. Jesus asked Peter, "Do you love me?" and Peter replied, "Yes, Lord, I like you." "Peter, do you love me?" "Yes, I like you." "Peter, do you just like me?" "Yes, Lord, you know everything."

"Jesus is simply asking for a genuine relationship, for a person who's humble enough to say, 'That's as far as I can go at this moment, but, Lord, I do go that far.'"

Why did he say *like*? Why couldn't he say, "Yes Lord, I love you?" Because it would have been dishonest, because he had finally reached the point where he wouldn't say something untrue. Throughout his life, he'd made big claims for himself. He would say things he later discovered he could not live up to. It was only three weeks before this incident that he had said, "Lord, these other disciples may all run away, but I won't. I'll go with you to the death, Lord. I love you." But he hadn't, and Jesus asked Peter, "Do you love me more than these then? You said you'd go to the death. Do you love me more than these?" But Peter didn't say "more than these"; he said, "Lord, I like you."

So Jesus left out the "more than these" and came nearer Peter's position. He said, "Peter, all right, I won't ask you if you love me more than these others, but do you love me?" but Peter still answered, "I like you very much. I'm fond of you." So Jesus took another step to where Peter was and asked, "Peter do you like me?" Peter's reaction could be paraphrased like this: Lord, I can't hide anything from you; you know everything. You knew I was going to deny you even before I did. I can't say something that's not true now. I know my own heart now. I'm not going further than is true. So I do like you. I am fond of you but to say I love you when I've let you down as I did is something I can't bring myself to say. I just can't.

But notice the wonderful thing. Jesus' words signified that all was now right: "Look after my sheep." In other words: Peter, all I want is an honest relationship with me and you can look after my flock. I'm not looking for someone who's perfect; I am looking for someone who knows his own heart accurately and is genuinely willing to go with me as far as he can go. So tend my lambs, look after my sheep and feed them. Jesus is simply asking for a genuine relationship, for a person who's humble enough to say, "That's as far as I can go at this moment, but, Lord, I do go that far," and Jesus replies, "Right, you can look after my sheep." So Peter became not the first pope but the first pastor: the first pastor of the church of Jesus Christ was Simon Peter and that's made him a rock.

Interestingly enough, back in Galilee on the seashore where Jesus had first called Peter, he had said to Peter, "Simon, Simon," [the two names mean "a reed; something easily shaken in the wind"], "Simon, I'm going to call you rock." Tough; strong; stable. But on this occasion it was as though Jesus was taking Peter back to the beginning. Let's see if those three years have made any difference. Let's retrace our steps. Go back to the beginning when I first called you. How far have you come since then? "Simon, do you love me?"

Sometimes it is a good exercise for every Christian, however many years they have been a Christian, to go back to the first day they met Christ and ask themselves how far have they come since then, being completely honest about the answer and then go on from there with Jesus. Go back to your conversion and ask yourself honestly, "How far have I come?" Not are you busy in the church or are you known as a Christian here and there, but simply, "How far have I come in my relationship with Jesus?" Can you say, "I love you, Jesus," which would mean you would go to the death for him? Would it be honest to say, "I have become very fond of Jesus," but there's room for a deeper love yet? That was Peter and he became the first pastor. Jesus wiped out the three denials with three acts of trust in Peter. The message was: Peter, I'm going to leave my sheep with you. I'm going to change you from a fisherman to a shepherd.

Then Jesus spoke to Peter about his future. The real trouble all along with Peter was that there had been too much self-will. He had done what he wanted to do, went where he wanted to go. "When you were young, you decided what you wanted and you did it." That had been the problem. Every time Jesus tried to do something for Peter, he had tried to tell Jesus what to do. He had introduced his own ideas. When Jesus wanted to wash Peter's feet, he had wanted him to wash his head and hands. Peter had always tried to tell Jesus what to do. "Peter, a day is coming, when you are older, when they will make you do what you don't want to do. They're going to tie your hands up and carry you somewhere where you don't want to go." Peter knew what that meant: only one future could be described in those words: being put on a cross.

So, for the rest of his life, Peter lived with the knowledge he was going to die on a cross like Jesus. Can you imagine living with that knowledge, knowing that you'd have to go through that? But the one thing it did for Peter was that it killed his self-will, because it takes a cross to kill self. Nothing less can deal with self but crucifixion. Peter went out from there to do Jesus' will.

JOHN: WHOM JESUS LOVED (21:20-25)

Jesus then walked along the beach, saying, "Follow me; come with me," and Peter walked along but he also turned round and noticed John coming. Here the old Peter came out again, inquisitive about others and impulsive about himself. Would he be the only martyr? Would he be rather special? But John was coming along too.

Jesus now let Peter know: "I'm going to deal with John differently from you, Peter. You are going to come to a dreadful death quite soon but he might live a long time. I could even keep him alive until I come back to earth. I might want that. If I wanted to keep him alive until I returned I could do that." In this way, Jesus gave a hint that John would live longer, and in fact he did. All the other apostles died before John. John was the only apostle who died peacefully in old age in bed. He was the only apostle who lived to see old age and who was carried into church by young men every Sunday to worship. As they carried him in the door, he used to look round the congregation and say, "Little children, love one another." Dear old John died years later. He was going to have a long life: he was the last of the first-hand witnesses to Jesus on earth.

"Peter," said Jesus, "it's none of your business if I decide to do that." One of the lessons we can learn from this is simply that Christians should mind their own business. Our task is to follow Christ and not compare our task or experience with other Christians. We are to keep our eyes on Jesus Christ and off other Christians, if we are going to make comparisons with them, especially unfairly.

"Peter, if I want him to stay alive until I come, that's none of your business." That little statement started a rumour in the early church which John's Gospel corrects, that Jesus would actually return in John's lifetime. Now that isn't what Jesus said. He said, "If I wanted that, it's none of your business." But I'm afraid some people made it their business and spread the rumour. That can happen when you're too interested in other Christians. You spread rumours and things go wrong. "Peter, you follow me."

Why did Jesus want John to live a long life? Peter was a man with a big heart, a man of tremendous affection. He could die on a cross, and he did. There was only one difference and maybe it was a return of the old Peter. When they came to lift the cross with Peter on it he said, "No, not this way, upside-down please." It's the old Peter still saying, "You know, I want to say how it's to be done." But he was doing it for the right reason: he didn't want to share the honour of Jesus. So they hung him upside down and put the cross head first into the socket in the rock.

But John was a man with a deep, cool head, a man of insight. Peter grasped things with his heart and sometimes his heart let him down and it ran away with him but John grasped it with his mind deeply. Jesus wanted one of the disciples to stay alive a long time to make sure as long as possible that while the gospel was preached one man remembered what Jesus really was like. This was because people quickly began to get the wrong idea of Jesus afterwards. Some people said he was only a human being. Some people said he was only a divine being and not human. But it was John, the aged apostle, who said that Jesus is the man who was God. Both fully divine and fully human. "The Word was with God and was God and became flesh."

As long as Jesus was alive, John could always tell people, "You're wrong about Jesus. I knew him; I saw him; I touched him; I walked with him." But the day came when John got too old and knew he wasn't going to live to see the Lord's return and so he took a pen and wrote down what he knew. He wrote down this Gospel. He has written the deepest, most thoughtful, most understanding, accurate account of Jesus in the world. He wrote it all out and some of the elders of that church published it after he had died. They wrote a postscript: "This very disciple of whom this was said, 'If I want him to stay alive till I come back,' was the one of whom this was said and who wrote these things down and we know that what he said was true." So the elders of the church wrote that postscript. They wrote another too, because when they read the book that John had written, some asked, "Is that all? Surely, there was more that Jesus said and did." So they realized there was much more and added another little note: "If everything were written down that Jesus did, the whole world could not contain the books." Do you think that's exaggeration? It isn't. You couldn't hold the record of Jesus in the whole universe, or his glory, because he made the universe. It is less than he is.

Yes, there are many things we don't know about Jesus. For example, for thirty years of his life we have only one incident of three days. Jesus did many other things even during his three years' public ministry: some day he may tell us about the other miracles he performed, the other sermons he preached, the other people he touched and saved. Maybe we will know but we have got enough for now.

On the wall of a cell in a mental institution behind the Iron Curtain these words were found written in pencil: "Could we with ink the ocean fill / And were the skies of parchment made, / Were every stalk on earth a quill / And every man a scribe by trade, / To write the love of God above / Would drain the ocean dry. / Nor could the scroll contain the whole. / Though stretched from sky to sky."

The Lord Jesus Christ knows everything. He knows how much you love him or how much you don't. He knows whether we have even started to love him at all. May he help each one of us be honest and start where we are and follow him from this day forward, for his name's sake.

EBOOKS

Most books by David Pawson are also available
as ebooks from:

amazon.com and amazon.co.uk Kindle stores.

**For details of foreign language editions
and a full listing of
David Pawson Teaching Catalogue in MP3/DVD
or to purchase David Pawson books in the** UK
please visit:
www.davidpawson.com

Email: info@davidpawsonministry.com

Chinese language books by David Pawson
www.bolbookstore.com
and
www.elimbookstore.com.tw

2621224R00266

Printed in Great Britain
by Amazon.co.uk, Ltd.,
Marston Gate.